PROJECT
Management

A Strategic Planning Approach

Paul D. Gardiner

palgrave
macmillan

First published 2005 by
PALGRAVE MACMILLAN

Palgrave Macmillan in the UK is an imprint of Macmillan Publishers Limited,
registered in England, company number 785998, of Houndmills, Basingstoke,
Hampshire RG21 6XS.

Palgrave Macmillan in the US is a division of St. Martin's Press LLC,
175 Fifth Avenue, New York, NY 10010.

Palgrave Macmillan is the global academic imprint of the above companies
and has companies and representatives throughout the world.

Palgrave® and Macmillan® are registered trademarks in the United States,
the United Kingdom, Europe and other countries.

ISBN-13: 978–0–333–98222–8
ISBN-10: 0–333–98222–3

This book is printed on paper suitable for recycling and made from fully
managed and sustained forest sources. Logging, pulping and manufacturing
processes are expected to conform to the environmental regulations of the
country of origin.

A catalogue record for this book is available from the British Library.

A catalog record for this book is available from the Library of Congress.

11
10

Printed and bound in Great Britain by
CPI Antony Rowe , Chippenham and Eastbourne

Contents

About this book

Learning objectives

After reading this chapter you should be able to:

- understand the structure and purpose of the book
- plan and manage your own project management learning
- benefit from the special features in the book
- access the companion website and its resources

Why study project management?

The practice of project management is not an exact science and there are wide variations of method, approach and terminology, reflecting the 'youthfulness' of project management as a discipline. This book explores many of these differences and reveals something of the richness and continuing evolution of the subject.

Projects come in all shapes and sizes and involve many participants. At one end of the spectrum there is personal project management, the everyday juggling of meetings, calls and things to be done and managed so that the focus is always on the tasks with the greatest contribution to the desired goal. At the other end of the scale is the megaproject, involving international consortia, joint ventures and vast sums of money. These projects are highly complex and challenging to plan, budget and schedule. Most projects lie between the two extremes.

As organisations grow and adapt to their environment, they undergo change at all levels. The ability to conjoin vision, strategy and strategy implementation, using a robust, flexible and responsive delivery methodology, is essential. On this journey, organisations may need to manage stand-alone projects, those that are subprojects of larger projects and others that have been bundled into a portfolio of managed projects.

So who needs to know about project management? Is it the newly appointed project manager, the project champion, the client representative, the sponsor, the chairperson of a users' committee, the spokesperson for an environmental action group, the project manager's manager, the finance director, the team leader, the consultant or independent advisor, the contractors or subcontractors? In fact, it is all of these. The experience and requirements of project management may be different in every case but the principles remain the same.

This book will help you to:

- select and apply the right balance of project management tools, techniques and theories to projects
- link individual projects to broader business strategy, IT and programme-level issues
- decide which techniques and methods are most relevant to who and under what circumstances.

Who should use this book?

Project Management: A Strategic Planning Approach is written with an international readership in mind – balancing the unique aspects of project management with the softer business strategy and people skills. It presents a comprehensive and integrated account of the theory and practice of managing projects for undergraduates, postgraduates and practitioners.

For the undergraduate degree student, this book will support compulsory or elective courses in project management. It provides a comprehensive approach, with many examples and illustrations, and a greater depth of knowledge than competing undergraduate titles.

For the MSc student studying for a specialist degree in management, engineering, science or medicine, the book offers a practical, well-referenced and transferable approach to managing projects.

For the student studying for an MBA degree, the book provides critical discussion of contemporary issues and several in-depth, longer case studies, giving an integrated view of project management in practice and an opportunity for critical evaluation and analysis.

For executives and managers, there are best-practice examples and templates showing how to apply project management techniques in practice and a companion website providing access to a wide range of additional useful resources.

Key features

The book has many attractive features, including:

- a clear and well-structured style, with learning objectives and end of chapter summary points for clarity and learning efficiency
- learning aids throughout the text to illustrate key points, explain important concepts, provide insights from industry and show project management in action
- multiple choice questions for each chapter on the companion website for self-assessment against learning objectives
- alignment with published project management bodies of knowledge
- well-referenced critical discussions on contemporary topics such as critical chain project management
- a choice of longer case studies for analysis, interpretation and deeper learning
- a skills-oriented approach, with the academic rigour demanded from a study text
- simple tools and models that can be quickly learned and applied in practice.

Companion website

This is an essential complement to the book and is referred to frequently. It can also be browsed independently as a resource in its own right.

Visit the website

http://www.palgrave.com/business/gardiner

▶ to access a wide range of supporting resources

Resources on the website include:

- multiple choice questions (MCQs) and answers
- suggestions for supplementary reading
- tools and templates that can be downloaded
- links to websites on key topics
- reference material that did not find space in the book
- selected additional case studies
- a matrix showing how the contents of the book map onto the elements of the Association of Project Management's *Body of Knowledge* (BOK) and the Project Management Institute's *Guide to the Project Management Body of Knowledge* (PMBOK), which can be used to help prepare for professional development and qualifications
- a form for feedback about the book and companion website.

Learning aids

 and

These boxes engage the reader in reflective thinking and provide an invitation to test your understanding of a topic before continuing to the next topic.

insights from INDUSTRY

Every chapter has a selection of fairly short and lively Insights from Industry stories and examples that demonstrate relevance.

CRITICAL CONSIDERATIONS

These develop critical thinking skills on important and contemporary topics.

These boxes supplement the text in places, helping to explain key terms and concepts.

PROJECT MANAGEMENT
in action

Longer case studies situated at the end of the chapters, with questions to aid understanding and discussion, some of which are quite long and lend themselves to rigorous analytical treatment, for example the cases at the end of Chapters 3, 7 and 8.

How to use this book

Project management is a science that integrates business, management and operational disciplines to deliver organisational benefits through projects and programmes which, in real life, are messy and unpredictable. In this book, the topics have been separated into discrete chapters with an accompanying Project Management in Action case for ease of learning and to help you stay focused on the links between individual topics.

Although the sequence of topics follows a logical structure, each chapter is self-contained and can be studied independently or in whatever sequence is appropriate to your course or individual interests, allowing a flexible approach to learning and teaching. As a guide, the following clusters of chapters and Project Management in Action cases may be studied together usefully.

Introduction to projects

Chapter 1   Introduction to projects and project management   *City technology college*
Chapter 2   A systems view of project management   *PC banking*

Commercial project management

Chapter 3   Strategy and governance   *Scottish Qualifications Authority (SQA)*
Chapter 4   Investment decision making   *'Roadkill' the movie*
Chapter 6   Organisation and procurement   *Virtual teamwork at BP* and *Maritime helicopter procurement process*

Planning and control systems

Chapter 8   (part) Project initiation   *DataSys knowledge transfer programme*
Chapter 9   Estimating, scheduling and budgeting   *Albion Sugar Company*
Chapter 10   Control, closure and continuous improvement   *The $26 million 'Oops!'*

Integrated project management and meta skills

Chapter 5   The project manager, sponsor and other stakeholders   *Easy Finance Ltd*
Chapter 7   Managing risk and quality   *Taj Mahal cycle taxi project*
Chapter 8   (part) Team building   *DataSys knowledge transfer programme*

Each chapter has a set of multiple choice questions on the companion website to test your understanding of the learning objectives for that chapter. If you cannot answer these, you should revisit the relevant parts of the chapter. Use the questions at the end of the case studies to guide you through the logic of analysing the issues in the case. To develop your critical thinking skills, each time you analyse one of the case studies, start off by referring to and using the key themes below to help to structure your analysis.

Key themes

- *Systems analysis* – providing a systems-based understanding of the complexity of projects with inputs, outputs, mechanisms and constraints.
- *Project life cycle* – highlighting the unique aspects of the different stages in a project and how to exploit these differences to manage projects successfully.
- *Link to strategy* – providing a link to the relationship between strategy planning, strategy implementation and the realisation of benefits through projects and programmes.
- *Interdisciplinarity* – emphasising the tendency of projects to cross multiple functions and disciplines in an organisation and the consequent need for well-developed communication and integration strategies.
- *Internationalisation* – demonstrating the wide application of project management at a global level.

Resources for lecturers

The resource website for lecturers includes:

- web links to the companion website, for ease of reference
- example learning and teaching strategies
- PowerPoint slides for each chapter, fully customisable
- additional Project Management in Action case studies
- additional case studies not on the companion website
- example examination questions relating to each chapter
- a form for feedback about the book and resource/companion website.

CHAPTER 1

Introduction to projects and project management

Learning objectives

After reading this chapter you should be able to:

■ differentiate between a project and a programme

■ compare and contrast the role of a project manager with that of a programme manager

■ elucidate the characteristics of projects, including the three primary characteristics

■ recount the historical development and evolution of project management

■ discuss the importance of project management training, qualifications and associations

Introduction

This chapter introduces the concept of a project and the discipline of managing projects. Consideration is given to the wide variation of project size and the breadth of scope and application of project management. The characteristics of projects are compared to those of nonproject activities. A definition and overview of project management precedes a brief look at its key management functions and the difference between the so-called 'hard' and 'soft' aspects of project management. The relationship between project management and programme management is outlined.

The penultimate section gives a potted history of the development of project management; its origins, practice and development as a professional and academic discipline, followed by an introduction to project management associations and other useful resources, some of them web-based. Finally, consideration is given to the development of education and training in project management for those seeking further qualifications.

The Project Management in Action case at the end of the chapter about a city technology college challenges the reader to identify examples of good project management practice.

What is a project?

This may seem like an easy question to answer; most people probably think they can recognise a project when they see one. Actually, there is a fairly broad interpretation of the term. For example, the Project Management Institute defines a project as:

a temporary endeavor undertaken to create a unique product or service. (PMI, 2000: 6)

Another definition is given by the British Standards Institution:

A project is a unique set of coordinated activities, with a definite starting and finishing point, undertaken by an individual or organisation to meet specific objectives within defined schedule, cost and performance parameters. (BS 6079-1, 2000: 2)

Then again:

a project is a task with a beginning, a middle and an end, which you as a manager need to complete. (MacLachlan, 1996: 2)

And so the list goes on. One of the difficulties of defining a project arises from the enormous variation in size that is possible, ranging from the very small, say, writing a letter, consisting of only a few tasks and basic materials, to the gigantic, such as creating the Anglo–French Channel Tunnel, involving thousands of tasks, hundreds of people and complex plant and machinery.

Whatever the size of a project, the same principles of project management apply. Of course the level of effort required to project manage writing a letter will be vastly different from that required to build the Channel Tunnel. The concept of scale is one of the challenges faced by anyone studying project management. Small personal projects can be managed by an individual with simple common-sense planning, while larger projects may require many contributors, sophisticated tools, techniques and management practices.

By considering how a project is defined, it is possible to discern the features and characteristics that are true for most projects. But be warned, the difference between projects and other activities is not always crystal clear.

Recognising projects

Use the definitions above to help you decide which of the following are projects:
- Building a bridge
- Designing an information system
- Planning an election campaign
- Swimming
- Making a television programme
- Solving a problem
- Doing a crossword puzzle
- Working in an office
- Writing an essay
- Getting a job

See shaded box for a suggested answer.

ANSWER suggested

They are all projects except 'swimming' and 'working in an office' which are too general and nonspecific to be called projects. However, by simply replacing the term 'swimming' with the phrase 'win a swimming race' or 'learn how to swim', this too can become a project. Similarly, within an office environment, there may be several projects that need doing, for example create a new brochure or update a catalogue.

Characteristics of projects

There are three primary characteristics of projects that set them apart from other activities. Projects are temporary, unique, and require progressive elaboration. Like desert flowers that burst magnificently into bloom when the rain falls and then disappear, projects also have a season. The first primary characteristic of projects is that each one is a temporary endeavour that exists for a limited period only; although temporary does not imply of short duration and a project's end products may endure indefinitely. For example, the historic monument Stonehenge, in Wiltshire, England, has been around in its current form for over 1500 years. Getting from the beginning to the end of a project can vary from only a few days to a few years, depending on its size and complexity. In ancient civilisations, large building projects would often take longer than a decade to complete; it is estimated that Stonehenge was in various stages of construction for 3500 years before it was finally completed around 1500 BC (Britannia, 2002).

The duration of a project partly depends on how the beginning and end points are determined. For example, a manufacturer of mobile phones may wish to include design, development, operation and future

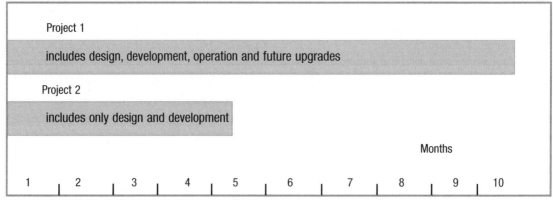

Figure 1.1 Project duration varies according to how a project is defined

upgrades in a project, resulting in a duration significantly greater than a project which included only design and development (see Figure 1.1).

Ideally, every project should have a clearly defined beginning and end, although in reality these boundaries can become rather fuzzy. In practice, the end is reached when the project's objectives have been achieved and validated, or when it becomes clear that the project's objectives will not or cannot be met, and the project is terminated. Some of the difficulties of identifying and reaching the end of a project can be seen in the two Insights from Industry boxes below.

---

insights from INDUSTRY

THE ABSENT-MINDED PROFESSOR

Twelve years ago a language professor approached our development talent support office, seeking support for the development of a simple application to assist students learning new sounds. His idea appeared to have some potential, so a small amount of support was provided to help him develop some prototype lesson modules.

The prototypes were used with students and did accomplish what the professor had intended. Two years later he submitted a proposal for financial support for the acquisition of new hardware and the development of newer and more elaborate lesson modules. The professor was regarded by several committee members reviewing the proposals as what we would now call an 'early adopter' and although his ideas were now much more grandiose, they still appeared to have potential. The committee members approved financial support for the acquisition of some of the new hardware and the development of new modules. The new equipment was acquired and the new modules were developed.

Two years later the professor submitted another proposal seeking support for newer, more elaborate equipment and substantial help with enhancements to existing lesson modules. Limited funding was again provided. This cycle has gone on and on and on. Over the years this professor has returned to the office six times, seeking and receiving financial support and consultation.

The process of development and consultation with the professor has not been easy. He has many characteristics of the absent-minded professor. When he decides, for example, that he wants to change something in his programme, he makes the change, forgets what he has done, and has to seek help to correct the digital chaos he has created. He also frequently forgets what has been determined to be the solution to the problem he has created and will return again and again with a look of hopeful expectation seeking assistance with the same problem. This has been his pattern for several years.

Two weeks ago, once again the door opened and in came the professor. All he wants this time is $4,000 more, and he'll be able to finish the project ... or so he says.

Source: Frank Gillespie, College of Saint Benedict and Saint John's University

Questions

1. Will this project ever end?
2. Does the story describe a project or a programme?
3. What lessons will the professor learn?
4. What role did the support unit play?

---

insights from INDUSTRY

A MULTIMEDIA PROJECT FOR NURSING STUDENTS

Prior to 1992 I was neither computer-literate nor dependent – I am now both. Ryerson School of Nursing has not historically used computers as teaching tools. My interest in developing new teaching methodologies, and in how and with what effect the new technology could be used, led me to an opportunity in 1995 to develop multimedia courseware as part of a pilot project.

The construction of multimedia is dependent on a diversity of talents working on different parts of the project. This project has involved professional experts and students in software programming, filming, nursing, communications, software design and graphics. While continuing to learn about the construction of software, my primary role is one of content developer and director. The director is limited, however, by a lack of experience in this medium, and the vision of the finished programme has undergone several permutations as new ideas have been integrated along the way. Unlike other projects that have clear timelines, expectations and outcomes, the development of multimedia is dependent on others' expertise and time and the hardware resources being available (and working!). There is uncertainty about the timing of the deliverable and the 'how' of the delivery.

The project includes an evaluation of the multimedia courseware from both students and faculty on the value of the programme, the ease of use and suggestions for additions/changes. Since the programme has been developed over several months there is an ongoing need to update materials and information. Unlike making a quick change in a lecture note, overhead or handout, revisions in a multimedia programme require changes throughout the 'multi-media', that is, more time in the sound studio to redo audio portions as well as deletion and additions of new material in the text.

In the meantime, I still don't know what the final product will look like – the programme is in a constant state of change. There is always the fear when dealing with technology of whether it will work or not. 'Glitch'

has become a standard in my vocabulary. Will it live up to my and others' expectations? Will we have working workstations and how many? Where will they be located? Will they be accessible? Will this programme bore the students to death? Will this project ever be finished! I have decided that a sense of humour is key to the development of a multimedia project.

Source: Judy Britnell, Ryerson University

Questions

1. Does the story describe a project or a programme?
2. In what way do you think Judy's experience is typical for project managers?
3. What are the key challenges in this project?
4. How you would try to manage them?
5. What can be done to reduce uncertainty?

The finite and transitory nature of projects often appeals to individuals and businesses, encouraging them to adopt a project mindset. Once a specific need has been identified, creating and managing a project to completion can fulfil it. In a cost-conscious society, projects are seen as a means of increasing control over scarce resources. Many companies are adopting a 'management by projects' approach (discussed in Chapter 3) to conducting business as a way of shortening product development times, lowering costs, and increasing quality, reliability and profit margins (Meredith and Mantel, 1995: 9).

The second primary characteristic of projects concerns their uniqueness; one way or another projects are all different. For example, there are hundreds of McDonald's hamburger restaurants worldwide and although a hamburger purchased in Moscow may taste the same as one purchased in Manhattan, reflecting the standardised and repetitive processes used to make them, it does not change the fundamental uniqueness of each restaurant – whether it is different size, different design, different location or different features. Each new restaurant has the familiar McDonald's brand feel about it but remains a project in its own right, needing to be planned, executed and controlled; they do not simply roll off the assembly line the way electrical goods do in a factory.

The third primary characteristic is that projects take shape through a process called 'progressive elaboration' in which the work required is gradually defined, with increasing detail being added over time. The process of elaboration is more noticeable and

pronounced for larger and more complex projects. For example, in a project to build a new housing development, the number and size of the houses to be built will be determined at an early stage. The exact style of each house may be determined a little later. The layout and orientation of rooms may be fixed later still and the precise details of fixtures and fittings to be included may be decided after construction work has started, perhaps in consultation with potential buyers. Finally, decisions about the internal colour scheme and external landscaping of each house may be left until most of the building work is completed and a buyer has been found.

In addition to the three primary characteristics of projects, there are several other traits that projects often exhibit. For example, projects tend to:

- carry risk and uncertainty
- be organisationally complex, requiring the interaction of many people, departments and other organisations
- be managed against time, budget and human resource plans
- suffer conflict due to competition for resources required by other projects and nonproject work
- have single point responsibility provided by the project manager
- require teamwork and the ability of participants to use effective leadership skills.

Even the objectives of projects are fundamentally different from those of other activities (PMI, 2000: 5);

for example, whereas a project seeks to complete a well-defined set of objectives and then formally close, an ongoing activity seeks to continue by developing new objectives on a regular basis. For example, in the office environment mentioned earlier, individual projects come and go while general office activities continue indefinitely.

Project management explored

At its simplest level, project management can be defined as the discipline of managing projects successfully. (APM, 2000: 14). This is a reasonable starting point but we need to know more. What is involved? How are the different parts related to each other? Who is involved in the process? What are their roles? What is meant by the terms 'hard' and 'soft' project management skills? Why is a project life cycle important and how does viewing a project as a system help us? These questions will be answered in due course but first take a look at how the British Standards Institution defines project management:

Project management is the planning, monitoring and control of all aspects of a project and the motivation of all those involved in it to achieve the project objectives on time and to the specified cost, quality and performance. (BS 6079-1, 2000: 5)

This definition contains new information explaining the two key words from the earlier one which were 'managing', that is, to plan, monitor, control and motivate, and 'successfully', that is, achieving the project's objectives on time, to cost, quality and performance. Actually, the concept of project success is a well-debated subject and one we shall be returning to in Chapter 10.

Some organisations prefer to use their own definition of project management. For example, this one is taken from the *US Fish & Wildlife Service Manual* (1994: 1) for automated information projects:

[Project management is] The management process that establishes the standards, techniques, and tools used to ensure that requirements are well defined and reflect end-user performance needs; that the project satisfies the defined requirements; that the products are thoroughly tested; that development costs are properly managed; and that the criteria for implementation, training, modification, and documentation are well defined and appropriate.

Notice that none of the definitions say anything

about doing or managing the 'work' on a project. This is an important point. Project management is about managing a process and the people who participate in it. The project manager may or may not also be involved in doing the work to create the project's end products, whether goods or services. Project managers essentially manage people, resources and the delivery of products, not the work itself. The work of a project is done, and is managed, en passant by the participants (Turner, 2000a). The management task in project managing a project concerns four activities in particular:

- Planning
- Organising
- Controlling
- Leading and motivating.

Each activity is described briefly below, while the Project Management in Action case at the end of the chapter gives examples of them from a real project. Later chapters will examine each topic in detail.

Planning

Every project needs a plan explaining how it is going to proceed. The participants need to know the goal, the steps to achieve it, the order those steps take and when those steps must be complete. A major cause of poor project management arises from failures at the planning stage leading to a series of subsequent alterations and clarifications that increases cost and creates delays (BS 6079-1, 2000: 5).

At the start of a project, it is important to ask the right questions:

- What needs to be achieved and why?
- When should it be done by?
- How will it be done?
- What will be the order of cost?

Different people provide different parts of the answers:

- The people who pay (project sponsors)
- The people who benefit (end users)
- The technical experts (knowledge workers).

The answers to these questions can be used as the basis for a feasibility report, which gives an outline of the project and its formal justification, that is, the business case for the project. The project manager works out what needs to be done, and how to do it within the constraints of time and cost. Everyone who is involved has got to agree on what the project is trying to achieve and be committed to it.

Any project has to satisfy three feasibility criteria:

- The *technical* criterion – is it going to work?
- The *business* criterion – are the cost and timescale right for the business as a whole? Is the return big enough to justify the risk?
- The *functional* criterion – will the result satisfy the end users?

Approval to go ahead with the project should not be given unless it satisfies these three criteria. Once it has been decided that the project is feasible, the rest of the planning activities can be carried out.

There are many planning documents in project management, including:

- the *activity plan*, showing the timescale of the project activities in each phase, with their resulting end products (deliverables)
- the *resource plan*, showing what skills are required, and thus who will be involved in the project
- the *budget plan*, detailing all the costs for the required resources.

A small project may only need a few planning documents, but more complex projects will require many different plans at various levels of detail. It is generally best to start by producing overall plans for the entire project, to provide the 'big picture', and then fill in the detail through a process of progressive elaboration, with the most detailed plans often progressing on a rolling-wave basis, that is, one or two time periods ahead of project execution.

Organising

Simply stated but not simple to achieve, organising is about arranging the people, material and support resources in a project to meet the project's communication, integration and decision-making needs to achieve on-time project delivery. Organising includes identifying the project tools, methods and templates to use, the reporting relationships and even the types and frequency of meetings. Increasingly, projects cut across departmental boundaries and the appropriate organisation will often be a temporary arrangement, consisting of a project manager supported by a team of staff drawn from

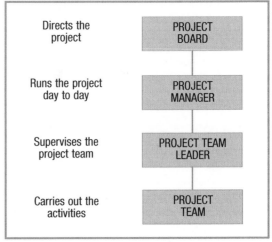

Figure 1.2 Simple project organisation structure

various quarters with the appropriate skills for the needs of the project (BS 6079-1, 2000: 5).

At the start of a project, an organisation structure should be set up which defines for everyone:

- what their role is
- their responsibilities
- who to report to.

The right structure is important to ensure that everyone:

- is committed to the project
- knows what is happening
- communicates effectively
- has common objectives.

A simple project organisation structure is illustrated in Figure 1.2. The responsibilities of the project board are to direct the project and make sure that everything is proceeding according to the plan. It is the project manager's responsibility to run the project on a day-to-day basis and ensure that the objectives and milestones are met on time and within budget.

Controlling

Controlling means making sure that the project is managed as specified in the planning documents and that attempts at organising become a reality. In this way planning and organising are used to transform resources (inputs) into tangible deliverables (outputs), not just something jotted down on a piece of paper and forgotten.

The project manager should meet with the project team regularly, to review progress and sort out minor problems. If each activity is planned carefully, progress can be monitored and control maintained more effectively. Any problems will be easier to correct if they are detected early.

There should be an assessment by the project board at the end of each project phase (and also mid-phase if the phase is long or there are significant problems). A decision is made about whether or not to authorise the next phase of the project by confirming that all the end products of the current phase have been completed and formally signed off. This ensures that everyone is consulted and is clear about what is happening. These assessments, or 'stage gates' as they are commonly called, are also used to re-examine the project against the three criteria used during feasibility (technical, business and functional) by asking the questions:

■ Are we still going about the project in the right way? Are we within schedule?
■ Is the project still cost-effective? Are we within budget?
■ Are we still going to get what we want? Is the scope still the same?

If one or more of these criteria is not satisfied, the board can consider three options:

1. Continue with the project.
2. Stop the project.
3. Delay the project and rethink it.

Leading and motivating

Without leadership, the other activities (planning, organising and controlling) would not be possible. Leadership guru Warren Bennis (1985: 21) said: 'Anybody can do things right, but it takes leadership to get people motivated to do the right things.' Management needs to consider the motivation of staff, especially if project work means they are taken out of their normal departmental roles. Tangible rewards related to the achievement of the project may involve money, but other rewards might include the kudos of being selected to work on a project or promotion to wider responsibilities. Where staff are deployed to a project on a full-time basis, there should always be an understanding that, as a minimum, a return to previous duties is safe (BS 6079-1, 2000: 5).

Leadership and team-building skills are critical to successful project management and hinge on having a sound knowledge and understanding of the human factors in a project. Project leadership involves shaping goals, obtaining resources, building roles and structures, establishing good communications, seeing the whole picture and moving things forward to a successful conclusion. Project managers need to be able to use the skills of communication, negotiation, team building, political influence and creating owner-ship, in addition to those of rational problem solving and participative management, and to move between them as the need arises. These activities do not describe a careful and methodical analyst, working out to perfection the best solution for a project. They are more akin to the activities of the entrepreneur, determined to get things done within an often hostile, indifferent or highly political setting. The people in a project often have their own interests to pursue. These skills are quite different from those that figured in the original training of most project managers, which is often of a technical nature.

Project managers need to get things done in situations where their authority is, at best, ambiguous in relation to people in different units, reporting to different line managers. In reality, many project managers have very little formal authority, and what authority is delegated to them needs to be quite clear and communicated throughout the organisation. Without this authority the project manager may be thwarted by departmental intransigence (BS 6079-1, 2000: 5).

Project management covers a wide spectrum of activities and overlaps with general management principles and other application areas (PMI, 2000: 9). It is an integrated discipline.

Hard and soft skills

When people talk about 'hard' or 'soft' project management skills, they are referring to the nature of the skills concerned. The term 'hard skills' generally refers to the mechanical and technical skills of plan-ning, estimating, scheduling and controlling a project. Project management training courses often focus almost exclusively on teaching these hard skills, which reflects the historical development of project management as a discipline – see later in this chapter. Soft skills, on the other hand, are people skills, such as interpersonal communication, commit-ment to success, negotiation, consensus problem solving, leadership and motivation. These skills deal with human factor issues and, until recently, have been less well discussed in project management literature. The Project Management in Action case at the end of the chapter illustrates many of these skills.

Ironically, it is the so-called 'soft' skills that are much harder to learn and use effectively. Our ability to learn and use hard skills, for example drawing Gantt charts and networks, is partly linked to our IQ, which is established relatively early in life. Soft skills, on the other hand, are more related to our EQ (emotional quotient) or emotional intelligence, which can continue to develop as we mature or through training. The Key Concepts below explains briefly the concept of emotional intelligence.

 CONCEPTS Emotional intelligence

Studies on emotional intelligence indicate that people who are intellectually the brightest are often *not* the most successful, whether in business or in their personal lives (Salovey and Mayer, 1990; Goleman, 1995). Over the past few years, EQ has become widely accepted as a shorthand expression for the emotional intelligence equivalent of IQ.

At the individual level, Salovey and Mayer (1990) define emotional intelligence as 'the subset of social intelligence that involves the ability to monitor one's own and others' feelings and emotions, to discriminate among them and to use this information to guide one's thinking and actions'. An emotionally intelligent individual is able to recognise and use his or her own and others' emotional states to solve problems and regulate behaviour.

Emotions have long been considered to be of such depth and power that, in Latin for example, they were described as *moutus anima*, meaning literally 'the spirit that moves us'. Contrary to most conventional thinking, emotions are inherently neither positive nor negative; rather they provide useful information all the time that can help spark creativity, keep one honest with oneself and help develop *trusting* relationships (Cooper and Sawaf, 1997).

It is not enough, of course, just to have feelings. Emotional intelligence requires that we learn to acknowledge and value feelings in ourselves and others and appropriately respond to them in our daily life and work. Emerging research suggests that a leader with a high EQ is someone who picks up more deftly, and more quickly than others, developing conflicts that need resolution, and team and organisational vulnerabilities that need addressing (Cooper and Sawaf, 1997).

Over the past decade, management initiatives have helped increase competitiveness in the West, but often with significant hidden costs, including crumbling trust, increasing uncertainty, greater distance between managers and those they manage, stifled creativity, festering cynicism, increasingly volatile anger, and vanishing loyalty and commitment. Now, emotional intelligence is beginning to make a contribution to the understanding of successful leaders with respect to:

- decision making
- open, honest communication
- building trusting relationships
- teamwork
- customer loyalty
- creativity and innovation.

Sources: Cooper, R. and Sawaf, A. (1997), *Executive EQ,* Putnam, New York; Goleman, D. (1995), *Emotional Intelligence,* Bantam Books, New York; Salovey, P. and Mayer, J.D. (1990), 'Emotional intelligence', *Imagination, Cognition and Personality,* **9**(3): 185–211

The following example illustrates the importance of soft skills:

I remember recently sitting with the senior vice-president of human resources in a large organisation. Three months ago she had hired what seemed to be the most qualified applicant for a particular project management role. Yesterday, she was terminating this same person's employment contract. Two other candidates in the past two years had suffered the same fate. She asked, 'Why is it that we keep hiring these bright, technically-driven people, who, on their résumés, have all the right stuff, and then shortly after, we have to let them go?' As I queried her reasoning she replied, 'They're lacking some of the key fundamentals like respect, courtesy, treating others with dignity, willingness to return email and phone calls, and, above all, they often have a disturbing sense of arrogance.' (Rock, 2004: 1)

In this situation, the 'hard skills' were in place but the 'soft skills' were underdeveloped. In modern project management there is an increasing awareness of the criticality of the people factor to project success (see for example Graham and Englund, 1997). The criteria and determinants of project success and failure are discussed in Chapter 10; the main issue here is to raise awareness that both hard and soft skills are necessary – hard skills set the goals and procedures while soft skills make sure that people can meet those objectives.

Project management, then, is the managerial task of accomplishing a project on time, within budget and to agreed technical and quality standards in order to meet or exceed stakeholder needs and expectations by using an appropriate mix of hard and soft management skills.

Where do projects come from?

For most projects, their origin is linked to the identification of a need (for example 'a project responding to new government safety legislation'), a problem (for example 'a project to install a new machine to remove a bottleneck') or an opportunity within the organisation (for example projects originating from the creative ideas of individual employees or improvement teams). In the case of project-driven organisations, projects originate from customer requests, orders for work or invitations to tender (discussed in Chapter 6). The Insights from Industry box shows six different sources of IT projects at a major UK bank.

In general, projects are usually authorised as a result of one or more of the following reasons (PMI, 2000):

- *A market demand* (for example a supermarket chain opens a new store due to popular demand)
- *A business need* (for example a university authorises a project to develop a distance learning course to increase its revenues)
- *A customer request* (for example an electric utility authorises a project to build a substation to serve a new industrial park)
- *A technological advance* (for example a new computer chip spawns a project to produce the next generation of computers)
- *A legal requirement* (for example a paint manufacturer authorises a project to establish guidelines for the handling of hazardous materials as required by recent government legislation)
- *A crisis* (for example a market downturn forces a company to restructure itself)
- A social need (for example a nongovernmental organisation (NGO) in a developing country authorises a project to provide potable water systems, latrines and sanitation education to low-income communities suffering from high rates of cholera).

The next Insights from Industry box describes how a project for a charitable organisation was set in motion in response to an overload of paperwork.

Marketing, in its role of securing new business, is also a significant source of new projects (APM, 2000: 39). The relationship between marketing and other disciplines in new product development is well documented (see for example Hooks and Farry, 2000). Misunderstandings between marketing and other parts of an organisation can often result in poorly specified requirements and unrealistic expectations by the customer. These problems are often not discovered until quite late in the project life cycle, when it is particularly expensive to correct them.

It is also possible for a project idea to originate outside the organisation, for example from the results of a study carried out by a consulting firm. Other

---

insights from INDUSTRY

SOURCES OF IT PROJECTS AT A MAJOR UK BANK

1. **The mainstream project.** This project has (i) identifiable and quantifiable benefits, (ii) clearly defined start-up and running costs, (iii) a return on investment model (RoI) which shows that the project will exceed the company's hurdle for investment, (iv) project management processes in place that are known to work and which include adequate financial controls and reporting, and (v) a process for delivering the claimed benefits, measuring them and reporting on progress.
2. **The infrastructure project.** This project (i) benefits the company through the implementation of mainstream projects and/or growth in the utilisation of the service(s) provided, (ii) has an RoI model that shows that the savings made or value delivered to other projects jumps the hurdle mentioned above, (iii) has a process for delivering the claimed benefits, measuring them and reporting on progress.
3. **The regulatory project.** If you don't do this project, your industry's regulators and/or the courts force you out of business or your auditors get you fired.
4. **The speculative project.** This project occurs when (i) you have an idea that you believe is worthwhile, (ii) you can estimate what you need to spend to progress the idea, (iii) you can see how the benefit will be delivered but cannot provide adequate figures of the value for the creation of an RoI model.
5. **The incremental project.** This project includes all those projects whose total expenditure is below an agreed, small figure and which are generally changing or extending the function of systems already in use.
6. **The repair project.** It broke; you fix it.

Source: Personal communication with Stewart Stevenson, former IT manager at Bank of Scotland (now HBOS)

JUNIOR ACHIEVEMENT FACES GROWING PAPERWORK MOUNTAIN

Junior Achievement (JA) is a nonprofit economic education organisation that inspires young people to value free enterprise, business and economics to improve the quality of their lives.

The need, problem or opportunity

Before students can start learning, a lot of paperwork needs to be processed at the JA offices of the upper midwest, USA. Volunteers must telephone JA to submit their areas of expertise and review potential classes. New volunteers need to sign up for training prior to teaching their first class and with thousands of people involved, administration becomes an issue. Nichole Zack, information systems manager at JA (upper midwest) comments: 'We needed to find an alternative to telephone registrations or we would have to double our staff.' The amount of paperwork that needs to be processed is pulling staff time away from the volunteer recruiting process. When the national Junior Achievement office announced increased performance targets for servicing students,

Nichole knew they needed a plan to manage the workload and time was a key concern.

The project

In analysing the issues, the board of directors suggested a solution based on an interactive web-based approach, where volunteers rather than JA staff could enter much of the data needed. They envisioned a system that would eventually interconnect volunteers, participating schools and JA's back-end information systems. With this vision in mind, Nichole approached a JA volunteer company to help and a project was set in motion with four phases, the first phase being delivered in only 90 days.

Source: Shared Resource Management Inc., featured case studies, Junior Achievement of the upper midwest, 'Online registration system allows volunteers to register for classes on the web', http://www.srminc.com/case_studies/casestudies.htm

Questions

1. How would you classify the origin of this project – for example 'need', 'problem' or 'opportunity'?
2. What is the difference between these terms?
3. Why is it important to understand the origin of a project?

---

projects are born through the provision of grants and financial aid. Research councils and funding bodies have annual budgets to attract a selection of research project proposals. In countries that operate a national lottery, a proportion of the revenues generated are typically channelled into community and art projects. For example, awards for lottery-funded projects in the London arts region number 260 and are worth £230 million. Table 1.1 highlights a sample of them; notice the wide variation in project size – the amount of project management applied to these projects will vary considerably.

In many organisations the annual review of the business plan results in a list of projects aimed at implementing the organisation's strategy. To maintain a healthy flow of project ideas it is crucial that senior management keep staff informed of the strategic needs of the business and how these needs and business priorities may be changing over time.

Whatever its origin, a project should be more than just a good idea. It should always be possible to show how a project supports the strategic goals of the sponsor's organisation. This rule even applies to the so-called 'loss leader' project. These projects are

Table 1.1 Sample of lottery-funded projects for the London arts region

Organisation	Project	Award
African Caribbean Centre	Feasibility study	£90,000
Association for Jewish Youth	Purchase of a mini van	£16,000
British Film Institute	'IMAX' Cinema	£5,000,000
Chingford Parish Church Music	Improvement to electrical system of church organ	£54,000
Royal Albert Hall	Redevelopment of Albert Hall	£20,200,000

undertaken because of perceived future opportunities for business, or because they are expected to lead to other more profitable projects with some sort of competitive edge as a result of the first one. The value of the first project lies in the competitive advantage created or the increased market share generated (Hartman, 2000).

growing body of evidence that the single most important contributor to project success is to agree the success criteria with the stakeholders at the start of the project (Turner, 1999). Chapter 10 has further information on the determinants of project success and failure.

As a relatively young discipline, the challenge for the future of project management is to develop its theoretical basis. This does not mean continuing to develop and adding to the extensive list of tools and techniques already used by practising project managers, but rather developing a set of premises about:

- the purpose of project management
- the criteria and factors for judging and achieving success on projects
- what constitutes good project management practice.

Project management maturity models enable organisations to score themselves against key processes in project management. These models are developed by applying total quality management principles to best-practice project management. An organisation can use the results of a maturity model assessment to plan future improvements and enhancements to their project management practices. See also Chapter 10.

Associations, standards and journals

Project management associations and institutes

Associations and institutes exist to promote understanding and awareness of project management. They publish articles and books, create guides on the body of knowledge of project management, contribute to the further development of that knowledge by organising conferences and seminars, and they also provide certification against professional project management qualifications. A selection of associations and institutes are described below.

The Association for Project Management, UK
www.apm.org.uk
E-mail: secretariat@apmuk.demon.co.uk
The Association for Project Management (APM) exists to help its members and advance and promote the profession of project management, its skills and practice. It is the only UK-based organisation dedi-

cated to advancing the science of project management and the professional development of project managers and project management specialists. It is affiliated with the International Project Management Association (IPMA) based in Zurich, Switzerland.

International Project Management Association
http://www.ipma.ch
E-mail: ipma@btinternet.com
The International Project Management Association (IPMA) is a federation of independent national project management associations worldwide. IPMA is a non-profit-making, Swiss-registered organisation, with a secretarial office based in the UK. Its function is to be the prime promoter of project management internationally, through its membership network of national project management associations around the world.

Project Management Institute
http://www.pmi.org
E-mail: pmihq@pmi.org
The Project Management Institute (PMI), based in the USA, is a non-profit-making professional organisation dedicated to advancing the state of the art of project management. The PMI establishes project management standards, provides seminars, educational programmes and professional certification for project leaders. The PMI website contains many useful links.

Australian Institute of Project Management
http://www.aipm.com.au
E-mail: marisa@aipm.com.au
The Australian Institute of Project Management is the professional association for project managers and project management users in Australia.

For details of other project management associations visit any of the following links:

www.ctsolution.com.my/pmlinks.htm
www.ipma.ch/natassoc.htm
www.wst.com/library/pmlinks.html

Project management standards

There are several international and national standards that relate to project management in the UK and the USA:

- The International Organisation for Standardisation (ISO) (central@iso.org) has published two standards on project management, one about terminology and the other about quality guidelines:

- ISO 15188, 2001 *Project Management Guidelines for Terminology Standardisation*
- ISO 10006, 1997 *Quality Management – Guidelines to Quality in Project Management*.
- The British Standards Institution (www.bsi-global.com) has published a standard in three parts relating to project management:
  - BS 6079-1, 2000 *Project Management – Part 1: Guide to Project Management*
  - BS 6079-2, 2000 *Project Management – Part 2: Vocabulary*
  - BS 6079-3, 2000 *Project Management – Part 3: Guide to the Management of Business-related Project Risk*.
- The Project Management Institute Standards Program (www.pmi.org/standards) is a comprehensive approach to evaluating and developing project management standards which are useful and practical to the conduct, certification and understanding of the project management discipline. The mission of the Program is 'to assist in improving the understanding and competency of experienced and new project management practitioners and customers worldwide'. The PMI's *Guide to the Project Management Body of Knowledge* (PMI, 2000) is now approved as an American National Standard (ANSI/PMI 99-001-2000).
- Global Working Group on Project Management Standards (www.aipm.com/globalstandards) was established to facilitate communication between those committed to the development of project management as a global profession supported by globally accepted and relevant standards.

Visit the website

www.pmforum.org/prof/standard.htm

❱ for details of other standards relevant to project management

Journals

The following journals and magazines are useful for research and keeping in touch with the latest thinking about project management theory, tools and techniques:

International Journal of Project Management

www.elsevier.nl

This is a technical journal which focuses on the advancement of project management techniques and methodologies. It is the official journal of the International Project Management Association.

Project Management Journal

www.pmi.org/publictn/pmjournal/index.htm

The professional journal of the Project Management Institute. It aims to advance the state of the art of the knowledge of project and programme management. It covers both the theory and practice of project management.

Engineering News Record (ENR)

www.enr.com

ENR has a long history of being a resource to project managers with regular articles on project management.

PM Network

www.pmi.org/publictn/pmnetwork

This is the professional magazine of the Project Management Institute.

Project

www.apm.org.uk

The Magazine of the Association for Project Management. Contains short stories and articles related to project management.

Project Manager Today

http://www.projectnet.co.uk/pm/pmt/pmt.htm

A UK publication which keeps project managers up to date on project management techniques, tools and methodologies. The publication often includes reviews of the latest in project management tools.

Project Magazine

www.projectmagazine.com

Free online magazine dedicated to the practical side of project management.

Visit the website

http://www.palgrave.com/business/gardiner

❱ for details of project management discussion groups and other information resources on the internet

Personal training and education

'The majority of project managers do not know that they are project managers' (Hartman, 2000). With this in mind, and the growing number of people who find themselves managing a project, the need for good quality education and training is clear. Statistics show that projects continue to come in late and over budget (Standish, 1995). Organisations continue to abandon projects before they are complete. Some of this can be attributed to the failure by some project managers (many of whom began their careers as professional engineers) to realise that project management is first and foremost about people and then tools and techniques. Unfortunately, until recently, the majority of consultant-based training has been firmly focused on the latter, to the exclusion, or sidelining, of the former. Project management is a truly interdisciplinary and integrative subject (PMI, 2000; APM, 2000; Turner, 2000b). The range of subjects that effective project leaders need to be competent in is at least as broad as the academic syllabuses of many business and management degrees, including MBAs.

Although project management training cannot guarantee project success, it can help to avoid ignorant project managers. The huge increase in interest in the subject over the last few years means that there is a variety of training resources to meet a wide range of needs. Project management training can come in several forms:

- On-the-job experience. Project management is essentially a practical discipline and there is nothing like on-the-job experience to develop a project manager's skills
- Mentoring and work shadowing schemes giving one-to-one guidance
- Benchmarking studies; learning from the best practices of others
- Short courses
- Intensive courses
- A module in a degree programme (undergraduate or postgraduate)
- Professional certificates and qualifications, for example the PMI's Project Management Professional (PMP) certificate, the APM qualifications (APMP, MPMP, CPM), or the PRINCE Practitioner Certificate
- A diploma or degree by full- or part-time study at a university or other institution of higher education

- Competency-based qualifications. People with existing project management skills can work towards a competency-based qualification, for example the UK National Vocational Qualifications (NVQ) scheme. See also the Australian National Competency Standards for Project Management and the IPMA Competence Baseline (IPMA, 1999).

In many cases, training can be provided by distance learning, for example see the Insights from Industry box below, or via online registration, which can be very convenient for the full-time project manager. Some educational establishments and training providers are accredited by the relevant national project management association. This helps to maintain the quality of the training provided, and provides a measure of consistency and standardisation concerning the topics covered and the terminology used.

---

insights from INDUSTRY   **FUTURE LEARNING SYSTEMS**

Future Learning Systems provide project management training by distance learning to large and small companies. For example, ICL have recently placed a contract for a product called Project Curriculum to enable staff throughout the UK to increase their knowledge through the flexible learning provided by distance learning modules. The courses chosen by ICL cover planning, cost management, risk and the newly launched module in resource management. The contract comes on top of other recent new orders from Costain, Dunlop Aviation and Mirror Group Newspapers.

*Source: Project, 2001, **13**(10): 8*

PROJECT MANAGEMENT *in action*

The making of a city technology college

City technology colleges (CTCs) were conceived in the UK, based on the US model of 'magnet' schools.

We believe there is an urgent need to create more choice in education provision to broaden the educational opportunity in urban areas. I have therefore decided, with the enthusiastic backing of the prime minister and my colleagues, to launch a pilot network of new schools in the urban areas including disadvantaged inner cities. These will be called city technology colleges. *(Kenneth Baker, former UK education secretary)*

The following dialogue was taken from an interview with an architect about a project to build a new CTC. The project was one of several CTCs being built in the UK at that time.

The sponsor was a consortium made up of local businesses in partnership with the Department of Education and Science (DES). The architect telling the story was employed by the sponsor as an independent adviser. Most of the design work was done by a different firm of architects working for the building contractor.

Question: How did the project begin?

Answer: The original proposal from the DES was to refurbish an existing school. The DES had identified a site and produced preliminary plans. But the sponsor didn't want a refurbished school. They wanted a new school. The scheme proposed would have resulted in ten different level changes to the original building. It was a mess ... a complete shambles. The sponsor threatened to pull out.

Question: Then what happened?

Answer: Finally, at the last minute, the DES said: 'OK, you can have a new school, but you still only get the same budget and timescale.' So the DES scrapped the initial scheme they had proposed and turned it into what they called a 'design and build' scheme. In fact it wasn't strictly design and build, more of a merger of two different types of contract: a management contract and a design and build contract.

Anyway, the DES presented the new scheme to the sponsor. By this time the sponsor had already chosen their project manager, a guy called David Wright. A particularly talented guy. I've got to say his drive and vision are outstanding. He's extremely good.

He had been given the preliminary documents for the new scheme and decided with the DES's blessing that he wanted his own professional team to advise him, and so he appointed ourselves as architects, and the XYZ Partnership as quantity surveyors (QSs).

Question: Were there any problems?

Answer: Time. David gave us the project documentation (nothing detailed, just preliminary plans) and said: 'We are about to go to tender on this.' We were given just two days, the QS and ourselves, to work through it and respond.

Question: How did you get on?

Answer: We went back to him two days later and said: 'If you build this you have got a disaster on your hands ... or build it without us.' It was a load of rubbish. He accepted our advice and so we went back to the DES saying: 'This doesn't work'. Then we rewrote the method.

We received educational input from the educational advisor that worked for the DES. He was already in place and had his own architects and his own QS. Between us we were able to produce a project charter that was capable of being achieved in design terms with a variety of solutions. There were a lot of specifications but we left the design open. That's the whole point of a design and build contract. You tell the contractor what your requirements are and give him the freedom to come up with the best design. That way there should be fewer problems building it. Even so, the project charter was really big. You're talking 500 pages. We tried to give the maximum range of options to the architects of the contractors that were invited.

While we were drafting the new documentation, we did an initial trawl of potential building contractors, checking them out. The tenders (including the project charter) went out to ... I think it was six contractors.

Question: How did you narrow it down to just one contractor?

Answer: We had question and answer sessions during the tender period because the speed of response needed from the contractors was very, very fast and it was much quicker to set up a whole series of meetings to answer any questions than to set up a heavy paperwork process. They were very much treated as a design team member right from the word go.

When we had received the final submissions we carried out interviews to assess their suitability. The QS, ourselves, the DES, and the educational advisor, in particular, all had very strong assessment criteria. We set up a matrix of what we felt were the important criteria, and measured each scheme against them. It was a robust method of measurement. Each of us went through it and then we brought our individual assessments together, and came to an agreement.

Question: Were the contractors aware of the criteria used?

Answer: Yes. The criteria we used were written into the invitation to tender documents. The contractors answered various questions as they went. Some of them were quantitative, to do with floor

area, for example. Others were more subjective, to do with, say, their understanding of the brief.

We asked questions such as: How well did the building adapt to change in education? How is cross-curricula activity catered for? Is the management of the school dispersed or centralised? What's the ability of the building to extend? What's the ability of the building to alter during the construction phases, because we knew that we had gone so fast, and that we were going to actually continue designing whilst we were building. The programme needed to be flexible.

We also assessed the contractors by the team they put forward. We insisted on seeing the team, the actual people running it.

Question: Before you appointed them?

Answer: Oh yes. We insisted on having the project manager, and one of the site foremen, they would put on the job right from day one. We weren't too interested in their marketing manager. We'd also insisted on their QS being there, their architect being there, and their services engineer. We felt, right from the word go, that the project manager was the key. If he didn't want it to work, it wouldn't work. I mean I must say several of the contractors have got very good project managers, certainly I can think of three who would probably have done it.

Question: Was anything else important?

Answer: The chemistry needs to work, between the individuals involved. The system has to be there, but if the chemistry is right it makes the system work.

Interviewing gives you a start. I wouldn't like to say that it's fully robust because if somebody has a nervous breakdown, his wife has a baby or the company goes into receivership in the middle, well, their characteristics may change.

Question: What happened next?

Answer: Once the tender was accepted, the contractor was involved in the detailed design. He had his own architect, who worked extremely closely with us. We had interface meetings with the contractor and the contractor was very open with the design team. The only way to work was to be able to say between us, 'look, we can afford this by doing this', or, 'we've got money spare here but we haven't got enough money here'. So the design proposals and costings were constantly being renewed and refined. We are talking about less than every week.

The role of Dave Lynch, the educational advisor, was crucial. He is a former county education officer for various areas, and very well known and respected. He helped put together the curriculum. For example, when we did the design brief, we hadn't got any college staff, all we had was a headmaster who wasn't even in the post at the time. So Dave's role was vital to get the educational balance right. We then agreed to bring on board the head and the deputy on a part-time basis from Christmas ... sorry, from September, and then we brought some of the key staff on from Christmas. They did most of the educational development programme, resources and materials. They were doing a lot of that at the same time that we were building, so we were constantly able to expand our information base.

Question: In what ways would you consider the project as successful or unsuccessful?

Answer: The project was overwhelmingly successful. The reason it was successful was that everyone wanted it to work. And the criteria we had established helped solve all the problems. We knew how much money we'd got, we knew what time we'd got, and

therefore we agreed to make the best possible decisions in the time available.

We had no illusions that there was a perfect solution because there never is. We developed a phrase which basically was: 'Making a decision was sometimes more important than the quality of the decision.' If we were 85–95% correct, it would be there. Take the decision, get it built. And in fact it has been borne out, because the quality of decisions if we had waited longer would have been very little better if any better at all. For example, we could have waited for the DES to agree the design before contacting contractors. If we'd followed the conventional approval line, we'd have been waiting a very, very long time. They, inevitably, weren't capable of responding fast enough.

Question: Were there any problems regarding communication?

Answer: No, because when we started the project, we sat down with the project director and agreed what the communication lines were, and they were short. We had a project director reporting direct to the sponsor and the DES. We would attend as required to make presentations. There was a short link there. The sponsor's project director went to ourselves as architects on all technical aspects, QS on costing, and the educational advisor on education issues. If there was any major design or assessment to be done, it would be done by the four of us, at most. We would come to a conclusion and that would be the end of it. A lot of

it was done by minutes. We would have a meeting, decide something, and record and action it by minutes and that was it.

Question: Looking back, what is your impression of the level of harmony, trust and goodwill between participants?

Answer: Exceptional. You happen to have chosen the best project I have ever worked on for job cooperation.

We ran a day and a half project orientation exercise, before it even went to site, which the project manager, his leading foremen and the QSs and everyone else was invited to. It was fully attended. We did it so that they knew what we were trying to build and what its purpose was. They were told about national curriculum. They were told about the way of teaching. They were told about the concept of pupil assemblies. They were told about how children would use this space. So in fact they had a very clear view, not just of the bricks and mortar, but of the purpose and why the timetable was so tight and what they were being asked to achieve.

The project manager and others reckoned the orientation exercise gave them a major insight into the project, so they knew what they were trying to do. It wasn't just a lot of bricks and mortar. Right from day one, they knew what they were doing, which basically means, they knew what they were building, why and what it was all about. And that does give purpose to many of the operatives, particularly to the people that supervise the site operations.

QUESTIONS TO AID UNDERSTANDING AND DISCUSSION

1. There are several examples of good practice in this case. Which of the following can you find?
   - commitment to project success
   - communication and feedback
   - early assignment of the project manager
   - fast tracking
   - integration of different participants
   - leadership
   - risk management
   - scope change
   - short communication lines
   - team building
   - use of advisors with expert knowledge.

2. What impact would you expect each practice to have on the project?

3. Are there any examples of poor practice?

Summary points

- Project definitions vary widely, reflecting the huge variation in size of what people call projects.
- The same principles of project management apply whatever size a project is; the amount of project management resource required, however, varies with size and complexity.
- Every project should have a clear beginning and end; in reality these boundaries are often fuzzy.
- Three primary characteristics of projects that set them apart from other activities are that they are temporary, unique and require progressive elaboration.
- Other characteristics of projects are that they tend to carry risk, be organisationally complex, trade between time, cost and function, compete for scarce resources, have single point responsibility and require teamwork and leadership skills to succeed.
- Project management is the planning, monitoring and control of all aspects of a project and the motivation of all those involved in it to achieve the project objectives on time and to the specified cost, quality and performance.
- The management task in project management concerns four activities in particular: planning, organising, controlling and leading/motivating.
- Hard project management skills are generally technical skills such as planning and scheduling; soft skills are people-related skills, such as communication, leadership and emotional intelligence. Project managers require competence in both.
- Projects originate for a variety of reasons such as market demand, business need, strategy implementation, customer requests, new technology, new legislation, operations management, a crisis or a social need.
- Programme management is the coordinated management of a portfolio of projects to achieve a set of business objectives.
- Programme management is particularly concerned with managing dependencies between projects such as strategic, technological, resource and budget.
- Five major influences in the history of project management are development of management thought, creation of special tools and techniques, development of information and communication technologies, socioeconomic and political influences and the expanding scope of project management.

- Project management is still an evolving subject. Although it is not yet recognised as a scientific discipline, it boasts many associations and institutes offering services to hundreds of thousands of members worldwide and continuing debate on the future of project management.
- A key challenge for the future of project management is to develop a set of premises about the purpose of project management, the criteria and factors for judging and achieving success on projects and what constitutes good project management practice.
- Project management maturity models enable organisations to score themselves against key processes in project management and plan for future improvements.
- Project management training cannot guarantee success but can help to avoid ignorant project managers and business managers, so that both can use and apply project management resources more effectively.

Visit the website

http://www.palgrave.com/business/gardiner

▶ to test your understanding of the learning objectives for Chapter 1 using multiple choice questions

In the next chapter we shall be considering projects as systems and introducing the life cycle of a project from generic and industry-specific perspectives. The importance of people in projects will be highlighted and the use of fast tracking and the PRINCE 2 methodology introduced.

References

APM (2000). *Body of Knowledge,* 4th edn, Association for Project Management, High Wycombe.

Bennis, W. and Nanus, B. (1985). *Leaders: The Strategies for Taking Charge,* Harper & Row, New York.

Brittania (2002). Accessed online 15 October 2002 from http://www.britannia.com/history/h7.html.

BS 6079-1 (2000). *Project Management – Part 1: Guide to project management*, British Standards Institution, Milton Keynes.

BS 6079-2 (2000). *Project Management – Part 2: Vocabulary*, British Standards Institution, Milton Keynes.

BT *Project Management Handbook*, Reference Manual, BT Programme Office, Issue 7 (10/94), Publication number: TPU 1159, published by MCS/Technical Publications Unit, London.

CCTA (1993). *An Introduction to Programme Management*, HMSO, London.

Graham, R.J. and Englund, R.L. (1997). *Creating an Environment for Successful Projects: The Quest to Manage Project Management*, Jossey-Bass, San Francisco.

Gray, R.J. and Bamford, P.J. (1999). 'Issues in programme integration', *International Journal of Project Management*, **17**(6): 361–6.

Hartman, F.T. (2000). *Don't Park Your Brain Outside*, Project Management Institute, Pennsylvania.

Hooks, I.F. and Farry, K.A. (2000). *Customer Centered Products: Creating Successful Products Through Smart Requirements Management*, Amacom, New York.

IPMA (1999). *ICB IPMA Competence Baseline Version 2.0*, International Project Management Association, Monmouth.

MacLachlan, L. (1996). 'Making project management work for you', Library Association Publishing, London.

Meredith, J.R. and Mantel, Jr, S.J. (1995). *Project Management – A Managerial Approach,* 3rd edn, John Wiley & Sons, New York.

Morris, P.W.G. (1988). 'Why project management doesn't always make business sense', *Project Management*: the Professional Magazine of the Project Management Association, Finland, **4**(1): 12–16.

Office of Government Commerce (OGC) (1999). *Managing Successful Programmes*, The Stationery Office, London.

PMI (2000). *Guide to the Project Management Body of Knowledge*, Project Management Institute, Upper Darby, PA.

Reiss, G. (1996). *Programme Management Demystified: Managing multiple projects successfully*, E & F Spon, London.

Standish (1995). *The CHAOS report*, The Standish Group, 196 Old Townhouse Road, West Yarmouth, MA 02673.

Themistocleous, G. and Wearne, S.H. (2000). 'Project management topic coverage in journals', *International Journal of Project Management*, **18**(1): 7–11.

Turner, R. (1992). *The Handbook of Project-based Management*, 2nd edn, McGraw-Hill, New York.

Turner, R. (1999). 'Project management: a profession based on knowledge or faith?', editorial, *International Journal of Project Management*, **17**(6): 329–30.

Turner, R. (2000a). 'Do you manage work, deliverables or resources?', editorial, *International Journal of Project Management*, **18**(2): 83–4.

Turner, R. (2000b). 'The global body of knowledge, and its coverage by the referees and members of the international editorial board of this journal', editorial, *International Journal of Project Management*, **18**(1): 1–5.

US Fish & Wildlife Service, (March 8, 1994) 270 FW 3, Information Resources Management, Project Management.

2

A systems view of project management

Learning objectives

After reading this chapter you should be able to:

- apply systems theory to explain the interrelations between project elements
- discuss the human factor and the role of feedback and feed-forward mechanisms in projects
- explain the effect of fast tracking on the project life cycle and its management
- characterise and interpret project life cycles in different industries
- use project classification tools to help select a project management approach
- explain the function and form of a project management methodology such as PRINCE 2

Introduction

An action, or failure to take an action, in one area of a project will usually affect other areas of the project (PMI, 2000: 29). In this chapter, systems theory is used to explain the project management life cycle. Breaking down a complete project into smaller inter-related parts enables more effective management of the project. The four major phases of a project, and their deliverables, considered here are: initiation and definition; planning and development; execution and control; and project closure. The use of feedback and feed-forward information, vital for all phases of a project, is introduced; and the myth of the 'fixed' project plan is exposed.

Project management has branched out from its early defence and construction roots to other industries and disciplines, such as software, banking, insurance, business transformation, new product development, event management, international development and the voluntary sector. Some of these have tailored the project life cycle to align it with their own way of working. This chapter considers several variations of the 'standard' project life cycle. Several approaches to classifying and comparing projects are also discussed.

A formalised project life cycle is often called a 'project management methodology' – a detailed guide for doing projects designed to bring consis-

tency and standardisation to managing projects in an organisation. An outline and discussion of PRINCE 2, a scaleable project management methodology, is included.

The chapter concludes with a Project Management in Action case about home and office banking – a rapid development project in a competitive environment, with an early benefit designed into the life cycle.

A systems approach

Introduction to systems theory

The development of a general systems theory in the 1950s and 60s gave birth to a new approach to understanding complex situations and events (Hall and Fagen, 1956; Johnson et al., 1963). Systems theory brings structure and order to an otherwise chaotic and unpredictable environment. The uncertainties and complexities of the early large defence and aerospace projects were prime candidates for the application of this new theory. To this day, it is generally accepted that project management can be studied more effectively with reference to systems theory because of its analytic and holistic approach.

The universal systems diagram, shown in Figure 2.1, illustrates the relationship between the three main parts of a system:

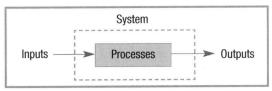

Figure 2.1 Universal systems diagram

1. *Inputs:* defined as energy in any form brought into the system.
2. *Processes:* defined as a series of actions, changes or functions that bring about a particular result.
3. *Outputs:* defined as the products or consequences that result from the processes performed.

The systems approach can be applied to a whole system or just part of a system. A large and complex system can be broken down into lower level subsystems as illustrated by the hierarchical structure of Figure 2.2. Using systems theory, a project can be decomposed into its separate phases, work packages and activities. These are lower level systems. When communicating project information, care should be given to match the level of the project system with the needs and desired result of the user. Most project management tools exploit the hierarchical property of a system. The project plan, the work breakdown structure, the cost breakdown structure, the Gantt chart and the project network can all be prepared for reporting purposes at different levels. Senior management usually find higher level reports, with less detail, more useful for strategic decision making, whereas contractors, subcontractors and

other work package owners use the greater detail provided by lower level reports to manage and control their work.

Key Concepts explains the nuances between the terms 'system', 'process' and 'procedure' which are often used incorrectly.

 Systems, processes and procedures

The definition of a system includes the idea of 'interrelated parts working in conjunction with each other in order to accomplish a number of goals'. On the other hand, 'a process is a series of actions bringing about a result' (PMI, 2000). The key difference is that processes are time-bound whereas systems are not. Systems contain processes which operate within a time frame, but systems themselves are not bound by a particular direction or sequence in time. The concept of sequence, however, is essential to a process.

Another related term is 'procedure'. A procedure is a formalised set of instructions, written down or passed on verbally, which inform people about *how* to do something. In manufacturing, for example, the correct use of a machine may be described by a standard operating procedure (SOP). A process, on the other hand, indicates *what* needs to be done rather than how to do it; and a system includes the relationships between the different parts – it provides the 'big picture' view of all the system elements and their environment.

Projects as systems

Systems theory was applied to organisations long before it was used to understand projects. Johnson

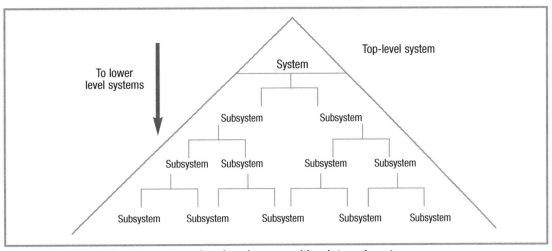

Figure 2.2 Hierarchy in a system showing decomposition into subsystems

et al. (1963: 10) describe a typical business organisation as:

a man-made system which has a dynamic interplay with its environment and many other agencies ... a system of inter-related parts working in conjunction with each other to accomplish a number of goals, both those of the organisation and those of individual participants.

Projects and organisations are open systems. This means that they interact with their environment – a condition true for most systems. The concept of an open system was used as early as 1951 by the biologist Ludwig von Bertalanffy to describe a living organism as a definite system and not just a collection of separate elements. From a systems perspective, projects and organisms share several traits. They are both:

- open systems which maintain a controlled state while matter and energy enter and keep changing
- influenced by, and influence, their environment while reaching, or attempting to reach, a state of dynamic equilibrium with the environment.

Later studies in the social sciences and psychology began to draw attention to the role of differentiation and its counterpart integration in business systems, particularly in large or growing systems. Differentiation and integration are also important in project management and will be explored in more detail in Chapter 6.

The components and relationships of the general project system are shown in Figure 2.3 and described below.

Inputs

There are six categories of resources necessary for a project:

- *business need and requirement* – these justify the existence of the project
- *human resources* – the people and skills available to manage and work on the project
- *physical resources* – equipment, materials,

energy, facilities and funds that are applied to the project
- *project constraints* – cost, time and technical constraints on the project and how they relate to scope, quality and safety requirements
- *organisational and environmental factors* – internal and external influences, structures, policies, regulations and procedures that affect the project
- *information resources* – historical data and information collected through feedback and feed-forward activities; used in scope definition, cost and schedule estimating, evaluation and control.

Outputs

Project results and end products vary according to the nature and purpose of the project. Examples of project results include:

- reports
- presentations
- new products and designs
- goods and services
- sporting and other events
- buildings
- software
- systems
- increased brand recognition and goodwill.

Project results include any outcomes, intended or not, that occur as a consequence of the project's activities. In a successful project, results comply with or improve on the critical success factors established for the project.

Processes

The project processes act on the resources to produce the project results. Since projects can be very complex, the management processes can also be complex. Conversely, for simple projects, such as a trip to the supermarket or making a cup of tea, no formal processes may be needed at all.

The APM's *Body of Knowledge* uses a universal

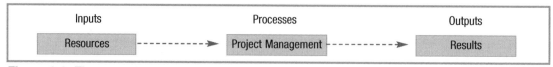

Figure 2.3 The general project system

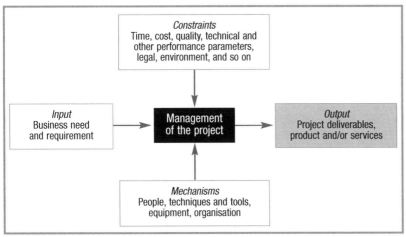

Figure 2.4 Project system showing constraints and mechanisms (APM, 2000: 15)

systems diagram, with added constraints and mechanisms, to represent the project management process (see Figure 2.4).

The human factor

It should be borne in mind that systems analysis is a model and tool to help people to understand and work with projects. A systems view is an abstraction of reality. In practice, projects involve real people with ideas, ambitions, strategies, strengths and weaknesses. The model is helpful providing it does not replace or undermine the good judgement and common sense of project leaders.

Hartman (2000: 121) draws attention to the glib way that project management is often described as being systematic, a systems approach, structured or phased, and how by so doing one can easily lose the 'most important single issue in managing projects: working with people'. He constantly reminds the reader that people are 'volatile, arbitrary, creative, and emotional' and that these traits make us 'exciting, challenging and, if we do it right, fun to work with'.

Feedback in a system

The importance of feedback

Feedback is important in a system because it can be used to regulate and control the system. This is achieved by comparing output information with control data and then making system adjustments to compensate for any variations observed.

 Feedback in a simple gardening project

Consider a gardening project in which one team prepares the ground for planting bulbs and a second team does the planting. The first team prepares the soil and drills correctly sized holes for the bulbs. The second team follows on some way behind, planting the bulbs and backfilling the hole with compost. Let us assume the team work all morning and make good progress, then the weather changes and it begins to rain. Due to the rain, the prepared holes begin to collapse before the second team are able to plant the bulbs.

To correct the problem, the second team pass information about the problem to the first team, who then take corrective action against the rain, perhaps erecting a temporary canopy for shelter or waiting until the rain abates.

In this project, control is achieved by comparing the output from team one (drilled holes in the soil) to the requirements of team two (holes suitable for planting bulbs) and issuing feedback information when a problem arises to invoke corrective action.

Effect of a time lag in a feedback system

Delays invariably occur between the output of a system and subsequent adjustments. Such time lags can substantially reduce the effectiveness of the control mechanism and under extreme conditions may actually cause the system to malfunction. The destabilising effects of a time lag depend on the duration of the lag and the strength or intensity of the feedback control correction (Dworkin, 1993). Consider, for example, the effects of a delay in the operation of a simple thermostat that regulates room temperature by turning on either a heating or a cooling unit. If the thermostat operates with a substantial time lag, it will permit the room to get too hot before activating the cooling unit. Likewise, it will permit the room to get too cold before activating the heating unit. Thus, time lags will cause increased oscillations in room temperature. Oscillation problems become especially troublesome if the feedback correction is particularly strong, for instance if very hot air is introduced to correct for a drop in temperature and very cold air is introduced to correct for a rise in temperature. Under these conditions, delayed feedback will exacerbate the destabilising effects of temperature fluctuations. Thus, time lags can seriously compromise the effectiveness of feedback regulation (Kalmus, 1966).

Feed-forward systems

Accurate prediction of a future event can only be based on how similar events took place in the past. For example, a weather forecaster predicts rain not on the basis of clairvoyance but on the basis of patterns of prior meteorological events. Thus, accurate prediction or feed-forward mechanisms are possible only with the existence of some kind of memory. Memory allows feed-forward mechanisms to anticipate output errors that have occurred in the past under similar circumstances. Through feed-forward mechanisms, a system can be 'corrected' before an output error actually occurs. In principle, feed-forward mechanisms are more useful than feedback mechanisms because they can reduce the destabilising effects of time lags in feedback regulation and adjust system functioning to *prevent* error.

In a feed-forward system, input information is compared with historical data from previous input data and its feedback control adjustments. Acting on this information allows adjustments to be made before errors occur.

 Feed forward in a simple gardening project

Returning to the gardening project above, if the team planting the bulbs knew that the weather forecast predicted rain, they could immediately consult their gardening records to determine what (if any) adjustments should be made to reduce the risk of problems occurring. The planting team could then feed forward this information to the ground preparation team, advising them to consider taking preventive action before it rains.

Feedback and feed forward in project management

Feedback is used as a means of changing a system through evaluation, part of the monitoring and control mechanism in a project. By comparing results with plans and objectives, the project manager can identify problems and fine-tune the system. Adjustments can be made by altering resources, revising management procedures or, if all else fails, redefining the project parameters. In project management, feedback:

1. helps each participant to learn about the project and their own contribution to it.
2. gives a participant information about how their contribution fits with and interfaces with all the other contributions and deliverables.
3. can be used by a participant to reflect on actions they have taken, learn from the consequences (positive and negative) and improve their performance.
4. helps ensure that everyone is working towards the same agreed project objectives, notoriously difficult to achieve.

Feedback involving the different stakeholders, on a regular basis, is the only assurance that the project manager and the main participants can get about how well they are satisfying the project stakeholders, especially the customer.

Feed-forward information serves two primary purposes:

1. It augments feedback information by alerting participants further down the project life cycle of events and decisions that are taking place in earlier phases. This allows participants of later phases to bring in their knowledge and expertise earlier than would otherwise be possible. The teams working in the earlier phases can benefit from this knowledge and adjust their outputs in a way that prevents errors and unnecessary (and expensive) changes downstream. This would be impossible with a feedback only control system.
2. Feed-forward information can help to shorten learning curves and accelerate the integration of the different disciplines working on a project. Everyone is able to contribute in a positive way to all phases of the life cycle. This is desirable in a project environment and can reduce the number of requests for change and rework, which in turn helps maintain or improve the cost–benefit ratio.

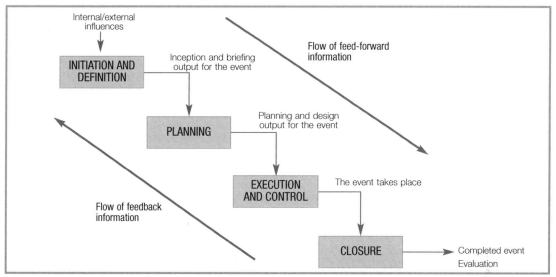

Figure 2.5 Feedback and feed-forward information flows in a sporting event

Project information is never 100% complete until the end of the project, therefore it makes sense to have in place both feedback and feed-forward systems of control. This allows the system to operate more efficiently and effectively under changing environmental conditions.

To summarise, feedback control acts to eliminate errors; feed-forward control operates to stop the error occurring in the first place. The system diagram in Figure 2.5 represents the life cycle of a sporting event and shows the different phases and information flows in the project.

Phases and characteristics of the project life cycle

The project life cycle

Projects typically move through a set of phases called a project life cycle. Each phase is marked by the completion of one or more deliverables, that is, a tangible, verifiable piece of work such as a feasibility report, a work breakdown structure, a project network or a project (or phase) end product (see Figure 2.6). Breaking a project up in this way aids its control, for example evaluation and approval points can be set up between phases. The progress of each deliverable can be monitored phase by phase and action taken as necessary to correct variations from the plan.

Using a life cycle approach to manage a project helps to ensure that:

- difficult issues will not be overlooked
- time and money will not be wasted
- resources will be more effectively employed.

The project life cycle defines the beginning and end of the project. This is useful because it makes it clear for everyone when the project has actually finished. Look again at the Insights from Industry: 'The absent-minded professor' in Chapter 1 as a reminder of how difficult it can be to pinpoint the end of a project.

In some projects, the life cycle is extended beyond the traditional phases to include operations, maintenance and logistics. Even decommissioning, disposal and replacement can be included in a project life cycle. In these cases the term 'total life cycle' or 'product life cycle' can be used to denote that both the initial costs and the future costs and benefits (savings) of the investment are included.

Each phase of the life cycle is discussed below in more detail.

Phase one: Initiation and definition

This phase represents the start of the project and defines the 'sum of the products and services to be provided by the project' (PMI, 2000). Scoping activities are performed to bound the project scope and define the interface between deliverables that are included in the project and those that are not. The justification for the project is firmly established with respect to the sponsor's strategic plan and the costs

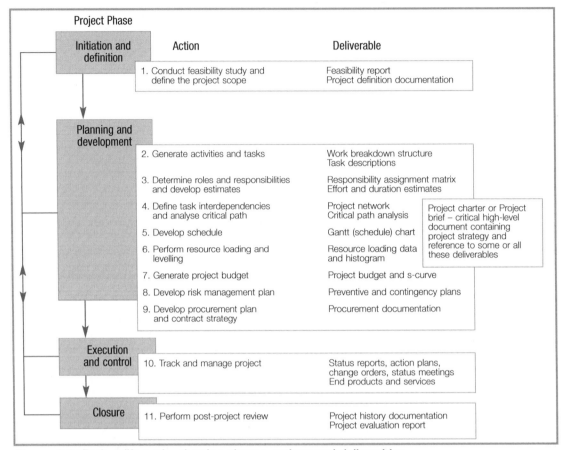

Figure 2.6 Project life cycle, showing phases, actions and deliverables

and benefits are investigated, usually by conducting a feasibility study and project assessment. The feasibility report provides vital information to help an organisation decide whether or not it should go ahead with the project investment. Frequently, funds are limited and a firm must ration the number of projects that are approved.

For a contracting firm, this phase is often split into two stages: marketing activities and exploration of project opportunities, followed by the 'go/no-go' decision to bid for the work.

In phase one, enthusiasm and an open-minded, creative approach to problem solving are important. Good practice requires the consideration of two or three alternative solutions.

It is often tempting, for the client and the performing organisation (when different), to rush some of the activities associated with the initiation and definition phase in an effort to start making 'real' or visible progress. However, this is almost always regretted later and rarely leads to a project finishing on time. The Insights from Industry box highlights evidence collected by KPMG on the importance of taking the time to conduct a feasibility study.

insights from INDUSTRY WHY BOTHER WITH A FEASIBILITY STUDY?

Feasibility studies are a time-tested practice, but they aren't used very much. A KPMG survey found that 84 per cent of companies that had suffered runaway projects proposed to use feasibility studies as one means of preventing future problems. This survey finding suggests that these companies had not performed feasibility analyses in their runaway projects. After all, if they had performed them in the past, why would they expect performing them in the future to make any difference?

Source: 'Runaway Projects – Cause and Effect', *Software World*, **26**(3) 1995

Phase two: Planning and development

By the time a project progresses from phase one to phase two, major decisions have been taken on the design of the project end products and how to obtain them, that is, the project strategy to be used.

Phase two focuses on planning and development issues that will form the basis of project control throughout project execution and delivery. There are three essential elements to phase two:

1. The creation of all the required plans to support the project including:
   - scope management plans, used to manage the expectations of project team members, support resources and other stakeholders
   - work plan and timeline
   - resource and budgetary plans
   - procurement plans and contract strategy
   - risk management plans
   - quality management plans
   - document management plans
   - project control plans, including project closure and handover
   - human resource management plans, including attending to any leadership and team-building needs, and training and recruitment needs.

   The information gathered and created during the initiation and definition phase is recorded in a document, often called a 'project charter' (in business and IT projects) or a 'project brief' (in engineering and construction projects). This document summarises the key points from the feasibility report and gives full reference to it. The project charter describes the background and decisions taken about a project, including what the agreed scope is, the project plan and strategy, the resources required, who is going to do the work and an agreed timescale. The agreement of the information in the project charter by the key project stakeholders is an important 'gate' through which the project should pass.
2. The mobilisation and organisation of all the resources required by the project: people, equipment, materials, knowledge, power, and so on.
3. The establishment of an infrastructure to support those resources and ensure that effective communication can be maintained across the network of project stakeholders.

Work done in the planning and development phase is effectively money in the bank, which alleviates the risk of the project manager having to operate 'on the fly' when project execution does not go as expected. Problems with project delivery are often known about early on in a project, but because it can be difficult, or unpopular, to address these issues at the time they are frequently ignored or put off till later. However, the popular adage that it costs more to fix things after implementation than it does to design and develop them right the first time holds true for most projects.

Because effective project planning is so critical to the overall success of the project, the project leader should ensure that all appropriate planning requirements have been addressed. This can be accomplished by ensuring that one of the 'gates' within the planning process is the approval of the overall project plan, which includes the project charter and all the additional planning documents. On a small project, this can simply take the form of a checklist to verify that all parts of the planning process have been addressed, or on a larger project, a more formal and in-depth review can be carried out.

Phase three: Execution and control

This is the phase in a project when the rate of expenditure is at its greatest. It is also the phase when the sponsor expects to see project deliverables arriving on time that meet or exceed expectations.

As a project progresses, new information and a better understanding of the client's circumstances can often lead to requests for change. It is often not until this phase that the client fully appreciates what the project outcomes will look like or how they will operate in practice. Although the aim of project planning is to 'get it right first time', the wise project manager knows that some changes are inevitable and even desirable.

Project management is about managing expectations and delivering an end result in keeping with those expectations. The ability to simultaneously plan and remain flexible, delivering to expectations quickly and without waste is a hallmark of effective project management.

Of course, there is a need to maintain control over any changes to project plans and minimise them to those that are required to achieve the project's critical success factors as laid down in the project charter or brief.

Phase four: Closure

Closure is a formal part of project management that is best planned at the start of a project along with the other activities. Closure represents the end of a project and is characterised by the closing of the project budget so that no more money can be spent on the project, completing the documentation and administration requirements of the project, including any final payments to contractors and suppliers, and arranging for the release of all the project participants. At handover, the finished product is transferred to the care, custody and control of the owner.

Delays to closure can occur when there are grievances between contracted parties that remain unresolved at the end of the project. Many otherwise good relationships can be marred by unpleasantness at the end of a project if parties are not willing or feel unable to come to agreement about disputes. Conflict and dispute management and resolution are covered in Chapter 8.

Closure provides an opportunity for formal project evaluation, which aims to review performance and learn from best practices and mistakes. In some organisations, benchmarking and knowledge-sharing processes are used to capture knowledge and learning and share this effectively with other projects and business units in the company. This is an effective strategy for strengthening competitive advantage.

However, the view that project evaluation occurs only at the end of a project is a dangerous misconception. Evaluation should be an ongoing process that examines interim results as the project progresses. A formal evaluation process may also be desirable at specified intervals, for example quarterly, at formal decision gates as well as at the end of the project.

Common life cycle characteristics

As a project moves through the life cycle phases, both its form and nature change. These changes require the project manager's watchful eye so that timely adjustments can be made to the style of leadership and management employed. The following life cycle changes are common to most projects:

- *Resources*. Consumption of resources begins low during initiation, gains pace during planning, is at full throttle during implementation and tails off rapidly at closure (see Figure 2.7, curve 1).
- *Staffing*. Staffing levels are low at the start, higher in the middle and drop quickly as the project draws to a conclusion.
- *Predictability of outcome*. The predictability of the project outcome, for example how successful it will be, is lowest at the start of the project. Predictability gets progressively higher as the project continues.
- *Opportunity to influence*. The opportunity for stakeholders to influence the final characteristics of the project without increasing the cost of the project is highest at the start and gets progressively lower as the project continues (see Figure 2.7, curve 2).
- *Organisational needs*. Each phase in a project has different organisational needs. For example, in the initiation and definition phase creativity and problem solving are important. During execution and control the emphasis is on turning carefully laid plans into reality – tight control of changes and rapid decision making are predominant needs.

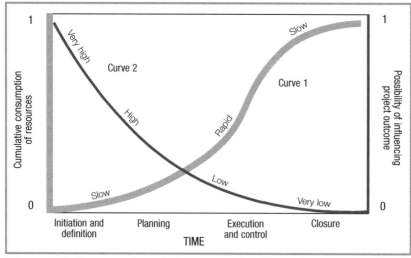

Figure 2.7 Common characteristics of project life cycles

 Project life cycle

The challenge for everyone involved in a project is to:

- maximise knowledge as quickly as possible
- reduce risk as quickly as possible
- preserve the ability to influence the final result for as long as possible
- minimise cost.

Information flows in a project

Managing information between different project phases is central to effective project management. Each phase has its own aims and objectives and moving from one phase to the next usually involves some form of technology transfer or handover, such as requirements to design, construction to operations, or design to manufacturing (PMI, 2000). In each case the outputs of one phase become the inputs for the next. Different people with different skill sets may be involved from one phase to the next. However, project management works best when information is available and able to flow freely between all phases at all times, not just at the

end of a phase. The different phases are strongly interdependent and each phase can be usefully informed by consulting with staff from the other project phases. When managed effectively, there is an open exchange of information (including feed-back and feed-forward information) between all the phases of a project. This helps the participants of each phase improve the quality of their processes and end products in a way that works together for the benefit of the whole project and therefore the end customer.

Figure 2.8 illustrates the relative intensity of information transfer that is typical within and between the various project phases over the entire project life cycle.

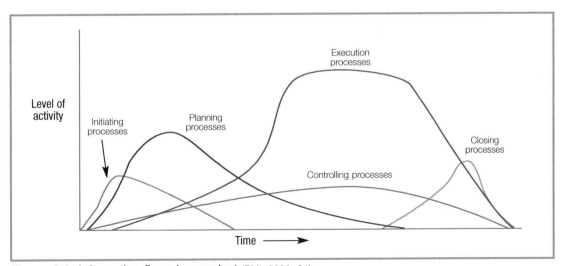

Figure 2.8 **Information flows in a project** (PMI, 2000: 31)

Fast tracking

Fast tracking is the shortening of the project life cycle by overlapping project phases. In some projects, a later project phase may be started prior to the completion and approval of all the previous phase deliverables. This usually occurs when the risks involved are deemed acceptable and are outweighed by the benefits. The practice of fast tracking is also known as 'concurrent engineering' and 'simultaneous engineering', especially in manufacturing projects. The concept of fast tracking is illustrated in Figure 2.9.

Fast tracking can reduce the duration of a project and its overhead costs. Revenue streams can begin earlier. Using this technique, the deliverables from one phase are passed over to the next phase on a 'rolling-wave' basis rather than waiting for each phase to have all items of work completed before passing them on. This means that for a time work is proceeding on several phases in parallel. Fast tracking gives the project participants at the receiving end something tangible to work

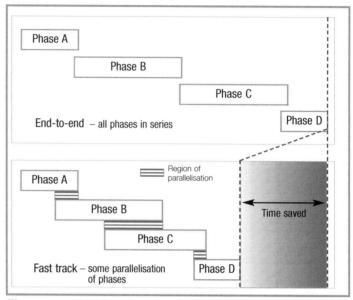

Figure 2.9 Fast tracking aims to shorten project duration

with much earlier, which can then help to smooth resources and accelerate the process of interfacing the different project phases. The Insights from Industry box 'Benefiting from fast tracking' shows how Lucas Girling and the Foinaven oilfield benefited from a fast-track approach.

---

insights from INDUSTRY   BENEFITING FROM FAST TRACKING

Lucas Girling

Brian Hindle, a project manager at Lucas Girling, an automotive parts manufacturer, describes how they introduced the concept of fast tracking into their operations:

> Traditionally we've tended to operate a manufacturing company where one department carries out its function, and then hands on the ball to the next department, who then carries out what it has to do to that project, and hands it on to the next one. So, if you look at the overall timing of the project, it's the time for each department to complete its work, added on to each other, plus some extra time, because obviously, as you hand it over they're not ready to start. What we are now trying to do is in fact to get the first department, say the design department, to start handing over its work to the next department, say the development department,

before it's completed the whole project – bringing to an end, hopefully, the old end-to-end 'relay-type' system, and bringing in what we now describe as the 'rugby-scrum' [fast-track] system.

Source: BBC Training videos, Managing Projects: Taking the Critical Path, 1988

Foinaven oilfield

Foinaven oilfield was discovered in 1992, some 190 kilometres west of the Shetland Islands. An oilfield development can be split into three phases, appraisal, engineering design and construction, with each essentially carried out in sequence. In the case of Foinaven, the time taken for each phase was shortened and then carried out in parallel to reduce conventional costs. For example, by drilling the appraisal wells back to back and using multiple drilling rigs, the full appraisal programme was completed in six months as compared to the normal estimate of two years.

Source: Atlantic Frontier Oil, 1999
http://www.gpuk.org/atlantic/library/oil/oilbrief.html

Warning about fast tracking

The benefits of fast tracking are not without their risks; the approach can lead to confusion, uncertainty and expensive rework when things go wrong. Be warned that the additional communication, feedback, and management control needed to maintain consistent and satisfactory quality from the outputs of each phase when fast tracking mean that in practice a fast-track project can (and many do) fail to deliver time or cost benefits and actually cause delays and cost overruns.

A contingency approach to project life cycles

If you are going to manage a software development project, a good starting point would be to go and talk to someone who has managed software development projects. The principles of project management apply in any discipline, but the chunking of a project or programme into life cycle phases will be shaped by the nature of the industry itself. This section explores the life cycles of projects in a number of different disciplines: software and systems development, building and construction, research and development, entertainment and events, and disasters and emergencies.

Although the jury is still out on whether project management should be viewed as a generic or domain-specific discipline (BPRC, 1997), no one denies that project management can be applied to any project in any discipline. The fundamental principles and underlying processes are universally, if not consistently, applied. However, we often hear people talking about 'construction project management', 'software project management', 'event project management', and so on, revealing a growing number of 'branded' project management approaches (see Table 2.1). The PMI (2000) includes several project life cycles, each illustrating a different application area. It also warns that although many life cycles have similar phase names with similar deliverables required, few are identical.

The project approach can be tailored to take into account some of the pitfalls and customer requirements in each discipline. This aids communication throughout an industry's projects. Familiarity with an acceptable model tends to perpetuate the implementation of that model, leading to possibilities for continuous improvement and the standardisation of the project delivery process. For example, project

Table 2.1 Results of an internet search for different 'brands' of project management

Search phrase used	No of hits 000s
software project management	152
construction project management	44
IT project management	68
building project management	44
organisational project management	13
business project management	19
critical chain project management	4
capital project management	5
manufacturing project management	3
strategic project management	3
event project management	2
pharmaceutical project management	1
lean project management	0.5

Source: Search conducted on Google.com, 19 June 2004.

participants in the movie-making industry will find that movie projects share similar characteristics. Film producers are faced with similar risks and constraints to others in the same industry. Customers and end users of the industry's products have similar expectations. In this way, collective experience shapes and forms the project life cycle.

Life cycles evolve as new processes are created to tackle particular problems and challenges. These are remembered and repeated by others (if they work) from one project to the next. However, project teams are typically created for a single project and then dismantled and dispersed after completion. Expert knowledge acquired over the duration of the project is therefore difficult to transfer to subsequent project-based teams (BPRC, 1997). The problem is compounded in traditional project management industries due to their conservative outlook, which generally means they are resistant or slow to embrace change, even when current methods continue to deliver late and/or over budget projects. Many organisations are turning to knowledge management and knowledge-sharing practices as important strategic imperatives for performance improvement in managing core business projects.

The lesson here is that there is no one right way to divide a project into its constituent life cycle phases to manage it. Rather, the concept of a life cycle is an artificial one created for the convenience of the participants concerned and to help project leaders manage the overall project system.

The downside of a discipline by discipline approach to project management is that it leads to unnecessary differences in terminology and practices between disciplines, which in turn hinders knowledge transfer and the development of new project management theories.

A range of different life cycles are described below. Those for software and systems development show how project life cycles evolve to reflect growing experience and understanding of a particular project environment.

Software and systems development project life cycles

Code and fix

Early software development projects followed a trial and error approach with little thought to project planning. A programmer creating a new application would jump straight into software coding, followed by a time of testing to identify bugs and then further coding to fix the bugs. More testing would be required to see if the bug fixes had worked and how many new bugs had been introduced. A typical project consisted of several iterations through the cycle: code, test and debug, until something 'acceptable' (in the programmer's mind) was produced. These projects included little in the way of forward or strategic planning and minimal user involvement, which was often left until the end product was almost ready (or the customer could wait no longer). The result was often a system that worked reasonably well some of the time but was not very close to what the user wanted or needed, or was too complex to use reliably without extensive training to get round the remaining bugs and human–computer interface problems that had not been addressed in the project. The approach was driven by the programmer with an attitude of: 'Let's see what we can do', a lot of misplaced hope and no clear requirements planning or management of expectations. Surprisingly, the method is still in use.

Waterfall model

The code and fix approach quickly hit problems as the complexity of software systems increased. A solution was found in a model used to develop complex hardware systems, called the 'waterfall model' – so named because of the way in which the discrete stages form a waterfall (see Figure 2.10).

The approach taken in the waterfall model is more structured and methodical than the code and fix approach. The number of phases can vary, but they are all based upon a systematic transition from one development phase to the next, until the project is complete. The method is document-driven and each phase is accompanied by documentation that is passed on to the next phase.

As a project proceeds, baselines are established that 'freeze' the products of the development at that point. The process takes the view that the business issues being addressed by the project will remain static during this time. Consequently, the method is

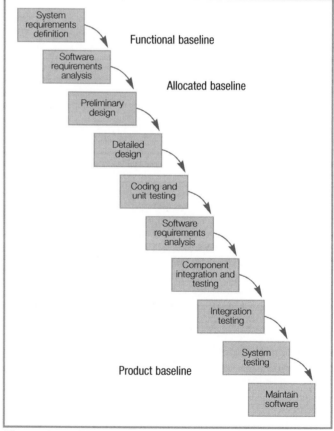

Figure 2.10 The waterfall project life cycle (Sorensen, 1995)

best suited to projects where changes to earlier phases are not normally required. However, when change is required, a formal change process is followed. The advantages and disadvantages of the waterfall model are as follows.

Advantages:
- The end of each stage provides a milestone for evaluating the project
- There is accountability for each stage of the project
- The model allows specialisation in each phase
- It is a well-established model and is supported by software engineering tools.

Disadvantages:
- Promotes a 'throw it over the wall' mentality
- Different teams handle each stage; this takes time, and for the customer patience is often a necessary virtue – a working version is not normally available till late in the project life cycle
- The long project life cycle makes dealing with new business issues difficult
- Improper analysis early in the project will mean that the final deliverable does not meet expectations; an issue compounded by the difficulty many customers have stating requirements clearly and explicitly early in a project
- Since decisions are frozen early, with limited opportunity for iteration, major problems can remain unnoticed until product delivery, with disastrous consequences.

Despite the disadvantages, the approach does have merit and is popular, particularly in situations where the requirements and their implementation are well understood.

Incremental model

The incremental model uses the waterfall approach in overlapping sections (see Figure 2.11). It attempts to compensate for the length of projects managed with a waterfall life cycle by producing usable products at the end of each section. This may involve a complete upfront set of requirements that are implemented in a series of small projects or the project model may start with general objectives. Then, some portion of these objectives is defined and implemented, followed by the next portion of the objectives until all the objectives are implemented.

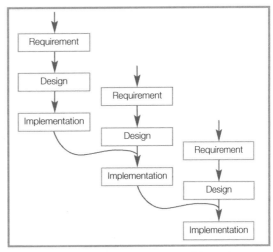

Figure 2.11 Incremental project life cycle

However, use of general objectives rather than complete requirements can be uncomfortable for management and, because some modules will be completed long before others, well-defined interfaces are required. Also, formal reviews and audits, an important quality control mechanism in many organisations, are more difficult to implement on increments than on a complete system. Finally, there can be a tendency to push difficult problems to the future to demonstrate early success to management.

The incremental model is particularly useful when the level of risk is too high to develop the whole system at once. Each complete increment delivers a benefit, including the option of continuing to the next increment.

Rapid prototyping

Rapid prototyping helps to provide a more thorough and complete understanding of the project's requirements than the waterfall model. In rapid prototyping the metaphor of the waterfall is broken by a cycle of iterations in which the creation of a system prototype is produced (see Figure 2.12). A prototype is an elaboration or trial model of the design that is built to test design decisions and identify potential problems. It is equivalent to the physical mock-up in engineering.

By interacting with the prototype, users can get a better idea of their information requirements. Once approved by the users, the prototype can serve as a template to create the final system. This involves a process of several iterations between prototype and requirements. After the prototype is complete, the waterfall model can then be implemented to complete the full system. Rapid prototyping is useful where requirements are difficult to specify; the early iterations allow a thorough exploration of require-ments using prototypes which can be produced rapidly and inexpensively.

Spiral model

The spiral model is another model developed in response to the problems with the waterfall model. In the spiral model, the linear approach of the waterfall model is replaced by a cyclic approach. The model is developed around a need for frequent interactions throughout the entire life cycle between the development team and the users. These back and forth iterations can be viewed as a spiral (Boehm, 1988) (see Figure 2.13). The spiral model explicitly includes risk analysis in the process, requiring management to manage the project risks.

The spiral model allows for significant evolution of project requirements from one cycle to the next. It is ideal where customer requirements are vague and incomplete. The advantages and disadvantages of the spiral model are as follows.

Advantages:
■ Many short processes rather than one long process, as in the waterfall model, and at each point the users can re-evaluate the system
■ Iterative, synergistic approach
■ Active customer participation
■ Enhances creativity.

Disadvantages:
■ Theoretical, not well supported by software engineering tools
■ No guidelines on when to complete a phase
■ No one knows when the system is finished, if indeed it ever is
■ Difficult to estimate costs
■ Requires strong project management.

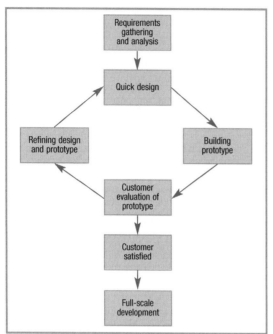

Figure 2.12 Rapid prototyping project life cycle

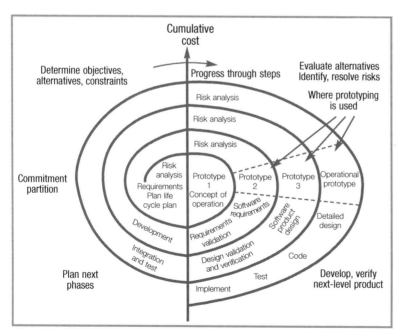

Figure 2.13 Spiral model of a project life cycle (Boehm, 1988)

Standards for software life cycle processes

The ISO/IEC 12207 Standard for Software Life Cycle Processes (1995), and its American equivalent IEEE/EIA 12207.0, describe the processes that are mandatory for a software development life cycle model. The standard can be applied to any software life cycle model.

 Software development project life cycles

Take a look at the Project Management in Action case: 'A PC banking project' at the end of this chapter. Which life cycle model do you think has been used?

See shaded box for a suggested answer.

Building and construction

As in the case of software development, there are many approaches to project management in the

This Project Management in Action case describes a project to create a Windows-based banking system for a UK bank's customers. The project was helped by the surprise success of a much smaller subproject, code-named QuickWin, used as a holding tactic to tap into a growing demand for PC banking and stave off competition from a rival bank until the main project was up and running. The life cycle is a hybrid one, containing elements of the incremental, rapid prototyping and waterfall models.

building and construction industry. Well-known methods include design and build, construction management and the traditional architect-led approach. The life cycle shown in Figure 2.14 emphasises the 'organic' nature of the design phase followed by the more 'mechanistic' nature of the production phase. The design–production interface is a major transition point in the project life cycle.

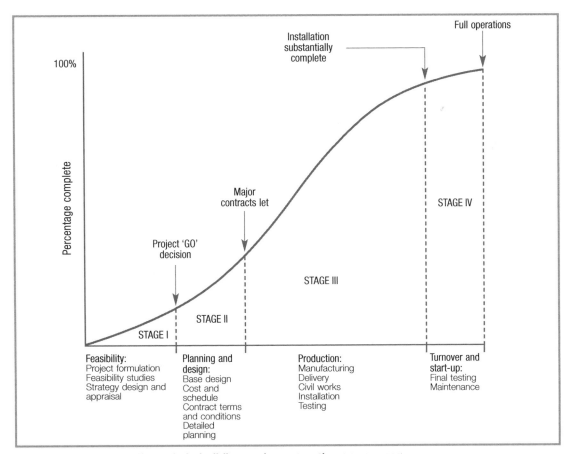

Figure 2.14 Project life cycle in building and construction (Morris, 1988)

DIRTY AND NOISY ... HIGGINS HALL, BOSTON COLLEGE

Executive Vice-President Frank B. Campanella speaks about a major construction project at Boston College involving a complex construction process, which will be executed in phases so that teaching and research can continue during the construction phase:

> There are two characteristics of construction projects that I am sure we are all familiar with. They tend to be dirty and noisy, and we appreciate the patience and tolerance that will be required of the Boston College community while this work goes on. Because the early part of any construction project – the excavation and foundation – tend to be the noisiest and most disruptive, we will try to accomplish as much of this work as possible over the summer. The project, therefore, will commence on May 11, two days after the last exam is held in Higgins.

> The first thing to be accomplished, Phase I, will be the construction of an addition across the front of the building, with the creation of an atrium between that addition and the existing building. Once that is accomplished, various elements of physics and biology will be moved into the addition, the remainder will be consolidated in the south wing and the north wing will be renovated. Then there will be further moving and consolidation in the north wing while the south wing is renovated. Overall we expect the project will take 36 months.

Source: Michael Seele, Boston College

Questions

1. Where in the project life cycle are noise and disruption likely to be a problem?
2. What measures are being taken to reduce this problem?
3. Where in the project life cycle do you think these decisions were made?
4. What is the duration of this project and why do you think it is so long?

There are many variations of the building and construction life cycle. A more detailed analysis of procurement in the construction industry is given in Chapter 6.

The Insights from Industry box draws attention to some of the issues that may need to be considered in a practical interpretation of the construction project life cycle.

Research and development (R&D)

R&D projects tend to be open projects, progressing in loosely structured teams with a strong emphasis on creativity and problem solving. This sometimes leads R&D workers to dismiss project management, as they fear that the resulting management control will interfere with and stifle creativity. In reality, project management training can help R&D workers to manage their own projects.

A typical R&D process has the following steps:

- research
- definition of a concept

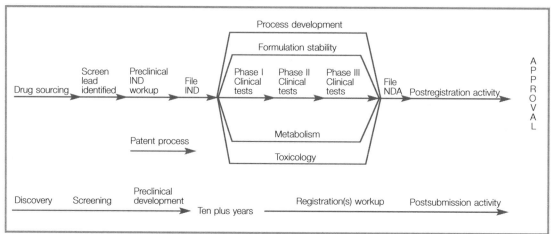

Figure 2.15 Pharmaceutical project life cycle (Murphy, 1989)

- feasibility testing
- development
- design of a product
- development of a prototype
- testing a pilot plant
- conducting market trials.

Murphy (1989) has developed an R&D project life cycle for the pharmaceutical industry (see Figure 2.15).

Entertainment and events

 Live entertainment

What time do you turn on the six o'clock news? How often does the curtain rise in the theatre to reveal last-minute costume preparations or a sign displaying 'Due to unexpected delays please return in two hours'? Live entertainment is an industry that delivers on time (virtually) all the time. Why is this?

See shaded box for a suggested answer.

Francis Hartman (2000), author of a book about SMART project management (where SMART stands for Strategically Managed, Aligned, Regenerative work environment and Transitional management), uses the entertainment industry as an example of a project-based industry that is more successful in its projects than the construction industry or the defence industry, both traditional users of project management. Live entertainment is also an industry that eschews traditional project management tools such as:

- work breakdown structures
- critical path method
- earned value techniques.

A focus on the project deadline puts a different emphasis on the project life cycle. Event projects work back from the date of the event, not forward from the first task. Another overriding constraint is the venue – the event site is vacated completely once the event concludes. This means that all work products have a transitory nature. Once again this is reflected throughout the planning of the event. Whatever is done has only a lifespan extending to the end of the event. There may be a legacy of the event, such as a cultural product or fixed facilities, but these are of secondary importance to the event.

The life cycle of a project in event management revolves around the ability to make decisions in a changing environment. It is this ability to function successfully in a volatile environment which gives the event industry a heuristic methodology which can contribute to the evolution of project management theory.

Managing in a changing environment relies on two key capabilities:

1. The capability to make optimal decisions quickly, which requires skills based on the experience and knowledge of alternatives.
2. The capability to communicate those decisions and have them carried out, which requires the qualities of leadership, delegation of responsibility and a pervasive culture of the urgency and importance of each task.

The Insights from Industry box highlights the role of teamwork and a partnership approach in Edinburgh's Hogmanay festival, currently the largest midwinter festival in Europe.

insights from INDUSTRY

EDINBURGH'S HOGMANAY FESTIVAL

Edinburgh's Hogmanay festival was launched in 1993 with three objectives – to attract tourists to Edinburgh in a traditionally off-peak period, enhance Edinburgh's national and international profile and provide a structure for local Hogmanay celebrations. The city centre street party on Hogmanay night quickly became the main public and media focus, although it is only one component of the event. The biggest project management challenge has been its huge popularity and rapid growth in a short space of time, as shown by the statistics below:

- In 1993, just under 50,000 people attended the

Hogmanay festival – in 2001 that figure was over half a million.

- In 1993, the budget was £237,000 – in 2001 it was £1.5 million.
- In 1993, the economic impact was insignificant – now it is around £30 million annually.
- In 1993, bed occupancy rates in city centre hotels at New Year were around 35% – in 2001 they were virtually 100%.
- In 1993, most shops, restaurants and visitor attractions were closed on 1 January – now nearly all are open.

So, how is this event project managed? The first thing to note is that no single person is dedicated full time to Edinburgh's Hogmanay. All the members of the project team have existing full-time jobs. Equally, there is no single door behind which Edinburgh's Hogmanay operates. Project management structures have had to be created around the capital and these have evolved over the years.

From the start, the festival has been developed as a partnership project, in which the city council has been the core funder and lead partner. The other partners are Scottish Enterprise, the police, the Tourist Board and the event contractor, Unique Events. This partnership continues to date, relying heavily on team building and teamworking.

Some would argue that a partnership approach to project management is a recipe for disaster – that the best you can hope for is 'to keep everyone equally unhappy'. However, experience with Edinburgh's Hogmanay suggests that this is not the case. There seems no doubt that a project like this would have failed without the partnership approach and the building of strong teams. A simple example is the involvement of the police as part of the project team – every decision along the way has police input and, ultimately, support. To develop an event on this scale and present it to the police at the eleventh hour simply would not have worked.

Source: Norman Ireland, 'Team building: Hogmanay – Celebrating the Celebration', 2001: 22

Disasters and emergencies

Disasters and emergencies are another type of project that require special consideration. Planning is vital in a rescue operation but time is a scarce resource and getting the balance right between planning and action is critical. The ability to respond rapidly to sudden events and change is critical in disaster management.

Contingency planning is important to large and small firms alike to enable them to continue conducting business in the face of a disaster. We shall be looking at contingency planning in more detail in Chapter 8; however, the Insights from Industry examples give a feel for some of the planning and decision-making capabilities needed in this special type of project.

DISASTERS AND EMERGENCIES

Lucky cow

Her Majesty's coastguard coordinates search and rescue through a network of 19 maritime rescue coordination centres, sub centres and sector bases. Its permanent staff are assisted by a corps of some 3100 volunteer auxiliary coastguards. The HQ branch, in Great Yarmouth, is responsible for the operational effectiveness of the coastguard, including procedures, compilation of statistics and memoranda of understanding. The press release below highlights an unusual rescue undertaken by the team.

Press Notice No: 260/01 7:30 pm, 2 August, 2001

Dramatic Animal Rescue on North Uist

At just after high water this morning, Stornoway coastguards were advised that a cow had fallen over the 60ft cliffs at Tigh Garre point on North Uist and into the water below. The cow, which was reported to be heavily pregnant and weighing 700 kilos, had somehow survived and managed to regain her footing at the base of the cliff. The animal was now stranded in an inaccessible bay and likely to drown on the next incoming flood tide.

The coastguard cliff rescue team from Benbecula were alerted and surveyed the site where it was intended to use lines to recover the animal to safety. They concluded that the cow was unlikely to survive the trauma. A veterinary surgeon was lowered down the cliff with the coastguard to provide a humane conclusion.

However, not to be beaten, the coastguard rescue helicopter *Hotel Lima* from Stornoway was brought in and used 'under-slung load techniques', normally used during counter pollution operations, to subsequently raise the sedated animal back to the cliff top and safety, cheered on by the local community.

Stornoway coastguard Watch Manager Duncan Mackay said:

'This was an excellent training opportunity for our rescue teams which proved the effectiveness of our equipment, procedures and their skills. The fact that we were able to save the life of the animal in the process was a real bonus'.

Questions

■ What special capabilities are required to execute these type of projects?
■ Where else might these capabilities be important?

How will you survive?

Disaster can strike quickly and without warning. It can force you to evacuate your home, your neighbourhood, your school or your workplace, or force you to be confined to your home. What would you do if the basic services you depend on – water, electricity, phones, gas – were cut off? In a large disaster, emergency officials cannot get to everyone at once. How will you survive until they reach you?

Where will you be when disaster strikes? You could be anywhere ... at work, at home, in university. Your family could be scattered all over town. How will you find each other? How will you know if everyone is safe?

Having a plan is the only way to make sure that you and your family know what to do, how to do it and when to do it when disaster strikes.

Questions

■ What natural or man-made disaster or emergency do you think you are at most risk from?
■ What steps and actions can you take to be prepared for such a disaster in the future?

Classifying projects

Why bother to create a classification system for projects? One good reason is that the same approach used to successfully manage one project is also likely to work with similar projects. Another reason lies in the creation of a learning organisation, where lessons learned from previous projects are made available to future projects; a classification system can help ensure that like for like comparisons are made. Thirdly, a project taxonomy can aid our understanding of project processes and may play a role in the development of new knowledge and theories about project management.

Projects can be classified in the following six ways:

1. participant mix – internal, external, mixed internal-external
2. degree of standardisation – concrete, occasional, open
3. project visibility – low or high
4. business need
5. size and complexity
6. industry.

Participant mix

Projects can be classified according to participant mix. For example, three categories in such a system might be internal, external or mixed internal-external. Projects can be self-contained within an organisation (internal projects), in which case the performing organisation is based inside the sponsor's organisation. For example, a project to amalgamate two or three departments in a university to form a single organisational unit may not require any input from external sources.

Alternatively, a project may be entirely contracted out to an outside organisation (external projects). For example, the building of an extension to locate a new manufacturing facility may be contracted out to a specialist building and design company. In this case, all the main participants are external to the sponsor's organisation. The management control system used in an external project is normally that of the main external participant (the prime contractor), although a sponsor may insist that their own system is used.

In other projects, subcontractors and consultants only take responsibility for parts of a project (mixed internal-external projects). In these projects it is important to harmonise the reporting, communication and control systems of the main participants, especially at the interface of the project phases. For example, the work breakdown structure of the client, the prime contractor and any subcontractors provide the greatest benefit when they are coordinated and can be viewed together as a single document.

Attribute	Concrete projects	Occasional projects	Open projects
Project deliverables	Clear and well defined	Usually less well defined, may take several iterations to finalise	Generally difficult to describe in detail, many unknowns often hamper early definition
Roles, systems, procedures	Clear, well defined and well understood	Often drawn up for the first time. Can be difficult to get acceptance from all team members	Roles and procedures are informal. Team members often rely on enthusiasm rather than written procedures
Project process maturity	Usually mature	Usually less mature or immature	Generally ad hoc, immature
Communication	Generally well-established communication infrastructure that meets the needs of the project	Often requires new channels put in place to meet cross-functional needs of the project	Informal communication common among principle participants, but not very well structured
Organisational change	Normally limited to minor changes	Often forms a large part of the project. Needs to be well managed to avoid damaging resistance	Less likely to form a major part of the project
Project team	Experienced, often dedicated project participants – some may be involved in several projects	Many participants have line management responsibilities in addition to project responsibilities	Participants usually have other nonproject responsibilities, and may depend on their own enthusiasm and creativity to maintain momentum
Example	An annual car rally	Refurbishment of a manufacturing facility	New product development

Table 2.2 Classifying project type as concrete, occasional or open

Degree of standardisation

This method of classification, adapted from Briner et al. (1996), classifies projects as being concrete, occasional or open and reflects the degree of standardisation applied to manage the project throughout its life cycle. Although not all projects fall neatly into one category or another, the technique does help to encourage critical thinking about the challenges posed by particular types of project. This classification system is summarised in Table 2.2.

Degree of visibility

Briner et al. (1996) also describe a classification system based on a concept called project visibility, in which projects can be categorised as having either high or low visibility.

High visibility projects:
- are seen to be critical to market position or organisational survival
- demand high-level, public commitment on the part of senior management

- have a higher risk of failure, with consequences damaging to the organisation's credibility and finance
- typically require a larger amount of organisational change.

Low visibility projects:
- are not seen to be critical or urgent
- receive little senior management attention
- have lower probability of failure, with less damaging consequences
- limit any organisational change to simple adaptations.

 Classifying projects

Combining the systems of project visibility and degree of standardisation gives a two-dimensional taxonomy of projects. The chart in Figure 2.16 shows five projects positioned according to their degree of standardisation and project visibility. You will notice that the labels have been removed from the chart.

Use your own judgement to match the project labels overleaf

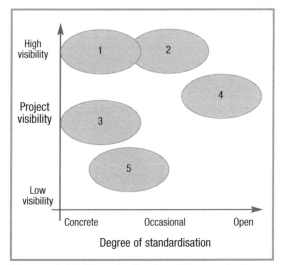

Figure 2.16 Exercise in classifying projects using a two-dimensional classification system

with the projects on the chart (where each numbered oval represents a different project). When you have finished, compare your answer with the suggested answer overleaf. The first one has been completed for you.

Project labels:
- An election campaign. Label number: 2 It is a reasonable assumption that this project needs to be highly visible to succeed. The project may be classed as occasional, occurring only once every few years.
- An email server upgrade in an organisation. Label number:
- A military exercise. Label number:
- A product development project. Label number:
- A product launch. Label number:

See shaded box for suggested answers.

Business need

Categorising projects according to business need can play a useful role in the prioritisation and funding of projects in a multiproject environment with limited resources. Hartman (2000) provides a classification system based on his interpretation of business need (see also Insights for Industry: 'Sources of IT projects at a major UK bank' in Chapter 1):

- *Exceptionally low-risk projects:* The project shows a low but solid return at a low risk; may be worthwhile depending on what else is in the project portfolio
- *Business imperative projects:* Projects that must be done or the business will be significantly

The following answers are a guide only. Putting a different interpretation on some of the projects may lead to a different classification. The reasoning behind each suggested answer is given:

- *Email server upgrade.* In a university, this project would have fairly low visibility, occurring largely in the background, invisible to most email users. If the people responsible for carrying out the project were familiar with project management techniques, this could be classed as a more concrete project, perhaps falling between concrete and occasional. Answer: Label number 5.

- *Military exercise.* This is a hard project to place because there are many different types of military exercise. Most, however, are very well planned and organised and so would be classed as concrete. In terms of visibility, military projects can span the whole spectrum. In this exercise the middle ground is taken. Answer: Label number 3.

- *Product development project.* These projects often take place behind closed doors. In the early stages there may be many false starts, with little consequence. Companies may be applying new processes and technologies and seeking new markets, so these would be classed as open projects. Answer: Label number 4.

- *Product launch.* A product launch needs to be highly visible and executed efficiently according to a clear plan. Answer: Label number 1.

damaged – requires thorough and careful risk analysis

- *Intuitively 'right' projects:* Difficult to evaluate objectively (proceed with caution) but do not dismiss all projects in this category, for example yellow Post it™ notes

- *Projects that exploit market opportunity:* Difficult to assess without market research data. In some circumstances, this information is not available and the project go/no-go decision must be based on the size of the market opportunity against risk exposure to the business

- *Projects that deliver technological advantage:* These projects can lead to new innovations, open up new markets or increase existing market share

- *Loss leader projects:* Undertaken because of perceived future benefits in new markets.

The Insights from Industry: 'Cutting-edge technology project' begins with a clear business need – a downturn in sales. The solution for Ted was a project to introduce new technology into his production

insights from INDUSTRY — CUTTING-EDGE TECHNOLOGY PROJECT

In 1981 Ted Montague, president of the Peerless Saw Company, a manufacturer of sawblades in Groveport, Ohio, was facing a difficult situation. In addition to the growing number of direct domestic competitors, foreign firms were moving into the market for higher volume sawblade models and offering equivalent quality off the shelf for lower prices. His sales were therefore down, yet costs were increasing and the old equipment in his plant was continuing to age and fail.

Ted had decided that he had no choice but to spend the hundreds of thousands of dollars to replace his worn-out punch presses. Yet he didn't see how that would significantly improve his ability to compete in the increasingly competitive sawblade market. At that point, Ted happened to see what the latest laser technology could do in cutting thin metals (such as sawblades), and that gave him hope. Originally, Ted had investigated laser cutting but, as he remarked: 'It looked as though an alligator had chewed on it.' Now, however, the cuts were thin, precise and well controlled. The only problem was that the laser manufacturers did not produce a means of easily controlling the laser cutter head.

Ted went to work on the problem. He knew what he wanted: a software program that was easy to use and which would direct the laser cutter head, automatically deciding where to place the blades on the sheet to minimise scrap and waste. Eventually, Ted approached Battelle Laboratories in Columbus to produce the software.

The implementation of the software-controlled laser cutter system was a disaster. As Ted remarked, 'It was just awful', but by persevering he eventually got the combined system working. And as Peerless started loading more and more of its work onto the laser cutter, and remarking to customers that their jobs were being produced with a computerised laser cutter, the firm began getting more orders. Not only were customers pleased that their jobs were being produced with such high-tech equipment, but they were also duly impressed with how fast they were able to get their work back. Soon they began ordering smaller batches more frequently, experimenting with slight changes in the blades to get another 1% improvement in quality, or 2% more productivity, out of the blades.

Before long, Ted had more business than he could handle, so he ordered another laser cutter, and then a third. He eventually set up a new division to investigate the potential for laser cutting other types of work. Now, because of Ted's willingness to take such a risk, Peerless enjoys the reputation of being the industry leader in a market that it had created.

Source: Adapted from Meredith, J.R. (1992)
The Management of Operations (4th edn),
John Wiley & Sons, New York

Questions

1. How would you classify this project according to business need?
2. What are the key management issues for such a project?

---

process. As with most new technology projects, there were difficult issues to resolve. However, creativity and perseverance helped achieve a positive result with clear benefits to Ted's business.

Size and complexity

Project size and complexity can also be used to classify projects. Larger and more complex projects (both product and organisational complexity) require greater project management effort. The number of tools and techniques that are used and the systems put in place for communication, integration and marketing will all be influenced by project size. Project management methodologies such as PRINCE 2 also take project size and complexity into account,

enhancing their versatility and scalability, rather than adopting a one size fits all approach.

Industry

The use of industry to classify projects, for example software, building and construction, and so on, has been described earlier in this chapter, see 'A contingency approach to project life cycles'.

The box below, Critical Considerations: 'Choosing a project management approach', shows how a consideration of a project's characteristics can facilitate choosing a suitable approach to managing the project.

CRITICAL CONSIDERATIONS

CHOOSING A PROJECT MANAGEMENT APPROACH

The best approach for managing a project will depend on the characteristics of the project concerned such as its degree of uncertainty or certainty. For example, deployment projects are generally well planned and highly organised before any work takes place; they are ordered, highly structured and tightly controlled. These projects were classified in this chapter as *concrete* projects. Development projects, on the other hand, are characterised by creative processes throughout the project and exist in highly uncertain, unstructured and unpredictable environments; but this is accepted and even viewed as a necessary part of the life cycle of these projects. These projects were classified in this chapter as *open* projects.

Examples of deployment projects are: construction, systems integration and installation. Their characteristics are:

■ Progress measured by deliverables
■ Waterfall (or similar) project life cycle is common
■ Investment objective is tactical efficiency
■ Leadership style will often emphasise supervisory command and control
■ Information systems are highly structured and capable of producing copious detail
■ Clear boundaries; task-oriented
■ Static environment.

Examples of development projects are new prod-uct development, software development, tional change, architecture. Their characteristics are:

■ Progress measured by uncertainty reduction
■ Many project life cycles used
■ Investment objectives include preserving strategic options and minimising regrets
■ Leadership style usually emphasises learning and dialogue
■ Information systems are relatively informal
■ Adaptive and evolving with permeable boundaries to sense and respond to changes
■ Dynamic environment.

Development projects are different to deployment projects due to their innovative and uncertain nature. There are four types of uncertainty in product development projects: organisational uncertainty, resource uncertainty, technical uncertainty, and market uncertainty.

A new product development (NPD) manager commented:

> NPD is very different from my former job in engineering, which had a finite nature. In NPD, there are higher levels of complexity and uncertainty. I have had to learn how to be patient and respond to ambiguity with more sophisticated project management tools.

Githens (2001) uses the concept of rolling-wave planning as an ideal tool for dealing with the high degree of uncertainty in development projects but warns that a rolling wave may backfire on deployment projects by making them *more* inefficient and slower.

Scaleable project management methodologies

A project management methodology is a structured guide or framework designed to help organisations manage large and small projects in a controlled and efficient manner. If everyone involved in a project works to the same methodology, this reduces communication and integration problems throughout the project life cycle.

While it is easy to identify the project management disciplines needed to send a manned mission to Mars and back (you simply use all of them), the challenge for most project environments is to tailor the approach for projects of lesser size, risk and complexity. This means smaller and less risky projects are not damaged by high project management overheads, unnecessary 'red tape' and can realise their benefits sooner. The point of project management is not to impose mountains of administrative overheads onto a project, but to provide techniques for thinking about project goals and risks, implementing plans and appropriate controls, and then adjusting them as needed.

One of the most widely used and accepted project management methodologies is PRINCE 2, which was commissioned by the UK government in 1996 and covers the organisation, management and control of projects.

Projects in controlled environments (PRINCE 2)

PRINCE, which stands for PRojects IN Controlled Environments, was developed by the Central Computer and Telecommunications Agency (CCTA, now part of the Office of Government Commerce) in 1989 as a UK government standard for IT project management. The latest version of the method, PRINCE 2, is designed as a generic and scaleable, best-practice approach for the management of all types and size of project. It is designed to be scaleable so that it can be used on both large and small projects. PRINCE 2 is the standard project methodology for use in UK government departments and is used increasingly in the private sector. An increasing number of overseas governments and multinational companies have also adopted the method.

There are eight processes in PRINCE 2, as shown in Figure 2.17, each with defined inputs, outputs and specific objectives to be achieved.

The method divides a project into manageable stages, according to the project life cycle, to enable efficient control of resources and regular progress monitoring throughout the project. The various roles

and responsibilities for managing a project are fully described and can be adapted to suit the size and complexity of the project, and the skills of the organisation. Project planning using PRINCE 2 is product-based which means the project plans are focused on delivering results and are not simply about planning when the various activities will be done.

PRINCE 2 incorporates the view that a project is driven by a business case which describes the organisation's justification, commitment and rationale for the intended outcome (see Figure 2.18). The method-

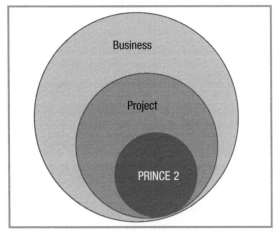

Figure 2.18 Relationship of PRINCE 2 to the project business case

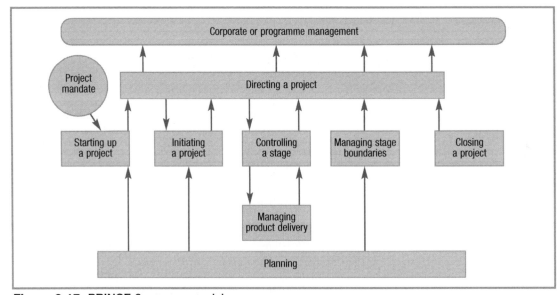

Figure 2.17 PRINCE 2 process model

ology allows for a regular review of the business case during the project to ensure that the business objectives, which can often change during the life cycle of a project, are still going to be met.

Visit the website:

http://www.palgrave.com/business/gardiner

▶ to view a summary of the PRINCE 2 methodology
▶ to access the PRINCE user group and related resources.

Chapman's project management scaleable methodology

Another useful project management methodology, developed by Jim Chapman and copyright of AMX International, is the 'project management scaleable methodology'. This provides a means for selecting the amount of project management needed by a project in ten different process areas (all nine process areas of the PMI's *Guide to the Project Management Body of Knowledge* (2000), plus multiproject oversight):

1. Integration
2. Scope
3. Time
4. Cost
5. Quality
6. Human resources
7. Communications
8. Risk
9. Procurement
10. Multiproject oversight.

Visit the website:

http://www.palgrave.com/business/gardiner

▶ to access Chapman's scaleable project management methodology.

The project described in Project Management in Action: 'A PC banking project' highlights some of the challenges relating to structuring and managing a project according to a systems view, with particular emphasis on communication and organisation aspects. When this project was carried out, the bank had recently reviewed their project management methodology and implemented changes to reduce the timescale from concept to benefit realisation, without increasing cost or compromising quality.

PROJECT MANAGEMENT *in action*

A PC banking project

Introduction

Some years ago, the Bank of Scotland (now merged with the Halifax Bank to form HBOS) developed HOBS (Home and Office Banking System), geared to the personal customer market, and Corporate HOBS (CHOBS) which, despite the name, is a totally different system geared towards corporate and business customers. This case study looks at the upgrading of HOBS and CHOBS to a Windows environment using rapid product development techniques.

Although the internet, with its variable response times and unguaranteed availability, is probably the least suitable delivery vehicle for banking products,

and one over which the Bank can have little control, it was the customers' preference. With this in mind, Gordon McQueen, UK banking acting general manager, asked the Management Services Division of the Bank (MSD) to produce a Windows version of HOBS and Corporate HOBS to bring these two systems into one modular PC banking product.

Structure and organisation

The project was formally set in motion by David Ball, the project director, who submitted a brief paper to the management board containing the project targets. The organisation structure of the project is shown in Figure 2.19.

The appointment of a project director by the management board was one of the innovations in this project. The pro-

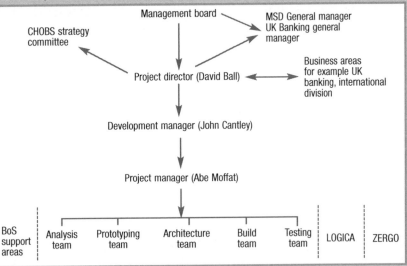

Figure 2.19 Management structure

ject director, David Ball, had the final say on project issues and executive authority to make decisions. The project was innovative for the MSD in the sense that there was actually a senior business unit manager heading up the project with very short lines of communication: 'If David can't make a decision, he just goes to one of the board members.'

The project director provided a single project focus:

I'm not a part of the management structure, so I can hopefully bring the different departments together. Whilst they should have an allegiance to the Bank, they also have an allegiance to their own departments. I can twist some fingers at a sufficiently senior level.

In this project, the project director was involved in some important decisions that helped to reduce the timescale of the project. For example, normally the Bank goes to tender for fairly substantial project contracts, but because of the short time frames being asked for in this project, the project director decided to approach Logica directly, and not go to tender. Another role of the project director was to make sure that all the different contractors integrated properly and that the Bank's element of the development integrated with the work of the contractors.

Development Manager John Cantley, however, points out that the new role of project director did cause some problems:

Although I'm getting a decision made more quickly, it can cause political problems because my line manager (two or three levels up) might not know what's happening. I tell David something, he passes it on to the MSD general manager, but my line manager may not know about it. He gets to hear about it from his manager, and he's not very happy. Now I make sure when I've seen David that I tell my line managers too.

John Cantley and Abe Moffat, the project manager, were key players in the project, responsible for coordinating everything to do with the applica-

tion build. They both had a lot of project management experience and were familiar with this particular application. They knew its weaknesses and were real hands-on guys.

John explains that:

The roles between development manager and project manager are not very distinct in terms of what they do. I'm more senior than Abe but we can mix and match. What tends to happen is that I tend to have the relationships with the outside parties, which are Logica and Zergo in this case. Abe is more concerned with the internal effort within MSD.

The project director also appointed a strong technical architect, 'who can look across all the different systems and work across some of the borders we have within the organisation group'. The technical architect agreed the system architecture internally with the Bank's own project team; he also rubber-stamped Logica's input and added his own expertise to it. John commented on the close working relationship between the architecture team and the analysis team:

They were working in parallel and feeding off each other for six months or so ... This is a fairly new departure for the bank, using the architecture department in this way. It's a recent innovation.

The fact that this project reported to the board meant that there was high project visibility and everyone was aware of that. David commented:

So if you ask for something to be done you get a better reaction than perhaps on other projects. That helps. I can call on that position if you like, although its not usually needed. It's there as a statement. And I think the people involved in the project do like the fact that the project is visible.

Another innovation in this project was the role of the customer help desk. They were empowered to have a substantial say in the design of the system and played a big part in developing prototypes.

Planning

Another innovation that worked very well was the Project Charter. It was used on one other project, where it was an outside party that introduced it. The Bank of Scotland tailored it for its own needs quite substantially. The Project Charter enabled the project to kick off a lot earlier.

David Ball, the project director, explained:

One thing which I did just after the initial paper went to the board was develop a Project Charter. The Project Charter is a very important tool. It says what the objectives are, what the resources are, what are the deliverables, the timescale, and who's responsible for what. The Project Charter makes it clear to everyone else what the board is accepting. It also indicated what subprojects would be within the main project, and their cost. It was the guiding light. Everything was in that Project Charter and put before the board.

The contents list of the Project Charter can be found in Addendum A.

John Cantley is also adamant that the Project Charter was crucial to the success of the project:

Typically what we do is go through a form C, which is an initial feasibility study. We didn't need to go through that process this time because we already had the business managers telling us that they wanted us to go ahead with it as a strategic development. Thereafter, typically, what happens is we do a Project Definition. Once that has been completed the project would often go to the management board for approval. To be able to do that would probably have taken, for a project of this size, six months. We were able to do the Project Charter in about six weeks. The reason for this massive time saving is that in a Project Definition, everything is specified down to a far greater level of detail and all sorts of business reasons for doing the project are included. There is a lot more analysis. In the Project Charter the focus is project infrastructure and what the aims of the project are rather than how it is going to be achieved.

The project also made use of rapid prototyping to help keep the project life cycle short. The prototyping carried out was designed to give a realistic look and feel to the product as opposed to any underlying logic to it. This was achieved by presenting the user areas with visual basic code to support screens to give the various business areas a flavour of what a Windows version would look like.

One of the largest phases in the project was the build phase. Most of the work in this phase involved moving from a three tier architecture to a two tier architecture, and thereby getting rid of a piece of hardware called a Tandem. The Tandem was used for CHOBS and HOBS and nothing else, and the Bank felt they lacked expertise in it. The system was costly in terms of software support and maintenance and from an operational point of view it was desirable to move out of this middle box.

Following the build phase was a series of systems tests, comprising the team's own internal testing, to make sure that the mainframe components were talking to each other, and tests with Logica and Zergo. There was also client acceptance testing which, according to John, was 'the full shooting match'. These tests took about four months to complete. Then, there was a certain amount of user acceptance testing in which representatives from the business areas were called in. Eventually, the system was piloted with a small number of customers in the Beta test. David commented that: 'If experience is anything to go by it will be something of a short pilot, say three or four months followed by a full-scale launch.'

Contractors
Logica, who were appointed without the usual tender process, were given a role to develop the customer access layer. John explains: 'We have got a two tier physical architecture; a mainframe and a network of PCs. Logica are responsible for the PC end. We are responsible for the mainframe element.'

The Bank's project team checked Logica's specification to see if it was up to their satisfaction before allowing them to go ahead with the build of the customer access layer software. A lot of time was saved there.

However, in terms of communication, there were some misunderstandings between the Bank of Scotland and Logica. John explains:

> We know our systems; in a short period of time we had to get Logica up to date on it. There's an awful lot of things to be explained, fairly complex things. Sometimes Logica haven't fully picked up on that and we have had to go back over things again. We tend to use workshops to get over that kind of information. When we are liaising with Logica, on some of the more complex things, it takes two or three times to get points across. I don't know how we can resolve that. We have probably held about a hundred plus workshops. As analysis issues come out during the build we hold additional workshops. We find the workshops very productive; they tend to involve three to six people.

Zergo, the other main contractor, developed a security application for the project. One of the Bank's requirements from a security point of view was to have encryption and decryption which the existing HOBS and CHOBS did not have in general. Zergo was brought on quite late in the project because a lot of work had to be done in terms of the architecture in order to bottom out what was needed from the security product. Once that had been done, Zergo was brought in to do the build of the security software. It had done some work for the Bank of Scotland previously. There was also a lot of interplay between Logica's personnel and Zergo's personnel, particularly on the architecture side.

There were a number of issues where decisions were made to pare back on the budget. Consequently, there was a bit of come and go with contracts in terms of what was fixed price and what was variable price, especially in areas that were difficult to define. The norm in difficult areas was to go variable so far,

then as soon as things got clearer, the Bank asked for fixed price.

The reporting mechanisms in place from the contractors and the Bank's development staff needed to be easy to read in terms of what were the critical issues such as cost variances, time variances and resource problems. A typical status report showing highlights and lowlights can be found in Addendum B. The reporting mechanism imposed a structure on the project. This was over and above any structures that the development manager had put in place, for example one-to-one meetings with people and weekly group meetings (often just short meetings to monitor progress and identify major issues).

Communication
The use of electronic media was essential for project control, and comprised email and Lotus Notes, a type of groupware database. Using electronic media helped to keep everyone aware of the costs and other issues. Contractors also had email but not Lotus Notes, the Bank did not want them to see a lot of the information on Lotus Notes.

Lotus Notes was set up in the project structure on day one. Infrastructure was classed as very important. Everyone in development had to have a PC so they could see the project director's instructions, and so the project director could not forget what he had asked somebody to do. Memos and requests were deleted as soon as they were answered. 'David doesn't keep anything. In his philosophy everything that has happened has gone.' However, there was a separate database to hold all key records, including weekly and monthly status reports from development, showing expense and progress, deliverables and definitions. To have an electronic medium was important because many of the parties were external to the Bank. To get information quickly demanded the use of electronic media. Contractors could also email their reports in.

The development manager commented:

> We've had mixed success with electronic media. David wanted to use Lotus Notes as a means by which information was exchanged. He made sure all the business areas were represented. There is a lot more accountability built in to this project than would be normally the case. The mixed success has been the fact that as a bank we haven't managed to get Lotus Notes running properly, some of my project team still don't have Lotus Notes. If a server goes down you are isolated because you have either got to go without information or put the effort into getting all the papers on hard copy, in which case it destroys the advantage of working with an electronic medium. But that aside it does let us get the documents out to everyone quickly. It also gives a responsibility to the business areas. David wanted them to be proactive. It has tended to be the case on previous projects that we were responsible for chasing up hard copies of documents. Lotus Notes allows everybody to see things at the same time, there's no delay in being able to see documents that are sent. There is a high visibility.

The Bank also had a commitment from Logica and Zergo to provide the project team with electronic copies of documents so they could be put up on Lotus Notes and be visible to all the project team, which wasn't the case in the past. In John's view it meant that: 'We are not continually hunting for somebody. They can go to Lotus Notes and get it.'

When asked about the future use of Lotus Notes, John replied:

> We've used Notes in a fairly simplistic way, we've got various categories, but we haven't tapped into its full potential. I think if we were going to be doing it again we would take more advice from a Lotus expert. One of the complaints of the very senior managers is that they don't have a quick guide as to what's going on, they would like a document giving a quick overview, with comments like 'if you want more information go to x, y, or z'.

QuickWin

The project was also helped by a separate miniproject which came to be known as 'QuickWin', which appeared six months after the start of the main project. QuickWin was a perceived need. There was a feeling that the Royal Bank was going ahead with a Windows product, and Barclays were also indicating that they were going to be bringing out a PC banking product.

The Bank of Scotland had identified that one of its existing HOBS customers had developed emulation software to put a Windows front end onto the existing HOBS system. So it bought it for a relatively small sum of money and spent a couple of months enhancing the software for its own needs, adding security and other features, before getting it onto the market quickly. John explained:

> The take-up of that product was quite staggering. It only went out to our PC customers, but new customers bought into it as well. It was more successful than anything we had anticipated.

HOBS for Windows, however, was a true Windows version, rather than an emulation, and the decision to go ahead with it was not influenced by QuickWin. 'Quickwin went on the market because of competitive pressures. It was a holding tactic. As it turned out the Royal Bank didn't have anything.'

That aside, QuickWin did help the Bank of Scotland assess how many of its customers were using PCs to access HOBS. And it was a higher proportion than it had originally thought.

Reflection

David and John both boast that the project ran pretty well to course, except perhaps for one thing:

> We didn't anticipate the complexity in the supporting software. That was well underbudgeted. We hoped to reuse existing software code which was really unsuitable, it wasn't up to the standard that we wanted. That was a problem. That was a decision taken and we then had to cut back in other areas.

There was no need to go back to the board, however, as the project remained within the budget laid down in the Project Charter.

John has had to accommodate a fair degree of change in managing this project. But it seems to have been change for the better. They have learnt much from the experience:

> Essentially, the first lot of client server developments were done on a trial and error basis to be honest with you. We are really learning from previous (old-style) projects in terms of having to look at all the project management issues from the outset. Some of the infrastructure used in this project is new to project management in MSD. This includes the use of a project director, a visible structure to board level, and the heavy use of a third party. One of the difficulties experienced in the Bank is generating real ownership; people will say, 'well that's his problem. It's his department. Not mine.' Everyone has got to be tarred with the same brush really. This place has tended to be very hierarchical.

John describes the management style as 'loosely structured', and admits:

> We don't follow any project methodology like PRINCE so to that extent it's not structured. It's always been this way. In general, in my view not a lot of effort has gone into project management training within MSD. It depends on the individual project manager. I've been a project manager for about six years and I've picked up things along the way. It should be more structured, we've got training programmes in the centre for programmers but once you've graduated from that there's not the same emphasis in the project management area so it depends on individuals. Having said that there is a lot more leeway for project managers in terms of how they manage projects. To a certain extent, in this project, we've had a discipline imposed on us by having a project director and having this kind of visible structure in place.

John explains that this type of structure has only been tried once or twice in the Bank in terms of MSD projects and its the first one that John has been involved in. But he is enthusiastic:

It's made a substantial difference to me in terms of getting very short lines of communication. I can go to David and get a decision right away. He's here on site. Prior to that, in a normal project in MSD what would happen is that, I could make some decisions as I can here, but any major decisions would have to go through a hierarchy within MSD. That hierarchy is about two or three deep. From MSD across to the customer area, say UK banking, for discussion with them. The length of time taken to make that decision is far greater. Not so in this case, decisions are made right away, and also there is support here from the management board. One of David's roles is to go to these guys and get decisions. So important decisions are made right away, and made with full knowledge and awareness of the board. That particular aspect has worked very well in my view.

ADDENDUM A
PROJECT CHARTER
Table of Contents

ADDENDUM B

Author:	Abe Moffat/MSD/BKSCOT
Composed:	29/10/95 10:56
Subject:	Logica Status Report – 20/10/95
Category:	Windows Development\Status reports

HOBS for Windows Weekly Status Report
Week Ending 20 October 1995

1. Overall Status
a *Highlights*
External Interfaces Specification first draft delivered on time. Second Draft of Project Plan and Quality Plan delivered. Requirements document produced. Fspec Table of contents established, and planning underway.

b *Lowlights*
Risk Reduction team not yet recruited (though we have started) WBS not brought to greater detail

2. Issues/Risks

Prototype timescale critical. Contract may not be ready by 31 October.

3. New Week Outlook – Key Areas for Attention
Issue final level of the plan for definition phase
FS workshop
Follow up on Contract
Bring detailed level of WBS to greater detail
Finalise Risk Reduction team

4. Resources
N/A

5. Budget
N/A

6. Overall Confidence Rating (Scale 1–10 – 10 high)
7.5

(*Note:* Native caution and a fear of nemesis prevents more optimism)

QUESTIONS TO AID UNDERSTANDING AND DISCUSSION

1. What was QuickWin? Was it a good idea?

2. How did the bank manage communication in this project? Was it effective?

3. Was this project tightly or loosely controlled? What evidence can you find?

4. How would you describe the life cycle of this project? Sketch it out on paper.

5. What evidence of innovation and enterprise can you find in this project?

6. What would a systems diagram of the project look like? Sketch it out on paper.

7. What influence did the bank's management culture have on the project?

8. The bank employed a major subcontractor without going to tender. What were the risks of doing this? Would you describe this as good or bad practice?

Summary points

- Projects are open systems which means that they interact with their environment.
- Using systems theory, a project can be decomposed into separate phases, work packages and activities.
- Breaking down a project into smaller interrelated parts enables more effective management of the project.
- As a system, each project or subproject is characterised by a set of inputs, processes, outputs, constraints and mechanisms.
- Although systems theory aids understanding about how projects work, the human factor remains the most important single issue in managing projects.
- Feedback, on a regular basis, involving the different stakeholders is the only assurance that the project manager and the main participants can get about how well they are satisfying the project stakeholders, especially the customer.
- Feed-forward information augments feedback information by alerting participants further down the project life cycle of events and decisions that are taking place in earlier phases, allowing adjustments before error occurs.
- A project life cycle is a high-level representation of a project showing the major phases, actions and deliverables.
- A generic project life cycle typically includes four or five phases – initiation and definition, planning and development, execution and control, and closure.
- In some projects, the life cycle is extended beyond the traditional phases to include operations, maintenance and logistics.
- As a project moves through the life cycle phases its form and nature change, requiring adjustments to the style of leadership and management.
- Project life cycle phases are strongly interdependent and each phase can be usefully informed by consulting with staff from the other project phases; this should happen throughout the project, not just at the end of each phase.
- Fast tracking is the shortening of the project life cycle by overlapping project phases. A fast-track project requires well-planned communication, feedback, and management control to maintain consistent and satisfactory quality.
- The principles of project management apply in any discipline or industry, but the chunking of a project or programme into life cycle phases will be shaped by the nature of the industry itself. This has led to a 'branded' or industry-specific approach to project management, for example event project management.
- Classifying projects helps us to refine our approach for particular types of project, improves our knowledge and understanding and enhances learning.
- Projects can be classified in many ways, for example by participant mix, degree of standardisation, project visibility, business need, size and complexity, and industry.
- A project management methodology is a structured guide or framework designed to help organisations manage large and small projects in a controlled and efficient manner.
- PRINCE 2 is the standard project management methodology for use in UK government departments and is used increasingly in the private sector and internationally.

Visit the website

http://www.palgrave.com/business/gardiner

▶ to test your understanding of the learning objectives for Chapter 2 using multiple choice questions

In the next chapter we shall be addressing the strategic nature of projects and how numerous projects can be managed simultaneously as a programme or portfolio, while sharing key resources.

References

APM (2000). *Body of Knowledge,* 4th edn, Association for Project Management, High Wycombe.

Boehm, B.W. (1988). 'A spiral model of software development and enhancement', *IEEE Computer*, **21**(5): 61–72.

BPRC (1997). 'Focus Group: Project Management, the Motivations and Conditions for Change', University of Warwick, http://bprc.warwick.ac.uk/focus12.html.

Briner, W., Hastings, C. and Geddes, M. (1996). *Project Leadership,* 2nd edn, Gower, Aldershot.

Dworkin, B.R. (1993). *'Learning and physiological regulation'*, University of Chicago Press.

Githens, G.D. (2001). 'Manage innovation programs with a rolling wave', *PM Network*, **15**(5): 35–9.

Hall, A.D. and Fagen, R.E. (1956). 'Definition of a System', *General Systems Yearbook of the Society for the Advancement of General Systems Theory.*

Hartman, Francis T. (2000). *Don't Park Your Brain Outside*, Project Management Institute, Upper Darby, PA.

Johnson, R.A., Kast, F. and Rosenzweig, J.E. (1963). *The Theory and Management of Systems*, McGraw-Hill, New York.

Kalmus, H. (1966). *Regulation and Control in Living Systems*, John Wiley & Sons, New York.

Morris, P.W.G. (1988). 'Managing project interfaces – key points for project success'. In *Project Management Handbook* by Cleland, D.I. and King, W.R. (eds), Van Nostrand Reinhold, New York.

Murphy, P.L. (1989). 'Pharmaceutical project management: is it different?', *Project Management Journal*, **20**(3): 35–8.

O'Toole, W. (2000). 'Towards the integration of event management best practice by the project management process', *Proceedings of Conference on Event Evaluation, Research and Education*, University of Technology, Sydney.

PMI (2000). *Guide to the Project Management Body of Knowledge*, Project Management Institute, Upper Darby, PA.

Sorensen, R. (1995). 'A comparison of software development methodologies', *CrossTalk,* Journal of Defense Software Engineering, January.

Visit the website

http://www.palgrave.com/business/gardiner

▶ for additional resources to explore the topics in this chapter further

CHAPTER 3

Strategy and governance

Learning objectives

After reading this chapter you should be able to:

- discuss the relationship between strategy and project management
- outline a typical strategic management process and argue why many organisations fail to implement their strategies successfully
- explain the concept of governance from a corporate, strategic, programme, IT and project perspective
- analyse a project case study using a model of strategic governance;
- explain the main stages of programme management and the key influences affecting them
- design and justify the use of an appropriate authorisation management process

Introduction

The importance of establishing strategy in organisations and implementing strategic goals and objectives is well known. It is also well known that few companies find this process easy to achieve (Johnson and Scholes, 1993).

The number of companies turning to project management as a way of adding value to their bottom line continues to grow, with projects increasingly viewed as 'building blocks' in the design and execution of the strategies of corporations and governmental agencies (PMI, 2000). A careful look at the activities of strategy planning, strategy implementation and the origin of projects reveals a strong link between strategic intent, project conception and project selection.

This chapter highlights the importance of the relationship between strategy and project management. A brief consideration of strategic management is followed by a detailed consideration of the precepts of good governance applied at the corporate, programme, IT, and project levels in an organisation.

Projects typically pass through many stages of authorisation before they are completed and these checkpoints or gates can be formally or informally managed, according to project size. Authorisation management, part of an effective system of governance, is discussed here because of its strategic importance, including the difficult decision of whether or not to continue or stop a project in the light of changing circumstances.

Projects and strategy

During the last 30 years there has been a surge in growth in corporate and business strategy subjects taught in business schools worldwide, with the aim of helping organisations create sustainable competitive advantage against their current and foreseeable competitors. A review of the literature reveals that most strategists have focused their efforts on various forms of strategic planning and, in particular, the strategic analysis and strategy formulation elements. The area of strategy implementation, which deals with operationalising strategic plans, has been largely neglected (Roberts and Gardiner, 1998). The process for converting strategic plans into the day-to-day actions by which they are realised is still largely a 'black box'. It is difficult to envisage how successful strategic plans can be devised in the absence of knowledge about how they are to be implemented.

A simple comparison of the definitions of strategic planning and project management provides an indication that the two disciplines are compatible. A typical definition of strategic planning is:

a set of decision rules which guide the company's resource allocation process, taking into account both the short and long term, with emphasis on allocating resources in uncertain conditions to achieve future objectives. The company which uses a form of strategic planning does not simply react to events in the present, but considers what should be done in order to achieve future objectives. (Scott, 1997)

Turner alludes to this through a rather succinct definition of project management as: 'the art and science of converting vision into reality' (Turner, 1996). The PMI also acknowledges a link between project management and strategy by stating that 'projects are implemented as a means of achieving an organisation's strategic plan' (PMI, 2000).

Hartman approaches strategy from the project manager's perspective, suggesting that 'the best project managers know how their projects support the corporate strategy and that they use this knowledge to help them obtain needed support and resources to succeed' (Hartman, 2000). The theory being that to obtain effective authority to manage projects, it is necessary to draw on the inherent authority granted by the organisation, authority which lies in supporting and assisting the corporate strategy and being seen to do so. Of course, whatever its origin, a project should be more than just a good idea. It should always be possible to show how a project supports the strategic goals of the sponsor's organisation … otherwise it consumes resources but fails to add value. There is little doubt that project management is an ideal tool for strategic planning and strategic implementation (Roberts and Gardiner, 1998).

Strategic management

Ten deeply ingrained concepts have dominated thinking on strategy since the 1960s, ranging from the early design and planning schools to the more recent learning, cultural and environmental schools (Mintzberg et al., 1998). Current understanding, however, suggests a need for strategy formulation to move away from these linear and static approaches, which suited earlier times of slow, linear and incremental change, to a wider systemic and eclectic perspective more suited to today's rapidly changing business environments.

The currently dominant view of business strategy – resource-based theory – is centred on the concept of economic rent and the view of the company as a collection of capabilities. This view of strategy has a coherence and integrative role that places it well ahead of other mechanisms of strategic decision making (Kay, 1999). In contrast to traditional strategy models which tended to focus on the company's external competitive environment, the resource-based perspective highlights the need for a fit between the external market in which a company operates and its internal capabilities. Hitt et al. (2002) state that:

Instead of focusing on the accumulation of resources necessary to implement the strategy dictated by conditions and constraints in the external environment, the resource-based view suggests that a firm's unique resources and capabilities provide the basis for a strategy. The strategy chosen should allow the firm to best exploit its core competencies relative to opportunities in the external environment.

The resource-based view of strategy emphasises economic rent creation through distinctive capabilities. Economic rent is what organisations earn over and above the cost of the capital employed in their business. It is a measure of their competitive advantage. The objective of an organisation is to increase its economic rent, rather than its profit as such. 'A company which increases its profits but not its economic rent, for example, through investments or acquisitions which yield less than the cost of capital, destroys value' (Markides, 1999).

Some researchers have even questioned the validity of strategic planning and whether having a strategic planning function adds value to an organisation or not (for example Mintzberg, 1994). The research results are ambiguous, because, although successful firms appear to have strategic planning functions, the causal relationship remains unclear, that is, do strategic planning functions lead to success or do successful firms establish strategic planning functions?

One outcome of the debate has been a decade or so during which strategic planning has been decentralised into the strategic business units (SBUs) of large organisations. In general, an SBU tends to be a unit that provides distinct products and services from those supplied by other SBUs in the same organisation. The dominant logic behind decentralisation is the belief that the SBU's closeness to its production processes, products, markets and customers would lead to better strategy formulation and implementation.

In the pursuit of competitive advantage, or in some cases just trying to catch up with competitors, SBUs have attempted to introduce a wide range of business change programmes to improve their performance, for example total quality management, enterprise resource planning, just-in-time, business process re-engineering, lean thinking and a host of others. However, there is mounting evidence that, in general, the majority of such efforts fail to result in the expected return on investment to the organisations undertaking them (Belmonte and Murray, 1993; Dreilinger, 1994; Hardy and Redivo, 1994; Kotter, 1995). Some observers suggest that more than 80% of change efforts fail. It has been suggested that these failures are often due to a failure by organisations to realign their internal infrastructures with changes in strategic direction (Roberts and Gardiner, 1998).

Most strategy models tend to follow a process similar to that laid out in Table 3.1. Although shown as a sequence, in practice it is often necessary to iterate between the different levels in response to additional information that is acquired or uncovered as the process unfolds.

In practice, most organisations carry out steps 1–3 in Table 3.1 in one form or another. However, formal and casual observations of more than one hundred companies suggests that most of them leap straight from step 3 to step 6 or 7 (Roberts and Gardiner, 1998). The vital 4th and 5th steps, identification of critical success factors and key business activities, are frequently missing. It is likely that this contributes to the gap between strategic planning and the operations functions which most often have responsibility for implementing the plans. The use of strategic project management approaches can help to ensure completeness, that is, that stages 1–7 are all covered during the planning and implementation phases.

Corporate governance

The role and importance of governance in organisations has increased steadily over the last ten years, spurred on by large corporate failures such as Enron and WorldCom. This trend reflects a commensurate rise in complexity and uncertainty of the internal and external environments that confront organisations. The principles of governance are important in business and large organisations because they underpin major ethical decisions in the face of uncertainty and tremendous competitive pressures. These same conditions are also faced by project directors and managers as they seek to apply a strategic and ethical approach to project management. As the section unfolds, the principles of governance are explored from a corporate perspective, a strategic perspective, a programme perspective, an IT perspective and finally a project perspective.

The principles and theories of governance continue to be debated (CCG, 2000; King, 2002; Garratt, 2003; Williams, 2003). They concern accountability, responsibility, direction and control, and are aptly expressed in the Asian Development Bank's annual report (1998) as four fundamental 'pillars' of governance:

- *Accountability* – the capacity to call officials to account for their actions
- *Transparency* – entails low-cost access to relevant and material information

Table 3.1 A strategy process model	
Model elements	Purpose
1. Mission statement	Establish the overarching purpose or vision of the organisation
2. Environmental scanning	Establish those things in the external and internal environments that provide threats or opportunities to achievement of the business mission
3. Strategy	Develop the medium/long-term plan towards achievement of the mission, taking account of the environment
4. Critical success factors	Identify the critical things that must go well if the organisation is to deliver its strategy
5. Key business activities	Identify the activities necessary to action the critical success factors
6. Structure and support system design	Design the organisation structures and support systems to facilitate the key business activities
7. Implementation	Operationalise the new designs and key business activities

Source: Roberts and Gardiner (1998).

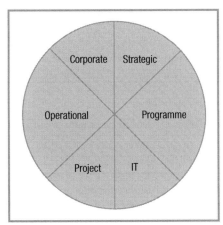

Figure 3.1 The governance wheel

- *Predictability* – results primarily from laws and regulations that are clear, known in advance and uniformly and effectively enforced
- *Participation* – needed to obtain reliable information and serve as a reality check and watchdog for stakeholders.

Systems of governance operate at many levels in organisations. Figure 3.1 shows some of the critical areas of governance, which often coexist in organisations, in the form of a governance wheel.

In its barest form, corporate governance is the system by which companies are directed and controlled, principally by a board of directors, to realise long-term shareholder value whilst taking into account the interests of other stakeholders (High Level Finance Committee, Malaysian Government, 1999).

As a system, corporate governance consists of:

- a *set of rules* that define the relationships between shareholders, managers, creditors, the government and other stakeholders
- a *set of mechanisms* to enforce these rules directly or indirectly.

The Cadbury Report (1992) has been particularly influential in developing best-practice governance systems focusing on the four key areas – see next Key Concepts.

 Corporate governance – Cadbury Report code of best practice

The board of directors

1 The board should meet regularly, retain full and effective control over the company and monitor the executive management.
2 There should be a clearly accepted division of responsibilities at the head of a company, which will ensure a balance of power and authority, such that no one individual has unfettered powers of decision. Where the chairman is also the chief executive, it is essential that there should be a strong and independent element on the board, with a recognised senior member.
3 The board should include non-executive directors of sufficient calibre and number for their views to carry significant weight in the board's decisions.
4 The board should have a formal schedule of matters specifically reserved to it for decision to ensure that the direction and control of the company is firmly in its hands.
5 There should be an agreed procedure for directors in the furtherance of their duties to take independent professional advice if necessary, at the company's expense.
6 All directors should have access to the advice and services of the company secretary, who is responsible to the board for ensuring that board procedures are followed and that applicable rules and regulations are complied with. Any question of the removal of the company secretary should be a matter for the board as a whole.

Non-Executive Directors

1 Non-executive directors should bring an independent judgement to bear on issues of strategy, performance, resources, including key appointments, and standards of conduct.
2 The majority should be independent of management and free from any business or other relationship which could materially interfere with the exercise of their independent judgement, apart from their fees and shareholding. Their fees should reflect the time which they commit to the company.
3 Non-executive directors should be appointed for specified terms and reappointment should not be automatic.
4 Non-executive directors should be selected through a formal process and both this process and their appointment should be a matter for the board as a whole.

Executive Directors

1 Directors' service contracts should not exceed three years without shareholders' approval.
2 There should be full and clear disclosure of directors'

total emoluments and those of the chairman and highest-paid UK director, including pension contributions and stock options.

3 Separate figures should be given for salary and performance-related elements and the basis on which performance is measured should be explained.

4 Executive directors' pay should be subject to the recommendations of a remuneration committee made up wholly or mainly of non-executive directors.

Reporting and Controls

1 It is the board's duty to present a balanced and understandable assessment of the company's position.

2 The board should ensure that an objective and professional relationship is maintained with the auditors.

3 The board should establish an audit committee of at least three non-executive directors with written terms of reference which deal clearly with its authority and duties.

4 The directors should explain their responsibility for preparing the accounts next to a statement by the auditors about their reporting responsibilities.

5 The directors should report on the effectiveness of the company's system of internal control.

6 The directors should report that the business is a going concern, with supporting assumptions or qualifications as necessary.

Source: The Cadbury Report: Report of the Committee on the Financial Aspects of Corporate Governance (1992) Gee & Co, London

Strategic governance

An organisation faces five critical challenges (Smith, 2002). These are represented in Figure 3.2 as lenses through which an organisation's strategy becomes increasingly focused, leading to the delivery of its potential value. Strategic governance is a process requiring ongoing focusing and refocusing of these five lenses in response to the prevailing internal and external environment. A description of the five lenses follows.

Lens 1: Decision making under uncertainty

Decision making is the first of the five strategic governance lenses and focuses on the ability of an organisation to exploit uncertainty and flux by making well-timed choices which move it nearer to its desired goal. Strategic decision making is bound up with effective risk planning (PMI, 2000) and the ability of organisations to differentiate between:

■ *high-risk decisions* which offer the greatest returns, carry the largest risk and require large-scale risk analysis. For example, at the time of writing, BP and the Iranian Oil Company are to invest about £350m in the development of the Rhum gas field in the North Sea (UK Activity Report, 2003) and Boeing have announced a multi-billion dollar product development effort to build and sell a new aeroplane, the 'sonic cruiser', flying faster, higher and farther than any current aeroplane (Boeing, 2003). These are both high-risk investment decisions.

■ *low-risk/low-reward decisions* which are important choices to identify because they do not offer significant value and so do not warrant large-scale risk analysis. Their contribution to value lies in being able to identify and respond to these risks quickly and efficiently.

■ *option pricing decisions* which involve situations where future paths can be narrowed down, but not completely eliminated. Managers move forward while deferring future difficult choices without substantially increasing their costs or risks, essentially optimising as circumstances evolve.

These types of decision typically involve a number of degrees of freedom. The strategy sets the framework within which future decisions will be made, but at the same time it leaves room for learning from ongoing developments and discretion to act based on what is learned. You can explore this concept further by reading the Critical Considerations box in which a garden of tomatoes is used as a metaphor to highlight

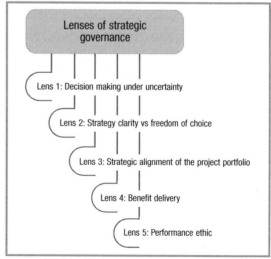

Figure 3.2 Strategic governance lenses

CRITICAL CONSIDERATIONS

STRATEGY AS A PORTFOLIO OF REAL OPTIONS

Managing a portfolio of strategic options, that is, projects, is like growing a garden of tomatoes in an unpredictable climate. Walk into the garden on a given day in August, and you will find that some tomatoes are ripe and perfect. Any gardener would know to pick and eat those immediately. Other tomatoes are rotten; no gardener would ever bother to pick them. These cases at the extremes – now and never – are easy decisions for the gardener to make.

In between are tomatoes with varying prospects. Some are edible and could be picked now but would benefit from more time on the vine. The experienced gardener picks them early only if squirrels or other competitors are likely to get them. Other tomatoes are not yet edible, and there's no point in picking them now, even if the squirrels do get them. However, they are sufficiently far along, and there is enough time left in the season, that many will ripen unharmed and eventually be picked. Still others look less promising and may not ripen before the season ends. But with more sun or water, fewer weeds or just good luck, even some of these tomatoes may make it. Finally, there are small green tomatoes and late blossoms that have little likelihood of growing and ripening before the season ends. There is no value in picking them, and they might just as well be left on the vine.

Most experienced gardeners are able to classify the tomatoes in their gardens at any given time. Beyond that, however, good gardeners also understand how the garden changes over time. Early in the season, none of the fruit falls into the 'now' or 'never' categories. By the last day, all of it falls into one or the other because time has run out. The interesting question is: What can the gardener do during the season, while things are changing week by week?

A purely passive gardener visits the garden on the last day of the season, picks the ripe tomatoes and goes home. The weekend gardener visits frequently and picks ripe fruit before it rots or the squirrels get it. Active gardeners do much more. Not only do they watch the garden but, based on what they see, they also cultivate it: watering, fertilising and weeding, trying to get more of those in-between tomatoes to grow and ripen before time runs out. Of course, the weather is always a question, and not all the tomatoes will make it. Still, we'd expect the active gardener to enjoy a higher yield in most years than the passive gardener.

In real option terminology, active gardeners are doing more than merely making exercise decisions (pick or don't pick). They are monitoring the options and looking for ways to influence the underlying variables that determine option value and, ultimately, outcomes.

Option pricing can help us become more effective, active gardeners in several ways. It allows us to estimate the value of the entire year's crop (or even the value of a single tomato) before the season actually ends. It also helps us assess each tomato's prospects as the season progresses and tells us along the way which to pick and which to leave on the vine. Finally, it can suggest what to do to help those in-between tomatoes ripen before the season ends.

Source: Luehrman, T.A. (1998). 'Strategy as a portfolio of real options', *Harvard Business Review*, September–October, 89–99

the importance of the effect of time on the potential value of a strategic option in the decision-making process.

Lens 2: Strategic clarity versus freedom of choice

In the second lens the focus is on the achievement of a balance between the policy of an organisation and freedom to act. Managers have an 'obligation to deeply understand their organisation's overall strategy, especially its key architectural elements' (Smith, 2002). They need to know where the organisation is going and how it is planning to get there. Ideally, they will be guided by a set of objectives with measurable targets, which people believe are important and to which they can readily aspire. At the same time, these managers must have the freedom to act within the context of their organisational area without feeling constrained or that they need to get approval before they can proceed. This is an important balancing process and is more difficult to achieve in public organisations where consultation and decision making by consensus are more common. This lens requires strategic thinking throughout the organisation, but especially at the operational level, so that managers can directly interpret and translate their understanding of the overall corporate vision into the appropriate lower level strategies. A similar process is described by Kaplan and Norton, called 'strategic mapping', which is used as an aid to help managers to select operational performance measures linked to business strategy for use in a balanced scorecard (Kaplan and Norton, 2001).

Lens 3: Strategic alignment of the project portfolio

The third lens focuses on the strategic alignment of the project portfolio. Any organisation can be thought of as a matrix with business and technology domains as shown in Figure 3.3.

The external focus (business and technology strategies) place the organisation in its market and industry context, while the internal focus (business and technology processes) define the operating model of the

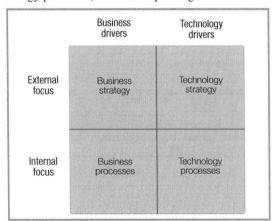

Figure 3.3 Business and technology matrix
(Adapted from Smith, 2002)

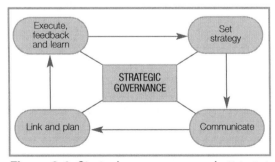

Figure 3.4 Strategic governance cycle (Adapted from Smith, 2002)

organisation. On the other hand, the business drivers determine where the organisation is going and how it will deliver value to its customers, whereas the technology drivers define the technology vision, direction, applications and infrastructure of the organisation.

Strategic alignment exists when all four domains are mutually supportive, that is, when all aspects of the business are executing towards a common and shared set of objectives. In other words, as the strategies change, the underlying processes must keep pace; and as the processes themselves evolve and improve, the strategies need to incorporate and exploit these changes. In the same way, as the business changes, the related technology areas must remain synchronised; and as technology advances to create new opportunities, the business domains must find new ways to assess, capture and leverage them.

To help to achieve and maintain alignment, a strategic governance cycle, such as the one illustrated in Figure 3.4, can be used.

The four stages of the cycle are:

- *Set strategy* – ensures that the organisation's strategy is relevant and focused on achieving the organisation's long-range goals
- *Communicate* – ensures broad dissemination and internalisation of the strategy. An important objective of this step is to achieve a sense of shared significance among people regarding the key ideas and consequences of the strategy
- *Link and plan* – ensures the strategy connects with the operating plans, budgets and project portfolio
- *Execute, feedback and learn* – ensures plans are put into action for operating the business and continuous improvement.

A business alignment model can unify a business and help to maintain its competitiveness in a changing environment.

Lens 4: Benefit delivery

Benefit delivery, the fourth lens, bridges the gap between strategy and strategy implementation. This lens uses portfolio management to ensure that the right set of projects are selected, and project management to ensure that these projects get done right to deliver planned benefits. The underlying benefit delivery philosophy is an important concept in strategic governance and is based on two simple principles:

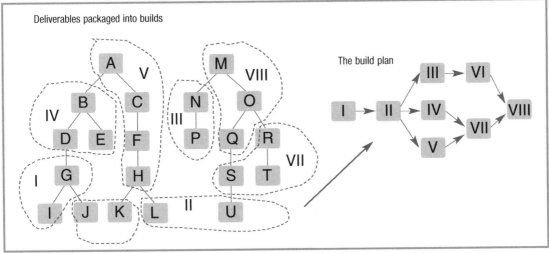

Figure 3.5 Creating a build plan for delivering business plan benefits (Adapted from Smith, 2002)

1. The use of deliverables to precisely define the value content of a project.
2. The use of a build plan to optimally package and incrementally deliver that value to the customer (see Figure 3.5).

Lens 5: A performance ethic

The fifth and final lens concerns the importance of establishing the right performance ethic for an organisation. This refers to the collection of habits, customs, understandings and relationships with which people work every day to operate and support the organisation and its customers and suppliers.

An effective value-driven performance ethic is characterised by a sense of urgency, stretch, commitment and delivery in all areas of the organisation, both internally (among various operating units and functions) and externally (among customers, partners and suppliers).

An example of a strategic governance system from the public sector in Australia is given in the Insights from Industry box.

Programme governance

A governance framework for programmes

Definitions of programme management were introduced in Chapter 1 and do not need repeating here. Suffice it to say that the projects in a programme are linked by a common programme objective. A portfolio, however, may contain one or more programmes and other projects unrelated to each other, but all supporting the organisation's vision and strategy.

Programmes consist of multiple projects with the following characteristics:

- Shared or scarce resources, demanding prioritisation and adjudication between competing projects
- Interdependency needing coordination and change management across projects and other ongoing nonproject work

SYSTEM OF GOVERNANCE WITHIN QUEENSLAND GOVERNMENT, DEPT OF PUBLIC WORKS, AUSTRALIA

The strategic governance process used by the Department of Public Works, Queensland Government is illustrated in Figure 3.6. The process is designed to ensure that there is a whole-of-government approach to the planning, management and delivery of state government building projects, which in turn will maximise value for money and contribute to a more effective service delivery.

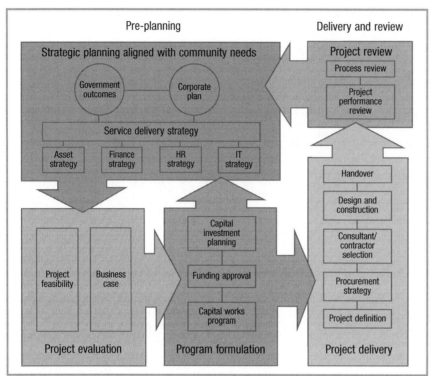

Figure 3.6 Strategic governance, Department of Public Works, Queensland Government (http://www.publicworks.qld.gov.au/home/home.cfm)

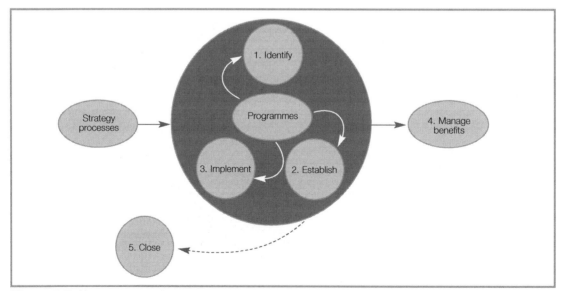

Figure 3.7 Key processes in programme management (Adapted from the UK Government's Gateway Process, http://www.ogc.gov.uk/sdtoolkit/index.html)

- Common infrastructure across more than one project, allowing cost and efficiency gains
- Shared risks and therefore opportunities to manage and contain risks across more than one project simultaneously.

In this section a programme governance framework is developed as an aid to help an organisation maximise its resources and implement its strategy. This framework reflects the view that a successful enterprise has a 'stream of projects' flowing through it at all times (Cleland, 1999); the aim being to enable a continuous balancing, trimming and improving of the project portfolio to ensure that it is the *minimal set* of projects and the *best set* of projects that advance the strategy.

A structured approach to programme management ensures that the interdependencies between projects are coordinated and the risk is managed across these interdependencies. The key stages in programme management, as used by the UK Government's Gateway Process, are illustrated in Figure 3.7 and described below.

Stage one: programme identification

This stage proceeds from the strategic planning cycle and focuses on the project proposals for implementation, including their anticipated benefits, risk, estimated costs, timescales and effort required. The process involves:

- examination of all relevant business plans and change strategies to define the benefits associated with change
- determination of the best grouping of projects into one or more programmes, evaluating planned benefits and economies of scale
- documentation of each programme grouping in order to support the business case and authorisation to proceed
- selection and appointment of a programme manager.

Stage two: programme establishment

This stage seeks to apply the appropriate level of controls and infrastructure to put the programme in place. The objectives of this stage are to:

- establish an effective programme governance regime

- communicate fully the programme-level objectives to all participants
- develop the programme design
- define the interdependencies between projects
- refine and consolidate the business justification for the programme
- establish a benefits management plan.

Stage three: programme implementation

The aim of this stage is to execute the project portfolio and facilitate strategic change. This process has the following objectives:

- maintain communication channels and conformity to programme objectives
- implement the project portfolio
- conduct periodic reviews at points of stability to test alignment with strategic objectives
- ensure the target business environment is adequately prepared to receive changes and in a position to take advantage of planned benefits
- monitor compliance with the programme design in order to ensure policies and standards remain consistent with organisation requirements
- ensure that the benefits and risks are properly managed throughout the programme.

Stage four: manage benefits

The purpose of this stage is to track the specific outcomes, which were identified at the start, and drive through the process of achieving these outcomes within the business operations during the life of the programme. Programme managers often remain with an engagement in order to assess implementation and satisfaction of long-term benefits, fine-tuning the programme in order to ensure that business benefits are achieved at the operational level. Project managers, on the other hand, tend to finish when the sponsor has signed off a project. The objectives of the manage benefits process are to:

- ensure the programme delivers the planned benefits and that these are fully realised
- make graded improvements or refinements through the programme, that is, fine-tuning
- provide corrective action in areas of significant shortfall
- seek additional areas of benefit.

Stage five: programme close

In order to establish and maintain a clear focus on achieving the end goal, a programme should have a predetermined end point and a formal closing down process. Benefits management may need to continue beyond the formal closure of a programme, particularly if the achievement of measurable improvements is to be part of ongoing business operations. This stage involves:

- confirmation that the changes defined at the start have been delivered and the programme's vision achieved
- completion of the learning process and ensuring that this is fully communicated to all interested parties.

Programme organisation

The organisation structure for a programme should have clear lines of sponsorship, authority and management, while being flexible enough to react to changes. Recommended roles are as follows (OGC, 2003):

- *Programme sponsorship.* Programmes require sponsorship from the most senior executives of the organisation or group of organisations committed to the programme to ensure support of the business case and its fit into organisational objectives. Sponsorship also includes senior management support for the changes introduced by the programme and commitment to achieve the required outcomes.

- *Programme management.* There are three primary roles for managing a programme:
  - *The programme director* who provides overall leadership and has ultimate responsibility for the successful delivery of the programme
  - *The programme manager* who carries the responsibility for day-to-day management of the programme's portfolio of projects and for ensuring these are focused on delivery of the required capabilities
  - *The business change manager* who is responsible for realising the required outcomes through the integration of the new capabilities into the business operation.

- *Programme support.* For most programmes, a programme support office should be established to assist with the management of programme information, that is, budget control, status

reports, programme documentation and the optimisation of resources and schedules across the programme to deliver programme benefits. Although a programme support office can serve both the programme and the individual projects within a programme, large projects are often supported by a separate project office. It should be borne in mind, however, that a programme office operates at a strategic level and seeks to optimise at the programme, business unit or organisation-wide level. This in turn may lead to some projects running suboptimally at a local level. The Insights from Industry box shows how a division of General Motors benefited from establishing a project support office.

USING A PROJECT SUPPORT OFFICE TO INTEGRATE SUPPLIERS

Poor supplier delivery was an issue faced by General Motors Powertrain (GMP) in the late 1990s. A string of late deliveries of critical parts such as engines and transmissions to its parent company, General Motors, caused General Motors to take notice and initiate corrective action to mitigate the risk of late product delivery to the customer.

A detailed assessment was carried out and key findings were identified in the areas of communication and project management processes for GMP and its suppliers. After careful analysis of the findings, it was decided to establish a project support office (PSO) as the most effective means of improving communication and deploying common project management processes. The major functions of a PSO are the development, execution and administration of project management processes, tools, templates, procedures and guidelines within an organisation. For GMP, the PSO would also provide the structure and environment to develop, train and house personnel with the skills needed to perform all required project management functions within the organisation.

Once established, the PSO served as a model for a common project management methodology that could be effectively and efficiently transferred to other divisions of General Motors.

Source: Couture, D., Gibbs, E. and Hresko, D. 'Manufacturing engineering project office: a critical link to supplier integration', PMI, *Manufacturing SIG*, 2001, **3**(2): 4–8

Management by projects

The terms 'management by projects', 'programme management' and 'project management' are not merely a twist on words. There are significant differences between them in concept, scope and capability. Table 3.2 summarises these differences.

According to the Project Management Institute, managing by projects 'is an organisational approach to the management of ongoing operations which treats many aspects of ongoing operations as projects to apply project management techniques to them' (PMI, 2000: 6). The principles of programme management also apply to organisations that manage by projects – the main difference being that the programme governance framework is organisation-wide.

These organisations tend to have management systems in place to facilitate project management. For example, their financial systems are often specifically designed for accounting, tracking and reporting on multiple simultaneous projects. On the contrary, nonproject-based organisations often lack management systems designed to support project needs efficiently and effectively. The absence of project-oriented systems usually makes project management more difficult. In some cases, nonproject-based organisations will have departments or other subunits that operate as project-based organisations with systems to match.

Management by projects is an organisational approach that has grown in response to these changes. One of the stated aims of the Institute of Project Management of Ireland reflects this trend: 'to promote the management by projects approach to service the needs and challenges facing business in today's competitive environment'. Since the mid-1990s, a growing number of organisations have discovered management by projects supports a more dynamic way of working which retains a strong customer focus.

Management by projects represents the confluence of strategy implementation, organisation behaviour and project management. Organisations are seeking to use management by projects as an important part of their long-term survival. According to Graham and Englund (1997), most future growth in organisations will result from successful development projects that generate new products, services or procedures. The Insights from Industry box below describes how Jo Hancock is changing the way services and operational activities are carried out in Thames Valley Police, London.

---

insights from INDUSTRY

THAMES VALLEY POLICE MOVE TOWARDS MANAGEMENT BY PROJECTS

Jo Hancock, newly appointed project and programme support manager, has set up a programme and project support office from scratch. Her role includes establishing the project management methodology for the force and assisting with a variety of projects relating to both support services and operational activities. She says:

> The relevance of project management within the police is being increasingly recognised as a structured way to develop new processes and IT which help to make better use of scarce resources. The next big challenge is to introduce programme management to coordinate portfolios of projects that achieve our strategic objectives.

Source: Project, 'Services: Police – Energy Force: PM Methodology for Thames Police' by Deborah Boyce, 2001, **13**(10): 14

Table 3.2 Differences between project management, programme management and management by projects

	Project management	Programme management	Management by projects
Concept	The direction and management of a project	The integration, prioritisation, communication and continuous control of multiple projects	The integration, prioritisation, communication and continuous control of multiple projects and operational schedules
Scope	Project-wide: a single one-off endeavour	Programme-wide: an ongoing operation for a given business unit	An enterprise-wide operating environment
Capability	A tactical issue	A strategic issue	A strategic issue

Source: Adapted from Boznak, 1996.

Perhaps the most important issue to recognise, and the reason why some organisations cope with complexity and change whilst others struggle, is that there are limited resources that must be shared between ongoing operations and all projects. Management by projects is about successfully handling this complexity which is extremely important to an organisation's success because what usually determines the success or failure of an organisation is not how brilliant the strategy is, but how well the plans are executed. Graham and Englund (1997) have studied the management by projects approach in Hewlett-Packard and have identified ten elements required for ongoing project success:

1. Change the organisation culture and way of working to a project-based organisation, a system based on teamwork at all levels.
2. Develop and emphasise the link between strategy and projects; essential to foster stronger and more robust motivation from all participants.
3. Understand upper management influence, and build this into the system, especially concerning support, negotiating deadlines and avoiding unnecessary interference.
4. Develop a core team process which integrates all the functions and departments from the beginning and remains intact throughout projects.
5. Organise for project management; structure influences behaviour and upper managers have responsibility to set up and maintain organisational structures that support successful projects.
6. Develop a project management information system; this maintains flexibility and keeps the project organisation intact.
7. Develop a plan for project manager selection and development; project management becomes a core organisational competence and not just a temporary annoyance.
8. Develop a learning organisation; a major part of managing by projects which drives competitive advantage.
9. Develop project management maturity; continue to improve and develop the organisation's capability in management by projects.
10. Develop project management throughout the organisation; continue to find new ways of using and applying project management to achieve strategic objectives.

IT governance

IT governance is positioned between programme and project governance in the governance wheel described earlier (see Figure 3.1). It is largely concerned with the enterprise and IT architecture that an organisation has in place. An enterprise and IT architecture identifies the main components of the organisation and the ways in which these components work together in order to achieve defined business objectives. The components include staff, business processes, technology, information, financial and other resources.

A well-designed enterprise and IT architecture can help give confidence to senior management that decisions made about IT will enable the organisation to 'join up' its IT, now and in the future, without risk of inflexibility or lock-in to a standard that may have been arbitrarily imposed. On the other hand, if decisions about components and their interrelationships are uncoordinated, ad hoc or localised, the result is likely to be duplication of effort and resources, poor coordination and control, problems with management and business performance, inability to share important resources such as information, and inefficiencies in operation. All these will hinder successful project and programme delivery.

There is now a growing realisation of a need for central IT coordination and planning, despite the rapid decentralisation of IT knowledge and increase in user power witnessed in the late 1980s (Grindley, 1991). Today, most routine tasks are automated and the focus within the majority of organisations is shifting to the creation of coherent information systems (IS) forming an efficient systems architecture for the entire organisation.

Pearlson and Saunders (2004) have developed a model to articulate the interdependencies between strategy, organisation and information, which they call the 'information systems strategy triangle' (see Figure 3.8). They suggest that all three points of the

Figure 3.8 IS strategy triangle (Pearlson and Saunders, 2004)

triangle should be in balance in any organisation, and if they are out of balance, then organisational tension, or possibly crisis, exists. The implications from the model are:

1. Business strategy should drive organisational and information strategy.
2. Organisational strategy must complement business strategy.
3. Information strategy must complement business strategy.
4. Organisational and information strategy should complement each other.
5. If a change is made to one corner of the triangle, it is necessary to evaluate the other two corners to ensure balance is maintained.

Given the strong relationship already discussed between strategy and projects, the IS strategy triangle suggests an implicit relationship between projects and information systems. Any framework for programme management must include the management of information and therefore the evolution of an enterprise and IT architecture. The Critical Considerations box illustrates the importance of enterprise and IT architectures in public sector programmes.

The development and exploitation of an enterprise and IT architecture will assist organisations to govern their IT investments and meet their business objectives. In particular, benefits can be achieved in the following areas:

- *Alignment:* ensuring that the design of the organisation and its information systems are aligned with the organisation's mission.
- *Integration:* ensuring that the business rules are consistent across the organisation, data resources are known and accessible as appropriate, interfaces and information flows are standardised and connectivity and interoperability are managed across the enterprise, and outside it where necessary.
- *Change:* facilitating and managing change to any aspect of the enterprise.
- *Responsiveness and efficiency:* reducing timescales for systems development, minimising requirements for new applications generation, reducing timescales for modernisation and reducing overall resource requirements for ICT.
- *Convergence:* moving towards enterprise-wide standards for infrastructure, data interchange and common applications.

CRITICAL CONSIDERATIONS

ENTERPRISE AND IT ARCHITECTURES IN PUBLIC SECTOR PROGRAMMES

Architectural frameworks for IS/IT development are becoming increasingly important in the public sector for the following reasons:

- The demands of e-government and the targets for electronic delivery of services.
- The requirements of 'joined-up' government and the need to consider interworking and information sharing beyond the boundaries of the organisation.
- The recognition of the importance of information as a key resource, and the pressures to exploit and share information resources.
- The continuing emergence of new technologies, including developments in mobile computing and support for home working.
- Pressures to re-engineer business processes to achieve improved efficiency and greater customer focus.
- The requirements for the ICT infrastructure to integrate legacy systems into newer e-business applications.
- The requirement for information systems and the underlying ICT infrastructure to respond rapidly to changes in organisation and the demands of the business.
- The development of elements of 'common' applications and infrastructure across government, such as the government secure intranet, the government Gateway Process, the knowledge network and the e-government interoperability framework.

Source: Office of Government Commerce (OGC) (2003). Successful Delivery Toolkit Version 4.0. http://www.ogc.gov.uk/sdtoolkit/

Governance failure in business change and IT projects is often associated with a lack of governance either at the concept stage where the justification is not fully thought through or once the system goes live and all governance processes cease. Failure can also occur when an organisation does not have the information or the courage to enforce a go/no-go decision at a gateway review for the project. This often results in late understanding of critical issues

CRITICAL CONSIDERATIONS

GOVERNANCE OF IT PROJECTS

Recent years have seen organisations investing large sums of money in information systems and associated technologies. However, there is conflicting evidence as to the contribution of these systems and technologies. As a result, the realisation has grown that heavy investment in IT can lead to poor financial performance if not properly managed, and that organisations should only fund projects and technologies which facilitate the attainment of business objectives. However, this places a requirement on IT evaluation procedures to incorporate not only the quantitative, tangible factors associated with such investments but also the less tangible, difficult to quantify, factors arising from applying technology to achieve strategic goals. Accordingly, the issue of IT evaluation and the techniques to use are becoming increasingly important issues.

Research confirms that capital budgeting techniques such as cost/benefit analysis, net present value and payback period are being overused in evaluating potential IT investments. This is at the expense of IT-focused evaluation techniques, such as value analysis and information economics. The result is a failure to incorporate intangible factors into the evaluation process and a failure to integrate corporate and IT governance on issues such as authority/responsibility within organisations for the sanctioning of IT expenditure.

As a result, large-scale projects with a strategic orientation are difficult to justify. The most important IT applications fall into this category. If this practice does not change, many innovative, business-led, strategically oriented initiatives will be rejected in favour of less important, short run projects which offer more immediate returns or savings.

One problem is that it is often financial rather than IT personnel who have responsibility for IT expenditure. This lack of authority on the part of IS personnel in deciding the level and direction of IT investment, while not affecting the profitability of organisations in the short term, helps to explain an absence of intangible, qualitative factors in the IT evaluation process, and thus hinders long-term profitability. Given the drawbacks associated with either the management information systems (MIS) or finance function having complete autonomy for IT project evaluation, joint authority by way of a multi-party committee (representing finance, MIS and senior management) has been proposed as an alternative governance arrangement to allocating the finance department sole authority to sanction IT expenditure.

Source: Casey, C. and O'Mahony, C. (1995) 'Current practices in information technology project appraisal: a need for change' ESRC, Paper Ref. 4/95, Business Information Systems, University College Cork

and resorting to project recovery mode to at least deliver some limited deliverables, with the promise that full benefits will be realised with the 'next release'. The case study at the end of the chapter is an example of such a project. Some issues in the governance of IT projects are highlighted in the Critical Considerations box.

Project governance

Project governance is the set of structures, systems and processes around the project that ensure the effective delivery of the project through to full utilisation and benefits realisation by the business (Lambert, 2003). There are four key influences on project governance structures:

1. *Risk planning* – balancing the extremes of risk avoidance and risk acceptance.
2. *Life cycle management* – ensuring a total life cycle approach, from concept to replacement, with authorisation management and well-defined strategic gateway reviews as appropriate. In some organisations, there is a tendency to have governance processes that finish once the project goes live or is commissioned. The risk here is that the project meets all its success criteria yet the outcomes are not realised over the longer term.
3. *Strategic change* – balancing the technical elegance of the solution against the organisation's capability to utilise the solution, taking into account the values and culture of the organisation – illustrated in Figure 3.9.
4. *Value management* – adopting consistent and repeatable processes that build in quality, remove

waste, add value and provide a strong customer goal-based focus and benefits delivery plan.

A project governance structure helps to ensure that:

- the scope of the project is defined so that the needs of all key stakeholders are adequately represented
- there is a clear understanding of the roles and responsibilities of everyone involved in the management of the project or programme
- a mechanism exists that ensures an organisation-wide perspective is brought to all project, programme and policy issues
- decision-making authority ultimately resides with an individual, not with a committee
- the budget for the project is adequate for the scope identified
- resources are available for carrying out the specific tasks
- there is a mechanism for escalation of issues
- overall project timelines are set and achieved.

Project management methodologies such as PRINCE 2 provide a complete solution to project governance. However, as the Project Management in Action case at the end of the chapter shows, it is only effective when the guidance given is put into practice. Also of interest to project governance are the recent developments in maturity models – discussed briefly in Chapter 10. A project management maturity model can be used to assess project governance maturity and plan future improvements.

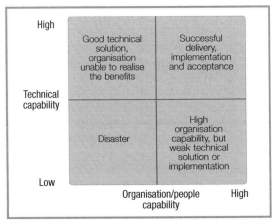

Figure 3.9 Balancing technical elegance and organisational capability to utilise the solution
(Lambert, 2003)

Authorisation management

Getting project go-ahead is about authorising and committing resources to meet a given need. The 'project charter' or its equivalent is usually the primary authorisation document. Other authorisation documents may include a 'contract' or 'customer order' in the case of work for external clients or an internal 'task sheet' for work for other business divisions in the same organisation.

Authorisation will normally be done at the start of a project and also at key 'investment gates' as part of a formal strategic review (APM, 2000). The business case for the project, which provides the project's original justification, should also be revisited as part of these staged reviews. The authorisation process is also critical as a way out of projects that have gone bad. Failing projects which are no longer going to deliver required or acceptable benefits should be stopped as soon as possible to avoid wasting time and resources (Staw and Ross, 1987). A formal mechanism such as a defined authorisation management process is necessary because many projects develop a significant inertia which is difficult to bring to a halt.

The process for approval to proceed to the next stage of a project (or to pull the plug on a project) will depend on the size and strategic importance of the project. Small value projects may be authorised by lower level managers. More senior management and directors will approve major cost and impact projects.

The completion of each stage frequently represents a project milestone, for example:

- authorise initial study
- authorise feasibility study and choose best solution
- authorise detailed planning
- authorise implementation
- authorise changes
- (authorise abandonment)
- authorise closure
- authorise follow-on project.

It is essential to understand any limitations or caveats that a project authorisation document may contain, for example feasibility study only; to design stage only; or turnkey to commissioning. The authorisation management process at Northumbrian Water and the gateway review process required for all new procurement projects in civil central government in the UK is given in the Insights from Industry box.

AUTHORISATION MANAGEMENT

Staged authorisation at Northumbrian Water

At Northumbrian Water, project authorisation procedures are published in a booklet containing a series of investment control forms. The following forms are used:

- Statement of problem
- Acceptance of feasibility study
- Request for project budget on completion of design
- Request to invite tenders/quotations
- Request to award contract
- Project completion report.

The booklet spells out that project progression is a step-by-step approach, with a stop at each stage requiring appropriate approval to proceed. The directors at Northumbrian Water stress the importance of following these procedures in making sound investments and emphasise the responsibility of the project manager to ensure that they are followed properly at each stage.

Source: Data collected during PhD research, Paul Gardiner. Used with permission

UK Government's Gateway Process

Speaking at the 'Gateway' launch in London at 12 Downing Street, Andrew Smith said:

> we now have a commercially minded reliable management system – the Gateway Process – that can be applied to every major government project. Such projects will pass through each 'gate', only when rigorous tests have been met.

Peter Gershon, the OGC's chief executive said:

> Historically there has been wide variability on the outcomes of major projects, with too many being late, over budget and not generating the planned level of benefits. The OGC Gateway Process is

based on techniques that have been tried and tested in the private sector and provides senior managers in government with the powerful tool to help manage these projects better in future. The introduction of project gateways will ensure that projects that have not met our rigid criteria will fail to proceed. This will enable appropriate corrective action to be taken.

The Gateway Process meets the requirements of the Gershon Report on government procurement and the Cabinet Office report *Successful IT: Modernising Government in Action*. It is also consistent with *Achieving Excellence in Construction*. The process is based on techniques that lead to more effective delivery of benefits together with more predictable costs and outcomes. There are six gateways at key decision points in the life cycle of a project, four before contract award and two looking at service implementation and confirmation of the operational benefits:

- Gate 0 – strategic assessment
- Gate 1 – justify business case
- Gate 2 – approve procurement method
- Gate 3 – approve award of contract
- Gate 4 – test whether project is ready to go live
- Gate 5 – identify if project has delivered planned benefits.

Gateway reviews are carried out at each key decision point by a team of experienced people, independent of the project team. The process emphasizes early review for maximum added value, providing project teams with advice and guidance from fellow practitioners. The Office of Government Commerce (OGC) has conducted gateway reviews of projects to a value in excess of £18 billion. The feedback from accounting officers, project officers and senior responsible officers has been highly supportive.

Sources: Office of Government Commerce, *Gateway Review: Leadership Guide*, 2001; UK Government press release, 20 February 2001, 'New government procurement technique will save £millions for front line services'

PROJECT MANAGEMENT
in action

The Scottish Qualifications Authority

By Paul D Gardiner, School of Management and Languages, Heriot-Watt University, Edinburgh, Scotland. Contact: P.D.Gardiner@hw.ac.uk
Presented at the 17th Nordic Conference on Business Studies, Reykjavik, Iceland, 14–16 August 2003

Introduction

On 9th August, 2000, 147,000 Scottish schoolchildren awaited nervously for their examination certificates. Normally, it is a day of celebration or disappointment, but in 2000 it was a day of confusion. Almost 17,000 pupils received inaccurate or incomplete certificates. The media were having a field day and the opposing government party demanded an investigation into the fiasco. It was 'the biggest failure and threat to the credibility of the Scottish education system in living memory' (Enterprise and Lifelong Learning Committee, 2000).

A major decision for the Scottish education sector

Before 2000, Scotland's secondary education system offered pupils two routes of study: an academic route, based on the Scottish 'Higher' qualifications and a vocational route based on modules and other vocational qualifications. From 1990 to 1992 a committee, chaired by Professor John Howie, was appointed to review the secondary education system in Scotland. The membership of this committee was drawn from a wide range of stakeholders (see Table 3.2).

The final report, known as the Howie Report, concluded that significant reform was necessary to have a fairer system for pupils. This was accepted by the government and became the first strategic decision in this multiproject.

The second decision was more controversial and concerned defining the nature and scope of the reform to take place. The proposals of the Howie Report – to adopt a twin-track education system, modelled on the Danish system – were 'almost unanimously rejected in the consultation that followed' (Raffe et al., 2001), in which much of the consensus was negative. In other words, members agreed what they did not want. The new qualification that was eventually accepted by the secretary of state in 1994, termed Higher Still, was the proposal that faced the least resistance; a questionable basis for strategic decision making.

The proposals that were eventually published, in March 1994, *Higher Still: Opportunity for All* (Scottish Office, 1994), proposed a 'unified curriculum and assessment system' based on provision at five levels, subsequently named Access, Intermediate 1, Intermediate 2, Higher and Advanced Higher. The system was to cover academic and vocational provision for all ages from 16 upwards in schools and colleges, but not higher education. Higher Still would provide a single, flexible, unified qualification system, based on a common pedagogy, that was suitable for high achievers and less able students alike, removing the previous divide between academic and vocational qualifications.

In the existing system, Scottish Highers tended to be in academic subjects, were delivered through a relatively traditional pedagogy, and were mainly assessed by external examinations. Modules were more vocational, at least in the sense of placing more emphasis on competence; their pedagogy was more student-centred and their assessment internal. The system was seen to be failing less able and able students alike. Students often mixed the two, and had to cope with their different pedagogies and styles of assessment.

The new unified system would have a single set of design rules for curriculum, assessment and certification and a greater balance between externally assessed examinations and internally assessed coursework. This in turn created an extra workload for the schools and colleges (known as centres) administering these assessments and for the new body responsible for processing the Higher Still system, the Scottish Qualifications Authority (SQA).

The decision to introduce Higher Still into the Scottish education sector was the start of a development programme that involved the largest consultation in Scottish educational history.

Although there was substantial support for the Higher Still from schools and colleges, there were also significant criticisms concerning:

- some features of the Higher Still model
- the speed with which it was implemented
- the leadership style of the Scottish Executive, the Schools Inspectorate and their agencies who designed the reform and carried it through.

Key concerns in the early decision-making process reflected the traditional style of governance in the Scottish educational sector under the leadership of Her Majesty's Schools Inspectorate which is perceived to be relatively centralised, 'top down' and linear (Raffe et

Table 3.2 Committee members involved in the initial Higher Still consultations

Stakeholders involved in the initial consultations:
Secretary of State for Scotland
Scottish Office Education Department
Education authorities
Scottish Further Education Unit
Scottish Consultative Council on the Curriculum
Teacher training institutions
Her Majesty's inspectors
Schools and colleges

al., 2001). The process in this project, however, did benefit from wide discussion and debate through the Howie committee and later consultations involved many stakeholders and informal groups and task forces.

Despite this consultation, gaps remained. A number of key risks were not addressed. No consultation paper was ever issued on assessment and reporting: 'the major debate which should have taken place not merely on the principles of the new assessment regime but on its practical operation failed to materialise' (Education, Culture and Sport Committee, 2000).

This was a major reform and consensus was always going to be difficult and conflict inevitable. Although these issues were not insurmountable, strong leadership was clearly going to be needed.

A low-key approach

Opportunity for All had abandoned Howie's proposed system, but it made little attempt to promote the principles underlying its own alternative. The logical leap from the post-Howie consensus to a unified system was assumed, not argued (Raffe et al., 2001). Indeed, far from selling a positive vision of a unified system, *Opportunity for All* presented it as a low-key technical response to the problems identified by Howie. This continued throughout the development and consultation process, during which school and college staff were being told that Higher Still would represent 'business as usual', and that, to begin with at least, their involvement would be just 'a toe in the water' (Raffe and Howieson, 1998).

The Inspectorate's ability to articulate its vision of reform was constrained by fears of losing teacher support or precipitating conflicts between different educational interests.

Existing award-processing bodies

Prior to Higher Still, there were two award-processing bodies in Scotland – the Scottish Examinations Board (SEB) and the Scottish Vocational Education Council (SCOTVEC). The SEB ran examinations – Standard Grade, Higher Grade (the Scottish Highers) and the Certificate of Sixth Year Studies. It was a statutory body, created out of the examinations branch of the Scottish Education Department in the 1960s. It was a self-effacing organisation with a strong public service ethos. Although a non-departmental public body (NDPB) with its own board, important decisions about the qualifications it offered were taken by government. Its budget had to be approved by COSLA (Convention of Scottish Local Authorities). As a consequence, it was run on a 'shoe-string'. SEB operated from offices in Dalkeith, near Edinburgh. It had recently converted its IT from an IBM mainframe to a relational database management system based on a Sequent platform. The system was built by external contractors.

SCOTVEC ran National Certificate modules and other vocational qualifications that were assessed on internally assessed units. It was created in 1986 as a company limited by guarantee and followed a private sector model, although financially supported by government. Unlike SEB, it promoted itself as well as its qualifications because it saw itself in competition with English awarding bodies (and SEB). SCOTVEC escaped COSLA control and was financially much better placed than SEB. It operated from an office block in the centre of Glasgow's business district (about 75 km to the west of Edinburgh). SCOTVEC had invested in a mainframe computer, an IBM AS400, with in-house software development.

The SQA – a new award processing body

Although the announcement to launch Higher Still was issued in 1994, it was not until 1995, after a consultation paper (on which 80% of respondents agreed), that the secretary of state decided a merger of SEB and SCOTVEC would be the most appropriate solution. It would be called the Scottish Qualifications Authority (SQA).

The two awarding bodies differed in their legal constitution, approach to assessment, culture, financial regime, IT architecture and location. However, after the decision had been made that the functions of the SEB and SCOTVEC should be merged, they were left without any guidance as to how this should be achieved. No one person had total responsibility for ensuring that the introduction of Higher Still would be successfully achieved by the SQA.

The SQA came into being on 1st April, 1997, three years after the launch of the Higher Still programme, with approximately 550 employees. It is governed by a board of management and the Scottish Executive, through two government ministers, the minister for enterprise and lifelong learning and the minister for children and education.

The statutory duty of the ministers is to approve the corporate plan, key objectives, performance indicators and the budget of the SQA. They approved the plan to introduce Higher Still into centres and implement a new computer system in the same year, whilst the integration of the formerly separate operations of SEB and SCOTVEC was continuing. The secretary of state for Scotland had already delayed the introduction twice before, from 1997 to 1999, because schools were not ready.

Also in 1997, the new Labour Government came into office and the strategy group, which had steered the development process thus far, chaired by the senior chief inspector, was replaced by an implementation group, chaired by the same person, with similar participation but with more local authority representation. The implementation group was supported by sector groups representing numerous stakeholders: schools, further and higher education colleges, and employment and training interests. However, as in the earlier stages of the process, committees tended to proliferate, and working groups and committees of varying formality and longevity took over much of the decision making from the groups that were formally responsible. In 1999, another significant political event exerted its influence on the project: the newly created Scottish Parliament challenged the system of governance of Scottish education, especially the role of the UK Government's Scottish Office and Schools Inspectorate.

Vision and leadership

Despite the consultation that had taken place and the apparent consensus, no overall common strategic vision was communicated to all the stakeholders. Therefore, a possible basis for conflict resolution was lost. School and college staff were not prepared for the scale of the changes, and reacted more strongly when these turned out to be much larger than had been suggested. The perceptions of the reform among the public, and among many educationists, remained incomplete and partial: in autumn 2000 it was still widely perceived as a reform only of the SEB Higher, but divorced from the wider reforms. The various sector groups, that were largely driving the project now, tended to have narrow and limited strategic vision, leading to a neglect of the broader reform issues and a failure to establish and communicate the 'big picture' effectively.

Consequently, Scottish education ministers were not prepared for the scale of the changes, and failed to recognise the need for political leadership on behalf of Higher Still until it was too late. This consequence was compounded by the change of government in 1997 (politicians are reluctant to campaign for a previous administration's policies) and by the separation in 1999 (due to the new Scottish Parliament) of educational responsibilities between two departments of the Scottish Executive, with Higher Still split between them.

The above issues also filtered down to the newly formed SQA. The vision and goal of the reforms were not clearly communicated to key stakeholders of the SQA. There were gaps and omissions in strategic clarity. The processes of assessment and reporting of Higher Still had not been debated, without which it was impossible to provide an early outline of the IT architecture to support and deliver the new system.

Staff from the previous two organisations were taking part in a stressful human resources project, with fewer directors than previously, none of whom had any significant IT experience. Despite these difficulties, a tight deadline had been imposed on the SQA without any large-scale risk analysis to support it. There was pressure from several sources to succeed, but a lack of strong leadership, communication of the strategic vision and open dialogue, together with restraining political influences, made it increasingly difficult to maintain high standards of governance.

Creating a new organisational structure

SEB and SCOTVEC had a total of eleven senior managers in 1990 and nine in 1996 just pre-merger. No director had qualifications or a background in IT, yet the SQA was to engage in one of the largest IT developments of its kind.

In January 1997, after open advertisement, the chief executive was appointed to the SQA by the board of management. His background was in educational policy not in operational management. He reappointed all six of the former directors of the SEB and SCOTVEC who had not opted for early retirement. However in 1998, the finance and services director retired early, and no effort was made to replace him. And in April 1999, the IT and operations director retired, leaving four directors to carry the responsibilities once carried by eleven. External interviews were carried out for one person to fill both these posts. However, the Finance, Planning and General Purposes Committee of the SQA decided not to appoint, but to split the work between the remaining directors. Both the IT and operations units were appointed to the director of awards. This meant he had responsibility for approximately half of all the staff in the organisation, although he had limited experience of operations or information systems.

Restructuring

In 1998, a huge project was undertaken to merge the personnel of the two companies. The chief executive's approach was to emphasise how much each individual was valued so every single person was matched in. If someone had a similar post in the original organisation, they were assigned to that, but if two or more people were suitable, competitive interviews had to take place. The heads of units were appointed in January 1998, nine months after the merger took place, and lower level appointments were completed in early 1999.

Location

Both pre-merger organisations occupied custom-built offices, reflecting their need for specialised warehousing space for the storing and dispatch of examination question papers and results certificates.

The advantages of moving to a new site were:

- speeding up the creation of a new SQA culture to supersede the cultures of the predecessor bodies
- enhancing business efficiency by facilitating face-to-face interaction and avoiding duplication of office services
- eliminating officer travel time between Glasgow and Dalkeith.

The disadvantages were:

- the cost of relocation (the government did not offer to fund it)
- the danger of losing experienced staff who would not move home or travel further to work.

The government offered no financial assistance to bring the two companies into one office so the chairman of the board of management and the chief executive of the SQA decided not to relocate everyone to one site or a completely new one but to remain at their separate sites.

The data-processing staff in SCOTVEC expected that they would have to move to Dalkeith but the chief executive decided that their work was in fact not data processing so that they could stay in Glasgow. This resulted in a lack of experience in Dalkeith which now had to process the former SCOTVEC modules with no SCOTVEC employees, and it reduced the expected staffing level of the department by a third. As the SQA was kept on two sites, the senior managers were also split between the two.

After integration was complete, no further efforts were made to help the organisation gel as a single unit. Communication between the two sites was limited to email and video conferencing in an effort to overcome geography.

IT architecture

Not only did the SQA have to introduce Higher Still to schools, it also had to implement a new information system, called the awards processing system (APS), to process the new qualification. In December 1996 external consultants were brought in who advised that an interim solution should be used, integrating the data sources of SEB and SCOTVEC. A single solution 'should only be achieved in the longer term, after the implementation of Higher Still' (Deloitte and Touche, 2000: 2). They suggested that bids from specialist companies for both developments should be invited. However, early in 1997 the SQA opted for a completely new system, based on the SEB's system, and to design it themselves. The IT department of the SEB had six members and had used external contractors to develop its previous applications. SCOTVEC's IT department had 13 members and had developed most of its packages in-house. Extra staff were brought in; however, only one person knew how to do each job as existing knowledge had not been shared among employees. The amount of money allocated was lamentably low and every-

thing had to be achieved in the two-year timescale set by the government.

A detailed plan was produced but no overall budget or measurable success criteria were set. An APS project board was set up in November 1997, and reported that the project was behind schedule in June 1998. However, no action was taken to address this.

Governance

The SQA is a non-departmental public body (NDPB) responsible to both the minister for enterprise and lifelong learning and the minister for children and education. The role of the ministers is to approve finance issues and corporate plans and give direction in situations of conflict. Two aspects make this NDPB unusual. First, it does not derive its income solely from the Scottish Executive, but receives fees from external sources as well. This means it is not dependent on the Executive for funding, so contact between the two bodies is not frequent. Second, because the SQA writes the examination papers and sets exam pass mark standards, it is measuring how the government performs on its education policies. Therefore the SQA must stay distanced from the government so that ministers are not able to interfere with the exam process.

Prior to 2000, annual meetings took place between the ministers, the chairman of the board of management of the SQA and the chief executive. Quarterly liaison group meetings were held between Scottish Executive officials from both departments and the senior management team (SMT) of the SQA. Below this level of governance, the board of management operates, representing schools, colleges, local educational authorities, training organisations and employers. The chairman of the board was responsible to the Scottish Executive through the ministers. However, this board was unpaid, had a variety of jobs and were members of other committees. The chairman was remunerated, based on one

day a week. The board met quarterly, its purpose being to bring an external viewpoint to the NDPB and represent the multitude of stakeholders involved in the SQA.

The board of management's role was to bring the experience and expertise of other organisations to the work of the SQA and contribute to the wider management of the organisation. It was designed to act as a safety net, challenging the chief executive and senior officers to ensure that the SQA fulfilled its function. However, no member was a specialist in IT, so they had limited experience of the issues arising from the introduction of the new computer system.

The board members and ministers were not issued with any management information so they had to rely on the SQA for information. However, senior managers of SQA lacked management information themselves, due to the delayed APS project, and so could not inform the board of the extent of the difficulties they were encountering. Queries to the SQA were being 'batted straight back, with the promise that concerns were being recognised and that everything would be alright on the night' (Enterprise and Lifelong Learning Committee, 2000).

In the minutes of the SMT's meetings between 13th January and 30th June 1999, there was generally no sense of urgency in dealing with the problems being encountered with the 2000 examinations, although on 3rd March 2000, an email was sent from the director of awards to the rest of the SMT, stating: 'I am reluctant to press the panic button but I am becoming very worried ... I think that we need to take full stock of:

- what is going wrong?
- why and whether we have remedial action in hand?
- what more we could do?
- how we best handle and resolve complaints?' (Deloitte and Touche, 2000)

SQA project deliverables and timetable

The key project deliverables for the SQA were:

- to merge the data sets already existing in the SEB and SCOTVEC
- design, develop and implement an information system to process the new qualification
- train schools on how to teach the new qualification
- delivery of the 1998 and 1999 examinations as normal using existing legacy systems.

The timetable leading up to the formation of the SQA and delivery of its goals was:

1994 Scottish Education Department announces Higher Still.
1995 The secretary of state for Scotland (prior to the Scottish Parliament) announces a delay of one year in implementation to give schools, colleges and the development programme more time. He also launches a consultation on what organisation should run Higher Still. The options were: give it all to one of the two bodies; split it between the bodies by age of student!; create a third body, possibly 'owned' by SEB and SCOTVEC; or merge SEB and SCOTVEC. The government's preference for a merger was agreed.
1996 The secretary of state announces another delay of one year in implementation.
1997 SQA comes into being in April. It inherits 200 staff in Dalkeith and 300 staff in Glasgow. It has a turnover of about £27m. Integration of the two sets of staff is a high priority.
1999 Higher Still courses start in schools and colleges.
2000 First Higher Still examinations: problems with issue of certificates affects 2.7% of results and 17,000 candidates.

IT project – the awards processing system (APS)

The introduction of the APS was based around the PRINCE methodology, which is a project management approach to managing large-scale change, popular in public organisations. A project manager controls the whole process and senior business users are appointed for each function, responsible for specifying their business needs. For the SQA, the head of operations was appointed as senior business user for five of the eight sections of the APS, at the same time as managing his own department. The appointed project manager had no previous experience of managing a large systems implementation, and was not high enough up the hierarchy to implement decisions on all aspects of the project.

PRINCE's guiding philosophy is that all data flows and all software is specified before a line of code is written. However, the IT department did not have the timescale for this. Instead, they had to start writing software for the first parts of the process, which registers the candidates, before the software for the exam results had been specified. The time pressure meant that the period for testing was shortened to near zero, which meant that issues were not identified until the system was live, when it was too late to make fundamental changes. Additional IT staff were recruited and an external IT contractor was brought in to speed up software writing.

Schools

Four different systems were used by centres (schools and colleges) to submit data to the SQA, depending on the region in which they were located. To be compatible with the APS, these systems had to be upgraded with new software. However, the SQA delivered test data late and changed specifications, so software suppliers could not provide upgrades for many schools until late 1999, or in some cases early 2000. This put data entry well behind schedule, which impacted on the recruitment of markers and the printing of exam papers, as this could not be finalised until the number of candidates registered for each course was known.

Data entry from centres (schools and colleges)

The process of data entry from centres is as follows:

- Authorisation of centres and the courses they provide
- Candidate registrations
- Candidate entries
- Unit entries
- Unit results.

Some centres did not submit the necessary data for the first part of the process, the authorisation of centres and their courses, so not all their courses were approved. This led to problems in the next stage, the submission of candidate registrations, because the system rejected candidates whose courses had not been approved. Previously, candidates could be entered into the system more than once, for example if they moved from one college to another they would be given a new number. This caused problems with the APS as its remit was to issue a cumulative certificate with a candidate's entire results history from 1994. Centres were asked to confirm that candidates had only one number, but some did not do this. To rid the system of this problem, a data-cleansing exercise was carried out in August 1999, but it was not done effectively and multiple entries for some candidates still existed.

The APS contained extensive validation checks. One of these was to reject data from new candidates already registered with the SQA (to avoid multiple entries of the same candidate) but this was lifted so that registration could go ahead quickly. This caused problems later on, because internal assessments could be registered to one number and the external assessment to another, making it look as though there was either missing data or that two candidates had only passed one part of the qualification. The validation checks resulted in a large amount of rejected data, which needed many man-hours to rectify, and, as individuals were doing this themselves informally, control was lost of data management. This resulted in different employees in the SQA asking centres to resubmit data that someone else had already requested from them.

Since the APS could only produce reports from the entered data, the delays in data inputting and processing, combined with the complexity, length, poor quality and unsuitable format of the APS reports, meant that management lacked information to identify the nature and extent of problems at an early stage.

Markers

Higher Still introduced new subjects, which required 1000 extra markers. In total 7000 markers were needed for the 2000 examinations. However, invitations to mark had to be delayed until late February and March, rather than the usual January, because delays in processing data meant that the number of markers needed for each subject was unknown. This late invitation, a marking period reduced from three to two weeks and low fees meant that more invitations were declined than in previous years. By April 2000, it became apparent that there were not enough markers, but it was not until mid-June, when 65,000 scripts were still left unallocated to markers, that action was taken by the SQA.

Data processing

David Elliot explained the data-processing problem:

> When packets of scripts come in from a centre they are 'turned round' and sent to the marker. There were major problems with this process in 2000 as insufficient markers had been appointed.

When the packets of scripts come back from the marker they are 'racked' (by data-processing staff) after the forms which record the marks for each script have been extracted. If this form is not removed, then the marks will not be recorded. However, the position is retrievable if the packet can be located on the shelf and the form removed later for processing. For some reason the initial check of the packet and its storing on the racks was not done to the usual standard. A packet in the wrong place is a packet lost. The lack of MIS made it difficult to identify the problem. Eventually, a complete check of the racking had to be carried out to retrieve all missing marks data. (Elliot, 2002)

This issue had not occurred in previous years; the data-processing staff had not changed.

Issue of certificates

On 17th May 2000, the head of operations reported to the Examination Diet 2000 Group within the SQA that the issue of certificates on 9th August might not be achieved. It was agreed that it was 'preferable to issue accurate certificates late than "suspicious" certificates on time' (Education, Culture and Sport Committee, 2000: 11). The SQA did not know if it would be capable of processing the remaining data until July, as centres had until 30th June to submit or amend unit assessment data. Huge amounts of data arrived for processing close to the deadline, so shift work and 60 agency staff were introduced to help enter the data. These extra staff had to be trained and supervised which took SQA staff away from their own functions.

On 27th June, the director of awards reported to the SMT that the software for results reporting was still outstanding. On 25th July, there were 8600 exam results and 61,000 unit results still to be entered into the system. On 31st July, at a meeting with the Scottish

Executive and Careers Central, SQA reported that results could be published without a delay but at least 5% of the certificates would be incorrect or incomplete. The next day the SQA confirmed that it would issue on time even though between 5000–6000 certificates were still missing. This action was contrary to the Examination Diet 2000 Group's decision on 17th May that it was preferable to issue certificates late than incorrect. Furthermore, its estimation was incorrect; in total 16,748 pupils suffered from inaccurate or incomplete certificates.

Acknowledgements

Thanks to Frances Young for data collected during her MA in Management dissertation, and Stewart Stevenson and David Elliot for interviews, presentations and discussions contributing to this case study.

Main sources: Deloitte and Touche, (2000). *A Review into Exam Results Issues Concerning the Scottish Qualifications Authority,* Scottish Executive Publications; Education, Culture and Sport Committee, Scottish Parliament (ECSC) (2000). *Exam Results Inquiry.* Volume 2: *Evidence,* SP Paper 234, The Stationery Office, Edinburgh; Elliot, D. (2002). Interview with David Elliot, former Director of Awards, SQA; Enterprise and Lifelong Learning Committee, Scottish Parliament (ELLC) (2000). *Report on the Inquiry into the Governance of the Scottish Qualifications Authority,* The Stationery Office, Edinburgh; Raffe, D. and Howieson, C. (1998). 'The Higher Still policy process', *Scottish Affairs,* **24,** 90–108; Raffe, D., Howieson, C. and Tinklin, T. (2001). 'The Scottish educational crisis of 2000: an analysis of the policy process of unification, Working Paper 2, Centre for Educational Sociology, University of Edinburgh, Edinburgh; Scottish Office (1994). *Higher Still: Opportunity for All,* Edinburgh

QUESTIONS TO AID UNDERSTANDING AND DISCUSSION

1. What was the SQA trying to achieve? Did it have a mission or vision? What was it?

2. Did the project have clear objectives? How were they communicated during the project?

3. What management and operational changes took place?

4. Was the timescale for the development of the award processing system appropriate?

5. What were the arguments for and against using an external IT company? What choice would you have made?

6. How was this project governed at the programme, project and IT level? Was it effective?

7. What contingency measures were in place? What else would you recommend?

8. Would a pilot scheme have been beneficial? What might it have consisted of?

9. How was staff morale affected during the project?

10. How would you summarise what went wrong for the SQA project? What were the key IS/IT issues?

Summary points

- The process for converting strategic plans into the day-to-day actions by which they are realised is still largely a 'black box'.
- Project management is an ideal tool to support strategic planning and achieve strategic implementation.
- It should always be possible to show how a project supports the strategic goals of the sponsor's organisation, otherwise it consumes resources but fails to add value.
- There is a trend for strategy formulation to move away from linear and static approaches to a wider systemic and eclectic perspective more suited to today's rapidly changing business environments.
- Many businesses have decentralised their operations and created SBUs to improve responsiveness and competitivity. However, a failure to realign their internal infrastructures with changes in strategic direction means that 80% of change efforts continue to fail.
- Many organisations fail to follow best-practice strategy planning and implementation models, causing a gap between strategic planning and the operations functions responsible for implementing the plans. The use of project management can improve the strategy process and help to reduce the gap.
- The principles of governance – accountability, transparency, predictability and participation – are important in business and large organisations because they underpin major ethical decisions in the face of uncertainty and tremendous competitive pressures.
- Governance principles apply at the corporate, programme, IT, project and operations level in organisations.

- Corporate governance is the system by which companies are directed and controlled, principally by a board of directors, to realise long-term shareholder value whilst taking into account the interests of other stakeholders.
- Strategic governance provides focus to an organisation though five lenses: decision making under uncertainty; strategic clarity versus freedom of choice; strategic alignment of the project portfolio; benefit delivery; and performance ethic.
- The aim of programme governance is to ensure a continuous balancing, trimming, and improving of the project portfolio to ensure that it is the *minimal* and best set of projects that advance the strategy.
- The UK Government's Gateway Process provides a structured approach to programme management towards ensuring that resources are optimised at programme level, interdependencies between projects are coordinated and risk is managed across these interdependencies.
- Management by projects is an organisation-wide approach that uses project and programme management principles for both projects and ongoing operations by treating many aspects of ongoing operations as projects.
- Any framework for programme management must include the management of information and therefore the evolution of an enterprise and IT architecture.
- An enterprise and IT architecture identifies the main components of the organisation and the ways in which these components work together in order to achieve defined business objectives. The compo-

nents include staff, business processes, technology, information, financial and other resources.

■ Project governance is the set of structures, systems and processes around the project that ensure the effective delivery of the project through to full utilisation and benefits realisation by the business.

■ The four key influences on project governance structures are risk planning, life cycle management, strategic change and value management.

■ Project management methodologies such as PRINCE 2 provide a complete solution to project governance.

■ Authorisation management concerns the process for approval to proceed to the next stage of a project (or programme). The level of scrutiny and authorisation required at each stage should reflect the size and strategic importance of the project.

Visit the website

http://www.palgrave.com/business/gardiner

▶ to test your understanding of the learning objectives for Chapter 3 using multiple choice questions

In the next chapter we shall examine the investment decision-making process – how to justify and present a case for project approval and how to prioritise between projects competing for a limited budget.

References

APM (2000). *Body of Knowledge,* 4th edn, Association for Project Management, High Wycombe.

Belmonte, R.W. and Murray, R.J. (1993). 'Getting ready for strategic change – surviving business process redesign', *Information Systems Management*, Summer: 23–9.

Boeing (2003). Sonic Cruiser Factsheet, accessed online [15 June 2003] at http://www.boeing.com/news/feature/concept/factsheet.html.

Boznak, R. (1996). 'Management of projects: a giant step beyond project management', *PM Network*, January, 1996.

Cadbury Report (1992). *The Cadbury Report: Report of the Committee on the Financial Aspects of Corporate Governance*, Gee & Co, London.

CCG (2000). Committee on Corporate Governance, 'The Combined Code: Principles of Good Governance and Code of Best Practice, derived from the Committee's Final Report and the Cadbury and Greenbury Reports', UK.

Cleland, D. (1999). *Project Management Strategic Design and Implementation,* 3rd edn, McGraw-Hill, New York.

Dreilinger, C. (1994). 'Why management fads fizzle', *Business Horizons*, Nov/Dec.

Garratt, B. (2003). *Thin on Top: Why Corporate Governance Matters and How to Manage, Measure and Improve Board Performance*, Nicholas Brealey, London.

Graham, R.J. and Englund, R.L. (1997). *Creating an environment for successful projects: The quest to manage project management*, Jossey-Bass, San Francisco.

Grindley, K. (1991). *Managing IT at Board Level: The Hidden Agenda Exposed*, Pitman, London.

Hardy, C. and Redivo, F. (1994). 'Power and organisational development: A framework for organisational change', *Journal of General Management*, Winter.

Hartman, F.T. (2000). *Don't Park Your Brain Outside*, Project Management Institute, Upper Darby, PA.

High Level Finance Committee on Corporate Governance (1999). 'Report on Corporate Governance', March 25, Malaysian Government, Malaysia.

Hitt, M.A., Ireland, R.D. and Hoskisson, R.E. (2002). *Strategic Management: Competitiveness and Globalization,* 5th edn, West, Minneapolis.

Johnson, G. and Scholes, K. (1993). *Exploring Corporate Strategy*, 3rd edn, Prentice Hall, Hemel Hempstead.

Kaplan, R.S. and Norton, D.P. (2001). *The Strategy-focused Organization*, Harvard Business School Press, Boston, MA.

Kay, J.A. (1999). 'Strategy and the delusion of grand designs', *Mastering Strategy, Financial Times*, Sep 27: 2–4.

King (2002). King Committee on Corporate Governance, 'King Report 2002', Institute of Directors, South Africa.

Kotter, J.P. (1995). 'Leading change: Why transformation efforts fail', *Harvard Business Review*, Mar/Apr.

Lambert, K. (2003). 'Project governance', *World Project Management Week*, 27 March 2003.

Markides, C. (1999). 'A dynamic view of strategy', *Sloan Management Review*, Spring: 55–63.

Mintzberg, H. (1994). *The Rise and Fall of Corporate Planning*, Prentice Hall, New York.

Mintzberg, H., Ahlstrand, B. and Lampel, J. (1998). *Strategy Safari: A Guided Tour through the Wilds of Strategic Management*, Free Press, New York.

OGC (2003). Office of Government Commerce, 'Successful Delivery Toolkit Version 4.0', http://www.ogc.gov.uk/sdtoolkit/.

Pearlson, K. and Saunders, C. (2004). *Managing and Using Information Systems – A Strategic Approach,* 2nd edn, Wiley, New York.

PMI (2000). *Guide to the Project Management Body of Knowledge* (PMBOK), Project Management Institute, Upper Darby, PA.

Reiss, G. (1996). *Programme Management Demystified*, E & FN Spon, London.

Roberts, A. and Gardiner, P.D. (1998). 'Project management and strategy implementation' in Proceedings of the 3rd International Research Network on Organizing by Projects, University of Calgary, Alberta, Canada, 6–8 July: 317–23.

Scott, A. (1997). *Strategic Planning*, Pitman Publishing/Edinburgh Business School, Edinburgh.

Smith, W. (2002). 'Maximising strategic value', Centre for Research in Information Management, Breakfast Roundtable Discussion Paper, University of Illinois at Chicago.

Staw, B.M. and Ross, J. (1987). 'Knowing when to pull the plug', *Harvard Business Review*, March–April: 68–74.

Turner, J.R. (1996). 'International Project Management Association global qualification, certifcation and accreditation', editorial, *International Journal of Project Management*, **14**(1): 1–6.

UK Activity Report (2003). Report dated 22 May, 2003, accessed online at http://www.ukbusinesspark.co.uk/.

Williams, T. (2003). *Corporate Governance: A guide for fund managers and corporations*, Provenance Investment & Financial Services Association Limited, Westpac Banking Corporation, Australia.

Visit the website

http://www.palgrave.com/business/gardiner

▶ for additional resources to explore the topics in this chapter further

CHAPTER 4
Investment decision making

Learning objectives

After reading this chapter you should be able to:

- explain the key phases and associated information flows in an investment management process
- explain the purpose of a feasibility study and how it relates to a business case
- prepare and analyse a feasibility study
- prepare and analyse a business case for a proposed project
- discuss a variety of approaches for project prioritisation
- use a range of techniques to help make investment decisions

Introduction

A project is an investment like any other and so can benefit from the same controls. This chapter describes a systematic approach to evaluating and selecting long-term capital investment projects. The importance of conducting a feasibility study and preparing a business case as part of the investment process is considered. Risk is an important factor in making investment decisions and is also introduced here. Finally, several prioritisation techniques are discussed as an aid to choosing between projects and arriving at go/no-go project decisions.

To survive in the long term, organisations seek to ensure that they do the right projects at the right time. The development and use of an investment management process can help organisations achieve this goal by providing an integrated and structured approach to managing their investments. A good example of an investment management process is the IT investment management process developed by the United States General Accounting Office (Accounting and Information Management Division) – see the Insights from Industry box.

IT INVESTMENT MANAGEMENT PROCESS, US GENERAL ACCOUNTING OFFICE

The investment management process has three phases – select, control, and evaluate (see Figure 4.1). Each phase forms part of a continuous, interdependent process rather than a series of discrete steps. Information from each phase is used to support activities in the other two phases.

The investment decision-making approach is a fluid and dynamic process. Selection decisions are based on an analysis of where needs are greatest and in line with the organisation's strategy. Projects that are stopped or delayed as part of selection decisions are evaluated immediately to allow the organisation to assess their impact on future proposals and benefit from any lessons that have been learned as quickly as possible.

Once selected and added to the portfolio, projects are subject to an investment control process. Investment control meetings are conducted on a regular basis throughout the year, including post-implementation reviews for all projects. The results of these meetings feed back into the following year's selection process.

The entire process is designed to focus senior management attention on three particular areas:

1. Institutionalisation of the management processes.
2. Regular validation of cost, benefit and risk data used to support investment decisions.
3. Ongoing focus on measuring and evaluating results.

Figure 4.2 illustrates the process in more detail, showing how these areas relate to the three phases of the model.

The full requirements of the model are demanding and the model guide acknowledges that 'it may be unusual to find an organisation that meets all of the requirements outlined'.

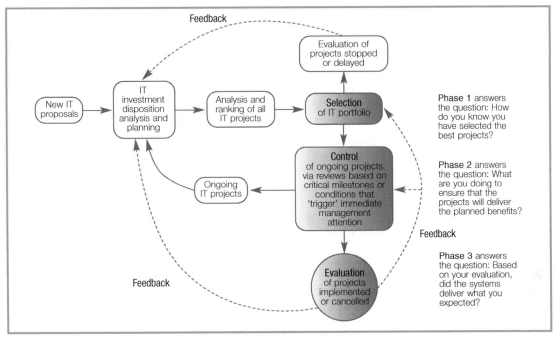

Figure 4.1 Investment management process (US GAO, 1997)

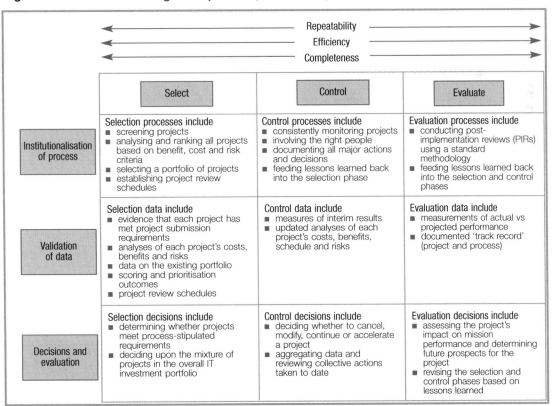

Figure 4.2 Components of the investment management process (US GAO, 1997)

Feasibility study

In some organisations a project is not formally initiated until after the completion of a feasibility study. Feasibility studies are typically performed before project initiation in support of the proposed business case, but can be also carried out at any of the key stage gates of a project. A feasibility study is often managed as a project in its own right.

The feasibility study report provides an accurate assessment of the factors which might affect a project or programme. A feasibility study enables a realistic evaluation of a project, incorporating both the positive and negative aspects of the opportunity. It evaluates both internal readiness and external opportunities available to successfully complete a project or programme.

The purpose of a feasibility study is to:

- determine if a business opportunity is possible, practical and viable
- provide a structured method:
  - to focus on problems
  - identify objectives

- evaluate alternatives along with associated benefits and costs
- aid in the selection of the best solution
- improve confidence that the recommended action is the most viable solution to the problem
- assure the sponsor that projects requiring significant resources can, should and will be done.

Feasibility studies are normally carried out for larger or riskier projects, or projects that are ill-defined. In some organisations all projects estimated to cost above a certain amount are subject to a feasibility study and cost/benefit analysis. In projects seeking external finance, funding agencies will require satisfactory feasibility study reports before committing significant funds to them, for example see the Insights from Industry box which describes the feasibility study requirements for development campaigns seeking government funding in China.

The feasibility study is the initial justification needed to determine if a project is 'doable'. The approach is frequently used to examine and appraise the technical, logistical, environmental, commercial and financial risks of projects requiring major investment.

FEASIBILITY STUDY REQUIREMENTS FOR DEVELOPMENT PROJECTS IN CHINA

As part of your preparation for a new endeavour in China, a feasibility study needs to be prepared and submitted to the local government agency for approval of the project. The feasibility study is a detailed analysis of your project proposal.

The feasibility study is part financial document, part legal document, part environmental analysis and part several other things. However, it is very detailed. A little advance work in this area could save serious tie-ups in the project timeline.

The feasibility study report (FSR) must provide an accurate summary of the results of the feasibility study. As with the study itself, the scope of the FSR must be commensurate with the scope and complexity of the problem or opportunity being addressed. Enough technical detail must be included in the FSR to show that the proposed response to the problem or opportunity is workable and realistic. The FSR must provide a basis for understanding and agreement among project management, executive management and programme

management, as well as satisfy the information requirements of state-level control agencies.

The FSR must provide a complete summary of the results of the feasibility study and establish the business case for investment of state resources in a project by setting out the reasons for undertaking the project and analysing its costs and benefits. Documentation provided by the agency must contain at least the following information:

- A description of the business problem or opportunity the project is intended to address.
- The project objectives, that is, the significant results that must be achieved for an alternative to be an effective response to the problem or opportunity being addressed.
- A thorough description of the selected alternative, including the hardware, software and personnel that will be used.
- A discussion and economic analysis of each of the alternatives considered in the feasibility study that meets the established objectives and functional requirements, and the reasons for rejecting the alternatives that were not selected.
- A complete description of the information technology capabilities and the conditions that must exist

in order to satisfy each defined objective.
- An economic analysis of the life cycle costs and benefits of the project and the costs and benefits of the current method of operation during the life cycle of the project.
- The source of funding for the project.

- A detailed project schedule showing key milestones during the project's life.
- A summary fact sheet must be prepared and included as the cover page of the FSR.

Source: http://chinaunique.com/bcase.htm

A typical feasibility study

A typical feasibility study checklist might include the following:

1. Detailed determination of the problem and underlying business need
2. Evaluation of
   - alternatives
   - market potential
   - cost-effectiveness
   - technical feasibility
   - implementation feasibility
3. Analysis of technology requirements
4. Assessment of internal capabilities
5. Identification and assessment of risks
6. Trade-off analysis (scope, time, and cost)
7. Identification of critical success factors, goals and objectives
8. Preliminary cost and time estimates.

The end result of a feasibility study is a management go/no-go decision on whether to proceed to business case development or, for a feasibility study conducted at a project stage gate, whether to terminate the project or approve its next phase. Although management can stop a project at any one of its phases, the decision is especially critical in the early stages before major resources have been consumed.

A feasibility study may be carried out by the project originator, a consultant, an independent project manager or a project manager who will go on to manage the rest of the project if the outcome of the feasibility study is favourable. In a high-risk project a project manager may consider using a risk consultant in order to obtain more facts and expert advice.

Business case development

A business case is prepared to ensure that projects put forward for funding reflect business strategy and will deliver the required benefits and returns to shareholders and stakeholders. The purpose of the business case is to:

- obtain management commitment and approval for investment, through a clearly presented rationale
- provide a framework for informed decision making in planning and managing the project and its subsequent benefits realisation.

A business case sums up the research from a feasibility study and presents it in support of the identified solution. Specifically, it is a tool used to convince the intended audience that a particular project should be implemented. The business case also details the reasons why, based on the results of a feasibility study, a particular project should be prioritised higher than some other project. This might be due to ease of completion, less risk or higher return on investment. The business case should also refer to the wider context of the organisation and any influence the proposed project may have on other current projects and programmes.

Key stakeholders (including end users where relevant) should be involved in the development of the business case. Their role is to influence decisions and provide a commitment to manage change in their own areas of responsibility. However, it is the investment decision maker who signs off the business case.

A business case is similar in many respects to a business plan used by entrepreneurs to secure finance for a new business idea. However, it is important not to confuse the business case with the project charter (discussed in Chapter 8). The business case should already be developed and the investment decision taken prior to creating the project charter.

Visit the website:

http://www.palgrave.com/business/gardiner

▶ to view a comparison of a business case, a project charter and project phase plans

The business case is maintained throughout the project, being reviewed at each key decision stage. If the justification for the project is no longer valid, the project should be stopped. The business case can be supported by further feasibility studies as required in response to new information and changing circumstances. The business case also provides the basis for a post-project review to check whether key objectives and benefits have been realised.

Business case perspectives

There are five main perspectives of a business case to consider in its preparation (OGC, 2003):

1. **Strategic fit**. This aspect investigates:
   - business need and contribution to strategy, including relationship to related projects
   - drivers for change
   - key stakeholders and the nature of their interest in the project
   - investment objectives, scope and desired outcomes
   - constraints
   - project fit with existing technological environment.

2. **Options appraisal.** This component investigates options for meeting the need with the highest ratio of benefits to cost, combined with an appraisal of risk. It includes:
   - clear and well-defined assessment criteria
   - SWOT (strengths, weaknesses, opportunities and threats) analysis of each option
   - more detailed assessment of options based on discounted cash flow analysis
   - comprehensive list and assessment of risks
   - sensitivity analysis of preferred option.

3. **Achievability**. This is concerned with the capability of the organisation to manage a successful project and any subsequent business change. It raises issues such as:
   - clear and well-defined critical success factors (CSFs)
   - risk management strategy and contingency plans
   - project management methodology
   - identified key players, indicating skills and experience
   - benefits realisation plan
   - plans for continuous improvement following post-project review.

4. **Commercial aspects**. This concerns achieving a viable deal for procurement projects and concerns issues such as:
   - assessment of the likely attractiveness of the project to providers

   - procurement strategy, method and timetable
   - preferred mechanism for payment
   - apportionment of risks identified
   - contract management plans.

5. **Affordability**. The final perspective is about financial aspects and availability of funding. It includes:
   - high-level affordability analysis to produce a financial model
   - reconciliation of the financial model with organisational finance arrangements in terms of budgets, balance sheets and cash flow
   - ability and willingness of budget holders to meet the resource implications of the project
   - statement of support from stakeholders.

Level of detail required

The amount of detail needed in a business case depends to a large extent on the total cost of the project. Two examples are shown below.

Small project:

- One-page project description, including a brief outline of the expected business outcomes
- Brief cost analysis, containing capital, recurring and non-recurring costs
- Brief benefit analysis
- One-page cost–benefit summary.

Large project:

- A project description, including a clear description of the problem the project is addressing
- A description of the alignment between the project and the organisation's business plan
- Description of the various stakeholders affected by the project, and details of their requirements
- Detailed description of the alternative ways to implement the project, and the rationale for the decision on each
- Thorough analysis of costs and benefits for the selected approach
- A description of the project's impact on business processes, staff and organisation
- Detailed risk analysis, including identification of the likelihood and impact of all risks, the consequences of each risk and the strategies to manage the identified risks
- Detailed recommendations for the IT project
- An executive summary describing the business

requirements that the project addresses, the recommended solution and a summary of project costs and other impacts.

Progressive development of a business case

For large-scale investments, the business case can be developed in progressive stages. For example, a three-stage process might generate the following components (OGC, 2003):

1. **Preliminary business case**. Provides key stakeholders with an opportunity to influence or reprioritise a project at an early stage, avoiding unnecessary effort in reworking. It focuses on business need, stakeholder commitment, scope definition and the identification of possible alternate solutions. The preliminary business case is particularly useful when:
   - there are many stakeholders
   - the project is novel, high risk or complex
   - the parameters of the project are ill-defined
   - there is a rapidly changing business environment.

2. **Outline business case**. The outline business case builds on the preliminary business case and in particular concentrates on the investment appraisal perspective to:
   - rigorously appraise options and support selection of a preferred option
   - provide robust estimates of cost, benefits and risks
   - demonstrate that the preferred option is likely to achieve value for money, is achievable and affordable
   - obtain senior management commitment and funding to develop the full business case.

3. **Full business case**. The full business case builds on the outline business case. It is accurate, complete and provides all the information required for senior management to make an informed investment decision. The full business case is approved before a contract is awarded, and must therefore provide sufficient assurance to senior management that a project can go ahead and resources can be committed. It is then maintained to reflect business changes throughout the project life cycle, and provides input to the post-project review following implementation of the project.

Capital budgeting

A financial manager must be able to decide whether an investment is worth undertaking and be able to choose intelligently between two or more alternatives. To do this, a sound procedure to evaluate, compare and select projects is needed. This procedure is called 'capital budgeting'.

Capital budgeting decisions often have an impact for many years and as such reduce an organisation's flexibility. This is an opportunity cost. For example, the purchase of an asset with an economic life of ten years will lock a firm into a ten-year investment period. During this time the firm has lost the opportunity to invest this money elsewhere, even if a better opportunity presents itself after only a couple of years. The large investment needed to acquire capital assets creates significant financial risks for a firm. The long-term nature of the capital asset also generates technological risk, for example investing in a new IT platform may lock a firm into a particular vendor's technology and there is a risk that this IT may lack the flexibility to integrate future IT products, which may in turn impact on a firm's ability to deliver business objectives.

Decisions on investments are based on the returns which that investment will make over time. Unless a project is for social reasons only, the investment needs to be profitable in the long run. Analysis of a proposed investment may reveal that it is more profitable putting the planned investment money into a bank to earn interest or investing it in an alternative project.

Timing is also important in capital budgeting – capital assets must 'come online' when they are needed. If a firm forecasts its needs for capital assets in advance through strategic planning, it will have an opportunity to create new assets when they are needed and can then enjoy the additional economic rent. If new assets come on stream late, an organisation may miss a competitive opportunity and even face paying large fines to customers who placed firm orders in advance.

For these reasons, organisations generally spend significant effort selecting projects in which to invest by performing project appraisals, usually as part of a wider feasibility study. Of course, analysing capital expenditure proposals also bears a cost. For certain types of projects, a relatively detailed analysis may be warranted, for others, simpler procedures should be used.

Project appraisals

The purpose of project appraisal is simply to assist an organisation in deciding whether a project concept is worth turning into reality. One of the most important questions to ask when appraising a project is: Are the benefits to be gained from the project sufficient to justify the costs of implementing and operating the project? A project appraisal is not an objective process that will always yield a 'correct' answer. Rather, it is dependent on a wide range of assumptions and judgements by the appraisers and, for an appraisal to have real value, it is important that these assumptions and judgements are clearly stated and understood. A frequent misuse of project appraisal is to use it as an *ex post facto* justification for a decision that has already been made. This is not difficult to achieve – by carefully adjusting the key assumptions upon which an appraisal is based, unscrupulous appraisers can easily produce the answer that they want.

Project summary

Project appraisal begins with a project summary. This organises information gathered about a project, indicating the purpose, history, value and cost of the project. The project summary contains an analysis of the relevant technical, process and commercial risks. It also considers proposed implementation dates. A particular project may be evaluated and reviewed for several years before it is funded. Recording the dates of each evaluation and review activity is important because it determines the time between project inception and initiation.

There are many project prioritisation and selection techniques. These are discussed shortly. However, there are several concepts to be considered first:

- Financial versus economic appraisal
- Externalities and their valuation
- Cash flows and sunk costs
- Cash flow analysis.

Financial versus economic appraisal

Project appraisal aims to weigh up the costs and benefits of an investment in order to decide whether to give it further consideration. Before starting on any appraisal, it is important to set the context by asking: On whose behalf is the appraisal being done, and whose criteria should be used for quantifying costs and benefits? There are two common answers to this question, which define two types of appraisal commonly conducted:

- The *financial appraisal* tries to determine if the project will work as a business proposition. In other words, it considers only those costs and benefits which are relevant to the business and those that will finance it.
- The *economic appraisal* seeks to decide if the flow of benefits is greater than the flow of costs, measured against broader socioeconomic criteria. Factors such as environmental impacts, employment effects, balance of payments effects and poverty alleviation might be taken into account.

The types of question typically asked are given in Table 4.1. Note that the distinction between each case is not simply one of private versus public sector. A public sector body should exercise at least as much financial discipline as a private firm, and will need to demonstrate this if it expects to be able to obtain loans from the financial sector. It should not use public money to support financially untenable investments unless there are compelling reasons.

Table 4.1 Economic and financial questions used in a project appraisal	
Economic appraisal questions	**Financial appraisal questions**
■ Does the project represent the most effective way for society to allocate scarce resources?	■ Is the project a sound business proposition?
■ Is the project the lowest cost way of meeting this particular socioeconomic goal?	■ Does the project earn a rate of return sufficient to satisfy shareholders?
■ Does the project bring particular benefits to the more disadvantaged sectors of society?	■ Is the cash flow of the enterprise (including the revenues earned from the project) sufficient to service any loans taken out to finance the project?
■ Does the project place an undue burden on particular sectors of society?	■ What assets are there that could serve as collateral for lenders?

Table 4.2 Matrix of possible outcomes from an economic and financial project appraisal

		Economic appraisal	
		Pass	Fail
Financial appraisal	Pass	These are 'ideal' projects that are both beneficial to society and attractive to private investors.	These projects are attractive to private investors, but impose costs on society (for example environmental impacts, adverse employment effects). In theory, government regulations should prevent this situation arising, but in practice such 'market failures' are common
	Fail	These projects are beneficial to society but not attractive to private investors. Some additional support is therefore needed to ensure they go ahead (for example 'soft' finance, subsidies, sovereign guarantees)	Projects in this category should be considered completely unviable, being neither beneficial to society nor attractive to private investors

Source: http://www.switched-on.org.

There are several possible outcomes of an economic and financial appraisal. These are summarised in Table 4.2.

Externalities and their valuation

An externality is said to occur whenever somebody who is not directly involved in a transaction incurs a cost or enjoys a benefit as a result of that transaction. The classic example of an externality is pollution: car exhaust fumes do not distinguish between drivers and non-drivers, but enter everybody's lungs indiscriminately. Car drivers reap the benefits of using petrol, but part of the cost is borne by those whose quality of life is affected by pollution.

The term 'externality' refers to the fact that the effect in question is external to the market. In the above example, the market for petrol determines what price petrol sells at, but the effects of the pollution that the petrol produces fall outside this market. Users of petrol do not pay for the privilege of being allowed to pollute, and the general public are not paid for suffering the effects of the pollution.

One of the most significant categories of externality, particularly in the context of the energy sector, is environmental impact. Environmental effects of projects are almost always negative, although it must not be thought that externalities are *always* negative – there are many cases where they can be positive. For example, a householder might decide to renovate and redecorate the outside of her or his house. Although only the householder pays for this, the whole neighbourhood benefits from the improvement in the building's appearance. Some of the benefits of the renovation and redecoration are therefore not reflected in its cost, they are external to the market.

Dealing with externalities

Ideally, government fiscal and regulatory policy should aim to internalise all externalities, by imposing taxes and charges to readjust prices so that they reflect true social and environmental costs. However, this is difficult to achieve in reality (both from a practical and a political perspective). In practice, therefore, many externalities will remain. Where a project is being appraised according to broader social criteria (rather than narrow financial criteria), it is necessary to take these externalities into account in the appraisal process. It is generally the case that the private sector is not interested in including externalities in investment appraisals as they are concerned only with the 'bottom line'.

Cash flows and sunk costs

In making business investment decisions, a manager is concerned with allocating resources over time. The question he or she seeks to answer is: 'How much shall I invest today for the prospect of cash inflows in the future?' To support the manager's decision it is the forecast cash flows which are important and the timing of when they are likely to be received in the future. A sale made on credit is only useful to a manager when the cash is actually received from the customer.

A typical project includes a stream of costs and a stream of benefits. Evaluating a project involves deciding if the benefits are greater than the costs. If they are, the project is viable. Generally, costs will be incurred at the beginning, with benefits being generated throughout the asset lifetime. There may be additional costs associated with 'decommissioning' at the end of the project. A typical cash flow profile is shown in Figure 4.3.

The cash flow profile of a project is an important factor in determining not just whether a project is economically viable but also whether it is attractive to potential investors. Because of the time value of money, costs or benefits that occur further into the future are worth less than those that occur closer to the present. The process of discounted cash flow analysis takes this into account when comparing costs and benefits.

Equally important for projects that are to be financed through loans is the question of how the cash flow profile of the project matches the repayment schedule of the loan. For example, the project illustrated in Figure 4.3 does not start generating significant net revenue for several years. If the loan repayments in the early years are too great, the viability of the project might be in question.

In financial terms, the key issue is how will the organisation's cash flows change over time if the decision is taken to accept the investment opportunity? If this can be forecasted, it will inform the manager of how the value of the business entity will change as a result of accepting an investment. In other words, in considering what the relevant cash flows are, with regard to a capital investment, the manager needs to include only those cash flows which will change as a result of accepting the capital investment. These are called 'incremental cash flows' and can be explained further by considering the following two types of cash flow.

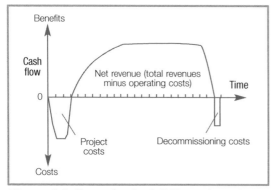

Figure 4.3 Example of a full life cycle cash flow for a project asset

Sunk costs

Costs which a business has already spent, or has contracted to spend, are not relevant to a decision made today about future capital investments. The decision to incur such costs has been already taken and, by definition, the business will incur these costs regardless of decisions taken today. They are 'sunk costs'.

For example, consider capital investments made in the pharmaceutical industry involving research into the development of drugs. There are defined stages in most research projects which involve expert assessment as to whether or not to invest in further research, usually with the aim of developing a product commercially. At each stage of development, the costs of research from the previous stage would be defined as sunk. Suppose, for example, a company, Eureka plc, is researching a new drug, Xanadu, and to date had spent £1 million in testing the drug. Current forecasts indicate that it will cost another £500k to develop the drug such that it can be sold on the commercial market. Estimated net revenues are expected to be £800k. The managers of Eureka plc are considering whether they should invest further in Xanadu.

On the face of it, the Xanadu project is forecast to be a failure, incurring a loss of £700k (that is, £800k − £1 million − £500k). However, if the decision today is to discontinue with the Xanadu investment, the loss will be £1 million. Using the principle of incremental cash flow analysis, the 'sunk costs' would be ignored in considering the decision whether or not to invest in the next stage of development. The £1 million costs to date are sunk and only the £800k revenue and £500k costs become relevant to the decision to invest. (Note that the timing of the future revenues and costs would also be relevant; for simplicity this factor has not been considered for the purposes of this illustration.)

Indirect cash flows

Incremental cash flows will also include any cash flows that may change from a capital investment, which are associated with existing projects in the business. So, for example, assume the drug Xanadu is being developed for sufferers of arthritis to improve their condition. Assume also that Eureka plc produce and sell an existing drug called Betadrug which is used to alleviate arthritic conditions. If the decision is taken to develop Xanadu commercially, its effect on the company's future cash flows from sales of Betadrug should be considered. Suppose that the new drug Xanadu would render Betadrug almost obsolete, this will cause a loss of revenue from reduced sales of Betadrug. If the loss of sales is expected to be greater than the expected incremental cash flows of £300k, the company would not be better off financially by developing Xanadu further.

The crucial question to be addressed in establishing the relevant cash flow information for capital investments is: What cash flows to the company will change in the future as a result of taking a decision to invest in the capital project today? To answer this question may require a manager to analyse the impact of the investment on the existing business activity and therefore the indirect impact on the existing cash flows.

Cash flow analysis

To establish the value of a project, a financial evaluation is carried out. Preliminary information required will include the evaluation period, project risk, an organisation's cost of capital and the cost of doing the project. Each of these is considered in turn below.

Evaluation period

The interested parties must agree upon the period of evaluation before starting a financial evaluation. Because they all compete for the same investment funds, the evaluation period for each project should be the same, otherwise their financial analyses will not be comparable. In such circumstances, special capital budgeting techniques can be used to ensure fairer comparisons.

Project risk

The risk associated with a project is also an important consideration as it will influence the variability or uncertainty of the project's return. The expected return of a project should be considered in conjunction with its return volatility – a measure of how much a project's actual return is likely to deviate above or below its expected return. See the Key Concepts for an explanation of expected return and return volatility.

 Expected return and return volatility

Definition
■ *Expected return* – the return expected on an investment based on a probability distribution, taking into account all possible return scenarios.
■ *Return volatility* – the variability or uncertainty of an asset's return, measured by its standard deviation.

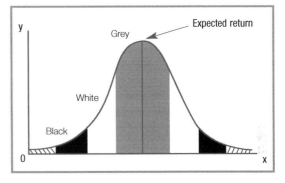

Explanation
Essentially, return volatility tells us how much an asset's actual return is likely to deviate above or below its expected return. Consider the probability distribution in the graph, where each segment represents one standard deviation:

■ 'grey' zone = 68% of area under the curve. This means that the asset's actual return has approximately 68% probability of falling within this zone (that is, within ±1 standard deviation of the asset's expected return).
■ 'grey+white' zone = 95% of area under the curve. This means that the asset's actual return has approximately 95% probability of falling within this zone (that is, within ±2 standard deviations of the asset's expected return).
■ 'grey+white+black' zone = 99% of the area under the curve. This means that the asset's actual return has approximately 99% probability of falling within this zone (that is, within ±3 standard deviations of the asset's expected return).

Example
Asset A has an expected return of 22%, and a return volatility (standard deviation) of 15%. With this information, we can infer the following:

■ Asset A has a 68% probability of achieving an actual return between 7% and 37% (that is, 1 standard deviation below and above expected return – represented by the grey area on the graph).
■ Asset A has a 95% probability of achieving an actual return between –8% and 52% (that is, 2 standard deviations below and above expected return – represented by the grey+white area on the graph).
■ Asset A has a 99% probability of achieving an actual

return between −23% and 67% (that is, 3 standard deviations below and above expected return – represented by the grey+white+black area on the graph).

The important point here is that the amount of risk, as defined by return volatility, can have a tremendous impact on actual return. The oft-quoted cliché, 'high risk, high reward', is only half the story. It fails to mention that high risk also means the potential for great loss.

Source: http://www.finportfolio.com/education/tutorial/tutorial_return_volatility.html

Cost of capital

The cost of capital is the minimum rate of return required from the project for it to be worthwhile. It takes into account the sources of project funding and the risk of the project. The cost of capital, as determined by an organisation's finance department, is used as the discount rate in the cash flow analysis; it must be established before starting a financial cost–benefit analysis.

The cost of capital is the opportunity cost of an investment, that is, the rate of return that an organisation would otherwise be able to earn at the same risk level as the investment selected. It is effectively the cost of passing up the next best choice when making a decision. For example, if capital is used for one purpose, the opportunity cost is the value of the next best purpose the capital could have been used for.

The cost of capital is also the rate of return an organisation must earn on the money it uses to finance the acquisition of new assets. This is determined by the return demanded by the people whose money the organisation is using. There are two sources of this money: equity and loans. For example, if the organisation finances an investment with new debt, the cost of capital must be the return demanded by these new loan providers (bondholders). If money is derived from the sale of new shares, the cost of this capital is the return that these new shareholders demand on their money. And if the organisation uses money that is on hand, the cost of this money is the return that existing shareholders require.

For example, suppose the bank savings rate is 10% per annum for fixed deposits and the bank lends money to a firm at, say, 16% interest. Also, suppose the firm has shareholders who have invested for the equity capital. Although they are not going to charge any interest, they have expectations about the performance of the company and they want to be rewarded

Table 4.3 Cost of capital example

Total investment	Capital	Interest	Total money payment
Equity	500,000	15%	75,000
Loan	300,000	16%	48,000
Deposits	200,000	12%	24,000
Total	1,000,000		147,000

for the risk that they have taken by investing in the company instead of putting their money in the bank or government bonds. If they were to keep the money in the bank, they would be getting a return of 10% per annum. Assume that the firm's shareholders want a return of 15% on the money they have invested. The firm also gets deposits from the lay public for which it pays 12% per annum. This information is summarised in Table 4.3.

Thus, in total the firm will have to pay out at the rate of 14.7% on the investment. In other words, the finance manager has to invest the company money in such a way that at the end of the year the company gets a better return than 14.7%.

Weighted average cost of capital

In the above example, each source of capital is weighted in the calculation according to its prominence in the company's capital structure. The result, that is, 14.7%, is the average cost of capital and is more formally known as the 'weighted average cost of capital' (WACC).

Risk adjusted cost of capital

An organisation's cost of capital can provide a useful discount rate (also known as a 'hurdle rate' or 'benchmark rate') of return for analysing and prioritising some types of capital investments, particularly strategic investments. However, there is another adjustment to consider before arriving at a suitable cost of capital. The weighted average cost of capital should be adjusted according to the 'riskiness' of the project by adding or subtracting a risk premium to reflect the project's specific risk characteristics. Using a risk adjusted cost of capital for the project discount rate helps to avoid two types of error:

1. relatively low-risk projects are rejected because

they are being discounted by too high a discount rate

2. relatively high-risk projects are discounted at too low a discount rate.

Cost of capital summary

Understanding an organisation's risk adjusted cost of capital is important for a fundamental reason – if an organisation is not earning a return at least equal to its cost of capital, it is dissipating its value. To ensure that an organisation's value is maintained or enhanced, the current asset base, in combination with additional capital expenditures, should be generating a return in excess of the risk adjusted cost of capital.

Cost of doing the project

Finally, a financial evaluation requires an estimate of the cost of doing a project. That cost will include capital and expense items, including the cost of personnel to work on the project.

Prioritisation techniques

There are many methods available for prioritising projects, most of which fall into one of the following categories (Martino, 1995):

- financial analysis
- decision tree analysis
- scoring and ranking
- portfolio optimisation
- simulation
- real options
- cognitive modelling
- cluster analysis.

Each category has advantages and disadvantages (Friedlob and Plewa, 1996) and is considered in turn below.

Financial analysis

Financial analysis prioritises projects according to profit contribution to a firm. This prioritisation method uses net present value (NPV), internal rate of return (IRR), payback period, discounted payback period and the profitability index (PI), or any combination of them, as comparison criteria. The projects are listed in order of financial return to the company.

Typically, projects are funded from the top of the list downward until no more funds are available.

Financial analysis is deterministic and indicates the value to a firm of each project. However, it uses financial measures that are derived from the cash flow analysis of the project. Unfortunately, cash flow analyses require information not readily available. Such analyses contain many assumptions and estimates that can only be substantiated once the project is funded. The need to confirm these assumptions and estimates and then update the cash flow analysis is another reason for reviewing projects every six months with senior management.

Most firms use one or more of the measures of financial analysis to prioritise projects; however, there is no single financial measure that is adequate for project prioritisation.

Net present value (NPV)

Think of a project as an abandoned suitcase containing money. If the amount of cash is positive, you will pick it up. If the suitcase contains 'negative cash' which would diminish your wealth you will leave it alone. (Marglin, 1963)

NPV simply states how much money is in the suitcase and whether it is positive or negative.

The NPV technique involves estimating the cash flows associated with an investment opportunity, discounting those cash flows received or paid in the future and deducting the cost of the initial investment. The steps involved in applying the NPV technique are:

1. Estimate the cost of the investment and all future incremental cash payments and receipts and their timings as a consequence of accepting the opportunity.
2. Estimate an appropriate discount rate (for example risk adjusted cost of capital) to apply to the future cash flows from the opportunity.
3. Discount all future cash flows at the appropriate rate to calculate their present value and deduct the cost of the initial investment.

All the business cash flows expected to change in the future as a consequence of accepting the opportunity should be included in the NPV estimate.

The decision rule of the NPV technique is as follows:

- For individual capital investments: Accept capital

investment opportunities which have a zero or positive NPV (that is, the present value of the future net positive cash flows from the project are equal to or greater than the initial investment cost).

- For ranking capital investment opportunities: Accept the capital investment opportunity which has the highest NPV.

In other words, if the investment opportunity has a return which is equal to or above the required rate of return (that is, the discount rate used), the opportunity is financially acceptable to the decision maker.

The formula for calculating the NPV technique is:

$$NPV = C_0 + \frac{C_1}{(1+i)^1} + \frac{C_2}{(1+i)^2} + \ldots + \frac{C_n}{(1+i)^n}$$

where:

C_0 = The initial cash investment
C_n = The total cash flows received or paid in period n
i = The appropriate discount rate for the capital investment opportunity

For example, consider a project to expand a bakery with the following cash flows over a five-year period (see Table 4.4). The cost of capital has been set by the financial manager at 12%. The table also shows the present value for each year using the terms of the above formula, giving a NPV of £43,929.

Applying the NPV decision rule, the bakery project is acceptable. The value of the bakery will increase by £43,929 in present value terms.

Intuitively, the NPV technique is appealing. If the bakery manager added up the NPVs of all of the bakeries operated by the company, he would find the NPV of the whole company's assets. This is an important distinguishing feature of the NPV technique not shared by the other financial analysis techniques.

NPV assumes that the timing and size of the cash flows are predictable. It also assumes that the discount rate (that is, the required rate of return or

cost of capital) is known and valid. If a project's NPV is positive, then its return exceeds the discount rate chosen for the financial evaluation. Thus, only those projects with a positive NPV require prioritisation. The characteristics of the NPV technique are:

- accounts for the time value of money as well as variable cash flow
- prioritises projects according to the total value earned during the project's evaluation period
- effectively identifies the best project in a set of competing projects
- allows the best set of projects to be identified since the NPV of individual projects can be summed to determine the NPV for a set of projects.

Internal rate of return (IRR)

IRR is based on the same assumptions used to calculate NPV, except that it does not require knowledge of the firm's discount rate. IRR provides a method for determining whether a project meets the chosen required return rate. IRR prioritises projects according to return rate rather than a monetary value. Using IRR, which is a percentage value, makes it difficult to determine the value of a set of projects, since their individual IRR values cannot be summed.

The IRR is a close relation to NPV, in that it too is a discounted cash flow (DCF) technique. The IRR technique involves estimating the cash flows associated with an investment opportunity, and finding the discount rate which, when applied to the relevant cash flows received or paid, produces an NPV of £0.

The steps involved to apply this technique are:

1. Estimate the cost of the investment and all future incremental cash payments and receipts and their timings as a consequence of accepting the opportunity.
2. Estimate an appropriate discount rate to produce an NPV of £0.

Table 4.4 Bakery project, example cash flows and NPV							
Period (years)	0	1	2	3	4	5	Total
Net cash flows	−56,000	17,500	26,250	39,688	27,891	30,672	
Present values	−56,000	15,625	20,926	28,249	17,725	17,404	
NPV at 12%							43,929

3. By trial and error continue to estimate a discount rate to produce an NPV of £0.

The decision rule for calculating the IRR of a capital project is:

- *For individual capital investments:* Accept capital investment opportunities which have an IRR greater than the required rate of return for the opportunity.
- *For ranking capital investment opportunities:* Accept the capital investment opportunity which has the highest IRR, provided that this is greater than the required rate of return for the opportunity.

The formula to use is:

$$£0 = C_0 + \frac{C_1}{(1 + IRR)^1} + \frac{C_2}{(1 + IRR)^2} + \ldots + \frac{C_n}{(1 + IRR)^n}$$

where:

C_0 = The initial cash investment
C_0 = The total cash flows received or paid in period n
IRR = The discount rate for the capital investment opportunity with NPV of £0

However, an IRR calculation can produce multiple answers, depending upon the cash flow assumed for the project. Multiple IRR values occur most often for uneven cash flows. An example of an industry with capital projects having this type of cash flow profile is mineral extraction. Late in the life of such projects the environmental area surrounding the mine needs to be relandscaped, which can involve a considerable cash outflow. Consequently, if cash flow is uneven, then the NPV method is easier to use since it always yields a unique result. Also, IRR does not indicate the monetary value of a project.

Payback period

The simplest financial measure to calculate is payback period. Dividing the initial costs by the cash flow per year provides the cash flow payback. It is the length of time required to recover the project's initial capital charges and expenses. The larger the cash flow payback (that is, the longer the payback period), the riskier the project. However, the payback technique does not take account of the important factors of the time value of money, risk and cash flows after the payback period. In other words, it

provides no information about the return rate for the investment made during the project.

The technique simply answers the question: 'When will this capital project repay the initial investment?' The payback technique involves estimating the cash flows associated with an investment opportunity, and calculating after how many periods the initial cost of the investment is covered by the investment's net positive cash flows. The steps involved to apply this technique are:

1. Estimate the cost of the investment and all future incremental cash payments and receipts and their timings as a consequence of accepting the opportunity.
2. Add or subtract the positive (or negative) cash flows received (or paid) after the initial cost of the investment.
3. Compare the cash flows received and paid for each period, starting with the first period after the initial investment, and compare the total with the cost of the investment.
4. If the cost of the investment is greater than the net cash flows received and paid up to the period in question repeat step 3. If the net positive cash flows are equal or greater than the cost of the investment, then this period becomes the payback period.

The decision rule for the payback technique is:

- For individual capital investments: Accept capital investment opportunities which have a payback period equal to or shorter than the target payback period.
- For ranking capital investment opportunities: Accept the capital investment opportunity which has the shortest payback period.

Both these factors are important, particularly in the case of long-term projects and those having cash outflows later in the life of the project. Table 4.5 shows the payback period for the bakery project introduced above.

The payback period is in period 3. If cash flows occur evenly throughout period 3, the initial investment should be repaid in 2.67 periods (56,000/83, 438); or approximately 2 years and 8 months (0.67 × 12 months), if the period is a calendar year.

Table 4.5 Bakery project, calculating the payback period

£

Period	0	1	2	3	4	5
Net cash flows	−56,000	17,500	26,250	39,688	27,891	30,672
Cumulative cash flows		17,500	43,750	83,438	111,329	142,001
Payback occurs				Here: £83,438>£56,000		

Discounted payback period

The discounted payback technique is similar to the above but uses a discounted cash flow. This helps to alleviate one of the fundamental problems of the payback technique by taking account of the time value of money. The technique still suffers from the same problem as the payback technique, in that it ignores cash flows received or paid after the discounted payback period.

The technique involves estimating the cash flows associated with an investment opportunity, discounting the cash flows at an appropriate rate of return (to obtain their present values) and calculating after how many periods the initial cost of the investment is covered by the investment's net positive discounted cash flows.

For relatively short life projects (such as the bakery project), the discounted payback period is unlikely to be significantly different from the payback period, unless the discount rate used is high. It may, however, produce a more noticeable difference in projects with a longer life and with projects where significant cash flows occur late in their life. Table 4.6 shows the steps involved to determine the discounted payback period for the bakery project.

The discounted payback period is in period 3. If cash flows occur evenly throughout period 3, the initial investment should be repaid in 2.86 periods (56,000/64,800); or approximately 2 years and 10 months (0.86 × 12 months), if the period is a calendar year.

Profitability index (PI)

Profitability index (PI), also known as present value index (PVI), is another technique for appraising capital projects which, being a DCF technique, is closely related to the NPV technique. The PI indicates a project's investment utilisation.

The steps involved in applying this technique are:

1. Estimate the cost of the investment and all future incremental cash payments and receipts and their timings as a consequence of accepting the opportunity.
2. Estimate an appropriate discount rate to apply to the future cash flows (excluding the initial investment) from the opportunity.
3. Discount all future cash flows at the appropriate rate to calculate their cumulative present value and divide by the cost of the initial investment.

The decision rule of the PI is:

■ For individual capital investments: Accept capital investment opportunities which have a profitability index of greater than one.
■ For ranking capital investment opportunities: Accept the capital investment opportunity which has the highest PI.

The PI technique yields the results for the bakery project shown in Table 4.7.

Table 4.6 Bakery project, calculating the discounted payback period

£

Period	0	1	2	3	4	5
Net cash flows	−56,000	17,500	26,250	39,688	27,891	30,672
Present values	−56,000	15,625	20,926	28,249	17,725	17,404
Cumulative cash flows		15,625	36,551	64,800	82,525	99,929
Payback occurs				Here: £64,800>£56,000		

Table 4.7 Bakery project, calculating the profitability index						
£						
Period	0	1	2	3	4	5
Net cash flows	−56,000	17,500	26,250	39,688	27,891	30,672
Present values	−56,000	15,625	20,926	28,249	17,725	17,404
Cumulative cash flows		15,625	36,551	64,800	82,525	99,929
Profitability index	= £99,929/£56,000 = 1.78					

Financial analysis summary

Most firms use two or more of these financial measures to prioritise projects. Since financial evaluations are done using spreadsheets, there is no reason not to calculate all these financial measures, and then use the appropriate ones during project prioritisation.

Decision tree analysis

In project management, decision trees provide a method for prioritising projects that require a series of decisions. They provide a structure to view different project options and investigate the possible outcomes of choosing each option. Decision trees take into account the estimated risks and rewards associated with each possible course of action; however, estimating the probabilities of each outcome can be difficult and is often subjective. Decision trees show the highest and lowest expected values for each project as well as the expected NPV. The following approach is reproduced with permission from MindTools and illustrates the process well.

Creating a decision tree

Start by drawing a small square towards the left of a large piece of paper. This represents the decision to be made. From this box draw out lines towards the right for each possible solution, and write that solution along the line. Keep the lines apart as far as possible so that you can expand your thoughts later. At the end of each line, consider the results. If the result of taking that decision is uncertain, draw a small circle. If the result is another decision that you need to make, draw another square. Squares represent decisions and circles represent uncertain outcomes.

Starting from the new decision squares on your diagram, draw out lines representing the options that you could select. From the circles draw lines representing possible outcomes. Again make a brief note on

the line saying what it means. Keep on doing this until you have drawn out as many of the possible outcomes and decisions as you can see leading on from the original decisions. An example of the sort of thing you will end up with is shown in Figure 4.4.

Once you have done this, review your tree diagram. Challenge each square and circle to see if there are any solutions or outcomes you have not considered. If there are, draw them in. If necessary, redraft your tree if parts of it are too congested or

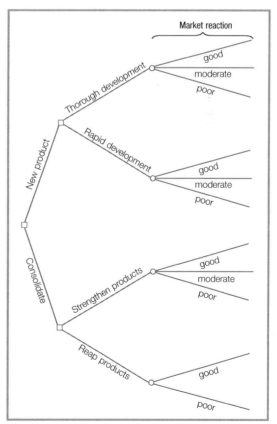

Figure 4.4 Structure of a decision tree

untidy. You should now have a good understanding of the range of possible outcomes of your decisions.

Evaluating a decision tree

Now you are ready to evaluate the decision tree. This is where you can work out which option has the greatest worth to you. Start by assigning a cash value or score to each possible outcome, how much you think it would be worth to you if that outcome came about. Next look at each circle (representing an uncertainty point) and estimate the probability of each outcome. If you use percentages, the total must come to 100% at each circle. If you use fractions, these must add up to 1. If you have data on past events, you may be able to make rigorous estimates of the probabilities. Otherwise write down your best guess. This will give you a tree like the one shown in Figure 4.5.

Calculating tree values

Once you have worked out the value of the outcomes, and have assessed the probability of the outcomes of uncertainty, it is time to start calculating the values that will help you make your decision. Start on the right-hand side of the decision tree, and work back towards the left. As you complete a set of calculations on a node (decision square or uncertainty circle), all you need to do is to record the result. You can ignore all the calculations that lead to that result from then on.

Calculating the value of uncertain outcome nodes

Where you are calculating the value of uncertain outcomes (circles on the diagram), do this by multiplying the value of the outcomes by their probability. The total for that node of the tree is the total of these values. In the example in Figure 4.5, the value for 'new product, thorough development' is:

$$0.4 \quad \times \quad £500,000 = £200,000$$
(probability good outcome) (value)

$$0.4 \quad \times \quad £25,000 = £10,000$$
(probability mod. outcome) (value)

$$0.2 \quad \times \quad £1,000 = £200$$
(probability poor outcome) (value)

$$= \textbf{£210,200}$$

Figure 4.6 shows the calculation of uncertain outcome nodes. Note that the values calculated for each node are shown in the boxes.

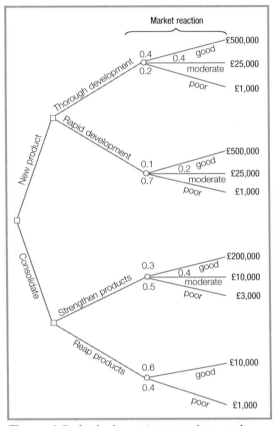

Figure 4.5 Assigning outcome values and probabilities to a decision tree

Calculating the value of decision nodes

When you are evaluating a decision node, write down the cost of each option along each decision line. Then subtract the cost from the outcome value that you have already calculated. This will give you a value that represents the benefit of that decision. Note that amounts already spent do not count for this analysis, these are 'sunk costs' and (despite emotional counter-arguments) should not be factored into the decision. When you have calculated these decision benefits, choose the option that has the largest benefit, and take that as the decision made. This is the value of that decision node. Figure 4.7 shows the calculation of decision nodes in our example.

In this example, the benefit we previously calculated for 'new product, thorough development' was £210,000. We estimate the future cost of this approach as £75,000. This gives a net benefit of £135,000. The net benefit of 'new product, rapid development' was £15,700. On this branch we there-

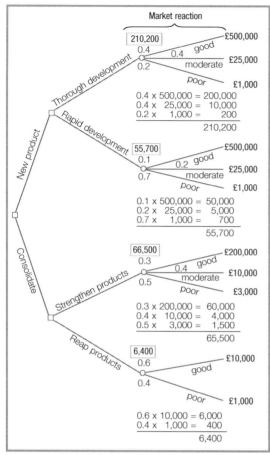

Figure 4.6 Calculating values for uncertain outcome nodes

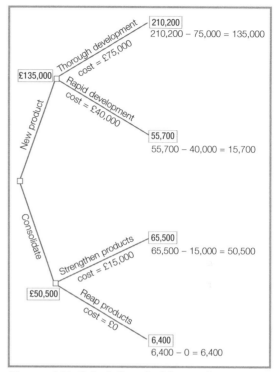

Figure 4.7 Calculating decision nodes

fore choose the most valuable option, 'new product, thorough development', and allocate this value to the decision node.

Result

By applying this technique we can see that the best option is to develop a new product. It is worth much more to us to take our time and get the product right, than to rush the product to market. It is better just to improve our existing products than to botch a new product, even though it costs us less.

Key points when using decision trees

Decision trees provide an effective decision-making method because they:

- clearly lay out the problem so that all options can be challenged
- allow us to analyse fully the possible consequences of a decision
- provide a framework to quantify the values of outcomes and the probabilities of achieving them
- help us to make the best decisions on the basis of existing information and best guesses.

As with all decision-making methods, decision tree analysis should be used in conjunction with common sense – decision trees are just one important part of your decision-making toolkit.

Visit the website

http://www.palgrave.com/business/gardiner

▶ to access other decision making tools and resources from MindTools

Scoring and ranking models

Ranking involves a pairwise comparison of all the projects under consideration. Each comparison determines which of two projects is better. By repeating the process, many projects can be ranked in order of preference. Ranking procedures involve the comparison of two or more criteria (multi-criteria assessment) in which the comparisons are scored using an agreed method. All projects are compared against a set of common decision criteria to weigh the relative merits of each project. The projects are then ranked from highest to lowest and projects are funded from the top of the list downward until no more funds are available (a form of capital rationing).

Ranking methods are simple to understand and easy to use. However, such prioritisation methods can pick the best of a bad lot and they do not indicate the value of doing one project over another project. In addition, the final scores often tend to cluster, making it difficult to rank the projects objectively.

Examples of scoring and ranking models are (Keeney and Raiffa, 1976; Bunn, 1984; Goodwin and Wright, 1999):

- Analytic hierarchy process (AHP)
- Simple multi-attribute rating technique
- Elimination by aspects
- Lexicographic
- Satisficing.

The criteria used should consist of elements related to three essential areas – benefits, costs and risks. Often organisations will establish a few key criteria related to these three areas and then develop more specific sub-criteria. For example, an organisation may establish risk as a key criterion and then include schedule risks, cost sensitivity, technical risks, organisational risks and risks if the project is not undertaken as sub-criteria.

Using an assortment of decision criteria to make decisions allows an organisation to take into account and compare the different subtleties of a wide variety of projects. Decisions should rarely be made based on one criterion.

An organisation may also assign weights to each of the criteria to help prioritise those factors that the organisation considers to be the most significant (for example a company with limited experience developing systems may give technical risk a greater weight than projected cost). These weights will vary from organisation to organisation and should take into account the organisation's unique mission, capabilities and limitations. In addition, different weighting approaches may be used for different kinds of projects (operational, infrastructure, applications development projects, and so on). Table 4.8 illustrates an example project scoring template.

An important point for an organisation in developing a scoring model or decision support tool is to define precisely the scoring elements (that is, define what constitutes a 1 versus a 5). The purpose behind these definitions is to ensure consistency in the scoring process and eliminate widely varying interpretations. Using common decision criteria across an organisation provides greater assurance that the organisation is selecting projects consistently and helps to avoid 'apples versus oranges' project comparison problems.

Portfolio optimisation

Ranking and decision theory prioritise projects individually; portfolio optimisation manages and prioritises sets of projects. It establishes the overall benefit from the interaction of each project in the set with all the other projects in the same set. Each project set can also be subjected to sensitivity analysis. Sets of projects are then compared to identify which set provides the greatest benefit to the organisation.

There is no single approach to portfolio optimisation that works in every organisation, industry or culture (Bridges, 1999). There are many different relationships between projects and they simply cannot be modelled in a single model to reflect the actual decision-making process (Aalto, 2001). Nevertheless, most authors agree there are three key tasks in portfolio optimisation:

1. Prioritisation and selection of projects in the portfolio
2. Resource allocation of projects in the portfolio
3. Evaluation and optimisation of the portfolio based on the portfolio's value, balance and strategic fit.

The role and purpose of a portfolio optimisation tool is described by Poskela et al. (2001) as:

- to establish a set of projects that reflects the organisation's strategy
- to balance overall risk, focusing on go/no-go risk and portfolio risk
- to optimise resource allocation across all projects
- to implement the organisation strategy.

Aalto (2001) draws attention to three portfolio management frameworks in particular:

Table 4.8 Example project scoring system template

Criteria (weighting)	Sub-criteria	Description	Maximum score
Risk (= 20 points)	Schedule risk	Evaluate the probability that this project can be completed on schedule.	4 points
	Cost sensitivity	Evaluate the sensitivity or quality of the cost estimates; consider project complexity, completeness of cost estimates, software development requirements.	4 points
	Technical risk	Evaluate the risk to complete the system from a technical point of view.	4 points
	Organisational risk	Assess the risk that the proposed system will fail due to organisational disruption due to change; has training been carried out?	4 points
	Risk of not doing it	Assess the risk to the organisation for not proceeding with this project.	4 points
Organisational impact (= 10 points)	Personnel and training	Assess the impact of the system on the knowledge, skill and training of organisational personnel if the system is implemented.	3 points
	Scope of beneficiaries/ cross-functional	Is the project a cross-functional project? Does it serve multiple offices, the public, and so on?	4 points
	Quality of work life	Measure the improvement in quality of work life expected for the systems.	3 points
Mission effectiveness (= 20 points)	Improve internal customer services	For example the system might improve the timeliness of financial reporting throughout the organisation.	10 points
	Improved service to the public	For example, delivering a service with fewer mistakes, increasing the availability of a computer system for customer use.	10 points
Strategic alignment (= 25 points)	Business model	Assess the degree of alignment with the organisation's business model.	7 points
	Level of interest	Assess the level of interest by senior managers.	12 points
	Business process redesign	Assess the degree this system enables the organisation to do business in a better way.	6 points
Cost–benefit impact(s) (= 25 points)		Any cost–benefit ratio less than one, that is, costs exceed the benefits.	0 points
		Cost–benefit ratio of one.	1 point
		Cost–benefit ratio of 1.5 to 1.75.	5 points
		Cost–benefit ratio of 1.76 to 1.99.	10 points
		Cost–benefit ratio of 2.0 to 2.99.	15 points
		Cost–benefit ratio of 3.0 to 3.99.	20 points
		Cost–benefit ratio of 4.0 or greater.	25 points
Total			100 points

Source: 'Selection processes', US General Accounting Office, http://www.gao.gov/policy/itguide/sel_proc.htm.

- the framework by Archer and Ghasemzadeh (1999)
- the strategy table model of Spradlin and Kutoloski (1999)
- the strategic buckets model of Cooper et al. (1997).

Each framework adopts a slightly different approach to portfolio management and optimisation, although the underlying principles remain the same. The framework in Figure 4.8 is adapted from the Archer and Ghasemzadeh framework.

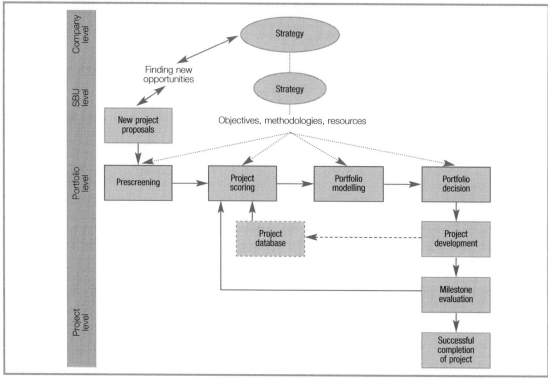

Figure 4.8 A modified project portfolio management framework (Aalto, 2001)

Simulation

Simulation, as a prioritisation method, can be thought of as time-dependent portfolio optimisation. It evaluates the outcome of a project or portfolio of projects for a sequential series of events. Simulation determines the outcome of alternative paths, each possessing a different payoff depending upon the chance outcome of each alternative. The outcome of each event is calculated using a Monte Carlo technique. The most likely outcome is then determined after performing a specified number of Monte Carlo calculations. The spread of each outcome is also determined by this prioritisation method. The project or portfolio with the greatest benefit to the company is then funded. However, estimating the probability range for each outcome can be difficult, and frequently the probabilities are determined subjectively.

Real options

Business decisions in many industries and situations can be implemented flexibly through deferral, abandonment, expansion, or in a series of stages that in effect constitute real options. Recognising real options can help decision makers assess the probability of new projects and understand whether and when to proceed with the later phases of projects that have already been initiated, particularly when they are close to breakeven. Real options are especially valuable for projects that involve both a high level of uncertainty and opportunities to reduce this as new information becomes available.

The real options approach frames the valuation process differently from traditional methods. It views a project as a process that managers can continually reshape in light of new information as the project progresses. For example, the opening of a new oilfield involves a series of decisions about whether to lease an area, how to explore it, what wells and pipelines to build and so on. This perspective contrasts with the traditional view of a project as a set of decisions made once at the beginning and unchanged during the life of the project.

The real options approach practically always leads to higher values for the same project than traditional methods, precisely because the options perspective recognises that managers make future decisions about a project as uncertainties become resolved.

They will terminate projects that are not working out and expand on those that are performing well. Real options methods incorporate this avoidance of losses and exploitation of gains in the analysis and therefore necessarily lead to a higher perception of value of 'risky' projects. This recognition and exploitation of the value of flexibility 'unlocks' the fundamental value in projects that carry high risk.

Designers can also design real options into projects and products, giving managers options, and the capability to improve performance, they otherwise would not have. For instance, engineers can build power plants to use several types of fuel, for example oil or natural gas. This flexibility costs money, but provides the potentially valuable option to switch from one source of supply to another according to relative fuel prices. Manufacturers can build product platforms that can support many different models, or flexible manufacturing facilities that can switch rapidly from one type of product to another. This requires careful design, but gives management the opportunity to follow markets and orders as they develop, rather than run the risk of over- or under-producing their products (Neely and de Neufville, 2003).

Real options takes the view that NPV assessments are conceptually wrong because they assume that the initiation of a project entails a complete commitment to the cash flow specified. An NPV valuation assumes that implementation always occurs, even when the early results are not promising. This ignores the reality of management control.

Cognitive modelling

Cognitive modelling prioritisation methods analyse the cognitive decision-making process and determine its components. These methods attempt to analyse the decision process of an organisation by analysing the decisions made by individual managers. Cogni-tive modelling strives to replace management in the decision process with a statistical model. This statistical model is derived from the historical decisions made by each manager. With cognitive modelling, the project manager never discusses the list of projects with the organisation's financial managers. Rather, the project manager or engineer calculates the various parameters required by the statistical model, inputs the parameters and then tabulates the results. For obvious reasons, managers are not enamoured with this prioritisation method. Cognitive modelling studies the entire decision-making process of a firm, which is an advantage. However, it assumes rational organisational behaviour and chooses projects in the absence of a decision maker.

Cluster analysis

Cluster analysis is a technique that aims to optimise an organisation's strategic position by identifying the set of projects best aligned with a firm's strategy. However, projects are not ranked and financial measures do not form part of the selection process.

Summary of prioritisation techniques

The prioritisation techniques used should reflect the following considerations:

1. The degree of business risk involved.
2. The organisation's internal and external environment.
3. The corporate governance regime (for example balance of shareholder versus stakeholder focus).
4. Cost of prioritisation activities compared to expected project returns.

The Insights from Industry box describes three examples of prioritisation from different sectors.

 **PRIORITISATION IN PRACTICE**

A high street bank

The following account is from a senior manager in a major high street bank in the UK:

Basically projects are categorised and cost-benefited. They are then tracked throughout their life. Now not every project has a cost-benefit – for example if the law changes you do the project to stay in the business.

Basically we seek to deliver projects which will improve the business. The rate of return on investment (RoI) has to exceed that which the company already delivers from its capital. Do projects less than that and the company is worse off. In the Bank, this means that projects with an RoI over 30% gross (19% net of tax) normally get done. Our actual return on capital is lower than 30% but this cutoff point generally leaves more than enough projects, which are then ranked and chosen.

There is a cross-functional committee of senior managers who select which projects of those over 30% will get done. The idea (if not necessarily the practice) is that senior business managers know where the business is going and are in a position to avoid inappropriate investments in nonstrategic areas. The final constraint is what the Bank can afford to invest each year. This is determined by the trading position for the company, market conditions and 'rule of thumb'. There are also allocations for nonstrategic projects made to each functional area so that even those that didn't win 'in committee' can still feel able to 'do something' and thus keep their own staff motivated and on side.

Source: Personal research interviews

Local authority

In pavement management, we utilise many factors to prioritise projects, with particular attention to field condition data. Those data are obtained from visual inspection of surface condition, machine measurements of friction, traffic volume counts, safety reports, and projections of deterioration. In bridge management, the process includes assessments of structural deterioration, analysis of functional adequacy, and a life cycle cost analysis. The safety programme annually reviews the top 30 worst locations, using an 18 accidents over three year threshold, and subjecting the data to critical accident ratio analysis. The top ten locations are then selected and incorporated into the regular program.

Priority setting is a fundamental step in the overall planning process. The priority that is assigned for any given project can and should be established as a direct expression of the impacts that the project produces in categories of greatest interest to citizens and decision makers. Priorities established in this way are then introduced into the budgeting and programming process that results in an endorsed list of projects to be undertaken over a specified time period. The budgeting and programming functions exist to advance those projects that emerge from the planning process

as having the greatest merit or highest priority. In short, the prioritisation process is the most important tool in making programming decisions ... but it cannot be the only consideration.

Although the priorities assigned to projects as a result of assessing their impacts in the planning process are the primary factors considered in budgeting and programming, there are other determinants that must be considered when committing limited resources to a discrete number of projects. These determinants stem from both the need to assess trade-offs among groups of prioritised projects in allocating scarce resources, and principles of prudent management. These determinants include:

■ deliverability due to schedule risk
■ fiscal resource impacts due to size of projects
■ human resource availability
■ current government policy.

Source: State of Delaware, Department of Transport, Financial Investments Program, 1998, http://www.deldot.net/static/invest/

An electric utility

An electric utility desired a new IT system for allocating its $250 million operations and maintenance budget. The organisation had a decentralised decision-making structure, and the IT application involved allocating funds across different business units run by managers who have line authority to decide how to spend their own project budgets. A centralised, project ranking system was unacceptable, since it would be inconsistent with the existing decentralised decision-making structure. The selected system used an alternative approach that evaluated alternative funding levels for each department, based on the projects that would be conducted under each funding level. This design allowed area managers to retain authority to prioritise and select projects within their respective areas while rewarding managers who proposed projects consistent with corporate objectives.

Source: M.W. Merkhofer (2003) 'Tools for Prioritizing Projects and Selecting Project Portfolios', *Proceedings of the First Annual Power Delivery Asset Management Workshop*, New York, June 3–5

PROJECT MANAGEMENT *in action*

Roadkill the movie

The following case study describes the trials and tribulations of a team of movie enthusiasts from Canada who began and finished a successful, low-budget, feature film called *Roadkill*. There are many lessons to be learned from their experiences, retold below in a jocular style by the film's creator Colin Brunton, an independent film producer.

How we made *Roadkill*

I made a short film called *The Mysterious Moon Men Of Canada*, a mock-documentary about a couple of Canadians who flew to the moon in 1959 but, because they were Canadian, were too modest to tell anyone about it.

Bruce McDonald was the editor. We had a lot of fun making the film, and when I entered the Genies (jokingly referred to as 'Canada's Oscars'), I listed him as 'co-producer'. To our surprise, it won the Genie for Best Live Action Short Drama. As we accepted the award, we'd already been thinking about this 75 minute docu-drama Bruce wanted to make called *All The Children Are In*.

On the Genie podium Bruce told the audience that we were in the process of raising money ... and would start by going through people's pockets in the cloakroom. We didn't look or act like normal Genie winners I guess, and were flattered when people told us that we added a little funk to the whole dreary affair. My acceptance speech, in its entirety was 'Uh ... thanks a lot ...'

Bruce's idea was to make a documentary about this local rock band called 'A Neon Rome', notorious for, among other things, putting up posters praising the use of drugs. Bruce then started thinking about building a bit of a story to go along with it, because then we'd have, like, a *real movie*. He hooked up with a struggling local playwright called Don McKellar, and Don worked out a basic storyline. We brought our good friend Al Magee on as story editor, which didn't entail actual 'editing' but rather helping us figure out the story itself. As Don would write pages, he'd pass them on to Bruce, Al and I, and we'd add our two cents' worth.

I thought of creative ideas as well as budget problems, and helped eliminate scenes that were too 'big' and tried to come up with clever alternatives. Al was an enormous help, and would constantly ask us mind-numbing questions like 'Why do you need this scene?', 'What's this scene all about?', and the funniest of all, 'I *am* going to get paid, right?'

Somewhere along the line several things happened: a light bulb went off in my head, and seeing the word roadkill in the 'script', thought it would be a better title than *All The Children Are In*. The lead singer of A Neon Rome decided to take a 'vow of silence' and this led all of us to think that this might cause him some problems with the dialogue, and we started to hunt for someone new. Don finished a 25-page document that was somewhere between an outline and a script. It wasn't a complete script, but we thought it sufficient to make a film out of, and we were confident we could fill in the gaps as we shot it.

Bruce had received Canada and Ontario Arts Council grants worth about $70,000, so we produced a little press-kit style book for a couple of grand and figured out how we could *get the film shot* for the measly $70,000 we had.

At the same time, we had heard of this place called the OFDC (Ontario Film Development Corporation), and decided to fill out an application form and have fun with it. We applied for about $120,000. We explained as best we could exactly how we were going to make a worthwhile feature film for under $200,000. The scriptwriter would not only act in the movie, he would act as continuity person as well. We would steal/borrow props and wardrobe, 'cause our art directors, Geoff and Jim Murrin, had the keys to a Toronto production company's warehouse. The script was structured to encourage improvisation (that is, we didn't really have all the dialogue figured out yet). The crew for the film would play, for the most part, the crew in the film, and we had lots of friends and relatives who would help us out.

We stuffed fake American hundred dollar bills in the application form as blatant bribes. We wrote a weird and cocky cover that expressed the 'gonzo' spirit and enthusiasm we had, sent it off and crossed our fingers, but really didn't take it too seriously. We really didn't think this OFDC place was going to go for it.

As producers, Bruce and I wanted to ensure that we had a sort of 'gender-balanced' crew, an equal amount of guys and gals. We had a woman from Montreal lined up to be our sound recordist, but she had to drop out at the last minute. I contacted a guy called Herwig Gayer who I knew from my involvement in LIFT, the Toronto Filmmakers' Co-op, and asked him if he would like to take a stab at recording sound on his first feature film. Herwig was pretty enthusiastic. I then told him our concern of being 'politically correct' and told him that he could have the job, but on one odd condition: he had to record the whole movie dressed as a woman. Desperate to get a chance to work on a feature, Herwig reluctantly agreed. He toughed out the whole shoot in a dazzling variety of outfits, and played the sound recordist in the film as well. No reference or mention was made about why the sound recordist for the film crew in the movie was dressed in drag, and I don't even know if that many people noticed it. Herwig's real test came when we went up to the Sudbury region, an area not especially famous for it's transvestites, but even up there, no one seemed to notice, or if they did, they didn't care. Maybe they thought this was to be expected of a film crew from Toronto.

We planned to be midway through day one of principal photography before we got the 'Yes' or 'No' from the OFDC. Again, we didn't worry about the application, nor did we expect to receive any money from them. But we warned them sternly (with tongues planted firmly in cheeks) that if the OFDC *didn't* help us out, *they'd* be the losers, not us. We were gonna get this film done somehow, with or without their help. And to counter our funky, film makers-from-hell attitude, we tempered that with a clear and concise budget, and pages of written material that anticipated any questions or misgivings anyone might have.

Luckily for us, there was a brave and bright kindred spirit at the OFDC: Louise Clark. She thought we were crazy and overambitious and impracti- cal and dreamers – and she thought that just maybe we were film makers too. Against the better judgement of others at the OFDC, Louise fought for and won approval to help fund this little black and white 'rock'n'road' movie. A last-minute phone call of endorsement from none other than Norman Jewison (Bruce struck up a friendship with Norman while working as his driver on *Agnes Of God*) helped convince the OFDC that we had what it took to make a feature film.

We now had enough money to not only get the film shot, but to edit it and make a print as well! We shot the film in May, had it edited throughout the summer, and finished it in time for the Festival of Festivals in Toronto, where much to our surprise it was selected to open the Perspective Canada series. We were voted The Most Outstanding Canadian Film at the Festival and won $25,000 cash. Bruce shocked the assembled bigwigs, suits and corporate sponsors by announcing that we would use the money to buy a big chunk of hash. It was the best press anyone could hope for. And not bad hash.

QUESTIONS TO AID UNDERSTANDING AND DISCUSSION

1. Would you have invested money in this project?

2. Was the project a success or a failure? Why?

3. Who was the sponsor?

4. What were the key investment decision points?

5. Was a feasibility study and business case prepared? What role did they play?

6. How did the investment process influence project planning and control?

Summary points

■ A project is an investment like any other.

■ Once selected and added to the portfolio, projects are subject to an investment control process – an integrated and structured approach to managing investments.

■ The three main phases of an investment management process are selection of the portfolio, control of ongoing projects and evaluation of completed or cancelled projects.

■ Techniques such as conducting a feasibility study and preparing a business case are used to justify the authorisation of projects – each project is assessed to determine whether or not it will add value to the organisation.

■ A feasibility study is a structured method that provides an accurate assessment of factors that might affect a project or programme.

■ The key purpose of a feasibility study is to determine if a business opportunity is possible, practical and viable.

■ A business case is prepared to ensure that projects put forward for funding reflect business strategy and will deliver the required benefits and returns to shareholders and stakeholders.

■ The principle purpose of a business case is to obtain management commitment and approval for investment, through a clearly presented rationale.

■ A business case provides a framework for informed decision making in planning and managing a project and its subsequent benefits realisation.

■ The five main perspectives of a business case are strategic fit, options appraisal, achievability, commercial aspects and affordability.

■ Capital budgeting is a set of techniques used systematically to evaluate, compare and select projects.

■ Capital budgeting decisions often have an impact for many years and as such reduce an organisation's flexibility – an important opportunity cost.

■ The purpose of a project appraisal is to assist an organisation in deciding whether a project concept is worth turning into reality.

■ When conducting a project appraisal, the following

concepts are important: financial versus economic appraisal; externalities and their valuation; cash flows and sunk costs; and cash flow analysis.

■ A cash flow analysis requires preliminary information about the evaluation period, expected return and return volatility (risk), the organisation's cost of capital and the cost of doing the project.

■ Project selection is closely related to an organisation's long-term strategy and business plan.

■ There are at least eight approaches to prioritising projects: financial analysis; scoring and ranking; decision tree analysis; portfolio optimisation; simulation; real options; cognitive modelling; and cluster analysis.

■ The prioritisation techniques used should reflect the following considerations: degree of business risk involved; the organisation's internal and external environment; the corporate governance regime (for example balance of shareholder versus stakeholder focus); and the cost of prioritisation activities compared to expected project returns.

The next chapter takes a close look at the role and responsibilities of the project manager and other key players in a project.

Acknowledgements

Part of the section on project appraisal has been adapted with permission from the MoneyTalks series of articles at http://www.switched-on.org/MoneyTalks/Projectappraisal.htm. © 2001 IIEC-Europe Ltd. Some of the financial analysis examples have been adapted with permission from *Corporate Finance* by M.A. Kerrison, part of the Heriot-Watt University Programme of Management Education, Heriot-Watt University, Edinburgh, Scotland, 2000.

Visit the website

http://www.palgrave.com/business/gardiner

❱ to test your understanding of the learning objectives for Chapter 4 using multiple choice questions

References

Aalto, T. (2001). 'Strategies and methods for project portfolio management'. In Artto, K.A., Martinsuo, M. and Aalto, T. (eds) (2001), *Project Portfolio Management*, Project Management Association (PMA) Finland, Helsinki.

Archer, N. and Ghasemzadeh, F. (1999). 'An integrated framework for project portfolio selection', *International Journal of Project Management*, **17**(4): 207–16. Reprinted in Dye, L.D. and Pennypacker, J.S. (eds),

(1999). *Project Portfolio Management: Selecting and Prioritizing Projects for Competitive Advantage*, Center for Business Practices, West Chester, PA.

Bridges, D.N. (1999). 'Project portfolio management: ideas and practices'. In Dye, L.D. and Pennypacker, J.S. (eds). *Project Portfolio Management – Selecting and Prioritizing Projects for Competitive Advantage*, Center for Business Practices, West Chester, PA.

Bunn, D. (1984). *Applied Decision Analysis*, McGraw-Hill, New York.

Cooper, R.G., Edgett, S.J. and Kleinschmidt, E.J. (1997). 'Portfolio management in new product development: lessons from the leaders II', *Research Technology Management*, **40**(6): 43–52.

Friedlob, G. and Plewa, F. (1996). *Understanding Return on Investment*, John Wiley & Sons, New York.

Goodwin, P. and Wright, G. (1999). *Decision Analysis for Management Judgement*, Wiley, New York.

Keeney, R. and Raiffa, H. (1976). *Decisions with Multiple Objectives: Preferences and Value Trade-offs*, Wiley & Sons, New York.

Marglin, S. (1963). *Approaches to Dynamic Investment Planning*, North-Holland Publications, Amsterdam.

Martino, J. (1995). *R&D Project Selection*, John Wiley & Sons, New York.

Neely, J.E. and de Neufville, R. (2003). 'Hybrid real options valuation of risky product development projects', *International Journal of Technology, Policy and Management* (in press) [accessed online 13/6/03 at http://msl1.mit.edu/mib/dsp/curricula.mit.edu/~dsplan/Docs/Papers/hybrid.pdf].

OGC (2003). Office of Government Commerce, Successful Delivery Toolkit Version 4.0. http://www.ogc.gov.uk/sdtoolkit/.

Poskela, J., Korpi-Filppula, M., Mattila, V. and Salkari, I. (2001). 'Project portfolio management practices of a global telecommunications operator'. In Artto, K.A., Martinsuo, M. and Aalto, T. (eds), *Project Portfolio Management*, Project Management Association Finland, Helsinki.

Spradlin, C. and Kutoloski, D. (1999). 'Action-oriented portfolio management', *Research Technology Management*, **42**(2): 26–32.

US General Accounting Office (1997). 'Assessing risks and returns: a guide for evaluating federal agencies' IT investment decision-making', US General Accounting Office, Accounting and Information Management Division, GAO/AIMD-10.1.13.

Visit the website

http://www.palgrave.com/business/gardiner

❱ for additional resources to explore the topics in this chapter further

CHAPTER 5

The project manager, sponsor and other stakeholders

Learning objectives

After reading this chapter you should be able to:

- identify, organise and categorise a wide variety of project stakeholders
- explain the relationship between the project manager and other stakeholders
- differentiate and discuss the role of the project manager from three perspectives
- generate balanced selection criteria for key project management appointments
- discuss the changing role of major stakeholders throughout the project life cycle
- analyse and evaluate a sponsor's ability to fulfill its obligations
- understand and argue the importance of shared expectations in a project
- perform a step-by-step approach to stakeholder analysis

Introduction

Projects involve many people and almost as many roles and titles; even the term 'project manager' has a myriad of meanings between organisations. There are sponsors with significant experience of projects and others with virtually none. This chapter is about the people who have a vested interest or stake in a project, whether it is the newly appointed project manager, the project champion, the contractors and subcontractors, the client representative, the sponsor, the chairperson of a users' committee, the spokesperson for an environmental action group, the project manager's manager, the finance director, the team leader, the consultant or an independent advisor. The experience and knowledge requirements of project management may be different in every case, however, the principles remain the same. This chapter provides a reasoned and balanced approach that clarifies which techniques and approaches are most relevant to whom and in what circumstances.

Project stakeholders

Project stakeholders are individuals, groups and organisations who are actively involved in the

project, or whose interests may be positively or negatively affected as a result of the project. Stakeholders can be internal or external to the project. Owners and funders, banks providing capital, senior management, government agencies and media outlets, individual citizens, temporary or permanent lobbying organisations and society at large are all potential project stakeholders. Figure 5.1 shows an example set of stakeholders for a project.

The project manager is an important link person between the different stakeholders, especially between those who direct the project (the project board) and those who carry out the activities (the project team).

The people involved in a project and their role vary according to the size of the project and the approach used. In this chapter the following roles are examined:

- *project manager* – the individual ultimately responsible for managing and leading the project to its successful conclusion
- *sponsor* (or *client* or *owner*) – the individual, group or organisation that provides the financial resources, in cash or in kind, for the project
- *project board* (or *steering committee*) – directs the project on behalf of the sponsor, and makes sure that everything goes according to plan

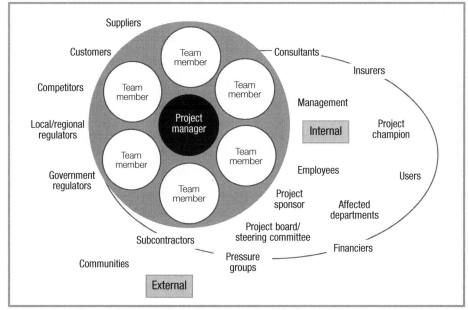

Figure 5.1 Example stakeholders for a project

- *finance providers* – provide the finances required by the project over and above that contributed directly by the client
- *project champion* – someone who strongly supports the project and communicates enthusiasm and charisma about it to others
- *consultant* – provides specialist advice, information and consulting services for a fee
- *performing organisation* – the organisation or organisations whose employees are most directly involved in doing the work of the project
- *customer* (or *end user*) – the individuals or organisation who will use the end product. The terms 'sponsor', 'client' and 'customer' are sometimes used indiscriminately, however, sponsor and client usually refer to whoever is paying for the project, while customer usually means the end user of the project's end products or services
- *project support office* – where present, supports the project team as required with requests for information and training.

Leadership role of the project manager

Who is the project manager

Identifying the project manager is not always as easy as it sounds. There may be several people working on the project from different organisations with the job title 'project manager'. Also, on large projects, different people may take on the project manager's role as the project progresses through its major phases. For example, in a project to build a new chemical plant there may be a feasibility project manager, a design and construction project manager and a commissioning and operations manager. Add to the above, natural turnover and the problem of identifying 'the' project manager becomes clear.

The role of the project manager is both simple and multifaceted – 'to attain the project objectives'. The project manager must simultaneously see to the needs of the sponsor and other stakeholders, manage the project life cycle and the performance of the project team, including his or her own performance. It is a role that entails a mix of competencies, combining management with leadership and political awareness (Pinto, 2000). The International Project Management Association (IPMA) has developed a project management competency baseline, consisting of 42 elements of project management knowledge and experience (IPMA, 1999).

Some organisations use the term 'project leader' to denote the more senior and responsible job requirements of leading, managing and decision making, and 'project manager' for someone carrying out the more detailed day-to-day management of project activities. However, it is more common to use the title 'project director' for the more senior management position. The Key Concepts below shows a set of example job descriptions for the roles of project director, project manager and project leader. On a large or complex project, the project manager may require the help of one or more assistant project managers to work alongside him or her.

key CONCEPTS Example job descriptions in a large project

Project (or programme) director
This is a senior management position in the organization. Responsible for the direction of a very large project with major sub-projects or a program of interrelated projects, ensuring integration, coordination, and consistency of process throughout

Accountability
- Sit on the project review panel and/or liaise with the program's sponsor
- Keep aware of the external environment and facilitate public relations in support of the program
- Ensure satisfactory liaison with customers at all levels
- Establish consistent project management policies and guidelines for the overall program
- Plan and prioritize sub-projects to meet the overall program goals and objectives
- Oversee selection and appointment of services and resources to the sub-projects
- Approve the major commitments on behalf of the performing organization
- Resolve resource conflicts
- Facilitate regular reporting, reviews and audits
- Organize the transfer of 'Care, custody and control' of the entire works upon completion
- Ensure proper closure and archiving of program records

Skill requirements
Strategic planning, program management, group motivation and discipline, imagination and diplomacy

Project manager
Unfortunately, 'project manager' is almost a 'default' title and is often applied to anyone who happens to be in charge of a project of whatever size and type. Responsible for managing one or more projects within the constraints of scope, quality, time, and cost, to deliver specified requirements and meet customer satisfaction

Accountability
- Liaise with project's sponsor and/or customer
- Ensure all project requirements and/or objectives are properly documented in a Business Case and/or Project Brief, as appropriate, and vigorously pursued
- Establish or confirm guidelines applicable to the project
- Obtain and manage all necessary services and competent staff for the project
- Ensure timely activity, integration, productivity and efficient use of resources to meet requirements
- Facilitate communication as appropriate to all involved and 'manage' the stakeholders

- Establish appropriate Key Success Indicators and manage trade-offs between scope, quality, time and cost
- Approve or recommend all required commitments
- Approve all appropriate project expenditures
- Track and report progress and forecast final targets
- Document, obtain approval, and track all changes in project parameters
- Document all obstacles, delays, and claims
- Ensure satisfactory transfer of 'Care, custody and control' of product upon completion
- Close all project documentation and archive appropriate records

Skill requirements
Goal orientation and action-focused, pragmatic and self-disciplined, good at project planning, organizing, communication, team motivation and delegation

Project leader
This title is typically given to a person not qualified to be a formal project manager, but nevertheless is put in charge of a smaller project, or large project-type activity. Responsible for managing a smaller project within the constraints of scope, quality, time, and cost, to deliver specified requirements and meet customer satisfaction

Accountability
- Liaise with project's sponsor and/or customer
- Ensure all project requirements and/or objectives are properly documented in a Business Case and/or Project Brief, as appropriate, and vigorously pursued
- Establish or confirm guidelines applicable to the project
- Coordinate assigned project team members, ensure timely activity, integration and efficient use of time and resources to meet requirements
- Facilitate communication as appropriate to all stakeholders
- Establish appropriate Key Success Indicators and recommend trade-offs between scope, quality, time and cost
- Track and report progress and forecast final targets
- Document, obtain approval, and track all changes in project parameters
- Document all obstacles and delays, and try to find 'workarounds'
- Complete all wrap-up activities upon project completion

Skill requirements
Goal orientation and action-focused, self-disciplined, good at project planning, communication, team motivation and delegation

Visit the website

http://www.palgrave.com/business/gardiner

▶ to discover Max Wideman's Project Management Wisdom website, which includes a comprehensive list of job descriptions relevant to project management

Project managers may also be supported by a project support office that provides a range of services, for example a company-wide project management methodology tailored for in-house use, project management templates, data collection and analysis services, and the preparation of project planning, control and evaluation documentation. The use of a project office was discussed in Chapter 3.

The detailed responsibilities of a project manager can be more easily understood by considering them alongside the three perspectives indicated in Table 5.1 – overall responsibility, early project responsibility and ongoing responsibilities. The project manager's role is quite extensive and can often seem daunting, especially to new project mangers. While there are no silver bullets in project management (and beware of sources that say otherwise), two useful guiding principles are:

1. All decisions should be directed towards achieving the project objectives.
2. Only the remaining work in the project can be managed.

The first principle is reflected in the project manager's overall responsibility in Table 5.1. The second principle is a call to manage the project's remaining time and resources wisely and in the light of today's circumstances which may be significantly different to those at the start of the project.

 TIME out The well-prepared project manager

Create and sketch a cartoon caricature to symbolise the readiness of the well-prepared project manager. Emphasise the more important features by drawing them to a larger scale.

Table 5.1 The three perspectives and responsibilities of the project manager's role	
Overall responsibility	■ To achieve the project's objectives within the time, cost and quality, performance and any other constraints imposed by the sponsor
Early project responsibilities	■ Establish the client's objectives and priorities ■ Identify the stakeholders and determine what their needs and expectations are ■ Develop effective communication procedures ■ Select, build and motivate the project team ■ Create a suitable project organisation structure and procurement strategy ■ Develop the project scope from the client's objectives ■ Develop the project schedule and budget ■ Advise on the selection of participants
Ongoing responsibilities	■ Manage and influence the expectations of the key stakeholders, especially the project sponsor ■ Respond to the changing requirements of the project as it progresses through its life cycle ■ Serve as the principal point of contact between the sponsor, management and contributors ■ Understand the importance of organisational politics and how to make them work for project success ■ Keep the sponsor and senior management well informed of progress in all phases of the project and alert them to problems – especially if these could have an impact on the project achieving its business objectives ■ Provide motivation and leadership skills throughout the project ■ Establish and develop teamwork between participants ■ Convene and chair meetings as appropriate ■ Ensure that the project structure is working as intended ■ Make or force timely decisions to ensure the project's success ■ Recommend termination of the project to the sponsor if necessary ■ Manage subcontractors ■ Monitor and control the project through to completion, for example against objectives and milestones ■ Carry out project evaluation activities at key project stages

Selling the project idea

The project manager is also a marketeer. A project needs to be well packaged and marketed if people are going to take an interest in it and buy into the idea, or at least go along with it. The merits of a project are not necessarily self-evident to everyone working on it, or indeed to large numbers of people in the sponsor's organisation, many of whom can help or hinder the eventual success and value obtained from the project. Important project marketing activities for the project manager include:

- planning and executing a marketing campaign throughout the project's life cycle to ensure it receives the attention and recognition it needs – a one-off activity in the start-up phase will be easily forgotten
- organising presentations (both formal and informal), particularly to explain why the whole project is important to the company, how it will be carried out and how people can help, for example the Insights from Industry box illustrates some early marketing to staff at Boeing, as they begin development of the Boeing 777 airplane
- agreeing with all stakeholders what the return to them will be as a result of the project
- encouraging the sponsor and any other project champions to create a 'good feeling' or positive image about the project
- making sure that news of the project regularly reaches the eyes and ears of the influential; informed stakeholders are happy stakeholders (or their concerns can be addressed early). This can be achieved through formal reports, updates and newsletters
- involving stakeholders in decision making wherever possible – ownership creates commitment
- demonstrating progress, using bulletins, drawings, models, prototypes, demonstrations and so on
- maintaining the confidence of key stakeholders by planning for an early project success, providing a taste of real benefit to stakeholders; for example QuickWin was an early deliverable for the Bank of Scotland PC banking team (see the Project Management in Action case at the end of Chapter 2).

Meeting the needs of the sponsor

The sponsor is the strongest project stakeholder. It is the sponsor who controls the purse strings and has the greatest interest in championing the project

 insights from INDUSTRY   SATISFYING YOUR CUSTOMERS IS REALLY HARD WORK

In 1991 the Boeing Company decided the world was ready for a new airplane, the Boeing 777. Alan Maloney, vice-president of engineering, addresses a mass meeting of company employees to communicate this news and encourage everyone to give their best effort:

> The airlines of the world told us they wanted an airplane bigger than the 767, but they wanted it smaller than the 747. We said: 'Why don't you buy 767s?' They said: 'We want an airplane that's bigger than the 767 and smaller than the 747.' So we said: 'Well, that costs a lot of money, to make a new airplane.' And of course you know what they said again: 'We would like an airplane that's bigger than the 67 and smaller than the 47.' … And do you know what else he said? 'Airbus was just here.' Boy! Satisfying your customers is really hard work!

Source: BBC television series, 21st Century Jet: *The Making and Marketing of the Boeing 777*, 1995, directed by Karl Sabbagh

outcome. The sponsor is also the project manager's boss. Managing the project and taking decisions to meet the needs of the sponsor will be easier if the project manager has established a good relationship with the sponsor and knows why the sponsor has initiated the project. This may involve considerable dialogue with the sponsor and careful probing. For example, unless it is clear why an organisation has launched a project to install a new information system, the uninformed project manager may tread on a number of sensitive toes and find it impossible to complete the project successfully.

The following leadership activities can be employed to increase the probability that a project will meet the needs of its sponsor:

- Asking questions to ensure that the sponsor understands the strategic direction and anticipated impact of the project, for example, 'Why are you doing this project?', 'What should the end result look like?' and 'What are your measures of success and critical success factors?'
- Designing with the project sponsor the most effective organisational structure and processes to run the project.

- Designing with the project sponsor the most suitable approach to involve stakeholders to ensure that they are continuously integrated into the project life cycle, and that they also understand the strategic direction and anticipated impact of the project.
- Negotiating directly with stakeholders regarding their level of input and involvement.
- Helping to clarify risks and identifying any gaps in the assessment of risks.
- Representing the project to senior management and clients, undertaking active internal marketing.

Meeting the needs of the other stakeholders

All projects have a client, an end user (who might be different from the client) and possibly a number of other external stakeholders (such as suppliers and subcontractors). Such parties have expectations of the project which the project manager must seek to meet and it is often the case that they all want something different. Establishing who the stakeholders are in a project and what they really want is never simple. The first thing to do is to ask lots of questions. People are rarely clear in their first pronouncements and a good project manager can rapidly build credibility by helping them to clarify their ideas. Another aspect of this leadership role is to point out where their expectations clash with those of others and encourage the parties to talk to try to resolve areas of conflict. When developing a new product, for example, reconciling the expectations of finance directors, design engineers, production people, marketing *and* customers involves many leadership skills. The project manager often acts as a broker or negotiator to try to find a best-fit formula that meets as many needs as possible. Without this, it is hard to succeed.

Managing the project life cycle

Another leadership role of the project manager is progressing the project through its various phases – managing the inputs, transformations and outputs at every stage of the project life cycle. This does not mean doing all the work, although on small projects, project managers may find that their role includes executing many of the project tasks as well.

The project leader has the responsibility to ensure that all team members perform well, both individually and collectively. However, for many project managers it is all too easy to become totally absorbed in the day-to-day tasks of a project and forget that their own performance also has a big impact on the overall progress. Many project managers admit to getting a 'buzz' from the stress and challenges of the job. However, left unchecked, escalating stress can severely impair personal health and performance. Project managers have a responsibility to avoid accepting totally unrealistic expectations, for example by listening and responding to their own internal 'counsellor'. See also Key Concepts: 'Emotional intelligence' in Chapter 1.

Typical life cycle responsibilities include:

Early phase:
- Helping the sponsor to prepare a project agreement or charter and obtaining commitment to it from the other stakeholders.
- Establishing an appropriate organisational structure for managing the project, and assigning and detailing roles and responsibilities identified in the project charter.
- Negotiating and obtaining written agreements with participating departments for project-specific resources.
- Planning and organising the project with the help of suitable tools. This involves:
  - preparing a work breakdown structure, responsibility assignment matrix, and project schedule
  - estimating benefits and costs for project alternatives
  - estimating risk and planning for risk reduction
  - tracking key objectives for the project
  - implementing adequate configuration control
  - implementing a systematic method to report progress to management and other key stakeholders as required
  - drafting a communications plan and keeping it up to date
  - preparing and maintaining a quality plan for the project.

Mid phase:
- Monitoring and control of progress using a project performance management system appropriate to the size and complexity of the project to ensure that targets are met and team members learn from mistakes.
- Preparing a timely request for consideration of amended project objectives when it is clear that the existing ones cannot be met.
- Identifying stage gates in the work plan where

withdrawal or termination would be practical, should the project cease to be viable during execution.

- Responding to inquiries from the media and the general public on high visibility projects.
- Preparing documentation for dialogue with senior management or project participants as necessary.

Late phase:

- Submitting a final evaluation of the performance of the project within a reasonably short period of time following project completion (for example, three months).

A survey of project leadership skills

The following list of 26 project leadership skills is based on a UK/USA survey to determine the 'excellent' project manager on large government projects (see Table 5.2). 'Excellent' in this instance means the top 0.2% of project managers who always seem to complete their projects on time and on budget. The project managers were asked to list, in order of importance, the key attributes of a project manager. The results highlighted a clear difference between the best project managers, average performers and those who had never been the manager of a large project.

Table 5.2 Project leadership benchmark results

Project leadership skills	Ranking by excellent project managers	Ranking by other project managers
To assume ownership for the mission, and to refer to it at all times	1	17
To have long-term vision and the ability to anticipate problems	2	6
To know how to delegate and how to lead the team	3	2
To be conscious of the political aspects, to know the major players and their interests and to be able to work with them	4	21
To know how to analyse and to select the best alternative	5	5
To manage by results	6	8
To know how to analyse problems methodically	7	3
To encourage innovation and personal initiative	8	11
To demand excellent individual performance	9	9
To be action-oriented and to stress urgency	10	10
To develop good relations with the major stakeholders: clients, users, suppliers	10	14
To be a good coach and mentor	12	12
To know how to find and to manage information	13	15
To be persuasive in order to overcome obstacles and to obtain support	14	23
To be imaginative and creative	15	3
To show self-control	15	13
To be able to assess the motivation and commitment of people	17	18
To know how to manage	18	16
To establish one's authority and to defend the project in all circumstances	18	24
To be positive and optimistic	20	24
To have a sound technical knowledge	21	1
To be sensitive to other people's needs	22	22
To pay attention to detail	22	7
To concentrate on the critical aspects	24	20
To have a good sense of priorities	25	18
To be competitive	26	26

Source: Stokes, 1997, *Training for Project Management*: Volume 1 – *Skills and Principles* Gower, Aldershot.

Table 5.3 Top differences in leadership skill rankings between excellent and average project managers

Project manager's skill	A Ranking by excellent project managing	B Ranking by other project managers	Difference B − A
(a) To have a sound technical knowledge	21	1	−20
(b) To be conscious of the political aspects, to know the major players and their interests and to be able to work with them	4	21	17
(c) To assume ownership for the mission, and to refer to it at all times	1	17	16
(d) To pay attention to detail	22	7	−15
(e) To be imaginative and creative	15	3	−12
(f) To be persuasive in order to overcome obstacles and to obtain support	14	23	9

 Key differences between excellent and average project managers

Table 5.3 shows the six leadership skills of project managers in the leadership survey having the greatest difference in ranking between excellent project managers and other project managers. Can you explain why these six skills in particular should be ranked so differently?

See shaded box for a suggested answer.

Project managers need 'soft' skills

The role of the project manager is central to a project and the sponsor can avoid many downstream problems if the project manager is identified and assigned sooner rather than later, certainly before execution, and preferably as soon as the project has been conceived.

The core competencies required by project managers can be divided into two categories: soft

---

ANSWER suggested

(a) The best project managers require people skills over and above technical skills. It is an erroneous belief that the project manager needs to excel at the functional skills required in a project. A threshold level of technical knowledge allows the project manager to converse intelligently with technical specialists. However, being an excellent engineer or other specialist does not imply excellence at project management.

(b) This also emphasises the importance of the human factor in project management. Projects run into trouble because the project manager is not able to 'tune-in' to the subtleties and nuances concerning people and politics. These are often of equal importance to the more familiar project management skills, such as creating schedules and networks.

(c) It is easy for a project manager to get caught up in a myriad of day-to-day problems, all 'urgent' and 'critical' according to someone, and lose sight of the big picture. The best project managers have the project mission imprinted on their minds and engraved on their fore-heads.

(d) Monitoring the big picture, and paving the way for progress, managing the stakeholders and project team, mean that the best project managers must delegate much of the project detail to others.

(e) There is nothing wrong with having creativity and a good imagination. However, it is not high up on the skill list for the best project managers who are happy for others in the project effort to provide such qualities. The excellent project manager sees that the job gets done, but is happy for others to do it, offering support, encouragement and leadership as needed.

(f) This is one of those leadership skills which isn't needed all the time, but, when it is called for, it helps to maintain the momentum of the project and keeps the project team committed to the project while increasing their trust and confidence in the project manager.

and hard skills. Soft skills involve behaviour, attitudes, communication styles and leadership. Hard skills are easier to acquire than soft skills, but both are necessary to successful project management. Hard skills set the goals and procedures while soft skills make sure that people can meet those objectives. This section outlines the soft skills required by the project manager. A useful starting point is the five skills below which according to the PMBOK are 'highly likely to affect most projects' (PMI, 2000: 21):

- Leading
- Communicating
- Negotiating
- Problem solving
- Influencing the organisation.

A more detailed description of these and other soft skills is given below – see also the Critical Considerations box which lists behavioural characteristics for project managers as specified in the Association for Project Management's *Body of Knowledge* (2000):

- *Visible leadership.* This is about creating a vision and achieving it with tenacity; getting team members and stakeholders enthused for action.

Behavioural research suggests that the best way to do this is through influence rather than mandatory edicts (Kotter, 1985).

- *Flexibility and alertness.* The ability to adapt and deal with situations and manage expectations during periods of change is critical to the project manager's image as a leader, especially in the eyes of the project stakeholders.
- *Sound business judgement.* There are many business interfaces between a project and its sponsor, for example accounts, personnel and finance. Project managers who make decisions with a sound knowledge of the business purpose of a project and an awareness of the wider management, political and cultural issues are more likely to deliver a successful project.
- *Risk taking/avoiding.* The project manager's attitude towards risk should be neutral in order to maintain objectivity and rationality in decision making. The project manager should be aware of project risks and be able to identify the potential benefits of accepting any risks.
- *Trustworthiness.* Stakeholders will want to be assured that the project manager represents a low risk because of his or her track record, credibility and ability to build relationships.
- *Communication awareness.* Project managers influence people to take action. This requires an

---

CRITICAL CONSIDERATIONS

BEHAVIOURAL CHARACTERISTICS OF PROJECT MANAGERS

Characteristics of an individual's personality generally recognised as important in project management are:

- *Attitude* – an open positive 'can-do' attitude which encourages communication and motivation, and fosters cooperation.
- *Common sense* – the ability to spot sensible, effective, straightforward, least risky, least complex solutions, that is, 90% right on time is better than 100% far too late!
- *Open mindedness* – an approach where one is always open to new ideas, practices and methods, in particular giving equal weight to the various disciplines involved on the project.
- *Adaptability* – a propensity to be flexible where

necessary and avoid rigid patterns of thinking or behaviour, to adapt to the requirements of the project, the needs of the sponsors, its environment and people working on it – to ensure a successful outcome.

- *Inventiveness* – an ability to discover innovative strategies and solutions from within oneself or by encouragement with other members of the project team, and identify ways of working with disparate resources to achieve project objectives.
- *Prudent risk taker* – a willingness and ability to identify and understand risks but not to take a risky approach in an unwise or reckless fashion.
- *Fairness* – a fair and open attitude which respects all human values.
- *Commitment* – an overriding commitment to the project's success, user satisfaction and teamworking. A strong orientation towards goal achievement.

Source: APM, 2000: 7

ability to communicate in a style appropriate for the individual concerned. For example, to get action from a person who is risk-averse, slow to act and detail-oriented, a leader needs to provide more detail and demonstrate how the action is low risk so that the person is comfortable with taking that action. To get action from an action-oriented person, by contrast, the challenge is to get him or her to listen to the details of what needs to be achieved before plunging into action. Being able to recognise each team member's communication style and adapt to it is an important skill.

- *Acts as a coach and mentor.* A project manager who builds trust will encourage team members to give and receive feedback. The project manager who knows the strengths and weaknesses of the team is better able to utilise the team members to complement and support each other.
- *Active listening skills.* Project managers listen. They read body language and perceive group dynamics. By listening well, project managers achieve a better understanding of team members and others, which promotes trustworthiness and helps in the management of both spoken and unspoken expectations.
- *Setting and managing expectations.* Managing stakeholder expectations is a key skill for all project managers.
- *Constructive project negotiations.* Project managers must have the ability to say 'no' and know when to say 'no'. This means being able to build win–win situations and constructive agreements among stakeholders.
- *Issue and conflict resolution:* Developing and following a conflict resolution model and being able to cope with finding a resolution, and any resulting stress, is an important skill.
- *Technological awareness.* Knowledge and understanding of current technologies may be thought of as a strategic asset that allows the best and proven technologies to be used within a project. Identifying new technologies allows a project manager to test their value to the organisation.

It is probably unrealistic to expect to find anyone who excels in all these skills. Although some skill gaps can be filled by providing selected training courses, others only come with maturity and experience.

 TIME out I know a project manager …

Think of a project that you have taken part in or one with which you are familiar. How well does the above list describe the project manager (or your boss) in this project? What evidence is there to support your thinking? Which skills were missing? What effect did this have on the project, the project team, the sponsor and any other stakeholders?

The project sponsor

The project sponsor pays for the project; the end users enjoy the benefits of the project. For example, a local government funds a new library, the local residents are the end users; a manufacturing company commissions the development of a new design of motor car, the end users are the people who purchase and drive the car.

Sponsors can be:

- *private individuals*, for example a celebrity commissioning an artist to do a portrait
- *several private individuals*, for example a group of investors opening a new city centre restaurant
- *corporate*, for example a bank commissioning a consulting firm to oversee a merger with another bank
- *government*, for example the updating of the UK Passport Office systems
- *mixed government–private* (for example the building of some hospitals and prisons is managed as a public–private partnership)
- *multinational* – common on very large engineering and aerospace projects which are usually too expensive and risky for any one sponsor to act alone. For example the Channel Tunnel had sponsors in England and France and the development of the Eurofighter was financed by several European countries.

The users in a project can also be represented by multiple groups. For example:

- a new information system in a university will have many kinds of user, including teaching staff, research staff, administration staff, undergraduate students, postgraduate students, conference delegates and other visitors, part-time staff and students, as well as distance learning students.
- the customers for a new pharmaceutical product may include the doctors who prescribe it, the

patients who take it and the health service or insurers that pay for it.

The sponsor and users are key participants in the project life cycle. If the users are not satisfied with the end product, chances are they will choose not to use it, preferring an alternative or reverting to the 'old system'. This is exactly what happened in the Project Management in Action case study at the end of this chapter called 'Easy Finance Ltd', in which one of the shortcomings of the project was a gross lack of effective consultation with the eventual users of the system during the development of a new information system.

Sponsors want a return on their investment in the project. The role of the sponsor is therefore to assess the need and feasibility of the project, to authorise the expenditure of resources on the project and ensure that an appropriate management structure is in place for the project to be undertaken. The sponsor is a key decision maker in the project life cycle. It is the sponsor who ultimately gives or takes away approval for a project to begin, and to continue until completion or termination. Users vote with their feet. Get it right and everyone is happy. Get it wrong and the project may be a disaster. Determinants of success and failure in project management will be examined in Chapter 10.

The person or group of people who represent the sponsor in a project will have an important bearing on how the project is managed. For example, an executive sponsor will be empowered to make key decisions about the project quickly, whereas a non-executive sponsor will often have to refer major decisions back to a project board or steering committee for approval. The culture and organisational arrangement of the sponsor and its impact on a project will be discussed in more detail in Chapter 6.

In some industries the role of the sponsor and the users is considered so important that detailed guidelines are laid down, for example in the construction industry, the Latham Report states that 'clients are at the core of the process and their needs must be met by industry'. The construction industry has produced many publications to help to educate building and construction clients about the procurement process and how to fulfill their responsibilities within it (Latham, 1994). The experience of the client can have a huge bearing on the project process (see Figure 5.2).

The Project Management in Action case at the end of Chapter 1, 'The making of a city technology

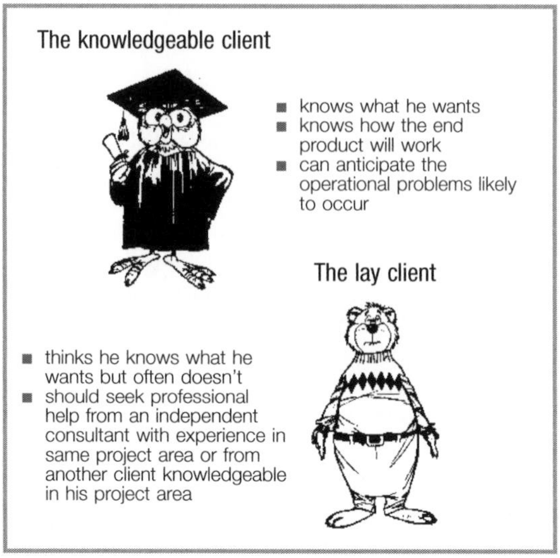

The knowledgeable client

- knows what he wants
- knows how the end product will work
- can anticipate the operational problems likely to occur

The lay client

- thinks he knows what he wants but often doesn't
- should seek professional help from an independent consultant with experience in same project area or from another client knowledgeable in his project area

Figure 5.2 The knowledgeable versus the lay client

college', is an example of a project in which the sponsor was a consortium made up of local businesses in partnership with the DES. It illustrates how stakeholders can create tensions in a project by pulling in different directions. In the end good management and strong leadership helped to keep this project on course for a successful outcome. In contrast to this is the Project Management in Action: 'The $26 million "Oops!"' in Chapter 10, where weak leadership by a public sponsor led to confusion, delays and mistrust.

Senior management

The project manager needs the participation of senior management because much power resides with them. Senior management decide whether the project will proceed. They also determine the extent of support the project will receive relative to other projects. If they do not view the project as having much strategic importance, senior management will allocate resources to more 'significant' endeavours.

The importance of senior management's participation becomes clear when there is a split over how important a project is. This may give a project a 'stop and go' mode of operation which can result in poor productivity and low morale. The problem can become even worse if management withdraw their support.

For example, senior management may waver in

support of a project due to changing market conditions. One month they support the project; the next month they give priority attention to another one. People with special skills may be pulled from the original project and sent to another and then returned later. As a result, the employees start feeling insignificant rather than valued and contributing members of the project and ultimately the company.

Senior management's participation is critical but what is even more important is the style of participation. If they participate in an overbearing, authoritative manner, senior management may constrain the project manager and, consequently, the project. Senior management must do what they do best – manage. They should not tell members of the team how to do their jobs. If senior management want the project to succeed, they must allow the project manager and team members the latitude to do the job. That means delegating, something many senior managers fail to do.

Senior management must not, however, adopt a policy of benign neglect. They must keep abreast of what occurs on the project. The emphasis is on what, not how. Feedback up and down the chain of command is absolutely essential.

The project board

A project board or steering committee is a group of people, usually from within the sponsor's organisation, who have been given responsibility for making executive-level decisions on behalf of the sponsor, throughout the project. The project board oversees the planning and execution of the project. The project board meets regularly with the project manger to review project progress and consider issues that cannot be resolved by the project manger.

Some project boards are primarily there to consider issues and make recommendations, acting in an advisory capacity. At other times the project board or steering committee is responsible for making decisions concerning budget and expenditure.

The project schedule can be adversely affected in a project where everything must be passed before the steering committee for approval. Committees that consist of more than three or four people are difficult to convene at a convenient time for all, consequently they generally meet infrequently. This can cause hold-ups where the board must make a decision before further progress can be made. Some sponsors will appoint an executive chairperson to the board who can make decisions quickly and efficiently

between meetings of the project board. It is important to safeguard the sponsor's investment so a balance is required between speed and efficiency and the reduction of risk.

Another disadvantage of a large project board is that often there are large differences of opinion that are difficult to resolve. Meetings tend to be prolonged and progress can be slow. The development of the UK millennium dome was managed by the New Experience Company, but was required to seek advice and approval on many issues from a variety of panels and boards. The people doing the work were often frustrated at the number of meetings and boards that their contribution had to pass through before they could actually get on and execute their plans (Wilhide, 1999).

The project champion

A project champion is someone who grasps the benefits of and is enthusiastic about the project. Both empirical research and anecdotal evidence have long supported the importance of the champion for successful project implementation (Pinto and Slevin, 1989). The role adopted by project champions is typically nontraditional and often contains one or more of the following elements:

- *Cheerleader* – providing the needed motivation (spiritual driving force) for the project team
- *Visionary* – maintaining a clear sense of purpose and a firm idea of what is involved in creating the project
- *Politician* – playing the necessary political games and maintaining the important contacts to ensure broad-based acceptance of the project on the part of the rest of the organisation
- *Risk taker* – being willing to take calculated personal or career risks to bring the project to fruition, for example Louise Clark, in the Project Management in Action: 'Roadkill the movie' at the end of Chapter 4
- *Ambassador* – maintaining good contacts with the three groups external to and affecting the project (intended users, top management and the rest of the impacted organisation).

Anyone can be a project champion; however, there are several characteristic traits to look out for in potential project champions. They:

- have some personal or positional power in the organisation
- are willing to use that power to benefit the project
- use their power somewhat nontraditionally or entrepreneurially
- go well beyond their expected and traditional job responsibilities to help the project.

While it is common to find senior managers serving as champions and having the necessary influence, mid-level employees who 'have the ear' of senior management and are empowered to make decisions and deliver results can also play the role of champion, and become powerful assets to the project, helping to keep the project a priority on the firm's agenda and the necessary resources committed. At other times it is the project manager who must assume the role of project champion.

According to Pinto and Slevin (1989) there are four types of project champion.

1. *Creative originator* – an engineer, scientist or similar such person who is the source of and driving force behind the idea.
2. *Entrepreneur* – the person who adopts the idea and actively works to 'sell' the project throughout the organisation, eventually pushing it to success.
3. *'Godfather'* (or *Sponsor*) – a senior-level manager who does everything possible to promote the project, including obtaining the needed resources, coaching the team when problems arise, calming the political waters and protecting the project when necessary.
4. *Project manager* – the project leader who handles the operational planning and day-to-day details, for example independent film producer, Colin Brunton, who played a key role as project manager and project champion in the making of *Roadkill* (see Project Management in Action at the end of Chapter 4).

The Insights from Industry box shows how two project champions assisted a technology project at different times and in different ways to help to ensure success for a medium-sized manufacturing company. The initial champion was the creative innovator, who originally conceived of the idea for the project and led the early push for project development. Later, during the project's full development and implementation, a senior executive effectively took over the championing role as the project's 'godfather'.

insights from INDUSTRY

MULTIPLE PROJECT CHAMPIONS HELP ENSURE SUCCESS

A medium-sized manufacturing firm initiated a project to install a comprehensive computer-aided design and manufacturing (CAD/CAM) system for its shop floor operations. Successful development of this project was forecast to reduce front-end production process times and costs by almost 15%. The original champion role was filled by a senior production engineer who effectively lobbied upper management for the innovation and then worked throughout the conceptualisation and project planning stages to eliminate objections, budgetary roadblocks and scheduling conflicts.

While originally viewed as something of a nuisance, his single-minded energy eventually won over enough support to initiate pre-development studies and then project development funding. Once the project was under way, the championing role was assumed by the vice-president of manufacturing, who by now had perceived the many benefits of successful implementation. His primary assistance to the project came in the form of smoothing the political side of the implementation effort and ensuring continued funding, even in the midst of an economic downturn. Furthermore, he enlisted support for the project from the engineering department, probably the most important group of eventual users of the CAD/CAM system.

Source: Pinto, J.K. and Slevin, D.P. 'The project champion: key to implementation success', *Project Management Journal*, 1989, **20**(4): 15–20

Consultants and contractors

Consultants

The role of the consultant (for example architect, management consultant, occupational psychologist, designer) is to act on behalf of the client to deliver a service, usually with deliverables in the form of (Turner, 1995):

Advice:
- information not easily available
- impartial interpretations of information
- special know-how
- provide management with arguments to justify fait accompli decisions

- provide temporary intensive help

Information:
- published information
- multiclient studies
- specially commissioned studies

Assignments:
- marketing research
- commercial research
- technical development

Contractors

The people who do the work on a project can be internal or external to the sponsor's organisation. External participants are commonly referred to as 'contractors', 'subcontractors' and even 'sub-subcontractors':

- *contractors* – organisations brought in to provide some or all of the project deliverables, for example a software house. Where there is one contractor with a lead role in the project, the term 'prime contractor' may be used.
- *subcontractors* – organisations brought in by the contractor to provide specialist services in certain areas of the project, for example a security firm. Where a sponsor specifies a specific subcontractor which a contractor must use, the term 'named subcontractor' applies.
- *sub-subcontractors* – firms brought in by a subcontractor, for example an equipment and plant hire firm.

Traditionally, contractors, unlike consultants and other participants, are often appointed to conduct an activity which has already been clearly defined by others. They are therefore less able to influence the sponsor's requirements as far as their contribution to the project is concerned. However, there are variations to this general rule that are discussed in Chapter 6 on procurement.

The importance of managing expectations

There are often many stakeholders in a project and dissatisfied or disillusioned stakeholders can cause a project to fail. Managing stakeholder perceptions and expectations is about generating agreement and harmony between the different views and beliefs held by the stakeholders. The Critical Considerations box highlights the difficulties of perception between two married people; how much more difficult for a project manager to be sure of the thoughts, feelings and attitudes of a project's stakeholders.

When all the stakeholders are 'dancing to the same tune', the project moves towards a successful outcome. One of the amazing wonders of nature is the way that insects such as ants, termites, and wasps can create intricate, delicate and wonderfully made structures. These 'projects' are executed successfully despite varying conditions and all manner of natural obstacles in their way. At each stage in these projects, hundreds or thousands of 'project participants' seem to know what to do, when and where; and seem able to make their own micro-contribution fit within a

---

CRITICAL CONSIDERATIONS

PERCEPTION

A few years ago I met a good friend while in a local restaurant. I asked the friend how things were going. 'Fine,' he said, 'the job's good, and the family couldn't be better.' He went on to say that in these days of shattered families he was lucky to have such a good marriage. He and his wife were very close and felt terrible for all the couples they knew who had separated. I agreed, and said how pleased I was that things were going so well.

As you might have guessed, the next time I saw my friend, some six weeks later, he was ashen-faced, haggard and visibly shaken. He said that a week after our previous meeting, his wife had told him that she was very unhappy and wanted to separate. After some intense conversations and several sessions with a marriage counselor, they did just that. Now he was on his own, living in a small, furnished apartment until they could arrange a settlement. He shook his head and wondered aloud how he could have been so blind as not to see his wife's unhappiness.

Understanding what is happening inside someone else, even a spouse, requires information, energy, time, and an empathetic view of the person. In addition, it requires an ability to perceive reality as it is rather than as we would like it to be.

Source: R. Block *The Politics of Projects*, Yourdon Press, Englewood Cliffs, NJ (1983)

single overall project objective. If only all projects shared these same characteristics.

In reality, most projects have stakeholders that look at the project from different perspectives and hold different expectations. Newcombe (2000) reports that project performance continues to be viewed in contrasting ways by different stakeholders. For example:

- the manager of a department that has requested a new information system may desire basic functionality and low cost, the system architect may emphasise technical excellence and the programming contractor may be interested in maximising profit
- a director of research may link new product success to state-of-the-art technology, the operations director may define it as world-class practices and the marketing director may be more concerned with cramming in as many new features as possible
- the owner of a property development project may be focused on timely performance, local government may wish to maximise tax revenue, an environmental group may wish to minimise adverse environmental impact and nearby residents may hope to relocate the project altogether.

These differences are not necessarily undesirable. Correctly managed, different perspectives can promote creativity, which is often how the best solution eventually emerges (Amabile, 1998). However, as a project progresses beyond the early planning stages, significant residual differences between the main stakeholders can be harmful and may interfere with the successful completion of the different phases of the project life cycle. Figure 5.3, although fairly well worn, illustrates this effect in a humorous and effective way by considering ten views of the same project through the eyes of its stakeholders.

With congruence between stakeholders, the project manager can be more confident that all effort is being directed towards the same project goals, and the project is less likely to suffer wasted time and effort, inefficiencies, scope changes, harmful conflict and unhappy customers. One of the difficulties of managing this process is that many of these differences can remain hidden for a time. Stakeholder analysis, discussed below, is a technique that can be used to help to identify project stakeholders and discern their values, beliefs, assumptions and expectations at the start of a project. The stages involved are:

- identification and analysis
- mapping stakeholders according to their impact on the project
- response and resolution of issues.

Stakeholder identification and analysis

Identifying a few of the stakeholders in a project is easy, finding all of them can be fraught with difficulty. In addition to the more familiar technique of brainstorming, other useful problem-solving techniques that can be used are brain-writing and the Crawford slip method (Newell, 2002), both adaptations of brainstorming.

Visit the website

http://www.palgrave.com/business/gardiner

▶ for help and advice on using three problem-solving techniques for project managers: brainstorming, brain-writing and Crawford slip method

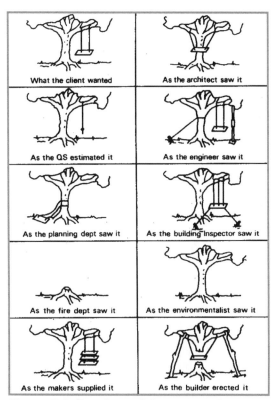

Figure 5.3 Ten views of the same project through the eyes of its stakeholders

What the client wanted

As the architect saw it

As the QS estimated it

As the engineer saw it

As the planning dept saw it

As the building inspector saw it

As the fire dept saw it

As the environmentalist saw it

As the makers supplied it

As the builder erected it

Establishing what stakeholders really want and expect is far from straightforward. The process can be aided by asking them lots of questions. People are rarely clear in their first answers and a good project manager can build credibility rapidly by helping stakeholders to clarify their ideas. Furthermore, each individual stakeholder is embedded in some form of organisational culture that will fuel and/or influence their perception of and behaviour towards the project. Consequently, it is also useful to have some appreciation of the types of organisational culture to which they belong. Handy (1993), for example, defines culture along the lines of power, role, task and person, although a more intricate 'cultural web' is discussed in Johnson and Scholes (2002). An informative collection of articles on culture and cultural change can also be found in the *Harvard Business Review on Culture and Change* (2002).

Another aspect of the task for the project leader is to identify where one stakeholder's expectations clash with those of another and encourage the parties to talk to each other with a view to resolving areas of conflict. For example, when developing a new product, reconciling the expectations of finance directors, design engineers, production teams, marketing consultants and customers is a high-level leadership skill. In these situations, the project manager often acts as a broker, or negotiator, trying to find a best-fit solution that meets as many needs as possible.

Projects that exhibit chronic or irreconcilable differences between the needs of the various stakeholders are best redefined, shelved until a later date or abandoned altogether. In these cases, the probability of success (through anyone's eyes) is extremely low.

Mapping the impact of stakeholders onto the project

Once the stakeholders and their expectations have been identified, they can be organised by mapping them in relation to their likely impact on the project. For example, it is important to know:

- whether or not they are likely to support or oppose the project
- the power and means available for them to do so
- the predictability of their behaviour and expected level of interest in the project.

These factors can be evaluated using matrices which aid the sponsor and project manager in understanding the various threats and appropriate management approaches to apply (Lederer and Sethi, 1991). The three matrices presented here are similar in their approach. After the mapping is completed, managers

can develop tactics or strategies to deal most appropriately with each stakeholder. Example responses for all three matrices are also shown below.

Position/importance matrix

This matrix, shown in Figure 5.4, categorises stakeholders according to their level of support or opposition to the project and their relative importance to the project sponsor.

Four categories of stakeholders result from analysis with this matrix (Nutt and Backoff, 1992: 196–8; Bryson, 1995: 284–6):

A Problematic stakeholders oppose the project, and are relatively unimportant to the organisation. *Response:* Target moderate stakeholders with educational programmes, adjust project plans to accommodate stakeholders, and prepare defensive plans if coalitions of stakeholders form.

B Antagonistic stakeholders oppose or are hostile to the project and are important to the organisation. *Response:* Identify potential coalitions and take defensive action, prepare for undermining supporters, anticipate nature of objections and develop counterarguments, and engage selected stakeholders in bargaining, and determining planned changes to gain support.

C Low priority stakeholders support the project and are relatively unimportant to the organisation. *Response:* Provide educational programmes and promote involvement with supporters.

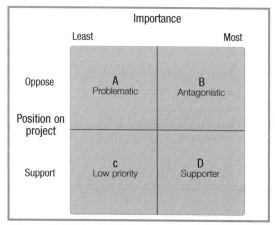

Figure 5.4 The position/importance matrix for project stakeholders (Nutt and Backoff, 1992; Bryson, 1995)

D Supporter stakeholders support the project and are important to the organisation.
Response: Provide information to reinforce position, and ask supporters to influence indifferent stakeholders.

Power/predictability matrix

This matrix, shown in Figure 5.5, maps stakeholder power against predictability and shows where political efforts are best channelled during the project.

As with the position/importance matrix, project managers should develop strategies to influence stakeholders or counter the power of stakeholders. The four possible types of stakeholders are:

A Highly predictable stakeholders with low power that present few problems.
Response: Not critical, little or no action required.

B Unpredictable stakeholders with low power that are manageable.
Response: Although not critical, these stakeholders should not be ignored as they might have an influence on the attitude of the more powerful stakeholders.

C Powerful stakeholders that are predictable.
Response: These stakeholders are problematic but sponsors should attempt to influence their stance by formulating strategies that will address their expectations or demands.

D Powerful stakeholders with low predictability that present the greatest danger or opportunity for the organisation.
Response: These are the most difficult to manage stakeholders. They are in a position to block or support new strategies or programmes. The sponsor should test out project ideas with this group of stakeholders prior to detailed planning or execution.

Power/interest matrix

The third matrix (Figure 5.6) maps stakeholder power against expected interest in the project and helps to determine the best strategy for managing stakeholder expectations.

The four possible types of stakeholders are:

A Stakeholders with low power and a low level of interest.
Response: No immediate action required – monitor carefully in case their position in the matrix changes.

B Stakeholders with low power and a high level of interest.
Response: No immediate action required – keep informed and monitor carefully in case their position in the matrix changes.

C Stakeholders with high power and a low level of interest.
Response: These are the most challenging stakeholders to maintain relationships with as, despite their lack of interest in general, such a stakeholder might exercise its power in reaction to a particular project or initiative.

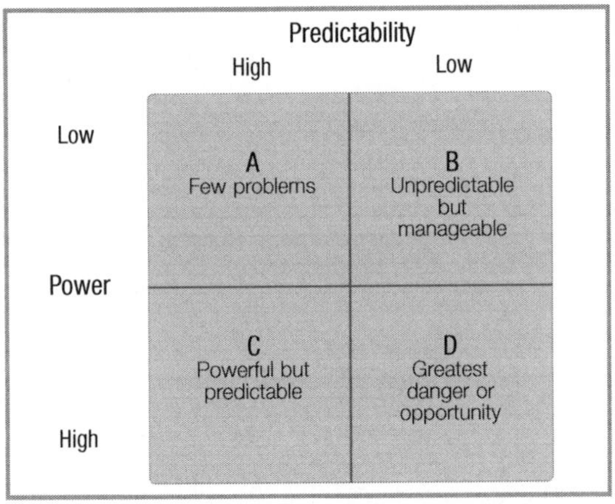

Figure 5.5 Matrix of stakeholder power versus predictability (Johnson and Scholes, 2002)

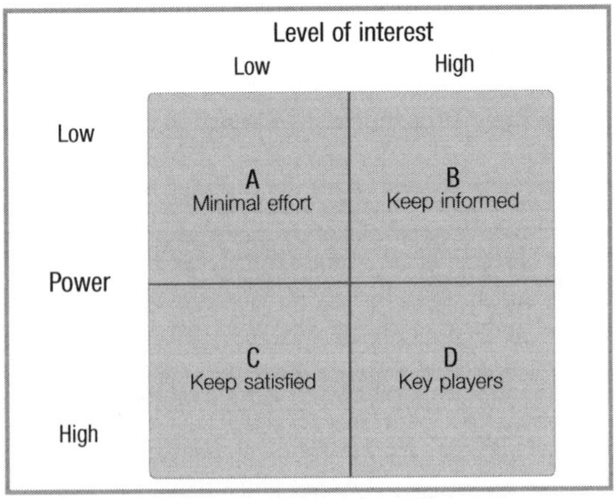

Figure 5.6 Matrix of stakeholder power versus level of interest (Johnson and Scholes, 2002)

D Stakeholders with high power and a high level of interest.

Response: These stakeholders are the 'key players', their reaction towards the organisation's projects and initiatives must be given primary consideration.

From 'managing' to 'collaborating with' stakeholders

Recent research and consulting efforts have focused on changing the relationship between the project and its stakeholders from 'management' to 'collaboration'. Stakeholder management emphasises mechanisms of how an organisation can identify, monitor and respond to its stakeholders. The mechanisms include issue analysis, consultation, strategic communication and formal contacts. The impression created here is that managers can direct and control the interactions with stakeholders, and that the main purpose is to buffer the organisation or project from negative or challenging stakeholder activities. In the organisation, the responsibility for stakeholder management is generally assigned to functional departments rather than senior managers or executives.

The collaboration approach, on the other hand, focuses on building stakeholder relationships that are reciprocal, evolving and mutually defined, and that are a source of opportunity and competitive advantage. Collaboration is a meta-capability to establish and maintain relationships which allows the organisation to tap into a powerful source of creative energy, a large pool of innovative ideas and a wider network (Liedtka, 1996). The goal here is to increase the organisation's environmental stability and enhance control over changing circumstances. This approach is more integrated and company-wide, with responsibility for stakeholder collaboration assigned to a senior executive (Svendsen, 1998: 2–5).

PROJECT MANAGEMENT *in action*

Easy Finance Ltd

Easy Finance is a small company providing tailor-made financial products for its customers. Although relative growth had been slow over the past few years, Easy were in a strong position in their particular market segment, targeting customers who were routinely refused finance from other sources.

Managing Director, Sol, had purchased a low-budget PC for his grandson and, watching him play with the machine, was astonished at the speed with which the grandson had mastered the complexity of the software and was delighted to see the hours of fun the young lad was having. Whilst waiting for the bus to work, it occurred to him that if his staff showed a similar amount of enthusiasm and commitment towards the office business, he could give the competition a very hard time.

At 9.30am the same day, he called a meeting of his staff to discuss their views on information technology. Four people were present at the meeting:

Raymond Slick, the sales manager, Gordon Grabbitt, financial director and company accountant, and William Wolf, the marketing manager. He put the question to Gordon Grabbitt: 'What should we be doing about information technology? I understand that we can save at least 20% of our operating costs, and improve our application processing time by up to 50% if we purchase an integrated computer system'.

Raymond Slick and William Wolf eyed each other nervously and shuffled in their seats, glad that Gordon Grabbitt was to answer the question.

Grabbitt cleared his throat nervously, stared Sol in the eye and said, 'I have no idea!'.

'Well, find out' said Sol, and here the meeting ended.

Among his close friends, Gordon had a number of accountants who had introduced computer systems into their companies and so his first reaction was to phone them and ask their advice. After all morning on the telephone, he had narrowed it down to three suppliers in the area. He duly phoned them and asked them to send a list of their products with prices. He then phoned Sol who seemed pleased with the speed with which things were moving. The next day, and before the glossy brochures had arrived, Gordon was sitting behind his desk performing endless calculations on the back of an envelope.

'Mr M Byte from BOW to see you Mr Grabbitt.'

'Send him in', said Gordon.

Mr Byte was a fresh-faced young man who seemed to talk more quickly than he had ever heard anyone talk before and in a language which seemed more like a Chinese dialect than English.

'It appears to me, I've got what you need', said Martie Byte. 'You must spend a lot of time with calculations in this company. We have just the machine for you which is compatible with all the big names. It should perform all those calculations before you can say "double entry". Fortunately, this month there is a 20% reduction in price for anyone who wants to buy two'.

'Yes! But what does it do?' asked Gordon.

'Well! It has revolutionary DVD-R capability, a GeForce3 graphics card and LAN interface options. What more could you want?', said Martie.

'Oh! I see', said Gordon, not wishing to appear unknowledgeable. 'But what can it do for me?'

'Never mind that', said Martie. 'It can do everything but boil eggs!' he added on reflection.

During the next week two more salesmen visited Easy, who seemed to talk in the same strange Chinese dialect, leaving Gordon exhausted and bewildered.

'What am I to do?' he thought. 'I can't make a technical assessment and neither can anyone else in the firm, so I suppose the best thing to do would be to go for the company which is going to be around in five years time, that is offering the cheapest machine.'

So Gordon placed an order with BOW (Better Off Without) and the two machines arrived the following week. The first thing Martie did when he delivered the machine, was plug it in. Easy had agreed that BOW should provide the sales team with two days training on the system.

'Right', said Martie, 'gather round.'

Six startled sales advisors gathered round in silence, whilst Martie ran through what they had to do to operate the system. It was clear, however, that after half an hour, he had lost everyone, as the team had started talking amongst themselves. Nevertheless, BOW had contracted to give them training, and training was what they were going to get. Everyone understood by the end of the day how to start the machine and load the software application.

'All they had to do', thought Martie, 'was read the manual and follow the instructions.'

Two months later, Sol requested a computer printout.

'Anything will do', said Sol. 'I just want to see what the machine can do.' Twenty four hours later, the report was ready. Sol stared aghast at the volume and wondered quietly how many trees had been chopped down to provide him with this report. Flicking through the pages it became clear that there was information on everything under the sun, but it meant nothing to him. He

rang Gordon, William and Raymond and asked them what information the computer was providing them with.

They all said together, 'Lots.'

'But what does it all mean?', asked Sol.

'I have no idea', they all said, not wishing to be associated with too many decisions.

'Well. How are you making your decisions?'

'Seat of the pants', said Raymond.

'As usual', said Sol.

'Inspired guesswork', said William.

'Well I work it out with a pencil', said Gordon. 'And where does the information come from?', asked Sol.

'From the files', they all said.

'Which files?', asked Sol, exasperated.

'The manual files', said Richard.

'So you mean to say that we spent £30,000 on all this new IT equipment and we are still using the manual files?'

'Yes', they replied with one voice.

QUESTIONS TO AID UNDERSTANDING AND DISCUSSION

1. What role did Sol play in this project? How well did he perform?

2. Who were the other stakeholders in the project?

3. Would the use of stakeholder analysis tools help to predict the behaviour of any stakeholders in this project?

4. Why did this project fail?

5. What recommendations would you make to Sol?

6. Is the use of project management justified for a small company like Easy Finance?

Summary points

■ Project stakeholders are individuals, groups and organisations who are actively involved in the project, or whose interests may be positively or negatively affected as a result of the project.

■ The role of the project manager is 'to attain the project objectives'. In doing so the project manager must simultaneously see to the needs of the sponsor and other stakeholders, manage the project life cycle and the performance of the project team, including his or her own performance.

■ The core competencies required by project managers can be divided into two categories: soft skills (for example leading, communicating, negotiating, problem solving and influencing the organisation) and hard skills (for example planning, scheduling and controlling).

▓ Two useful guiding principles are that all decisions should be directed towards achieving the project objectives and only the remaining work in the project can be managed.

▓ A project needs to be well packaged and marketed if people are going to take an interest in it and buy into the idea.

▓ Sponsors can be notoriously complex organisations, with many formal and informal relationships between different functions and business units. There may be hidden agendas and power struggles going on. Managing a project amidst this uncertainty is one of the more difficult leadership requirements of the project manager's role.

▓ Project managers often have a small number of key players around them who constitute their core team. This will include representation from the sponsor and, depending on the size of the project, assistant project managers, contract managers, project management support staff and professional advisors.

▓ Other key stakeholders are the project board (or steering committee) and project champions. In the wider context, stakeholders such as contractors, government agencies, pressure groups and unions may also influence a project.

▓ It is important to know as much about project stakeholders and their likely behaviour as possible. A variety of techniques are available for identifying and analysing project stakeholders.

Visit the website

http://www.palgrave.com/business/gardiner

▶ to test your understanding of the learning objectives for Chapter 5 using multiple choice questions

In the next chapter we shall examine organisation structures and their influence on the project management process, as well as a range of procurement choices available for sponsors seeking to have some or all their project managed by a third party.

References

Amabile, T.M. (1998). 'How to kill creativity', *Harvard Business Review*, September–October: 77–87.

APM (2000). *Body of Knowledge* (4th edn), APM, High Wycombe.

Bryson, J.M. (1995). *Strategic Planning for Public and Nonprofit Organizations: A Guide to Strengthening and Sustaining Organizational Achievement* (rev. edn), Jossey-Bass, San Francisco.

Handy, C.B. (1993). *Understanding Organizations* (4th edn), Penguin, Harmondsworth.

Harvard Business Review (ed.) (2002). *Harvard Business Review on Culture and Change*, Harvard Business School Press, MA.

IPMA (1999). *IPMA Competence Baseline (ICB) Version 2.0*, International Project Management Association (IPMA), Monmouth.

Johnson, G. and Scholes, K. (2002). *Exploring Corporate Strategy* (6th edn), Prentice Hall, New York.

Kotter, J.P. (1985). *Power and Influence: Beyond Formal Authority*, Free Press, New York.

Latham, M. (1994). 'Constructing the team: final report of the government/industry review of procurement and contractual arrangements in the UK construction industry', HMSO, London.

Lederer, A.L. and Sethi, V. (1991). 'Managing organizational issues in information systems development', *Journal of Business Strategy*, **12**(6): 38–43.

Liedtka, J. (1996). 'Collaborating across lines of business for competitive advantage', *Academy of Management Executive Journal*, **10**(2): 20–37.

Newcombe, R. (2000). 'The anatomy of two projects: a comparative analysis approach', *International Journal of Project Management*, **18**(3): 189–99.

Newell, M.W. (2002). *Preparing for the Project Management Professional (PMP) Certification Exam* (2nd edn), American Management Association, New York.

Nutt, P.C. and Backoff, R.W. (1992). *Strategic Management of Public and Third Sector Organizations: A Handbook for Leaders*, Jossey-Bass, San Francisco.

Pinto, J.K. (2000). 'Understanding the role of politics in successful project management', *International Journal of Project Management*, **18**(2): 85–91.

Pinto, J.K. and Slevin, D.P. (1989). 'The project champion: key to implementation success', *Project Management Journal*, **20**(4): 15–20.

PMI (2000). *Guide to the project management body of knowledge*, Project Management Institute, Upper Darby, PA.

Stokes, I. (1997), *Training for Project Management: Volume 1 – Skills and Principles*, Gower, Aldershot.

Svendsen, A. (1998). *The Stakeholder Strategy: Profiting from Collaborative Business Relationships*, Berrett-Koehler, San Francisco.

Turner, R.J. (1995) *The Commercial Project Manager: Managing Owners, Sponsors, Partners, Supporters, Stakeholders, Contractors and Consultants*, McGraw-Hill, London.

Wilhide, E. (1999). *The Millennium Dome*, HarperCollins, London.

Visit the website

http://www.palgrave.com/business/gardiner

▶ for additional resources to explore the topics in this chapter further

6 Organisation and procurement

Learning objectives

After reading this chapter you should be able to:

- compare and contrast different organisational structures and their impact on projects
- discuss the procurement choices available in project management
- identify and describe the main parts of a procurement plan
- identify the key features of common contract types and explain the differences between them
- select appropriate contracts and justify their use in a range of situations
- explain what is meant by incentive contracting and perform basic financial calculations
- differentiate between common partnering arrangements, their merits and pitfalls

Introduction

Project organisation is about structuring and integrating the internal project environment through careful planning and organisation design. The relationship between participating organisations and the interface between their respective functions and departments affect all aspects of project management. Theories of organisation design have resulted in a variety of organisational forms and approaches to procurement. Each has its own advantages and disadvantages. In particular, the effectiveness of different forms of matrix organisation and their management are elaborated. The increasing use of virtual organisations is also discussed.

Project organisation leads on to procurement as a means of implementing projects using external resources and expertise for all or part of a project. The procurement process is considered from a supply chain perspective. The chapter includes a look at a variety of approaches that can be used to engage and organise the parties to a project. Procurement is bound up with contracts and contract law and these are also dealt with briefly. The advantages and disadvantages of the more common forms of fixed price, cost plus and international contracts are examined.

The relevance of organisation structure

The internal environment of a project consists of the people, groups and organisations that are directly involved in the project. This includes the way in which the major stakeholders of a project are organised and how they relate to each other and their environment.

The project's organisation structure defines the reporting structures, processes, systems and procedures of the project. There is no such thing as a perfect organisation structure, in all cases there are advantages and disadvantages. Important issues in the structuring of a project include the degree of project-functional orientation, the extent of project management authority, collocation of project members, the allocation of resources, work packaging and interface management, and the definition of control, authorisation and reporting procedures and systems (APM, 2000: 47).

Projects are carried out in a myriad of organisational forms. These organisation structures have evolved in response to the major structural dilemmas faced by all organisations (Bolman and Deal, 1997: 60–1):

- differentiation versus integration
- gaps versus overlaps
- underuse versus overload
- lack of clarity versus lack of creativity
- excessive autonomy versus excessive interdependence
- too loose versus too tight – vertical and horizontal
- diffuse authority versus overcentralisation
- goalless versus goal-bound
- irresponsible versus unresponsive.

These dilemmas in turn relate to the five organisational principles espoused by the classical theorists (Robbins, 1993):

1. departmentalisation
2. unity of command
3. span of control
4. division of labour
5. authority and responsibility.

Table 6.1 shows how modern day dilemmas map onto the principles of the classical theorists. Not much has changed; modern day companies continue to struggle with organisational issues in their projects. This is well illustrated in the Insights from Industry box which shows an extract from a project audit performed at one of the sites of a large European defence contractor.

There are two basic organisation structures (Burns and Stalker, 1994):

1. *mechanistic structures*, which are command and control based
2. *organic structures*, which are open and less rigid and where value is placed on using special knowledge with open communication.

Modern structures tend to adopt more of the organic characteristics, whilst older legacy structures tend to be more mechanistic, reflecting their traditional and classical origins. Even when a project is about creating a new organisation, for example joint ventures, the project will still be influenced by the organisations that set it up. This is typified by the Project Management in Action: 'The Scottish Qualifications Authority' in Chapter 3, where the organisational maturity of the main participants, that is, their project management systems, culture, style, structure and project management support, had a

insights from INDUSTRY

ORGANISATION AND COMMUNICATION ISSUES FOR A DEFENCE PROJECT CONTRACTOR

The comments below relate to a large European defence contractor. They were highlighted during some recent research using capability maturity models for performance improvement:

- Mechanical engineers are not involved early enough in projects, especially at the bidding stage
- Information is not forthcoming when it needs to be
- Despite some improvement, there is still a lack of involvement of design-for-manufacture (DFM) personnel in the early design stages
- The matrix system was generally regarded as a positive organisational approach to manage scarce resources effectively; however, losing the advantages of collocation is a heavy price to pay and limits concurrency
- The matrix structure does not cope well with resource peaks
- The manufacturing and quality departments feel isolated from mechanical design
- Mechanical design feel isolated from systems, software and electrical/electronics
- Few team-based tools are in use for generating creative ideas and problem solving
- There tends to be dissatisfaction with the managers and project lead engineers going to project meetings all the time and not allowing others to get involved.

Table 6.1 Similarities between classical organisational theorists and modern day organisational dilemmas

Classical theorist principles	Equivalent modern day issue
Departmentalisation	Differentiation versus integration
Unity of command	Excessive autonomy versus excessive interdependence
Span of control	Too loose versus too tight
Division of labour	Vertical and horizontal
Authority and responsibility	Diffuse authority versus over-centralisation

major influence on the project management process (PMI, 2000).

The following sections examine four organisational structures: functional, product (or projectised), matrix and, a newer organisational form, the virtual organisation.

Functional structure

The functional structure (see Figure 6.1) is by far the most common organisational form used by companies. It is also referred to as the traditional structure or classical structure. In a functional structure people are grouped by discipline and their level of authority in a top-down hierarchy. Traditionally, as an organisation grew in size, it recruited more supervisors to keep control and manage its workers in each of its disciplines. Then, as the number of supervisors grew, the functional manager would appoint assistant managers to manage and control the supervisors. And so it went on.

The main characteristics of the functional structure are:

■ deep structures with many levels and bosses with impressive titles – career progression is an upward struggle, ascending through the various levels one by one.
■ relatively weak coordination and communication between functions – issues that involve more than one function often take a disproportionately long time to resolve. Sometimes it is hard to track down who the problem owner should be. The decision-making process may have to go up and down the different functions and levels several times before an issue is finally resolved. This is time-consuming and detrimental to the progress of project work through the organisation.
■ no customer focal point – since the main focus is on the management and control of the separate functions and not the customer, customer care is often poor or lacking altogether. The business processes are not organised to benefit the customer. Even when a customer support function does exist, it is often in name only and may have difficulty resolving issues quickly and to the satisfaction of the customer.
■ allegiance and commitment are to the function and not to the projects passing through the function – scheduling and control of project work is often haphazard, with little emphasis on maintaining deadlines and customer delivery promise dates.

Its main advantages are that:

■ there are vertical communication channels within the functions – communication and decision making within a function may be good, although where decision-making responsibility is retained by more senior managers, the process can still be slow.
■ the functional manager has complete autonomy and control over manpower resources, budgeting and cost control – this means the function is extremely flexible and able to deal with large fluctuations in workload since the functional manager simply assigns and reassigns manpower as he or she sees fit.
■ there is often a large concentration of specialists providing the organisation with competitive advantage, enabling the firm to offer more complex and technically challenging services than smaller organisations.
■ there is often investment in function-specific technology – the cost of expensive specialists and technology can be spread across many projects.

On balance, the functional organisation is not very well suited for rapid and efficient execution of projects because:

■ work typically passes through the organisation in an uncoordinated suboptimal manner, often without a project manager being assigned. Each time a job passes from one functional section to

Figure 6.1 The functional (or traditional) organisation structure

another, a new manager or supervisor becomes responsible for getting the next part of the work done, and then moving the job on to its next destination. When a company has many projects in progress at the same time, it is common for some jobs to lie waiting at different stages (sometimes for long periods of time) to suit the scheduling needs of the function.

■ the customer often finds it a battle to get work done quickly, and may feel that no one really cares about delivery promise dates. The system can seem to be inflexible and inefficient, even though the quality of the end product may be consistently high.

■ genuine projects may have project managers assigned to them but these project managers may still not be given priority by the functional managers concerned. This makes the project manager's job extremely frustrating, but with little recourse for action.

Over time, functional structures can become bureaucracies; consider the structure of any government. As layers and layers of middle management build up, there is less and less horizontal or vertical communication taking place. Two employees in two different departments may have to contact five people before they can talk to each other.

The functional structure is slow to respond to environmental changes. For example, several years ago, when IBM first reorganised, they moved from a functional structure to a divisional structure. Under the functional structure, every time there was a proposal for a new product it had to go through several functional departments, slowing down new product development to a point where some new products never left the warehouse.

Product (or projectised) structure

In a product structure, people are organised according to the product line, programme or project, they belong to. Figure 6.2 illustrates the product structure; referred to as a projectised structure in the PMI *Body of Knowledge* (PMI, 2000).

The characteristics of the product structure are:

■ employees on a particular product or project are generally collocated

■ the participants work directly for the product or programme manager – who therefore has full control over the deployment of resources.

Resource conflicts can be resolved by the programme manager according to project priorities (rather than functional priorities)

■ strong communication channels – communication is (or should be) well developed at all levels of the product, providing a quick and efficient decision-making environment

■ loyalty to the product – participants give their allegiance to the product line they belong to

■ rapid reaction time to problems and issues – participants are focused on a single product or programme so can respond quickly and appropriately when a situation arises.

Its disadvantages are that there is:

■ a tendency to retain a full complement of personnel for each product, covering each discipline, long after they are all needed; personnel are associated with a particular activity (product) and therefore identify strongly with it, leading to a risk that the closure of a product line will be delayed, despite a declining market, in a bid to avoid facing future uncertainties and unwelcome change.

■ a risk of low innovation and application of new technology over time – without the specialist focus provided by functions, the latest technological advances in a discipline may not be considered and applied, or may lag behind other organisations. Product managers may not have sufficient capital to finance expensive new technology, unlike a functional manager who can

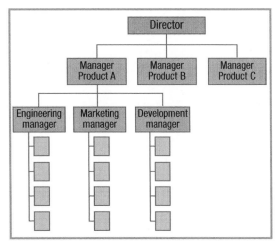

Figure 6.2 The product (or projectised) organisation structure

draw from deeper pockets, spreading the cost across many products and projects.

■ a danger that management costs might escalate – as an organisation grows in size and develops new product lines and commensurate structures to accompany them, resource requirements become duplicated and there is the inevitable drop in overall efficiency. In a traditional organisation each project has to share the same pool of resources per function or discipline, a more cost-efficient model.

Studying the characteristics of the traditional and the product structures reveals advantages and disadvantages for both forms. The functional approach is more resource-efficient and provides greater specialist knowledge. However, communication and project control are generally better developed in the product structure.

Some organisations have reorganised into a divisional structure, an organisational form similar to the product structure. Division takes place on the basis of strategic business units – a similar concept to the 'family of products' discussed above. The key advantage of the divisional structure is its rapid response time. In the case of IBM, the firm reorganised into several divisions, for example the PC division and the mainframe division. Any proposal for a new PC would be sent to the PC division and persons from manufacturing, marketing and so on responsible for PCs only would evaluate it. This was

a significant improvement over the old system of sending it through each functional area.

Matrix structure

The third organisation structure to consider is a combination of both the above forms. It is called the matrix structure, a term that generally refers to the 'project matrix' described by Galbraith (1971) and clarified by Gobeli and Larson (1987). The matrix structure attempts to integrate a projectised structure with an existing traditional structure (see Figure 6.3). It was designed to dispel the disadvantages of each while retaining their advantages. Many large companies use this method of management, including British Aerospace and Renault. In a matrix structure, vertically organised functions still exist, but these are overlaid with a cross structure of projects and project managers – two structures merged into one.

The aim of the matrix structure is to give greater visibility and management control to projects within a larger, often traditionally organised company, allowing the company to 'maintain high levels of expertise in disciplinary and functional areas' (Chambers, 1989).

Many companies endorsed the matrix structure in the late 1970s and 1980s. The matrix structure provided a way for project managers to move horizontally between departments, enabling them to

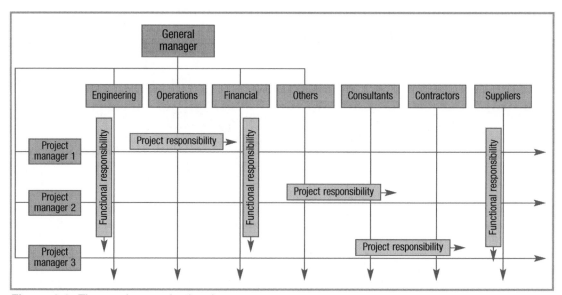

Figure 6.3 The matrix organisational structure

manage their projects more easily using participants from a wide range of functions within the organisation and across organisations. To many, the concept is simple and seems to offer great potential. However, getting it to work can still be a struggle. Insights from Industry: 'The Twingo project' describes how Renault benefited from a matrix-type structure introduced in the late 1980s and partly responsible for the success of the Twingo, a highly innovative small car. The matrix structure gives project managers a method for managing and planning, but it does not necessarily provide the goodwill (from the functions) required to do the job effectively. Project managers, hoping to take their project on to timely completion, soon realised that having a matrix structure did not guarantee cooperation.

---

insights from INDUSTRY THE TWINGO PROJECT

At the World Automobile Show in October 1992, Renault announced the launch of a small car, the Twingo, in spite of the fact that the company was already in this market with a leading product, the Clio. The new model, with its highly innovative concept, design and monobody architecture, was an enormous media success.

This project was to be first to try out new project management procedures set up in late 1988 during internal reforms in Renault. There was no strong project management in the 1970s and 80s: this role was played by a tripartite team (product, engineering and industrial production departments) in charge of coordination and reporting back to corporate decision makers sitting at the tops of the pyramids of the various departments making up the corporation.

The 1988 reforms introduced a measure of unity into project management, giving it strong enough status to carry on an equally matched dialogue with top departmental echelons. The project management role was entrusted to experienced executive personnel. The project manager was surrounded by a team comprising departmental project supervisors (products, engineering, industrial production, purchasing, sales, quality, personnel relations) with one foot in each hierarchy and operating within a matrix-type model.

The application of the above structure to the Twingo project was to be a decisive factor in enabling it to assert its unique identity and arrive at balanced choices on the product and its technology. Previously, projects had to integrate the broad lines of the strategy defined by corporate technical departments and those lines were not always consistent or suited to the specific problems to be resolved. Now project management could negotiate solutions with due regard for the project's particular constraints and opportunities. On the sales side, the work done by project management led to innovations in distribution modes and communications; these led in turn to major savings in programme costs.

The changes affect the actual working practices of all those involved, right down to the industrial draftsman at his CAD console, the industrial methods technician, the corporate buyer, the foreman and so on. Project teams do not make the automobile themselves, they enable others to make it.

From that starting point, project managers set out to implement organisational structures and working methods aimed at mobilising more effectively the many contributors to the project, enhancing communications between the various expert workers in order to anticipate possible problems, improving the trade-offs between the various logical systems involved and so on. All these principles can be summed up under one generic heading: 'concurrent engineering'.

These principles first took concrete form in the project scheduling. Formerly, the work of the various experts was performed sequentially, starting with marketing and design, going on to engineering, production methods, materials purchasing and serial production and ending up with sales. On the Twingo project, contributors traditionally playing 'downstream' roles (plant personnel, outside suppliers, sales personnel) were involved right from the beginning. The aim of this was, firstly, to enrich input into the search for solutions while some freedom of manoeuvre still existed and, secondly, to contract for solutions with those who would later be responsible for their implementation. The symmetrical opposite was also true: 'upstream' players (engineering and production methods design) were increasingly called on to implement downstream what they had designed.

Those same principles were also concretised by physically gathering together all expert personnel, to the maximum extent possible, in the same location – known as the 'project platform' (*plateau du projet* in French) – with the physical media and tools for development near at hand: drawings and models at the beginning, prototypes later and, finally, the production machinery. Formerly, workers on a project stayed where their departments were physically located, which often meant that they were far apart. Physical proximity therefore enabled time measured in weeks to be saved in solving interface problems, in particular the management of modifications dictated by industrial feasibility.

Source: C. Midler, *A management revolution at Renault,* Centre de Recherche en gestion de l'Ecole Polytechnique, (1994)

Questions

1. How did Renault manage projects before 1988?
2. How did Renault manage projects after 1988?
3. In what way did the role of the project manager change?
4. The change conferred several benefits to the project management system. What were they?
5. What evidence is there that feedback and feed forward are important in the new structure?
6. What is concurrent engineering and how did it help the Twingo project?

Laying a horizontal structure over an established traditional structure did not solve the problem of how to create effective project organisations.

The matrix structure is considered the most complex form of organisation structure, providing for maximum information exchange, management coordination and resource sharing, but at a price. By having dual management accountability, the matrix structure has sacrificed the principle of unity of command found in most bureaucracies and increased the need for integration. Both project and functional managers have authority and responsibility over the work: the functional or line manager is responsible for the 'what', 'how', and 'by whom'; the project manager decides the 'when' and 'for how much'.

However, it is well known that matrix structures have a tendency to generate conflict and can suffer from constantly changing boundaries and interfaces. Team members inside a project matrix find themselves being pulled in two directions at the same time. The functional manager and the project manager are not always able to agree regarding the deployment of resources. The inevitable result is friction and conflict at the points of intersection in the matrix structure (see Figure 6.4). This issue is compounded in a multiproject environment.

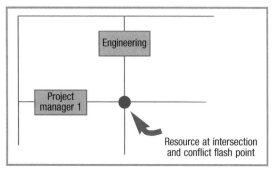

Figure 6.4 Conflict flash points in the matrix structure

Weak matrix structure

The occurrence and intensity of conflicts in a matrix organisation depend largely on the underlying culture of the organisation. When a functional culture still predominates, there is a higher risk of project conflict or project delays. The project manager has a mandate to execute a project but may have a low level of authority compared to functional managers. This represents a weak matrix structure. Such a set-up can still work but only if the functional managers accept the importance of a project and give their cooperation and goodwill to it. In a weak matrix structure, the interpersonal and project marketing skills of the project manager are critical.

Strong matrix structure

On the other hand, in an organisation where the traditional demarcation lines have become less visible, and there is a stronger process or customer focus, the project manager will have more influence in the organisational minefield. Project managers in this type of organisation are sometimes referred to as 'heavyweight project managers' (Hayes et al., 1988). Of course even in these cases good interpersonal skills are an advantage, the difference being that the rewards in terms of project success are probably greater.

Table 6.2 summarises the project-related characteristics of the different types of matrix structure and their relatives, the functional and projectised structures.

Discussion of matrix management

Matrix management is an organisational alternative to the functional silos and deep hierarchies that can adversely affect innovative and new product development projects, as highlighted in the Insights from Industry: 'Silos and hierarchies'.

Table 6.2 Influence of organisation structure on projects

Project characteristics	Organisation Structure				
	Functional	Matrix			Projectised
		Weak matrix	Balanced matrix	Strong matrix	
Project manager's authority	Little or none	Limited	Low to moderate	Moderate to high	High to almost total
Percent of performing organisation personnel assigned full time to project work	Virtually none	0–25%	15–60%	50–95%	85 – 100%
Project manager's role	Part-time	Part-time	Full-time	Full-time	Full-time
Common titles for project manager's role	Project co-ordinator/ Project leader	Project co-ordinator/ Project leader	Project manager/ Project officer	Project manager/ Programme manager	Project manager/ Programme manager
Project management administrative staff	Part-time	Part-time	Part-time	Full-time	Full-time

Source: PMI, 2000: 19.

insights from INDUSTRY SILOS AND HIERARCHIES

New product development (NPD) projects

The functional organisation is less effective for achieving important new product development (NPD) project goals than alternatives, such as a matrix with a strong project manager or a project organisation. When the NPD project manager is seeking to build a cooperative, multifunctional project team, he or she is commonly confronted with functional silos and the attendant tribal loyalties.

This is especially true in a company producing long-lived products. In these organisations, routine ongoing manufacturing is frequently seen as the producer of the goods being sold and thus the source of the resulting income. In this view, any new product is merely a disturbance to the smooth functioning of the production operation and, worse, a generator of scrap and accounting variances. Conversely, of course, such manufacturing hegemony is less prevalent in companies dominated by short product lifetimes, where new products are commonly understood to be essential. In these companies, production operations personnel are often highly receptive and cooperative.

Source: M.D. Rosenau, Jr, (1995) *The new product development project manager's burden,* Product Development and Management Associationhttp://www.pdma.org/visions/oct95/mi.html

Tapping into the benefits of the matrix structure

The following example draws on a study of selected UK and Brazilian companies to illustrate the benefits of having strong cross-functional horizontal communication over traditional deep vertical functional communication.

In a functional organisation, departments are focused on meeting their own goals. In other words, departments do not own all of a process; they simply perform an activity and then pass the result on to another department. Evidence in this study has shown that the majority of wasteful activities occur at the boundaries of traditional departments. This is aptly revealed by the statement of a machinist on the shop floor at company A (UK):

> It might be better if while the design team are studying what they intend to design, they come down to ask us if that idea would work. Instead of which they just go ahead and produce a drawing that won't work here, either because our machines are not capable of doing that or because we cannot understand what they mean by their drawing.

Because business processes cross functional boundaries, many companies have been restructuring their organisation to facilitate the horizontal flow of knowledge and activities, as stated by the production manager from company B (Brazil):

> with many people driving a process it's impossible to avoid conflicts; that's why we've reduced our

Source: Belmiro, T.R., Gardiner, P.D., Simmons, J.E.L. and Rentes, A.F. (2000) 'Are BPR practitioners really addressing business processes?', *International Journal of Operations and Production Management*, **20**(10): 1183–202

hierarchy. We realised we don't need too many bosses. If you have a person with authority to cross functions as well as people from other functions working as a team you can have a more effective process, and consequently be more productive.

The matrix structure is more adaptable to rapid social change, more responsive to individual needs and closer to the democratic ideal than the traditional structure. In particular, it is well suited to organisations where there is:

■ more than one critical orientation to the operations of the organisation, for example where there is a customer need for unified direction of the project to avoid dealing with many managers and the company needs to maintain strong specialist departments for future projects
■ a need to process simultaneously large amounts of information, for example a local social services department seeking help for an individual will need to know where to gain help from outside agencies *and* who to contact from internal resources within the organisation
■ a need for sharing of resources, including staff.

The benefits and potential pitfalls of the matrix management system are summarised in Table 6.3.

Data obtained from a study of matrix organisations used by primary and secondary contractors to the military and aerospace industries found goal conflict to be the primary disadvantage of the matrix, leading to slow reaction time in making resource allocation decisions (El-Najdawi and Liberatore, 1997). Problems of communicating long-range programme objectives to functional managers was also a concern. A key issue is for project managers to interface and communicate with functional managers in order to ease conflicts and clarify goals. The programme manager must be adept in dealing with conflict, especially with functional managers, and possess a balanced perspective of long-range objectives versus short-range goals. The failure of the matrix, espoused by many authors, is often a result of the goal conflict between programme and functional managers rather than a fundamental problem with the matrix structure itself (McCollum and Sherman, 1993).

Peters and Waterman (1982) claimed that the tendency towards hopelessly complicated and ultimately unworkable structures

Table 6.3 Benefits and potential pitfalls of matrix management	
Benefits	**Potential pitfalls**
■ Better cross-fertilisation of ideas	■ Lack of commitment to project by functional personnel
■ Stronger project manager control	■ Lack of administrative control of personnel
■ Quicker decisions on project issues	■ Competition between projects for resources
■ Project manager has authority to commit company resources	■ Dilution of expertise and learning in disciplines due to fragmentation
■ Greater security and control of project information	■ Requires excellent communications
■ Better utilisation of time and money	■ Potential for conflict of authority/power
■ Avoids duplication of effort	■ More people required for administration
■ Project does not have to 'carry' people	■ Greater need for integration to overcome complexity
■ Opportunities for staff development	■ Lack of *esprit de corps*
■ Combines flexibility with stability	
■ Greater focus on objectives and the customer	
■ Can reduce design and development time	
Source: Adapted from Chambers, 1989.	

reaches its ultimate expression in the formal matrix organisation structure, which regularly degenerates into anarchy and rapidly becomes bureaucratic and non-creative.

However, McCollum and Sherman (1993), in a study of research and development environments, found that under certain circumstances the matrix can be effectively applied. They refute Peters and Waterman's aversion to the matrix organisation due to a lack of 'any hard evidence' and suggest that the balance of research opinion supports the view that

if properly implemented when the environment and integration requirements are appropriate, the potential problems that are unique to matrix structures can be successfully addressed.

This would appear to be the case in the Twingo project (see above). This view is also supported by the results of two surveys conducted by Gobeli and Larson (1986), which revealed that although the matrix endures ongoing criticism, it still enjoys a high degree of popularity among practising managers. It is also the dominant organisational mode for development projects.

However, companies do not necessarily have to choose one form over another. Skinner and Ivancevich (1992) suggest that an organisation can employ two different structures at once. A predominantly functional organisation may create a special project team to handle a critical project. Such a team may have many of the characteristics of a projectised organisation (PMI, 2000: 20). In this way, organisations are exploring the role of projects as a means of enhancing the communication between functions and overcoming compartmentalisation, one of the limitations of the functional organisation. The logical conclusion of this shift is the project-based organisation whose operations consist mainly of projects (see the section Management by projects in Chapter 3). These organisations tend to have systems in place to facilitate the project process, for example financial systems designed to control multiproject environments.

Virtual organisations

Another form of organisation is the 'virtual organisation' which comprises several project groups producing output based on a common understanding of business rules. Typically, each project provides resources, core competencies and knowledge in order to be more flexible and achieve quicker reaction times to changing environments. The project partners are connected by means of modern information and communication technologies. The virtual organisation is a model that rivals the matrix structure as an effective support for projects. Its two most marked characteristics are the relinquishment of central management functions and the use of IT systems to connect project partners. The benefits of virtual organisations include:

■ support for solving complex problems through group communication
■ allowing internal members and external partners to get involved in the early project phases
■ support by varied computer technologies.

An example of a successful virtual organisation in oil exploration projects is described at the end of the chapter in Project Management in Action: 'Knowing the drill – virtual teamwork at BP'.

Organisational boundaries in procurement

Projects typically involve numerous organisations with differing roles to play. These can be classified into four types of organisation according to their role (Gardiner and Simmons, 1992):

■ *Client system (CS)*. This term includes all the organisations which satisfy one or more of the following criteria:
  ■ has the authority to approve expenditure on the project
  ■ has the authority to approve the form the project has to take and/or its timing
  ■ will be the owner of the project
  ■ will be a major user
  ■ will administer or manage the project upon completion (Walker, 1996).

■ *Project organisation (PO)*. The temporary multi-organisation established for the limited and finite purpose of bringing the project into being from inception to completion, which consists of parts of several separate and diverse organisations drawn from the project participants (contractors, subcontractors, suppliers and also the client system), and whose members will eventually disperse, going back to their own organisations or on to some new project (Cherns and Bryant, 1984).

■ *Client project organisation (CPO)*. The intersec-

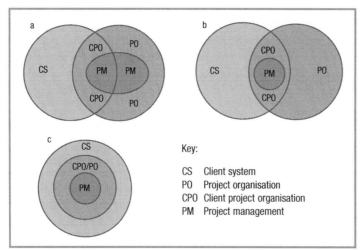

Key:

CS   Client system
PO   Project organisation
CPO   Client project organisation
PM   Project management

Figure 6.5 Example project organisational arrangements

scope, from outside the performing organisation. (PMI, 2000: 8)

In general there are two methods of realising a project. These are:

1. in-house (do it all yourself) – Figure 6.5c
2. procurement (pay a supplier for goods and/or services relating to the project) – Figures 6.5a and b.

Small projects and projects where the client has sufficient resources, knowledge and experience can be completed entirely in-house. In these projects, no contractual relationships are required. The organisation implements a project delivery system without external help. These projects were classed as 'internal' projects in Chapter 1.

More often, especially as projects increase in size, complexity or value, a project sponsor will decide to use the services of one or more suppliers. A sponsor can buy in a small part or all the goods and services required to realise a project. These projects were classed in Chapter 1 as 'external' and 'mixed internal-external' projects, depending on the amount of services bought in.

Managing the external relationships in the supply of goods and services has evolved into a major discipline called 'supply chain management', which integrates strategy, purchasing and quality management. Supply chain management is a fully integrated process extending from the supplier's supplier to the customer's customer, and is becoming an increasing focus of project operations, as shown in Figure 6.6. It includes all the contributors to a project including first tier users and second tier users, contractors and subcontractors and the management of the sponsor's internal supplier network. Supply chain managers search backwards throughout the entire supply chain to identify unnecessary or nonproductive costs that can be taken out of the system. They work with the entire supply chain to improve continuously the quality, service and delivery time. The output of any process in the supply chain affects every process and every customer in the supply chain downstream, which means that improving a process improves every process downstream, which results in cost savings accumulating throughout the supply chain.

tion of project organisation and client system; that part of the client system designated or assumed as having project responsibility.

■ *Project management (PM).* A subset of the project organisation whose responsibility includes one or more of the following management functions: boundary control; monitoring and maintenance activities (in connection with the activities of the project organisation); and project recommendation and/or approval powers (Walker, 1996).

Examples of how these four types can relate to one another are given in Figure 6.5. Figure 6.5a is typical of the majority of projects. The role of project management is shared between the client and other members of the project organisation. In Figure 6.5b the project management function is contained entirely within the client organisation; this is typical of project-oriented companies and those with substantial project management experience. The situation in Figure 6.5c shows a project organisation that is a subset of the client system. This arrangement would apply to small, in-house projects, for example an office move.

Supply chain management

Project procurement management includes the processes required to acquire goods and services, to attain project

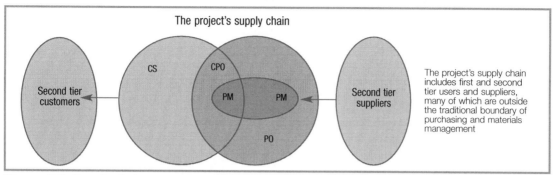

Figure 6.6 Supply chain management

Procurement planning

Procurement planning is determining what project deliverables to buy in and when. Contracts are required when goods and/or services are bought in – see Key Concepts: 'What is a contract?' for a description of a legally binding contract. The organisations supplying these goods and services are called 'contractors' and 'suppliers'; the organisation paying for them is called the 'sponsor', 'owner', 'client' or 'customer'. The purchasing process can be performed at a local departmental level or, in the case of most large companies, centrally through a purchasing function.

 **CONCEPTS** What is a contract?

A contract is an obligation, such as an accepted offer, between competent parties upon a legal consideration, to do or abstain from doing some act. A contract, to be legally binding, must show that:

- the two parties clearly intend to contract
- there is a clear offer and a clear acceptance of the offer
- the two parties are legally capable of contracting
- a price has been set that the buyer agrees to pay the supplier
- there is a purpose for the purchase which is clearly legal
- there is a clear agreement between contracting parties about the terms and conditions of the contract.

The purpose of a contract is to reduce to a formal agreement the respective responsibilities of the parties in the agreement. The contract must clearly state these responsibilities as they relate to the scope of the work to be performed, the deliverables, the results to be obtained, the reporting requirements, the performance monitoring activities and the price and payment methodology.

There are four phases to procurement:

1. *Requirements planning* – defining the need (to buy), for example deciding what to make and what to buy in for the project.
2. *Solicitation* – deciding which potential providers (contractors/suppliers) to approach, what to ask from them (to help decide whether or not to award a contract to supply goods/services) and how to evaluate their submission.
3. *Awarding* – making the award, that is, establishing a contractual relationship.
4. *Contract administration* – managing the contractual relationship, closing the contract.

A simplified procurement process is illustrated in Figure 6.7. Each element is described below.

Requirements planning

Requirements planning involves the definition of the content and boundary of the procurement. This should be established at an early stage in the project and clearly detailed in the project charter or its equivalent, for example the procurement plan. Requirements planning defines what parts of the project will be procured versus what parts will be done in-house – the make or buy decision. The following factors should be considered in each case:

Make decision:
- Less costly to use own skills and expertise if available
- Easy integration with existing operations
- Idle capacity available to use
- Maintain direct control
- Avoid unreliable supplier base.

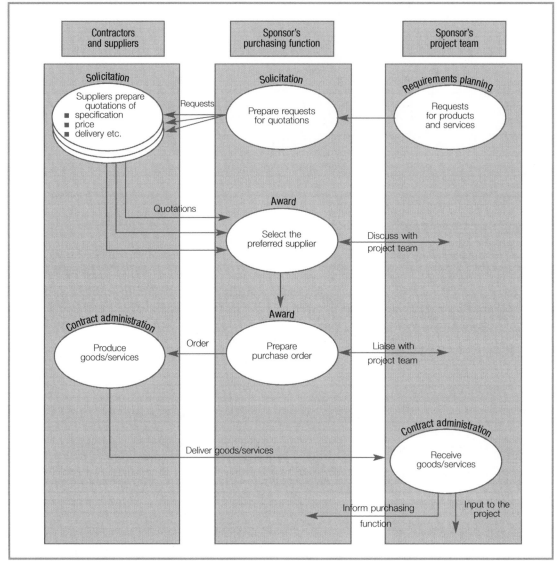

Figure 6.7 Project procurement process

Buy decision:

■ Cheaper to buy in if own skills and expertise are insufficient

■ Not enough capacity available

■ Quicker if well tried and tested solutions already exist (less design time).

An organisation can procure as much or as little of a project commensurate with its own needs and circumstances. For example, a client may procure:

■ the entire project, which is then often referred to

as a 'turnkey project' (common in the process industries)

■ design services only

■ equipment and project supplies

■ construction and manufacturing services

■ computing, systems engineering or electrical engineering services

■ project management services

■ contract management services

■ quality management services

■ risk management services

- independent advice – particularly important for the lay client (see Figure 5.2 as a reminder of the differences between a knowledgeable and a lay client).

In many organisations the buying process begins with a requisition from the sponsor – a document which authorises the purchase of goods or services, usually containing approval signatures and indicating funding commitment. At this stage in the buying process, the key factors that determine the requirement are questions of what is needed, what it should do, the delivery date and where it will be used. If these questions can be answered clearly, the requirement has been defined accurately.

The next stage is to develop a statement of work. The statement of work is a narrative description of the work required and stipulates the deliverables or services required to fulfil the contract. It defines the task to be accomplished or services to be delivered in clear, concise and meaningful terms. To ensure that the statement of work contains complete information, it is important to check that every aspect of the requirement has been verified, such as whether:

- the contract should be based on a fixed price or a per diem rate
- the work will be completed on or off site
- there is a need to make specific facilities, equipment, documentation and personnel available to the supplier
- travel will be involved
- the supplier is responsible for providing certain materials, equipment and documentation
- whether progress reports should be made and when.

The statement of work is important, as it becomes part of the resulting contract. Nothing should be assumed or left unsaid in the statement of work. If a conflict arises about the work required, the statement of work is one part of the contract always referred to in resolving disputes. As the key to all the other steps in the buying process and to the contract with a supplier, the statement of work must be accurately worded, carefully prepared and clear.

Solicitation

Solicitation is the process of identifying a supplier to provide the goods or services required. The process used will depend on the value of the purchase and the nature of the requirement, for example when the sponsor knows what it wants done and how it should be done, it is simply a case of looking for the best price. On the other hand, when the sponsor knows what it wants done, but not how to go about doing it, it will seek proposals on methods, performance, ability and price and it can then negotiate on the best method to achieve the best value.

Low value items can be purchased direct. This is a noncompetitive method and market conditions apply. Orders for goods/services are typically placed using supplier lists and paid for through purchase orders or company credit cards. Higher value goods and services are normally acquired through a solicitation process, in which sealed bids or proposals are invited from several suppliers, openly and competitively. However, in certain circumstances a single supplier (sole source solicitation) can be used without competition.

Bid and proposal solicitation

There are two ways of soliciting sealed bids and proposals for competition:

1. *Public advertising.* This is more common in public sector contracting than the private sector, because of the professional and legal obligation to obtain the best possible price or value in the public sector. The most visible method to meet this objective is through public advertising of contractual requirements. However, this is expensive. When publicly advertising, the purchaser can consider media advertising, for example trade and professional journals, public notices and internet web page tender information.
2. *Use of supplier lists.* Project teams, functional disciplines and the purchasing function will often maintain official supplier lists that are used to request firms to bid on competitive purchases not publicly invited. These lists are used as a basis for preparing a list of suppliers to be solicited for bids.

Sole source solicitation

Sole source solicitation is a noncompetitive method of buying. Many organisations, particularly public ones, try to avoid going to only one company with a bid or proposal opportunity. However, circumstances that warrant sole source buying occur when:

- the product or service is required immediately due to pressing emergency (for example natural

disaster or terrorist attack) and there is not enough time to issue a competitive tender or proposal
- it is not cost-effective to solicit bids competitively (low value purchases)
- there is only one qualified company, such as a business that has developed a patented or copyrighted product or service or a prototype
- (for governments) it is not in the public interest to hold a competition, for example for requirements of national security such as classified military or national defence projects.

Types of bid solicitations

There are four types of bid solicitation that can be used and each is discussed in turn.

Telephone-buy (T-buy)

Used for small competitive purchases that can be easily described over the phone and must be delivered quickly. Typically, the purchaser phones at least three companies including the last successful company from its source lists. They give their bids over the phone. The one that offers the lowest price and fulfils all the terms of the requirement wins the contract.

Request for quotation (RFQ)

RFQs are generally one-page documents that provide a description of the required goods or services and list the terms and conditions of the organisation. In response, suppliers provide a quotation document indicating price and delivery information. RFQs often take place by fax and telephone and are therefore considered a more informal method of tendering, which can easily be used for either the purchase of goods or contracting services and is considered a convenient way to survey the market for best price without incurring substantial legal obligations. The bid documents are kept simple so that the contract can be awarded quickly.

Invitation to tender (ITT)

An ITT is a more formal method of tendering than an RFQ, which is used for higher value purchases that have fairly straightforward requirements, such as a request for off-the-shelf goods. Tenders describe in significant detail through specifications what is expected to be supplied or the service required. An

ITT is sent out to any interested party who may submit a formal tender bid. The ITT approach is used when:

- two or more suppliers are capable of filling the requirement
- the evaluation of tenders can be done against clearly stated criteria
- tenders are all likely to have a common pricing basis
- the lowest priced responsive tender is to be accepted without negotiations and the contract awarded.

Of all the solicitation bid types, tenders are unique because they can be opened publicly – it is generally regarded as good practice to hold a public opening for any tender where the contract award will attract publicity, except for those that are classified.

Request for proposal (RFP) (negotiated contracts)

Similar to ITTs, the RFP is a formal method of obtaining price yet differs in that the RFP allows for numerous methods by which a project result can be achieved. An RFP is a negotiated contract – there will be discussions and the bidder may get the opportunity to change bid pricing, technical requirements and so on. Price is not the primary factor in evaluation. RFPs seek the best value for an organisation through the competitive bid process yet provide for both objective and justifiable reasons for its choices.

The RFP describes in detail the project to be completed, the intended result and the criteria for choosing a successful bid. It can propose a preferred method of completing the work or can ask the bidders to provide solutions, seeking the creative input of suppliers. Communication between prospective bidders and the sponsor is used to gain clarity. Negotiation gives the sponsor more flexibility in the selection process. Often, bidders may provide numerous methods by which the intended result can be achieved that may not have been considered prior to the release of the RFP.

RFPs can be as simple or as detailed as required, allowing greater flexibility in their design, yet must be evaluated according to the published criteria for evaluation. In other words, an RFP is an invitation to offer, seeking a specified requirement based on functional or performance specifications with scope for variety and innovation. RFPs are negotiated contracts that are used when it is impossible to fully describe the item, service or project. Price remains a key factor. RFPs cover:

- Advanced technology
- Complex areas of R&D
- Sophisticated systems, missile programmes, aircraft and weapons systems.

To summarise: a proposal is different from a tender – unlike a tender, an RFP is not an offer, but only contemplates an offer. Unlike the receipt of a tender, the receipt of a proposal is not an acceptance, and therefore does not result in a contract. For example, a marriage proposal does not always result in an agreement of marriage. See Key Concepts: 'When to use a proposal or a tender' for further clarification.

 When to use a proposal or a tender

Tender – know what and how
Use a tender if you know what you want done, how it should be done and are looking for the best price to deliver it, that is:

- if the good or service is clearly defined
- if there is a detailed methodology, procedure, or material and performance specification.

Proposals – know what, but not how
Use an RFP when you are looking for the best value solution to resolve a problem or deliver a good or service, but are not exactly sure how to achieve it, that is:

- if the good or service is not clearly defined
- if there is no detailed material or performance specification
- if you are looking for a general solution to a problem
- if the proponent's solutions are expected to be quite varied and/or difficult to evaluate
- if only one source is being solicited (remember that you send an invitation to tender to more than one supplier)
- you expect to have to negotiate with one or more bidders about certain aspects of the requirement.

With an RFP, suppliers are invited to propose a solution to a problem, requirement or objective and contractor selection is based on the effectiveness of the proposed solution rather than on price alone. Suppliers are usually expected to submit detailed technical, managerial and cost proposals.

Evaluation of proposals

Once a proposal is received, it is normally evaluated on relevant technical merit and overall best value, in accordance with the selection method and evaluation criteria specified in the RFP. Contract award may sometimes be made without discussions or negotiations. Normally, however, a competitive range is determined based on the technical evaluation results. Discussions are then held with the contractors in the competitive range and each contractor is given an opportunity to submit final proposal revisions. Offers submitted in response to an RFP are confidential and are not released outside the evaluation panel. Supplier relations are critical during contract negotiations; good previous experience and relationship rapport can shorten the negotiation process. All bidders are notified of the outcome of their proposals. Debriefings are provided to unsuccessful bidders on request.

Letter of interest

Preparing proposals is often costly to a business. To keep the total cost to business down and still ensure that all potential suppliers at least get to know about the requirement, and have a chance to compete, proposals can be solicited in two steps:

- Before issuing an RFP, suppliers are asked to provide *letters of interest* and qualifications, from which a short list is developed. This process might be appropriate where many potential suppliers are known; suppliers not submitting letters of interest are perhaps not interested
- During the second step, an RFP is issued, asking suppliers on the short list to submit detailed proposals.

Awarding

Awarding is about final contractor selection and contract award. The award normally goes to the lowest bidder, although sponsors are always concerned when one bid is much lower than the others. The award cycle results in a signed contract. Under normal conditions, the type of contract used and payment method is decided by the client through contract negotiation with the contractor. See below for details of several different contract types and payment methods. The objective at the award stage is to negotiate a contract type and price that will result in reasonable contractor risk and provide the contractor with the greatest incentive for efficient and economic performance. Unfortunately, negotiating the contract and preparing it for signatures may require months of preparation. If the customer needs the work to begin immediately or if long lead procurement is necessary, the customer may provide the contractor with a *letter contract* or *letter of intent*. This authorises the contractor to begin straightaway.

Contract administration

Contract administration is about managing a contractor until completion of the contract. The main contract administration functions include:

- contract change management
- specification interpretation
- adherence to quality
- warranties
- subcontractor management
- monitoring the work
- contract breach and resolution of disputes
- project termination, payment schedules and contract closeout.

Contractor – agent or vendor?

A contractor may be viewed either as an agent or a vendor. An agent represents the client's interest and has a fiduciary responsibility. A vendor delivers a specified product for a price. Consultants and independent advisors are usually viewed at the agency end of the spectrum and other contractors at the vendor end. But there are exceptions. When sponsors need guidance or advice, they typically choose an agent relationship. Sponsors who know exactly what is required typically form vendor relationships. There can be a conflict of interest if a contractor is both agent and vendor or if a contractor changes from agent to vendor in the course of a project. However, some owners do not worry about the conflict of interest and instead look for good reputations and continuity.

Number of contracts on a project

The number of contracts used on a project can vary considerably. For example, in the construction industry, the traditional construction process uses two contracts, one with an architect (or engineer) and one with a construction contractor. There are many alternatives to this. A design and build contract achieves the same result with only one contract. A construction management contract, on the other hand, involves a management contractor (management input only) and numerous additional contracts with the prime subcontractors (who perform the building and construction work). Alternatively, the sponsor may purchase building materials and equipment and arrange multiple labour contracts, which, on a large project, may result in thousands of contracts.

Multiple contracts enable a client to fast track a project (overlap design and construction). Direct purchase of labour and materials eliminates overhead mark-ups. Unbundling design allows selection of specialists, and unbundling construction allows careful selection of specific manufacturers and trade contractors. So, as the number of contracts increases, the opportunities to save time and money and improve quality also increase, but so does the risk. Clients who choose to manage multiple contracts must manage the contracts well (that is, they need to be experienced clients) or take the responsibility for management failures. Consequently, most clients package contracts under a general contractor or choose a construction manager to help if they use multiple contracts.

Insights from Industry: 'Hiring consultants' is about procurement, organisation and project team roles, with a particular emphasis on the use of consultants in projects.

The complexities of procurement for a large project are encapsulated in Project Management in Action: 'Maritime helicopter procurement process', at the end of the chapter. This case gives an in-depth look at procurement planning and decision making in a large Canadian defence project.

 **HIRING CONSULTANTS**

The project

In 1996 a major San Francisco bank was poised to roll out an application for tracking customer calls routed to its 'elite' group of customer service representatives who handled problem cases. Reports provided by the new system would be going directly to the president of the bank and board of directors. An initial product demo seemed sluggish, yet the consultants assured both the information system (IS) and the telephone banking division managers that all was well. They were wrong. 'The source code was so bad it took 20 minutes to load the program on the PC,' recalls Jim Daviner, the systems analyst on the project.

The problem

The system crashed constantly, could not support multiple users at once and did not meet the bank's security requirements. IS hired a new consultant to help rewrite the application, but after three months the project was killed – resulting in a loss of approximately $200,000 in staff time and consulting fees, and a bad rap for IS.

According to Daviner, the first mistake was the bank's failure to check references and work samples of the consulting firm. Daviner caught a major flaw in the database design in time, but as the project progressed, the programming team became increasingly isolated and hard to work with, refusing to release the source code to the project managers. Daviner says the programmers didn't want the bank to find out that they were, in his words, 'pretty inept'.

But the root of the project's failure was a complicated reporting structure that left no clear line of command. Between Daviner, the lead analyst from the business side, and the four consulting programmers located in Arizona, there were two other layers of management from IS. Another layer, Daviner's boss, was the lead project manager and sponsor – yet she had no direct contact with or control over the programmers and left the company in the middle of the project. Worse, the project correspondence was lost in the process of cleaning out her PC, Daviner says. At the same time, the bank's IS department was being reorganized. One of the two IS managers on the project resigned to go to another company, and the other was restructured out of a job after the project's problems came to light. In late 1996, with no leadership or business sponsor to rescue a coding disaster, Daviner had to mop up the mess.

The recovery

The project was never revived, and Daviner says the biggest loss for the bank is not having access to valuable customer information the system was to deliver. On a positive note, the business units are getting rid of unnecessary layers in projects. Today project managers have direct oversight of the programming consultants and approve all hiring of IS personnel. 'Things happen more smoothly now,' he says. Daviner (who, as an aside, says his reasons for leaving the bank were not related to this project) shares the following tips:

- Institute a formal review process for hiring consultants.
- Require change control documentation so that managers can see what changes were made during development, when and why.
- Ownership is essential. When sponsors or top players leave the company or the project, new owners should be identified immediately and supported with documentation.
- Assign a central manager for the project team who is the conduit for communication and decisions. Result: Everyone is on the same page rather than working in parallel and reporting to different managers.

In the end, a disorganized project team with unstable leadership wrought the ruin of an important customer application. Unfortunately, due to the ongoing IS reorganization at the bank, Daviner says that IS has not improved its project management practices – a clear example of chaos breeding chaos.

Source: P. Schneider, 'Too many cooks in the kitchen', *CIO Magazine*, Dec 1, 1998. http://www.cio.com/archive/120198/turk.html

Questions

1. What is the purpose of a demo or prototype in a project?
2. How did they use the information from the demo in this project?
3. At the end of the case, Daviner gives four tips. Do you agree with them and how would they have helped in this project?
4. By the end of the case nothing has changed – what do you suggest they do?

Contract terms of payment

There are numerous ways to structure the amount to be paid for work performed as required in a contract. Some pricing arrangements are used only in complex development and production environments, while others are quite common. Figure 6.8 shows the most frequently used types of contract.

It is, however, important to understand the distinction between cost and price. Price refers to the total amount paid, including profit. Cost, on the other hand, refers to the expenses of the contractor which, when added to a profit (also called fee), comprise the total price.

The two principal payment methods are fixed price and cost reimbursement contracts. Within the two basic types of contract pricing, there are several variations and some of these are discussed below.

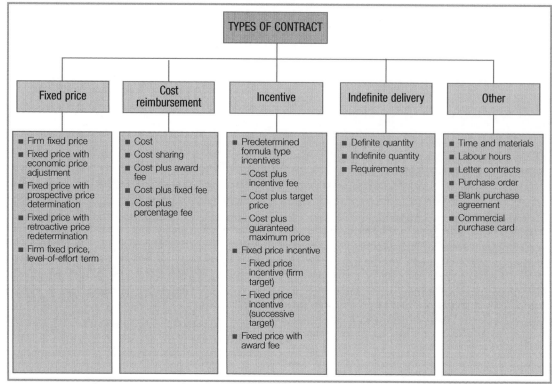

Figure 6.8 Common types of contract

Fixed price contracts

Firm fixed price (FFP)

This type of contract can also be called 'fixed price' or 'lump sum'.

A fixed price contract is by far the most common. It involves payment of a specific amount for delivery of specified supplies or performance of a specified service. In many cases, the customer may order incremental quantities of the service or supply, so that the total value of the contract may not be known at the outset, but the pricing is fixed on a per-increment basis. This is referred to as 'fixed unit price'.

The contractor is expected to earn a profit, but the profit is not guaranteed. Even if a loss is incurred, the contractor is required to perform the contract. In return for this rigidity, the fixed price contract constrains the customer from asserting control over the performance and any changes to the requirements may result in a claim for an *equitable adjustment* to the price.

Fixed price contracts have the virtue of being easily administered and are appropriate where the contract requirements can be well defined and performed without significant risk of failure.

The fixed price contract is inappropriate where the performance is fraught with unknown or unquantifiable risks, or where the customer will need to assert significant control over the performance efforts. For example, if the amount of contaminated soil to require treatment is twice the amount specified in the request for proposal (RFP), the fixed price contract would require a modification.

Note that, in a firm fixed price contract, the contractor's profit increases if the contractor's efficiency goes up and cost savings (not built into the contract) are realised.

Fixed price with economic price adjustment

This type of contract is not very common; it was developed during an era of high economic inflation. It remains available, however, for appropriate circumstances. Such an example might be where a specific commodity (a rare metal, possibly) used in a deliverable item is perceived to be at risk of becoming inordinately expensive at some point during the performance of the contract. The underlying concept is simple. The price can be adjusted to reflect inflation-induced changes in the contractor's cost of performance. These contracts are normally used only for long-term (more than a year) requirements.

Cost reimbursement contracts

Cost plus fixed fee (CPFF)

The most common type of cost reimbursement contract, the cost plus fixed fee (CPFF), involves two elements: an estimated cost and a fixed fee. The contractor is reimbursed its costs of performance and is paid a fee in addition to those reimbursed costs. It is particularly important to note that only those costs which can be fully documented by the contractor are reimbursed. It is quite easy for a contractor to lose money on a cost reimbursement effort.

It is also important to note that the fee does not change as the costs increase or decrease. It is *fixed*, and will change only if the overall scope of the work is changed and the fee is renegotiated. There is a limitation on the amount of fee that can be paid, based on the original estimated cost of the contract.

CPFF contracts are used where the risks of performance are high, or the customer requires a high level of performance control. Because of the high costs of administration, they are typically used only in higher value contracts.

Cost plus percentage of cost

In this type of contract, the contractor's fee is expressed as a percentage of the total costs expended. The fee grows with the expenditures and the structure is an invitation to the worst of inefficiencies. It should be avoided if at all possible. In some countries this contract type is illegal.

Other contracts

Time and materials and labour hours

The time and materials and labour hours contract types are closely related. In both, the contractor is paid for hours of service without regard to whether the desired task is accomplished. A specified hourly rate is used for payment. The time and material form also includes reimbursement for the cost of materials (plus a percentage mark-up).

Such contracts have the unfortunate aspect (from the customer's point of view) of being more expensive to the customer and having the least risk for the contractor of all contract types. For this reason, these types of contracts are usually restricted in use to fairly low monetary values and are normally used only where other types are not available.

Incentive contracting

Incentive contracting is about sharing performance savings with the contractor generating the savings. By determining the specific project parameters which are important to a client, an incentive agreement can be developed to enhance performance in these areas, for example cost, schedule, quality, safety and customer satisfaction. This promotes a win–win situation. Poor project execution costs a sponsor money and good-to-excellent project performance saves the sponsor money.

Since estimates and budgets are normally based on historical data (representing average or mediocre performance), it should be clear that incentive contracting can be entirely self-funded from the savings made. In addition, the client always reaps a positive benefit above any share of the savings from earlier production or higher returns on investment.

Incentive contracting:

■ is a contractual method that rewards performance
■ is about risk/reward sharing
■ promotes the project team concept
■ promotes a win–win opportunity
■ ensures project work is goal-oriented by promoting specific goals.

Incentive contracting has several inherent advantages. The client goals, objectives and expectations are well known by all the participants and are extensively emphasised in the incentive agreement. Contractors generally provide their best project teams on projects where performance can enhance contractor profitability. They frequently take pains to expedite the project. Project monitoring is kept up to date and there is a genuine concern by contractors to find ways to remove 'roadblocks' or 'stumbling blocks'. Any contract savings are shared with the contractor. The client gets a share of the savings plus all the benefits of early project completion – see Insights from Industry: 'Incentive-based savings pave the way for new projects' for an example project where savings were made.

Cost incentives take the form of a sharing formula

INCENTIVE-BASED SAVINGS PAVE THE WAY FOR NEW PROJECTS

The new Conway bypass, South Carolina, USA, opened recently at a well-attended ceremony. The project, a design and build partnership between Fluor Daniel and the state of South Carolina completed months ahead of schedule despite three hurricanes and a host of sensitive environmental issues requiring special methods of construction. The project also came in well under budget, with an industry leading safety record and a refund to the South Carolina Dept of Transportation of more than $250,000. These savings, along with other efficiencies realised during the project, have allowed the state to begin work on other transportation needs throughout the region.

generally expressed as a ratio. For example, if a 90/10 formula were negotiated, the client would pay 90 pence and the contractor 10 pence for every pound above the target cost. Similarly, the client would pay the contractor an additional 10 pence in the pound for every pound saved. Thus, it benefits both the client and the contractor to reduce costs, and expected profits can be increased by making maximum use of the contractor's managerial skills.

The more common incentive-type contracts are discussed below.

Cost plus incentive fee (CPIF)

These contracts are a variation of cost reimbursement contracts in which the fee paid depends upon how well the contract satisfies certain performance objectives. Other than the fee structure, the contract type is essentially the same as a CPFF. The fee includes an incentive which (as in a fixed price incentive contract) relates to objective performance criteria. The fee in a CPIF contract can include a fixed fee component, with the incentive portion being an additional amount. There is usually a limit on the maximum fee that can be earned under the contract. CPIF contracts are useful in developmental environments where it is deemed useful to reward particular performance characteristics of the final product design. They can also be used as an incentive to complete a contract by an immoveable delivery deadline date.

Cost plus target price

The contractor is paid actual costs plus a fee. A target price is set and the contractor shares in the savings or the overrun. The target price can be modified by a change order (a formal request for a change in a contract) as the contract progresses.

Cost plus guaranteed maximum price

The contractor is paid actual costs plus a fee; however, a maximum price is set. The contractor will share in the savings but will pay the entire overrun. The guaranteed maximum price (GMP) can be modified by change orders as the contract progresses. It is essentially a ceiling on a cost plus contract with a defined scope.

Example of cost plus incentive fee (CPIF) payment structure

In a cost plus incentive fee contract, the contractor is reimbursed 100% of the costs. However, there exists a maximum fee (that is, profit) and a minimum fee. The final allowable profit will vary between the minimum and maximum fee. Because there appears more financial risk for customers in a CPIF contract, the target fee is usually less than in a fixed price incentive contract and the contractor's portion of the sharing ratio is smaller.

Consider a cost plus incentive fee contract with a payment structure defined by Table 6.4.

In this example, the final fee and price for a contract where the actual costs are £9,000 are calculated as shown in Table 6.5.

A graph to illustrate the relationship between the various terms is given in Figure 6.9.

Table 6.4 Payment structure for example CPIF contract

Payment structure	
Target cost	£10,000
Target fee (profit)	£750
Maximum fee	£1350
Minimum fee	£300
Sharing formula (owner/contractor)	85/15

Table 6.5 CPIF calculation explained in three steps

Step 1		Step 2		Step 3	
Target cost [1]	£10,000	Target fee (profit) [4]	£750	Total price =cost+profit, [2]+[7]	£9,900
Actual cost [2]	£9,000	Contractor's proportion of underrun, 15% [5]	0.15		
Underrun, [3]=[1]-[2]	£1,000	Amount of contractor's share of underrun, [6]=[3]x[5]	£150		
		Contractor's total fee (profit), [7]=[4]+[6] (less than the maximum fee)	£900		

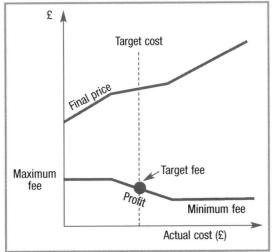

Figure 6.9 Example of CPIF contract payment structure

Fixed price incentive (FPI)

The FPI contract is a modified form of a fixed price contract. The 'incentive' in the name is a reference to the fact that the contract is structured to reward the contractor for certain performance accomplishments, for example how high an airplane can fly or how efficiently a heater works. Note that the incentive must be objectively measurable and must be linked to the final price paid in a calculable way, based on the measurement. Multiple incentives can be included in a single contract.

There are four components to the 'price' in an FPI structure. These are the target cost, target price, ceiling price, and sharing ratio. If the contractor succeeds in performance at the target cost, it is paid the target price. If its costs exceed the target cost, the price increases proportionately to the additional costs until it reaches the ceiling price, at which point addi-

tional costs are fully absorbed by the contractor. Similarly, savings in cost result in a proportionate decline of the total price. (This feature results in this incentive form being less attractive than a standard FFP contract.) The sharing ratio determines how much of the cost difference is absorbed by the contractor and how much is shared by the customer.

The FPI contract can be difficult to administer. It involves a great deal more intrusion into the contractor's cost accounting than is necessary in a firm fixed price effort and the incentive for efficient performance is often less than in a firm fixed price environment.

Typical applications of the FPI contract are when a new production effort is being undertaken and the contractor and customer have difficulty agreeing on a price. It gives the contractor some additional pricing room (at a lowered profit) should the costs escalate past expectations, while giving the customer a ceiling price to protect it from a total cost explosion.

Example of fixed price incentive (FPI) payment structure

Consider a fixed price incentive contract with a payment structure defined by Table 6.6.

The contractor has a target cost and target profit. However, there is a price ceiling of £11,500 which is

Table 6.6 Payment structure for example FPI contract

Payment structure	
Target cost	£10,000
Target profit	£850
Price ceiling	£11,500
Sharing formula (owner/contractor)	70/30

Step 1		Step 2		Step 3	
Target cost [1]	£10,000	Target profit [4]	£850	Total price =cost+profit, [2]+[7]	£10,150
Actual cost [2]	£9,000	Contractor's proportion of underrun, 30% [5]	0.3		
Underrun, [3]=[1]–[2]	£1,000	Amount of contractor's share of underrun, [6]=[3]x[5]	£300		
		Contractor's total profit, [7]=[4]+[6]	£1,150		

Table 6.7 FPI calculation explained in three steps

the maximum price that the contractor will be paid. If the contractor performs the work below the target cost of £10,000, additional profit will be made. For example, by performing the work for £9,000, the contractor will receive a profit of £1150, which is the target profit of £850 plus £300 for 30% of the underrun. The contractor will receive a total price of £10,150. This is explained in more detail in Table 6.7, just follow the three simple steps.

If the cost exceeds the target cost, then the contractor must pay 30% of the overrun out of the contractor's profits. However, the FPI contract has a *point of total assumption* beyond which all additional costs are burdened by the contractor. The point of total assumption occurs when the final price is equal to the price ceiling.

Figure 6.10 shows the relationship between the contractor's profit and the final cost. As the final cost increases, the contractor's profit decreases. The point

of total assumption is clearly seen. If the cost continues to increase beyond this point, all profits may disappear and the contractor may be forced to pay the majority of the overrun.

When the contract is completed, the contractor submits a statement of costs incurred in the performance of the contract. The costs are audited to determine allowability and any questionable charges are removed. This determines the negotiated cost. The negotiated cost is subtracted from the target cost. This number is then multiplied by the sharing ratio. If the number is positive, it is added to the target profit; if it is negative, it is subtracted. The new number, the final profit, is added to the negotiated cost to determine the final price. The final price never exceeds the price ceiling.

How to choose a contract payment method

The selection of a contract type is dependent upon the following factors:

■ Capabilities of the sponsor's project team
■ Level of detail available describing the project's scope
■ Firmness of the project's scope
■ Amount of risk the sponsor is willing to assume
■ Amount of time available to execute the project
■ Control the sponsor has over other divisions and departments in the organisation
■ Driving force or payout of the project.

The purpose of contract pricing is to reward the contractor for successful performance and minimise the costs associated with the contract, commensurate with the risks of performance. Risk is a critical component of contracting and the choice of pricing type generally reflects the degree of risk involved. As

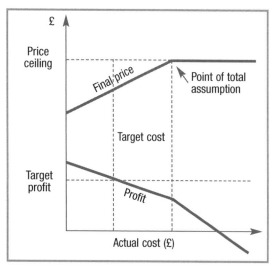

Figure 6.10 Example of FPI contract payment structure

a general rule, cost reimbursement contract types are used in anticipation of significant risk of performance. In this case, the risk represents the unknown factors, for example the length and depth of a contamination plume while conducting an environmental investigation. On the other hand, procurement of truck tyres over a three-month period would result in essentially no risk to the contractor, the customer being best served by a fixed price contract.

The contract method also reflects the capability of the customer to define and manage the project. The cheapest contractual method on a well-defined project for a client with an *experienced project team* is cost plus, because the client controls the project scope growth and project delivery methods and avoids paying the contractor's perceived risk for taking the project delivery risk. With an *inexperi-enced project team,* the cheapest contractual method is fixed price (lump sum); let the contractor be responsible for controlling scope growth and delivery methods.

Poorly defined projects should be executed cost plus until scope definition is firm; only at that time should they be converted to another contract method.

Visit the website

http://www.palgrave.com/business/gardiner

❯ to see a more detailed comparison of contract types and pricing arrangements

Insights from Industry: 'Contractors ask for more risk!' highlights an emerging trend in the USA in which some contractors are moving towards fixed price contracts for projects that carry significant risk.

---

insights from INDUSTRY CONTRACTORS ASK FOR MORE RISK!

In a business where sealing contracts with a handshake was standard, builders believed they could always work out jobsite problems, or settle disputes with a phone call or friendly chat. But just as handshake deals are now scarce, so are old attitudes toward risk and liability. These days, owners and project developers are asking – and even demanding – that contractors take on more liability, such as providing guarantees that a project will finish on time, despite such uncontrollable risks as acts of God. There is a concerted effort by owners to place risk on contractors that contractors have historically not accepted.

Traditionally, risks have been assigned to those who can best handle them. These risks normally are either insured against or priced to reflect the contingency. But industry observers see an imbalance looming that could simply drive up project prices, or worse, have the opposite effect. 'Some companies will take more risk for less reward and it will drive business down,' says Ron Oakley, president of Fluor Daniel's Aliso Viejo CA-based transportation group.

Of course, ramped-up risk isn't new in construction. 'You only have to look around for the companies that are no longer with us. If you dig down, you'll see they took huge risks and suffered severe consequences. There's always a price to pay.'

These days, public owners are asking contractors to take responsibility for such items as environmental issues, right-of-way, force majeure and subsurface conditions, among others. 'Owners know there is a point we won't cross, but they continue to push the envelope,' says Oakley.

Even the federal government is beginning to shift project risk. This time, however, it's the contractors who are actually asking for it.

The U.S. Defense Dept. still has thousands of acres at closed military bases that can be transferred to municipalities or private owners for redevelopment. But much of that property languishes while federal regulators move slowly through the quagmire of cleaning up environmental hazards left behind.

Some contractors think there is a faster way to get this job done and they are willing to take the sizable risks to do it. Some say they can predict the preferred cleanup strategy, design it, complete work under a fixed-price contract and win regulators' blessing for site reuse. The volume of cleanup site experience now allows contractors to comfortably specify acceptable remedies and significantly reduce project risk.

Source: Powers, M.B, 'Risky business has its reward', *Design-Build Magazine,* February (2001)

Questions

1. What is the relationship between contract strategy and risk?
2. What is unusual about the contract strategy here?
3. What are the advantages and disadvantages of this approach for sponsors and contractors?

International contracts

Increasingly, large projects are performed across international borders. This brings with it a need to find contracts that can be applied at an international level. These projects tend to be more complex to manage and their conditions of contract have been developed to facilitate and smooth out the contracting process for all parties. This section introduces two of the more common series of international contracts in use today.

NEC

The new engineering contract (NEC) is a legal framework of project management procedures designed to handle all aspects of the management of engineering and construction projects, large and small, national and international. The NEC was developed by the Institution of Civil Engineers in the early 1990s with the aim of introducing a new, nonadversarial form of contract strategy which would contribute towards the more effective and smoother management of projects. There are several options available including fixed price, cost plus, target, management and professional services.

The contract is designed to motivate all parties to apply improved practices to the project through the following two principles:

- foresight applied collaboratively mitigates problems and shrinks risk
- clear division of function and responsibility helps accountability, motivates people on the project and results in fewer disputes about who is to do what and how.

Although a legal document, the NEC is written in ordinary language. It has few sentences which contain more than 40 words and longer sentences are subdivided using bullet points to permit easier understanding.

FIDIC

The International Federation of Consulting Engineers (FIDIC) has long been renowned for its standard forms of contract for use between employers and contractors on international construction projects, in particular:

- Conditions of Contract for Works of Civil Engineering Construction: *The Red Book* (1987)
- Conditions of Contract for Electrical and Mechanical Works including Erection on Site: *The Yellow Book* (1987)
- Conditions of Contract for Design-Build and Turnkey: *The Orange Book* (1995).

The standard forms of contract published in 1999 are increasingly used for international construction and plant installation projects around the world. This new suite comprises:

- Conditions of Contract for Construction for Building and Engineering Works Designed by the Employer: *The Construction Contract*
- Conditions of Contract for Plant and Design-Build for Electrical and Mechanical Plant and for Building and Engineering Works Designed by the Contractor: *The Plant and Design/BuildContract*
- Conditions of Contract for EPC/Turnkey Projects: *The EPC/Turnkey Contract*
- Short Form of Contract – *The Short Form*

Visit the website

http://www.palgrave.com/business/gardiner

▶ to access more information on FIDIC international agreements and contracts

International contract law

The United Nations Commission on International Trade Law (UNCITRAL) was established by the General Assembly of the United Nations in December 1966, with the aim of furthering the progressive harmonisation and unification of the laws of international trade law (Davidson, 2000). In 1996, the Model Law on Procurement of Goods, Construction and Services was finalised by UNCITRAL. The Model Law deals with competitive procedures for selecting suppliers and contractors. Its main features are summarised below:

- *Economy and efficiency.* Transparent, competitive and efficient procurement is a driving force to improve public administration and sound commercial practices by the private sector
- *Competition.* Competition is generally regarded as the way to obtain the best value and quality available in the commercial market
- *Fairness.* The reality and the perception of fairness at all stages of the procurement are

important for private sector and taxpayer confidence in the integrity of the procurement system

- *Transparency.* Transparency (availability of information) is central to achieving the fundamental objectives of economy, competition, fairness and accountability. This includes the availability of information about:
  - the 'rules of the game'
  - procurement opportunities
  - the procurement requirement
  - what happened in the procurement proceedings
- *Accountability.* This objective is fostered by the provisions establishing transparency and the provisions on review. In addition, there should be no improper inducements, conflicts of interest or other unfair bidder conduct.

Visit the website

http://www.palgrave.com/business/gardiner

❯ to access more information on the UNCITRAL Model Law

World Trade Organization (WTO) procurement guidelines

The WTO is the only global international organisation dealing with the rules of trade between nations. At its heart are the WTO agreements, negotiated and signed by the bulk of the world's trading nations and ratified in their parliaments. The goal of the WTO is to help producers of goods and services, exporters and importers conduct their business by:

- supporting greater transparency at all stages of procurement
- reducing corruption (from biased pre-qualification of bidders or specifications, collusion in bid-rigging, over-invoicing or reduced quality in contract performance through to the unfair or often unavailable process for the resolution of complaints)
- promoting a uniform, transparent procurement system that promotes competition among qualified bidders and suppliers of goods and services. This will also help governments to maximise the opportunity to secure the best product at the most favourable price. Failure to do so diverts scarce government resources from important development objectives with a disproportionate impact on the poor.

Visit the website

http://www.palgrave.com/business/gardiner

❯ to access information on the International Trade Centre

(ITC), the technical cooperation agency of United Nations Conference on Trade and Development (UNCTAD), and the WTO for operational, enterprise-oriented aspects of trade development.

World Bank procurement guidelines

The World Bank finances more than 200 new development projects each year, each of which involves an estimated 30,000 individual contracts. The project cycle is a process jointly managed by the World Bank and the borrowing country ('the borrower'). The bank and the borrower work together to identify likely projects. The borrower prepares a set of documents for bank approval and revisions, and the bank evaluates the project for viability and economic impact. Negotiations on terms and conditions for the loan are held and, if the board of directors approves the project, it passes into the implementation phase.

The bank has found that, in most cases, their needs and interests can best be realised through international competitive bidding (ICB), which provides all eligible prospective bidders with timely and adequate notification of a borrower's requirements and an equal opportunity to bid for the required goods and works.

Visit the website

http://www.palgrave.com/business/gardiner

❯ to access information from the World Bank on the procurement of projects

Partnering and joint ventures

Partnering was one of the key recommendations of the Egan Report *Rethinking Construction* (1998: 9). This is the Report's definition of partnering:

Partnering involves two or more organisations working together to improve performance through agreeing mutual objectives, devising a way for resolving any disputes and committing themselves to continuous improvement, measuring progress and sharing gains.

Partnerings can take any of a number of forms such as a strong relationship with a major customer, a partnership with a source of distribution, a relationship with a supplier of an innovation or product or an alliance in pursuit of a common goal. Table 6.8 shows the different kinds of collaboration commonly formed, all of which require a degree of risk sharing.

The aim in partnering is to secure the best possible commercial advantage. The principle is that team-

Form	Purpose	Features
Table 6.8 Common types of partnership		
Horizontal forms		
Joint venture	■ win business	■ small number of partners ■ specific, time-limited business project ■ shared resources, risks, rewards
Strategic alliance	■ gain direct business advantage	■ as joint venture, but more open, longer term search for mutual gain
Business cooperative	■ save costs or create marketing opportunities	■ joint purchasing or joint marketing ■ potentially many members ■ usually a delegated management function
Vertical forms		
Supply chain partnership	■ deliver added value to customers	■ vertical relationship between purchaser and supplier – longer term focus than traditional approach to procurement ■ focus on driving quality improvement through systems, skills, communication and relationships
Networks		
Networking forum	■ learn from each other	■ vehicle for debate, exchange ■ loose and open-ended ■ driven by members' own agenda
Business association	■ promote member interests	■ as networking forum, plus … ■ consult and represent member interests
Sector group	■ promote competitive advantage of an industry	■ develop sector strategies and key projects ■ possible advisory role to government agencies
Cluster group	■ promote competitive advantage in related industries	■ as sector group, but involving a wider set of supplier and customer interests

work is better than combat. If the end customer is to be best served, the parties to a deal must work together and both must benefit. A partnering relationship works because the parties have an interest in each other's success.

Partnering is not just a form of contract. It is a structured management approach used to facilitate teamworking across contractual boundaries. Its fundamental components are:

■ Fostering of a mutual interdependence and trust rather than a blame culture based upon separately appointed and accountable designers and contractors and competitively tendered contracts
■ Establishment of agreed decision-making procedures
■ Commitment to continuous improvement (benchmarking and key performance indicators)
■ Development of teams that work together down the entire product and supply chain, with

suppliers chosen according to value and performance clearly measured
■ Benefits based upon open book accounting, with pain and gain shared on an agreed basis offering best value for money.

Partnering should not be confused with good project management practice, or with long standing relationships, negotiated contracts or preferred supplier arrangements, all of which lack the structure and objective measure that must support a partnering relationship.

Which projects can benefit from partnering?

Partnering is suitable for a variety of projects but is only appropriate between organisations that support the fundamental principles of partnering from 'top to bottom'. There is no point in upper management supporting partnering if others in a large project adopt an adversarial approach. It is important that all personnel are educated in a new culture. New systems are needed to capture the benefits of partnering rather than as a tool for monitoring and apportioning blame.

Partnering is most suited to the following circumstances:

■ Where there is an explicit problem which is best resolved by a team of expertise (BP adopted this approach for innovative offshore projects)
■ Projects which are repetitive in their nature and based upon a set of standard processes (this is known as 'strategic partnering') (Selfridges and McDonald's use partnering where tight construction programmes are more important than cost control and volume is more important than individuality or aesthetics)
■ Where time is a critical factor (Argent Developments Limited require projects to be developed as fast as possible to maximise their rate of return)
■ Where there is a rapid expansion or roll-out of a programme of related projects (for example Safeway and NatWest Bank)
■ Where there is a significant input required from specialist contractors or subcontractors (BAA Terminal 5 – significant benefits were derived from the involvement of specialists).

Partnering is less well suited:

■ When cost certainty is important – a client embarking on a project will only achieve price certainty once the design has been completed, by which time it is too late for the benefits of partnering to materialise
■ For 'one-off' projects commissioned by a 'one-off' employer – the benefits of team building and supply chain management cannot easily be achieved on a single project
■ Where the employer has little knowledge of the project process – partnering is a client-led process and needs the active involvement of a knowledgeable client.

Once a suitable partner has been found and relations established, it is common to formalise the intention to collaborate and work together using a memorandum of understanding (MOU).

Visit the website

`http://www.palgrave.com/business/gardiner`

❿ to see an example memorandum of understanding used as a statement of goodwill between the University of Alberta and other organisations wishing to form a partnership to generate mutually beneficial activities

Common pitfalls in joint ventures (JVs)

The following are some of the common pitfalls to be found in joint ventures:

■ *Mutual trust* – the most important factor affecting the success of a joint venture is the degree of mutual trust and cooperation that is achieved and sustained by the co-venturers throughout the joint venture's existence
■ *Communication* – communication between the co-venturers plays a crucial part in the success of a joint venture. In international joint ventures in particular, having a common business language that is understood and common to all those concerned is an important practical consideration. Failure to communicate inevitably leads to misunderstandings and disputes
■ *Profit motivation* – the joint venture needs to have some profit motivation by way of specific features or synergy gains (for example use of pooled know-how or intellectual property rights, or production of a product that neither party is capable of producing independently)
■ *Decision making* – the business of the joint venture may suffer because of the fragmentation of decision-making powers, leading to a lack of effective management and drift. See Project Management in Action: 'The Scottish Qualifications Authority' at the end Chapter 3.

Project-based joint ventures

Project-based joint ventures represent a particularly interesting group of JVs, with peculiar characteristics (Harrigan, 1988; Lorange, et al., 1992; Lynch, 1993: 26). First, they have a predetermined, limited lifespan. Their activities are oriented towards well-defined objectives. These JVs are terminated upon the completion of the given project. Such a limitation in time usually leads to specific managerial problems. For instance, there is obviously a pressure for rapid decision making. Also, given the project-specific nature of such ventures, the selection of an inappropriate, or poor, partner may be more likely than the case of ongoing JVs. Parent firms have less

Table 6.9 Comparison of project-based and traditional joint ventures

Area of comparison	Project-based JVs	Traditional JVs
Lifespan	Finite	Indefinite
Nature	Dissolving after project completion	Ongoing
Strategy planning	Short-term orientation	Long-term orientation
Time to rectify default	Within contract period	Ongoing process
Decision making	Relatively fast	Relatively slow
Management style	Task-oriented	Business-oriented
Partner relationship	Short-term orientation	Long-term orientation
Information flow requirement	Must be quick	Ongoing process
Product/service improvement	Defined by contract	Ongoing process
Control	Hierarchy	Teamwork
Primary objective	Completion of project on time	Business objectives
Potential benefits	Possible win–lose situation	Win–win situation

Source: Adapted from Lynch, 1993: 26.

time to understand the local environment and qualify thoroughly all their potential partners. In addition, there is a greater potential for culture-related conflicts, if adequate planning and deliberation do not proceed key partnership and venture formation decisions.

Table 6.9 shows a summary of the differences between project-based and traditional joint ventures.

BOOT, BOT and BOO arrangements

Many governments, particularly in developing economies, have sought to involve the private sector to participate in infrastructure projects. Urban infrastructure is composed of various sectors, which are needed for the proper running of cities, like water supply and sanitation, public transportation, roads, electricity and so on. The reasons for opening the infrastructure sector for private investment by these governments is to meet the huge financial demands and use private sector expertise in the construction and operation of the projects. Unlike conventional financing, private investment in public infrastructure projects needs to incorporate all aspects of risk and return on a project finance basis where there is limited public financing available. This is normally possible by establishing a special purpose vehicle (SPV) and justifying the return through the cash flows of these specific projects.

This section discuss briefly three popular arrange-

ments of private sector financing: BOT (Build–Operate–Transfer), BOOT (Build–Own–Operate–Transfer) and BOO (Build–Own–Operate). The differences between these arrangements can be seen through three phases of the project: development, operation and termination. The degree of privatisation increases correspondingly as we go from BOT to BOOT to BOO format.

- In a typical BOT model, the government entity enters into an agreement with a private sector company to finance, design and build a facility at its own cost. The private companies are then given a concession, usually for a fixed period, to operate that facility and obtain revenues from its operation before transferring the facility back to the government at the end of the concession period. This enables the project company to receive sufficient revenues to service its debts during this period. Road projects primarily opt for BOT format.
- In a BOOT project, the ownership is vested with the private developers, albeit temporarily, and a terminal payment is made to the project developer during the asset transfer process at the end of the concession period.
- Under the BOO format, the ownership of the asset is retained in perpetuity by the private developer. This is more popular in power plants, where the private developers own the plant and are governed by a power purchase agreement,

which is usually a fixed term contract. The physical assets of the project do not revert to the state after the concession period is over.

All these projects require bold decisions by governments for private participation in infrastructure development. People are often willing to pay a reasonable rate for better services like roads, power, water and so on. Infrastructure projects can be viewed as the engines for growth of an area; they can be major contributors to the overall development of an area, bringing direct and indirect benefits.

PROJECT MANAGEMENT
in action

Knowing the drill – virtual teamwork at BP

On a cold day on the North Sea in 1995, a group of BP exploration drilling engineers had a problem. Equipment failure had brought operations to a halt, and because they couldn't diagnose the trouble, they faced the prospect of taking the mobile drilling ship (leased at a cost of $150,000 a day) back to port indefinitely. Instead, they hauled the faulty hardware in front of a tiny video camera connected to a newly installed computer workstation. Using a satellite link, they dialled up a BP drilling equipment expert in Aberdeen. To him, the problem was apparent, and he guided them quickly through the repair. The downtime, as it turned out, lasted only a few hours.

The equipment aboard the ship was there thanks to a pilot project BP had just undertaken called 'Virtual Teamwork.' The name reflects the aim: to support collaboration across the barriers of distance and organizational structure, through the use of sophisticated technology.

The importance of coaching
A subgroup of the core team called the Change Management Team was responsible for helping participants understand both how to use the technology and how it could further their work. This effort was deliberately called 'coaching' rather than 'training': coaches work to get the best out of players, they don't simply present information to passive recipients. Only twenty percent of the coaches' time was designated for training people in

how to use the system. The rest would consist of challenging and helping them to exploit its capabilities to serve their business needs. The core team was so convinced that extensive coaching was essential to the success of the project that they spent approximately half the pilot's budget on it.

An unplanned experiment helped prove them right. Due to budget constraints, one of the projects, the new network of geoscientists and engineers, was set up without coaching. The members of what was called the Virtual Petrotechnical Team were given virtual teamwork (VT) equipment and essentially left alone to find uses for it. This project was the only one of the five that failed. The problem was not that the group couldn't make the technology work – it was fairly simple to operate. What they lacked was an understanding of why they should bother. Remarks from the team ('I don't see how this fits in with my work.' 'The people I want to talk to are not on the network.') were similar to those made initially by other teams. In part because there was no one to help the group explore the value of the system and overcome their scepticism, their VT network declined and eventually fell silent.

Certainly, virtual teamworking did not eliminate the need for meetings. Colleagues still needed them to establish mutual trust and to thrash out important issues involving large groups. Meetings were, however, significantly reduced. Having met once, participants found that videoconferencing maintained a richness of communication and a sense of direct personal contact that phone calls, email or memos could not match. Before long, even Trafalgar House praised the system.

But the quantifiable benefits on the Andrew Project went well beyond reductions in travel expenses and time. There were also measurable productivity improvements related to more efficient information searches and issue resolution, and less 'miscommunication.' One finding was that commitments made 'face-to-face' using the VT stations were honoured much more consistently than commitments made by phone or mail. (This underscores the point that the project was principally about behaviour, not technology.) Time frames were also compressed by things like the VT clients' application-sharing feature, which allowed teams to write memos jointly, avoiding hours or days of sending drafts back and forth. In sum, virtual teamworking contributed significantly to the project's meeting its target date and incurring a much lower total cost of steadily bringing forward first oil, a principal milestone in the development of a new field.

Unexpected uses
The VT team was even more encouraged by some spontaneous and relatively unstructured uses of the technology they observed. For example, VT users began communicating across projects, with members of the Andrew Project, for instance, contacting members of the Miller Team. The connection was important: much of the knowledge the latter team had gained from a now-mature oil field was highly applicable to work on the emerging Andrew field.

The 'hosts' of the Business Center Network, meanwhile, decided to hold weekly 'virtual coffee breaks.' The idea was to try to mimic a knowledge-sharing opportunity that collocated employees enjoy every day. Famously, 'water cooler conversations' are how people absorb corporate culture; they also bring about chance conversations that sometimes spark creative ideas. With no set agenda announced, these virtual coffee breaks have attracted up to twenty people at eight separate locations. Their expectation, and the company's, is that the conversations will pay off in unpredictable ways.

Source: D. Cohen (1997) 'Knowing the drill – virtual teamwork at BP', Perspectives on Business Innovation, Issue 1: Managing Organisational Knowledge, January. http://www.kmadvantage.com/docs/ km_articles/Virtual_Teamwork_at_BP.pdf

QUESTIONS TO AID UNDERSTANDING AND DISCUSSION

1. In what ways does this project qualify as being a virtual organisation?

2. What is the difference between a trainer and a coach?

3. Why was this important to the BP project?

4. Why can't virtual organisations function without meetings?

5. What were the unexpected benefits resulting from this project?

PROJECT MANAGEMENT *in action*

Maritime helicopter procurement process

On 17 August, 2000, the Canadian Ministers of Public Works and National Defence made a joint announcement that the Crown Project to replace the Canadian Forces' Sea King helicopter fleet would commence immediately. The 'Maritime Helicopter Statement of Requirement' which had been approved over a year earlier but kept under wraps, was also released to the public the same day. The announcement indicated that the procurement would be split; separate competitions would be held first to procure the helicopter and second for the mission systems. The Ministers also stated that selection would be based solely on the principle of 'lowest cost compliance' (LCC). Industry was also informed that a 'Letter of Interest' (LOI) would be made public, soliciting interest from helicopter and mission system suppliers wishing to participate in the two competitions.

The Letter of Interest was made public on the Department of National Defence (DND) website on 22 August. It established a project structure and an approximate schedule. Each competition is divided into two phases: a pre-qualification evaluation, which is itself multi-phased; and a proposal evaluation phase. Each bidder in the second phase must also include a bid for long term 'in service support' for which a separate contract will be awarded.

The pre-qualification process is designed to eliminate or mitigate the potentiality of a contender being judged technically non-compliant during the proposal evaluation phase. Presumably, although not clearly stated, any contender judged technically non-compliant during the evaluation will not be invited to submit a bid in response to the subsequent 'Request for Proposals'.

The selection of the helicopter and support system (called the 'Basic Vehicle') and the mission system and its support system (called the 'Maritime Helicopter Integrated Mission System') will occur at the end of the respective proposal evaluation phases and will be based solely upon lowest cost.

The government's stated objective is to have the competition for the 'Basic Vehicle' completed before the end of 2001, and to have the mission system competition completed before the end of 2002 – all with the aim of having the first fully integrated helicopter delivered by the end of 2005. All deliveries are to be completed by the end of 2008.

Of the original $2.9 billion announced for the project, the Letter of Intent allocates a maximum of $925 million for the 'Basic Vehicle' and a maximum of $925 million for the support systems. The allocation of the more than one billion dollars remaining is not explained.

The split and staggered process and the principle of 'lowest cost compliance' has set a precedent for the major procurement of complex military hardware in Canada. In the proposed process, the 'so-called' Basic Vehicle will be built and delivered according to specifications that cannot possibly take into consideration the size, weight, shape, power needs, and so on, of a yet-to-be-determined mission suite. It is not made clear who will pay for the modifications to the airframe that the systems contractor requires in order to fit the mission suite equipment into the basic helicopter. Nor is it made clear who will do the metal cutting and modifications and then re-certify the modified helicopter as airworthy once all of this is done. And who will pay for this? Moreover, who will be held accountable when all the extra modifications and work required result in 'unforecast' project and delivery delays?

Experience has shown that a single acquisition with a single prime contractor responsible and accountable for all aspects of the end product is a superior way to contain and minimise cost, schedule risks and all other associated project risks for a complex crown acquisition of this nature. No explanation is offered as to why the government elected a process containing built-in hazards that risk cost and schedule overruns as well as integration nightmares down stream.

The Letter of Intent states that the government 'is committed to utilising new and innovative procurement processes while adhering to the [Treasury Board's] Government Contract Regulations (GCR)' and that 'to this end, industry will be involved early in the procurement process'. However, there is no indication that all of industry was consulted in the development of the proposed procurement process. In fact, the opposite appears to be the case judging by the reactions of some to the procurement process. Furthermore, the Treasury Board's contracting policy contained in the contract regulations (GCR) clearly requires all government departments to seek 'best value' in their procurements and states that:

inherent in procuring best value is the

consideration of all relevant costs over the useful life of the acquisition, not solely the initial or basic contractual cost. Often, the goods and services offered by different suppliers are not identical. Assessments and evaluations should be made between different performance characteristics, costs, delivery dates, follow-on procurement and logistic support. Equally important are those cases in which a product or facility has been designed to meet specific government requirements. In such instances, detailed analysis of materials and components in terms of their function and price may be needed before the contracting process. This should clarify the requirement which should, in turn, result in best value.

It appears in the case of the Maritime Helicopter Project that the government has chosen to ignore its own procurement regulations – without explanation or accountability.

On Wednesday, 11 October, 2000, E.H. Industries, the Anglo-Italian consortium that makes the Cormorant helicopter, and which is already under DND contract for the supply of 15 helicopters to replace the ageing CF Search and Rescue Labrador helicopters, filed a complaint with the Canadian International Trade Tribunal stating that the Maritime Helicopter Procurement procurement process was flawed in not taking into account the obvious benefits and savings to the taxpayers of 'fleet commonality' and citing the government's own rules that the evaluation should be based on 'best value' principles.

A second contender, Sikorsky Air-

craft Corporation, has asked the federal government to reconsider and change one of the compliancy rules it has established. Specifically, Sikorsky questions the stipulation that helicopters offered must be certified airworthy by transportation authorities when the contract is signed in 2001. Sikorsky's new S-92 helicopter will not be ready for official certification until 2002, three years before the helicopters are to be delivered in 2005.

After cancelling the Sea King replacement project in 1993, the government promised in its Defence White Paper of 1994 to replace the Sea Kings 'by the end of the decade'. This did not happen. Then the government waited for over a year following the approval of the new Maritime Helicopter Statement of Requirement before announcing the Maritime Helicopter Project, wherein they indicate only a strong desire to have delivery of the first helicopter before the end of 2005. Now the government has issued a convoluted and controversial procurement policy that has prompted a reaction from two of the three leading helicopter contenders. This process does not bode well for a replacement project for the Sea King fleet, which is already long overdue.

Source: This article was prepared in consultation and cooperation with retired officers with extensive experience in military procurement and project management. Colonel (Ret'd) Lee Myrhaugen is the coordinator for the Friends of Maritime Aviation (FOMA). Reproduced with permission.

QUESTIONS TO AID UNDERSTANDING AND DISCUSSION

1. What procurement documents are referred to in the case and what is the purpose of each?

2. How would you describe the procurement strategy of the Canadian government?

3. What are the signs in the case that it is successful or unsuccessful?

4. What general lessons can you deduce from this case about large procurement projects in the public sector?

5. In what way do you think procurement in the private sector is managed differently?

Summary points

- Organisational requirements change throughout a project's life cycle.
- In the early life cycle phases, communication needs to be free and unhindered to encourage creativity and allow alternative solutions to be considered.
- Once a solution is selected, the unsuccessful ones are discarded and the chosen solution is optimised.
- During implementation, communication is aimed at keeping to scope and schedule, and controlling modifications and developments of the project plan.
- The traditional organisation has stood the test of time; based around functionally organised capital and human resources, information and materials are passed sequentially from one department to the next and finally to the customer.
- Attempts to improve the customer focus of the functional approach have led to a re-engineering of organisations according to process rather than by function, but this tends to compromise the efficiency of resource use.
- The matrix organisation aims to provide strong customer focus and resource efficiency. There are strong and weak forms depending on the level of authority vested in the project manager; it is sometimes seen as unstable and conflictual.
- Project management can be carried out entirely in-house or parts of a project can be procured using the help of other organisations.
- Project procurement requires a contractual relationship between a sponsor and a contractor. There may be many contractual relationships on a project. Contractors can also subcontract parts of the work to other companies.
- The four elements of procurement planning are: requirements planning – what is the project about, its requirements and boundaries; solicitation – approaching contractors and suppliers for bids and negotiation; awarding – evaluation and selection of suppliers, award and signature of contracts; and contract administration – managing contractors and suppliers until contract completion.
- Contractual arrangements allow for a variety of contract payment structures. These generally fall into two categories: fixed price – the price is fixed at the start of the contract, used when the project is fully and clearly defined; and cost reimbursable – the contractor is paid for costs incurred plus a fee, used when a project is started, before design is complete or the deliverables are exploratory.
- Incentive contracting, often used by governments and other owners procuring large projects, can be applied to both types of payment structure.
- An incentive contract has an additional payment formula built into it linked to one or more defined project performance criteria. A contractor gets more profit if the contract performance scores well against these criteria. Conversely, profit is reduced for poor performance.
- Fast tracking is the overlap of project phases to reduce the overall project duration. It can be applied to all types of contractual arrangements but needs careful management and control and is therefore not recommended for the lay client.
- Increasingly, large projects are performed across international borders. This brings with it a need to find contracts that can be applied at an international level.
- International projects tend to be more complex to manage and conditions of contract have been developed to facilitate and smooth out the contracting process.
- On an international contract, any law and process can be agreed, for example the use of UNCITRAL Model Law contract.

In the next chapter we shall investigate the importance of risk and quality management, and take a look at health and safety issues in project management.

References

APM (2000). *Body of Knowledge* (4th edn), Association of Project Management, High Wycombe.

Boleman, L.G. and Deal, T.E. (1997). *Reframing Organizations: Artistry, Choice, and Leadership*, Jossey-Bass, San Francisco.

Burns, T. and Stalker, G.M. (1994, reissue of 1961 edn) *The Management of Innovation*, Oxford University Press, Oxford.

Chambers, G.J. (1989). 'The individual in a matrix organisation', *Project Management Journal*, **20**(4): 37–42, 50.

Cherns, A.B. and Bryant, D.T. (1984). 'Studying the client's role in construction management', *Construction Management and Economics*, **2**: 177–84.

Davidson, F.P. (2000). *Arbitration*, Scottish Universities Law Institute, W Green & Son Ltd, Edinburgh.

Egan, Sir J. (1998). *Rethinking Construction,* HMSO, London.

El-Najdawi, M.K. and Liberatore, M.J. (1997). 'Matrix management effectiveness: an update for research and engineering organisations', *Project Management Journal*, **28**(1): 25–31.

Galbraith, J.R. (1971). 'Matrix organisation designs – How to combine functional and project forms', *Business Horizons*, **14**(1): 29–40.

Gardiner, P.D. and Simmons, J.E.L. (1992). 'The relationship between conflict, change and project management strategy' in P. Fenn and R. Gameson (eds) *Construction Conflict Management and Resolution*, E & FN Spon, London.

Gobeli, D.H. and Larson, E.W. (1986). 'Matrix management: more than a fad', *Engineering Management International*, **4**: 71–6.

Gobeli, D.H. and Larson, E.W. (1987). 'Relative effectiveness of different project structures', *Project Management Journal*, **17**(2): 81–5.

Harrigan, K.R. (1988). 'Strategic alliances and partner asymmetries', *Management International Review*, **28** (Special issue): 53–72.

Hayes, R.H., Wheelwright, S.C. and Clark, K.B. (1988). *Dynamic Manufacturing: Creating the Learning Organization*, Free Press, New York.

Lorange, P., Roos, J. and Bronn, P.S. (1992). 'Building successful strategic alliances', *Long Range Planning*, **25**(6): 10–17.

Lynch, R.P. (1993). *Business Alliances Guide*, John Wiley & Sons, New York.

McCollum, J.K. and Sherman, J.D. (1993). 'The matrix structure: bane or benefit to high tech organisations?', *Project Management Journal*, **24**(2): 23–6.

Peters, T.J. and Waterman, R.H. (1982). *In Search of Excellence: Lessons from America's Best-run Companies*, Harper & Row, New York.

PMI (2000). *'Guide to the Project Management Body of Knowledge'*, Project Management Institute, Upper Darby, PA.

Robbins, S. (1993). *Organisational Behaviour: Concepts, Controversies, and Applications* (6th edn), Prentice Hall, Sydney.

Skinner, S. and Ivancevich, J. (1992). *Business for the 21st Century*, Irwin Press, Homewood.

Walker, A. (1996). *Project Management in Construction* (3rd edn), Blackwell, Oxford.

Winch, G. (1997). *Thirty years of project management, what have we learned?*, Business Process Resource Centre, University of Warwick.

Visit the website

http://www.palgrave.com/business/gardiner

▶ for additional resources to explore the topics in this chapter further

CHAPTER

7

Managing risk and quality

Learning objectives

After reading this chapter you should be able to:

- discuss the importance of risk in a project and how it can be managed
- explain the processes of risk planning, risk assessment and risk control
- describe tools used in risk management and how to use them effectively
- explain the process of contingency planning in project management
- identify key health, safety and environmental issues in a project
- discuss the importance of quality to project management
- differentiate the meaning of quality in the context of product, service and process
- explain three important quality management processes
- outline key contributions to quality management by Deming, Juran and Crosby
- explain how to determine the total cost of quality
- describe simple tools used in statistical process control and how to use them effectively

Introduction

All projects carry some level of risk and how this is dealt with affects project success. The first part of this chapter looks at the nature of risk and risk management. The process of risk management is divided into a number of stages. Risk planning draws attention to the strategic role of preparing an overall approach to project risk. Risk assessment introduces techniques to help identify risks within the scope of a risk plan, leading to their analysis and prioritisation. The next stage considers risk control, including response planning, resolution, monitoring and reporting. The chapter outlines a number of useful tools to help manage risk and also considers the nature of contingency planning and how it can be used effectively.

Organisations have a statutory obligation to provide a safe working environment for employees, and this obligation extends to everyone working on a project. Health and safety issues are important factors in any project. They are considered here,

together with a look at the role of hazard and operability studies, performed as part of project planning in some sectors.

Quality is also a vital aspect of project management and is explored here with an initial focus on the different perspectives of quality, highlighting the fact that quality applies to the design and execution of processes in project management as well as to the end products and services. The process of quality management is explained with reference to the ISO 9000 and ISO 10000 series of standards on quality. Concepts of quality have been influenced by a number of well-known quality gurus and some of their thinking is presented here, along with a discussion on how quality management can complement project management. The chapter continues with a look at the total cost of quality, followed by a brief examination of some tools and techniques used in quality management and statistical quality control. The chapter closes with a consideration of environmental issues in projects and ISO 14000, the international environmental management standard.

Risk and risk management

A project risk is often described as:

any event with an undesirable outcome for the project that may happen sometime in the future.

However, there has been significant debate recently over the definition of a risk. The 2000 edition of the *Guide to the Project Management Body of Knowledge* (PMI, 2000) states that a project risk is:

an uncertain event or condition that, if it occurs, has a positive or negative effect on a project outcome.

The idea that risk can have a positive effect is also reflected in a recent survey of IT managers (see Figure 7.1) which revealed that although 49% of respondents regarded risk as a negative event, 22% of respondents held the view that risk can include positive consequences of some event as well as negative aspects (Charette, 2002). The same survey also indicated that organisations using formal risk management tend to favour the traditional definition of risk over definitions that allow the inclusion of negative and positive effects. These effects are also known as *downside* risk (negative effect) and *upside* risk (positive effect).

There are essentially two categories of risk:

1. *Speculative risk:* meaning a chance of a loss or chance of a profit. For example, an established business could expand and make more profit or it could go bankrupt, so buying stock in this company is a speculative risk. Most projects carry speculative risk.
2. *Pure risk:* meaning only a chance of a loss. For example, driving a car involves only the chance of an accident. Pure risks are insurable.

The success of many projects, particularly larger more complex ones and those that may be classed as highly visible or open, hinges on having in place an effective approach to risk and an appropriate risk

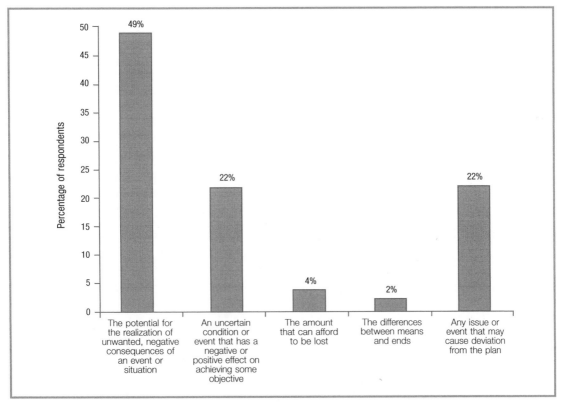

Figure 7.1 **Survey results – definitions of risk** (Cutter Consortium: Press Center: http://www.cutter.com/press/020606.html)

management plan from the beginning of the project. The risk management plan will take account of risks arising from three principal sources:

1. Factors under project control (for example poor design, ineffective management systems, poor performance by contractors).
2. Factors in the wider external environment which are only controllable by decision makers elsewhere (for example changes in government policy, institutional weaknesses, lack of political will).
3. Factors that are essentially uncontrollable (for example natural disasters, international terrorism, political instability, world prices, interest rates).

Whatever their source, project risks are characterised by the fact that:

- they are usually at least partially unknown
- they change with time
- they are manageable, in the sense that action may be taken to change their impact
- they exist only in the future tense – there are no past risks, only actual occurrences
- they exist in all projects.

Risk management is about balancing the harmful effects of risk against potential project benefits, see Insights from Industry: 'If you don't take commercial risks, you're not going to make any money'. Risk

---

 IF YOU DON'T TAKE COMMERCIAL RISKS, YOU'RE NOT GOING TO MAKE ANY MONEY

Currently, both the editors of books and their authors are wondering about the future. Galassi, translator of Italian poetry, says:

> It's a very unsettled moment in publishing right now. I have queasy feelings about the state of the marketplace. Until very recently I felt strongly that the backbone of the business was still the hardcover book, but that may be changing.

Making the consumer aware of new books – even those with large potential readerships – poses a growing challenge as our media-saturated society bombards the populace with information. Galassi says:

> There's just so much noise out there, drowning things out. If you are Procter & Gamble, you sell Colgate toothpaste year in and year out. But if you are Farrar, Straus & Giroux, it's like introducing 200 new products each year: how do you create brand awareness?

Books have been pushed out of the centre of the culture. It's not that they aren't still important, but they don't have the same primacy. At a dinner party, people used to ask, 'What are you reading?' Now, it's 'What have you seen?'

A drugstore that does not sell its Colgate toothpaste cannot send the tubes back to Procter & Gamble. But publishers have long allowed retailers to return unsold books for full credit. The practice began in the Depression, to encourage booksellers to carry titles in lean times, but it persists today and has become a mammoth problem. Returns ranged between 20 and 35% for many years, but now they are approaching 50%, and coming back to publishers with boomerang speed. Superstores track their inventories closely with computer software and often give new books a window of only a few weeks to make their mark – or else be shipped back.

Some publishers want to restrict returns, as the music industry did many years ago. 'The book chains are now often as big as the publishers, or bigger – so why should the publisher take all the risk of selling the product? The vendor and publisher should share the risk more equally,' Galassi says. Years ago, Harcourt Brace tried selling its books on a nonreturnable basis, but the move quickly flopped when no other houses followed suit and retailers gave the policy a predictably chilly reception.

Technology may someday solve the returns problem, in the form of a high-tech re-creation of the early days of publishing, when books were published by subscription. It is now possible to order a backlist book constructed on demand – custom-printed in a shop for as little as 30 to 50 dollars. Galassi says:

> This could happen with new books, too. Instead of printing 50,000 copies and getting 30,000 back, you send out just 6,000 copies to bookstores. If a customer sees the book and likes it, the bookstore will make a copy and have it ready in 10 minutes, or perhaps the next day – or send it to you. All of a sudden our distribution problems go away.

Such a system is only one step beyond current mail-order booksellers like the internet-driven Amazon.com, whose sales may soon surpass $100 million.

Even if the distribution risks in publishing eventually disappear, the editorial risks never will. 'Taste is what it's all about in publishing: taste and the telling, the ability to convey your enthusiasm,' says Galassi. 'In literary publishing, you've got to be able to smell something good, and then be able to promote it, to market it.' He praises Morgan Entrekin of Grove Atlantic Press and others who 'are swashbuckling it, doing it with panache, flair, savvy, shrewdness. If you don't take commercial risks, you're not going to make any money.'

He reflects:

The old-time gentleman publishers wanted to publish something good, and also hoped to make a living at it. The trouble now is that, in our economy, the product is often only a means of making a profit.

That's the problem with the way we do capitalism. What's often missing is a sense of commitment to the product. Instead of being intrinsic and fundamental, the product becomes incidental to the commercial transaction.

Source: Adapted from C.A. Lambert, associate editor, *Harvard Magazine*, Nov-Dec 1997, http://www.harvard-magazine.com/issues/nd97/books3.html

Questions

1. What are the risks faced by authors writing a new book?
2. Is the risk the same for all authors?
3. In what way is the statement 'If you don't take commercial risks, you're not going to make any money' relevant to project management?

---

management is a process of clear thinking and planning by careful evaluation and visualisation of the future. Modern business methods and entrepreneurship encourage some risk taking and accept, even expect, that occasional mistakes will be made. Success in business often requires quick, close to the edge decision making. These views are as true for project management as they are for other business situations. However, the careful prior analysis of risks, free from time pressure, makes each decision easier when, eventually, it has to be taken. Key Concepts: 'A family day out – identifying the risks' illustrates well the concept of risk using a simple story of a family stroll in the countryside.

 A family day out – identifying the risks!

Every decision leads to a range of possible outcomes. One of these is the expected outcome, but there are usually many other possible outcomes The poorer outcomes can sometimes be mitigated, through action taken in advance, though often this involves additional cost. For those risks which are not mitigated in advance, a good control system can often prevent adverse outcomes.

Suppose, for example, that you and your family are on holiday, and you are all discussing taking a country walk, before going to a show in the evening. First, you agree the objectives for the walk. Some members of the family may just want an enjoyable stroll in the sunshine but if a 12 year old wishes to see a steam engine, it is important to identify this at the outset when choosing the route. You then identify the risks involved in the walk, such as being caught in a thunderstorm, encountering a muddy path or getting lost.

You then analyse the likelihood of each such event and how serious the consequences might be.

The next step is to identify the risk mitigation options, such as carrying umbrellas and rainwear, wearing boots, or taking a mobile phone to call a taxi if necessary. In each case, there will be an inconvenience or cost factor and a decision will have to be made on whether mitigation is worthwhile.

Unless all the risks are mitigated in advance, some residual risks will remain. Suppose it is decided not to take rainwear. The residual storm risk will then have to be controlled by keeping an eye on the sky and heading for shelter in time if black clouds roll up. The time risk will likewise have to be controlled by occasionally looking at a watch so that the taxi can be called. If we take the mobile phone, this will introduce a secondary risk; as it might be lost or stolen.

Source: Lewin, C. (2003) 'Making the right decisions', *Finance/Risk Management*, PSCA International, January

Risk management planning

Risk management can be divided into *risk assessment* activities and *risk control* activities. Of course before embarking on either of these it is necessary to first consider the amount of effort that will be needed to develop an appropriate risk management plan. This is called risk planning. The PMI *Guide to the Body of Knowledge* introduced 'risk management planning' as a major process in 2000; without prior planning, it is difficult to agree when to stop risk analysis. The identification of risks becomes an almost infinitely lengthy activity leading, ultimately, to 'paralysis by analysis'. A simple form of risk planning involves developing a 'purpose statement' in the style of the one used during BP management training, which consisted of three components (Isaac, 1995):

- *Objective:* Why is the risk analysis being done? What outcome is needed? What decision is required? By when?
- *Project:* What is the project or programme being analysed?
- *Scope:* What are the boundaries or limits of the analysis, for example one work package or one project phase or a whole project.

The use of a purpose statement can be compared to the use of an agenda for a meeting; without one, a meeting can go on indefinitely, with one, there is a chance of a useful outcome. Risk management planning is primarily a strategic activity, rather than operational. Strategic and governance issues in projects are discussed in greater detail in Chapter 3.

Risk assessment

The following activities are associated with risk assessment:

- *Risk identification* – draw up a list of all the risks that could compromise the success of a project
- *Risk analysis* – study each risk to determine the relative exposure it brings to the project using quantitative and/or qualitative methods. Note that risk exposure is a measure of the impact of a risk to a project, programme or organisation
- *Risk prioritisation* – rank or prioritise each risk in order of importance.

Identification of risks

Risk identification is about determining all the risks (within the scope of the risk assessment) likely to affect a project and documenting their characteristics in an understandable way. It is an organised approach that aims to seek out any events associated with a project that may impair the achievement of that project's critical success factors. On the other hand, it is not a process of trying to invent highly improbable scenarios of unlikely events in an effort to cover every conceivable possibility of outrageous fortune – the risk purpose statement or its equivalent should prevent this kind of outcome.

The process of risk identification should:

- examine all areas of a project in a systematic manner
- be proactive rather than reactive
- use information from all available sources. For example:
  - previous lessons learned files and other historical information about the project and its context
  - all planning outputs to date including work breakdown structures, schedule and cost plans
  - the project charter, industry-wide and organisation-wide risk checklists
  - feasibility reports
  - trade-off analyses involving cost, time, quality and scope
  - interviews with experts and knowledge workers.

A risk checklist offers a summary of the common causes of risk, with examples of the nature of the source and its effect. These simple tools are often highly tailored to suit different organisations and sectors. They can help a group of people identify risks systematically across a project or programme; however, they are only a guide and should not be regarded as exaustive. The following checklist shows several areas where risk can often be identified:

1. Business impact and benefits – strategic impact, level of senior management support, shareholder confidence, costs/benefits expected.
2. Project management issues – funding, schedule, staff availability, materials, contractual relationships, political risks, stakeholder management.
3. Organisational impact – who is affected in the organisation, level of cultural change, resistance level of employees, communication infrastructure.
4. Technical risks and complexity – new technology, level of experience, reliability of suppliers, performance requirements.
5. Logistics – movement of people, equipment and materials, availability of space.
6. Production – coordination and integration of work packages, material availability.
7. Testing – compliance with specifications and standards, verification and validation of software and systems.

Project Management in Action: 'Taj Mahal Cycle Improvement Project', at the end of this chapter, is

---

SWOT Analysis

SWOT stands for Strengths, Weaknesses, Opportunities and Threats. The tool is ideal when dealing with complex situations in a limited amount of time, Helping to quickly get to those issues that have the most impact on the situation.

Ground rules for SWOT analysis

1. Take time to make lists about the strengths, weaknesses, opportunities and threats of your project, listing each of these subjects (with real thought and honesty).

2. The first two, strengths and weaknesses, apply internally to the project environment. The second two, opportunities and threats, relate to elements and events outside the immediate project environment but which may impact on it.

3. The process requires serious thought. You don't have to complete the process in one sitting.

It is often surprising to see the problems clearly identified in front of you. Even more pleasing are the obvious solutions to many of them that will be evident.

Figure 7.2 How to carry out a SWOT analysis

a complex project with many risks. The use of a risk checklist such as this would aid the identification of risks.

The risk identification process may involve team meetings, often called 'risk clinics', with key project members and stakeholders. A risk consultant or other subject expert can often add professionalism and thoroughness to the process. Tools to help to identify risks include brainstorming (see Chapter 5), SWOT analysis (see Figure 7.2), cause and effect diagrams and risk concept maps (both explained later in this chapter).

Some risks are easier to identify if related risks are grouped together by source. Often, people only recognise part of a risk. The act of classifying risks according to some predefined structure, or the project's work breakdown structure, can point out sets of risks that are multiple aspects of the same risk. These are called 'complex risks'. Dealing with this set and its source rather than individual risks can save time and reduce mitigation costs.

Analysis and prioritisation

The objective of risk prioritisation is to prioritise the identified risks for mitigation, compare identified risks effectively and provide a proactive perspective. The risk prioritisation method should consider the following three factors:

1. Probability of the risk occurring.
2. Impact of the risk – which can be broken down further, for example, into:
   - impact on schedule
   - impact on cost
   - impact on performance.
3. Cost and resources required to mitigate the risk.

Quantitative analysis is not always necessary. Many successful risk management practitioners rarely perform quantitative analysis. In fact during training in risk management at BP, the terms 'qualitative' and 'quantitative' were removed because they did not improve the clarity of what was to be achieved (Isaac, 1995). Indeed, some senior project managers expressed concern that the 'number crunching' detracted from implementing risk management – the assumption being that practitioners of risk management will gradually increase the sophistication of the modelling tools they use as confidence and experience grows.

Qualitative analysis of risk exposure (for example using a scale of 1–10, or designating high, medium or low to probability or impact) is sufficient to sort through a large number of risks to select the most important. Quantitative analysis can be reserved for those risks that require numerical justification or rationale for mitigation plan approval. They include:

- probability analysis
- decision trees (discussed in Chapter 3)
- Monte Carlo simulation
- sensitivity analysis.

Risk analysis is about establishing the probability of occurrence and the impact of occurrence of all identified project risks. Once these two variables have

Table 7.1 Risk assessment matrix				
Probability		**Impact**		
		Low **1**	**Medium** **2**	**High** **3**
Low	1	1	2	3
Medium	2	2	4	6
High	3	3	6	9

been determined, the risk exposure of the project to each risk can be calculated using the equation:

Risk exposure = probability of risk × impact of risk

A risk assessment matrix, as shown in Table 7.1, is a convenient way to categorise this information in order to assess the overall risk of 'project failure'. Each risk is placed in one of the nine boxes according to its assessed probability and impact. In this example, the exposure can take values between 1 (lowest exposure) to 9 (highest exposure). In the summary risk register of Table 7.3, exposure scores can range from 1 to 100.

In practice, the value of risk exposure attached to a given situation is influenced by the sensitivity to risk of the person performing the analysis. It is a reflection of the personality of the risk taker. Twenty people can look at the same situation and assign twenty different values of risk exposure to it. This is why it is always better to analyse risks with a group of project stakeholders in order to ensure a more balanced outcome.

A typical risk assessment workshop is described in Key Concepts below.

 CONCEPTS Risk assessment workshop

A useful way to organise a risk assessment workshop is to bring together a group of key stakeholders (but excluding any who are opposed to the activity) and ask participants, working in small groups, to undertake the following:

■ Draw a large risk assessment matrix on flip-chart paper and fix it on a nearby wall
■ Brainstorm all the risks to the success of the project that anybody in the group can think of, writing each risk on a Post-it note and placing them on a blank piece of wall
■ Take each risk in turn and discuss how 'critical' or 'dangerous' it is to the success of the project if it happened – classify all risks as either 'low', 'medium' or 'high' impact

■ Take each risk in turn and discuss how probable it is – classify all risks as either 'low', 'medium' or 'high' probability
■ Stick each of the Post-it notes into the appropriate box in the risk assessment matrix
■ Each group presents their risk matrix in a plenary session followed by discussion and agreement on one overall risk matrix. Table 7.2 shows how the distribution of risks in the final risk assessment matrix can help to indicate the overall riskiness of a project or programme

Finally, ask the group to consider if the project can be redesigned to minimise the most important risks; or if not, to identify how they can be managed.

Source: 'Tools for Development', Department for International Development, UK

Table 7.2 Overall assessment of project risk exposure	
	Pattern of risks in the risk assessment matrix
■ High-risk programme	One or more at 9 More than one at 6
■ Medium-risk programme	One or more at 4 One or more at 6 More than one at 3
■ Low-risk programme	One or more at 1 or 2 One at 3

Risk control

The output from a risk assessment is used in the second stage of risk management, risk control. Risk control is usually carried out at a more senior level in the project organisation structure than risk analysis. This is because risk control places high pressure on those involved who must make decisions with limited information.

Risk control consists of the following activities:

■ *Risk response planning* – the production of plans for responding to and controlling each risk
■ *Risk resolution* – the elimination of a risk by executing activities in the risk response plans
■ *Risk monitoring and reporting* – keeping track of the project's progress towards resolving each risk.

Risk response planning

The purpose of risk response planning is simply to bring organised purposeful thought to the subject of:

- eliminating risk wherever possible
- isolating and minimising risk
- developing alternative courses of action
- establishing time and money reserves to cover risks that cannot be avoided.

The output of this process is a risk response plan. There are six types of response to risk:

1. **Avoidance** – the cause of the risk is avoided completely and a different course of action chosen. For example, if the risk is that a small contractor would go bankrupt, use a larger contractor. For some risks, avoidance could mean abandoning the project altogether.
2. **Mitigation** – measures are carried out to reduce the probability or impact of the risk; this may require the use of additional resources, improved communications infrastructure or the holding of contingency funds to offset the risk. Using a variation of the risk assessment matrix, the probability and impact of project risks can be plotted on an isorisk chart to portray graphically

their relative importance and impact on the project, as shown in Figure 7.3.

The location of risks on the isorisk contour chart provides insight into the most cost-effective manner by which they may be mitigated. For, example Risk A is best mitigated by a strategy that reduces the impact of the risk, while Risk B is best mitigated by a strategy that reduces the probability of the risk.

3. **Acceptance** – the risk is acknowledged and accepted as a legitimate risk that cannot easily be avoided or provided for.
4. **Transfer** – the risk can be shared or transferred to another party, such as a contractor or risk insurance agency. Risks should be borne by the party best able to manage them. This could be an insurance company (through purchase of a policy), the market (through securitisation of the risk) or another party (for instance by contracting out some of the work).
5. **Absorption or pooling** – an example of which would be taking part in a project as part of a consortium or joint venture.
6. **Knowledge and research** – in which testing and simulation studies are used to improve the prediction of the most likely outcome; used during the Auckland International Airport Terminal Expansion, a megaproject in the 1990s – see Insights from Industry: 'Simulation studies at the Auckland International Airport terminal expansion'.

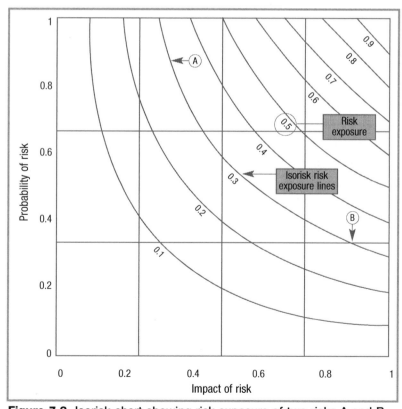

Figure 7.3 Isorisk chart showing risk exposure of two risks A and B

SIMULATION STUDIES AT THE AUCKLAND INTERNATIONAL AIRPORT TERMINAL EXPANSION

New Zealand-based international consultancy firm Beca Carter Hollings & Ferner (BCHF) played a key role in the recent Auckland International Airport (AIA) expansion which started in 1990 when it led a development-concept design study in order to determine the optimum expansion of the international terminal. Based on a projected increase in air traffic for the next 20 years, it was decided to adopt a staged expansion of the terminal.

Technology played a big role behind the scenes and aided the decision-making process at the design stage. When AIA wished to examine and verify the adequacy of proposed facilities and layouts for the passenger departure area, the BCHF systems technology group applied a custom-built discrete event simulation model.

The model considered various passenger processing procedures (departure fee inspection, emigration clearance and aviation security stations) and determined the likely length of queues and emigration processing times, under a range of aircraft departure and passenger processing scenarios.

Another model simulated Ministry of Agriculture and Fisheries (MAF) processing to establish what impact an increased use of X-ray treatment of passenger baggage processing would have on incoming international flights. The resulting analysis provided information which helped MAF identify the optimum screening strategy.

Due to its nature, size and complexity, the project presented substantial logistics and project management challenges. Peter McGregor, BCHF project manager, recalls: 'Right from the start the main concerns were ensuring safety and security at all times. We planned construction work so it allowed for the ongoing and virtually uninterrupted operation of the airport.' The ever changing layout of the terminal, for instance, had to be carefully planned to minimise disruption to the travelling public and avoid confusion to passengers.

Precisely planned and sequenced construction allowed the terminal, including the retail areas, to remain fully operational. Moving the immigration line, for instance, involved a carefully staged series of moves to ensure that all 16 counters were always fully operational. All counters had to be completely recabled and relocated three times before they could be moved to their final location. Flight schedules made this a very tight operation which had to be completed in the few hours between the last flight at night and first flight in the morning.

The terminal expansion was completed on time and officially opened on 8 December 1997, resulting in an overall increase of floor area from 39,000 m^2 to 77,000 m^2 as well as increasing the number of check-in counters from 51 to 80. Retail, restaurant and bar amenities were greatly improved and more duty-free and retail outlets were created. Critical success factors included a clear vision from the client, strong proactive management from BCHF and total commitment to the airport's safety and service delivery goals.

Questions

1. How did simulation studies help to reduce project risk in this project?
2. Who benefited from these studies the most and why?
3. What contract strategy would be appropriate for this project?

Risk resolution

Risk resolution is the primary goal of risk management. It is achieved by implementing the activities in the risk response plan to eliminate or reduce exposure to the identified risks. For example, if the loss of a key person in a project is classed as a high-risk exposure, an attractive reward package can be put in place and a replacement for that person identified to mitigate the risk (that is, reduce exposure to it).

The key to risk resolution is making sure that risk response plans are fully integrated into the project plans and actioned by the appropriate people in a timely manner.

Risk monitoring and reporting

Project risks can change at any time and so the risk response plan should be revisited regularly and updated throughout the project life cycle. For this reason, monitoring and reporting are vital parts of a comprehensive approach to risk management. Risk monitoring is about keeping track of progress towards resolving the risks in the risk response plan.

Risk management is most effective when it is done and redone as an integral part of normal project planning and management. Some of the more obvious times to revisit the list of identified risks and the risk response plan include:

■ in preparation for major decision points
■ in preparation and immediately following technical reviews and audits
■ after changes in schedule, cost, scope or quality.

Contingency planning – if all else fails ...

Even the best laid plans can fail. Management will want to establish contingency plans for tasks which are of vital importance and where there is more than a possibility that the task will not be completed in time. The identification and planning of alternative activities to be implemented in the event of a risk occurring is called 'contingency planning'. It is prudent to consider and develop contingency plans for tasks that are mission critical, as well as for resources that are mission critical. Of course contingency plans are only enacted if a given risk actually occurs, or seems increasingly likely to occur. For each contingency action there should be a defined condition which signals the go-ahead for the contingency action. This is called the 'trigger point'.

To summarise, a contingency plan should identify:

■ alternative resources and/or processes for completing mission critical tasks (for example using manual labour for a task that has been automated)
■ resources needed to launch and maintain such processes
■ lead time for the substitute processes to become functional
■ trigger point that causes a contingency plan to be activated.

Finally, contingency plans need to be revisited throughout a project to ensure that they are up to date and always reflect the best interests of the project.

Useful tools to help manage risk

Keeping a risk register

It is generally accepted that managers are more likely to act on written information than on verbally transmitted concerns. Likewise, project participants usually become more interested in tackling a risk once it has been listed and identified in a report. Accordingly, once the project risks have been identified and analysed, they can be described, recorded and tracked in the form of a risk register and standardised risk information sheets. Table 7.3 is an extract of a year 2000 summary risk register for IT managers tasked

Ref	Risk	Likelihood	Consequence	Exposure	Risk response
					KEY Probability: 10 – virtual certainty 1 – extremely unlikely Consequence: 10 – severe impact 1 – negligible impact Exposure: 100 – very high exposure 1 – very low exposure
1.	**Strategic**				
1.1	Poor awareness throughout the organisation, including the lack of a senior level sponsor	5	9	45	■ Formation of a Steering Group with a high level sponsor as chairman ■ Regular monitoring of progress at a high level and communications issued to all relevant personnel within the organisation ■ An appropriate reporting structure for the teams/personnel working on the project
1.2	Poor confidence amongst the customer and shareholder community which may be exacerbated by increased media reporting	5	8	40	■ Establishment of Year 2000 Project Office charged, inter alia, with the dissemination of 'comfort' messages to stakeholders ■ Sensitive information should be strictly controlled with restrictive circulation ■ The organisation's publicity department should understand the issues and be able to respond to any adverse publicity
1.3	Losses due to business failure of other organisations	9	9	81	■ Ensure that your financial exposure to other organisations is limited, for example closed Treasury positions
2.	**Human resources**				
2.1	Insufficient resources within the organisation to tackle the problem	10	9	90	■ Assessment of the scale of the problem in terms of effort required, which should be subject to reassessment in the light of findings during conversion work ■ Comparisons between planned and actual resources should be monitored and any shortfalls dealt with ■ Long-term arrangements made with contractors/suppliers as appropriate

Table 7.3 Extract from the Year 2000 Risk Matrix

continued

		Likelihood	Consequence	Exposure	
					KEY Probability: 10 – virtual certainty 1 – extremely unlikely Consequence: 10 – severe impact 1 – negligible impact Exposure: 100 – very high exposure 1 – very low exposure
Ref	**Risk**				**Risk Response**
2.2	Key people (which may be anyone working on the project) leaving the organisation	9	8	72	■ Provision of reward/bonus schemes to retain people up to the Year 2000
3.	**Planning**				
3.1	Failure to define what Year 2000 compliance means for the organisation	7	6	42	■ Compliance should be defined (BSI have already issued a useful definition) and disseminated to relevant personnel by the Year 2000 Project Office
3.2	Failure to determine contingency plans for systems which may not be renovated, or replaced, in time	8	9	72	■ Contingency plans may dictate that different conversion strategies will be required as the time progresses ■ For some critical systems it may be necessary to perform two parallel conversions using different conversion strategies (although it is doubtful that anyone has the time for this!) ■ Other possibilities include the use of vanilla packages with manual work arounds or the reversion to manual systems
4.	**Implementation issues**				
4.1	Failure to recognise interfaces between systems	8	8	64	■ All interfaces between systems should be recognised as part of the system inventory. These would probably be identified as dependencies, both before and after the specified system
5.	**Testing**				
5.1	Failure to perform sufficient user testing (including allocation of user time and other resources)	10	7	70	■ User testing should be scheduled. Users may require some assistance to determine test data
6.	**Project management**				
6.1	Use of inappropriate personnel to manage and coordinate the project	8	10	80	■ Ensure that project management personnel have a proven track record and experience of major projects
6.2	Poor segmentation of the project, and a consequent problem with elements which are too large	6	7	42	■ Detailed planning identifies how the project will be segmented ■ Responsibility should be allocated for every element in the plan ■ There should be measurable milestones which can be used as part of the progress reporting

Table 7.3 continued

Source: Wakeland, S. (1999).

with eradicating software bugs before the start of the new millenium and Table 7.4 shows a completed example of a risk information sheet. The consistent format of a risk register and risk information sheet helps everyone understand the real risk.

Risk concept map

A risk concept map (Bartlett, 2002) is basically a flow diagram, derived from soft system thinking principles, designed to show, in one picture, the total risk scenario for a project or programme. Figure 7.4 is an example risk concept map. The *risk drivers* can clearly be seen, leading to increasingly severe risk situations and impacts. Attached to the risk situations are individual risks, coded to entries in a risk register. Also attached, where applicable, are assumptions about the risk situations.

From the concept map it is possible to envisage not only the maximum impact of risk for the project or programme, but also the incremental situations leading to it. The map is not time-based, but represents participants' assumptions of the events that could occur in an uncontrolled environment. It is effectively a cautionary map, which warns that if mitigating or avoiding action is not taken at a particular stage, the impacts shown could arise.

Table 7.4 Risk information sheet			
ID: ABC 23	**Risk information sheet**		**Identified:** 2/3/01
Priority: 6 **Probability:** High **Impact:** High	**Statement:** With our lack of experience in X Windows software, we may not be able to complete the GUI code on time and it may not be the quality of code we need		
Timeframe: Near	**Origin:** G. Smith	**Class:** Personnel experience	**Assigned to:** S. Jones
Context:	The graphical user interface is an important part of the system and we do not have anyone trained in the X Window system. We all have been studying it, but it is complex and only one person in the group has any graphics/user interface experience and that was with a completely different type of system and interface requirements. There are other personnel within the company who have relevant experience and training, but they may not be available in time to support this project		
Mitigation strategy:	1. Update coding estimates and schedules to reflect the need for increased training and for hiring an expert in X Windows (changes due 1/5/01) 2. Coordinate with customer and get approval for changing schedule (approve by 1/6/01) 3. Identify an available expert from other projects in this division (hired by 15/6/01) 4. Bring in outside training source for current programmers (training complete by 30/07/01)		
Contingency Plan and Trigger:	*Plan:* Subcontract GUI development to LMN Corp. and accept the increase in our cost. £25,000. LMN has a level of effort contract with ABC Headquarters and can support with 1 week notice *Trigger:* If internal expert is not on board and training not completed by 30/7/01		

Status	Status Date
GUI code delivered on time, required quality	30/1/02
GUI code has been delivered for testing on schedule	13/11/01
Code 50% complete and 1 week ahead of schedule	15/9/01
Personnel completed 2 week training: will monitor progress and quality of work	15/7/01
Brown from project XYZ will be available on 5/6/01 to provide quality assurance, mentoring and critical path programmes	1/6/01
Customer approved revised schedule milestones	3/5/01
Revised estimates and schedule complete: indicates a worst-case 3 week slip if we get the additional expert	23/4/01
Approval: J.Q. Jones, ABC Project Manager	
Closing date: 15/2/02 **Closing rationale:** Code delivered on time. Acceptance test excellent. Risk is gone.	

RAMP

In July 1998, the Institution of Civil Engineers and the Faculty and Institute of Actuaries launched a risk management methodology known as RAMP (risk analysis and management for projects). The methodology was developed to address the failure of projects, characterised by delay, cost overrun, loss of life or other adverse consequences. Since then, HM Treasury has commended the methodology as a tool for use in the public sector, describing it as 'a proven method for managing project risks'. RAMP is not only useful for projects involving physical constructions, such as new hospitals or transport infrastructure; it is equally applicable to projects such as new training schemes or even an office move. It is a system for identifying, evaluating and managing risks that specifies the need to list the key assumptions made in a project appraisal and then to examine the risk that these assumptions may be wrong.

It is interesting to note that RAMP was the result of collaboration between the professional bodies of civil engineers and actuaries – both professions are concerned with the analysis of risk. For civil engineers, this risk is mainly structural, for actuaries it is more financial.

One of the main reasons for creating the RAMP process has been the shortcomings in existing approaches to risk management, particularly insufficient follow-through from initial risk reviews and inappropriate allowance for risks.

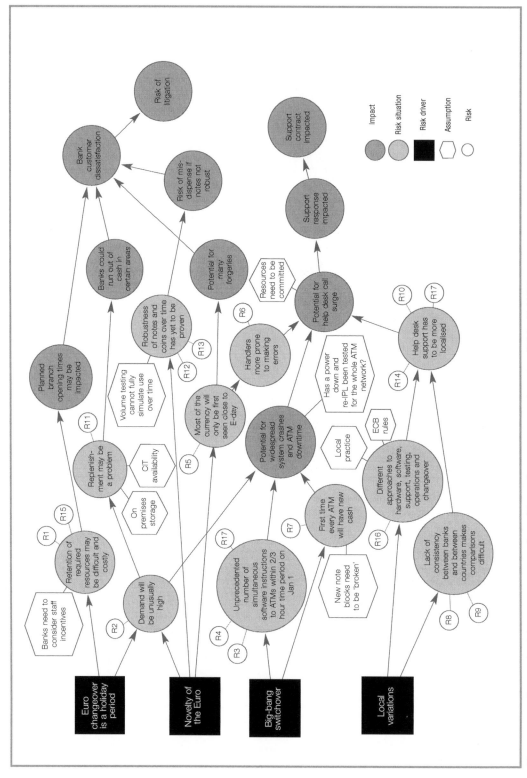

Figure 7.4 Example risk concept map for a Euro changeover project for ATMs © NCR

Visit the website

http://www.palgrave.com/business/gardiner

▶ to see an alternative layout for a risk register and risk information sheet
▶ to download and use two risk assessment tools in Excel

Health and safety

The APM *Body of Knowledge* (APM, 2000) discusses 'health, safety and the environment' in the context of project management, drawing attention to the need to ensure that applicable standards are respected and achieved in operation, and reviewed to ensure their continued validity. It also highlights the need for proper appreciation of the legal and corporate environmental controls and reporting procedures required for the project.

What is safety

Safety is defined as 'the freedom from unacceptable risks of personal harm'. (BS 4778). The harm referred to here may be immediate or longer term (for example from radiation, noise exposure or environmental damage) and it may be acting on an individual or groups of people, organisations, assets and the environment.

When considering safety in product development projects, it is vital to recognise that a system includes the software, human and procedural aspects as well as the system hardware. A system is a combination of physical components, procedures and human resources organised to achieve a function. This idea that a system is intended to achieve a function leads on to the concept of functional safety discussed below. A system cannot be considered in isolation from its environment. This includes the physical environment (for example location, weather, vibration) and also the other systems and utilities with which it interfaces, which all have an effect on the safety of the system of interest.

Physical safety concerns issues such as:

■ The working environment – noise, lighting, temperature
■ Dangerous materials and processes
■ Sharp edges, hot surfaces, electrocution, irradiation
■ Dropping, falling, crushing
■ Fire, explosion.

Physical safety aspects are usually directly recognisable by examination of the system and operating environment and they are often governed by health and safety legislation. Physical safety issues depend on the components making up the system.

In contrast, the functional safety of a system depends on the function which it is intended to perform, rather than the system components. Failure, malfunction or poor performance of the system can lead to safety problems. This means that safety problems may not be directly recognisable without deep investigation of possible malfunctions. It also means that an item which is 'safe' in one application may be 'unsafe' in a new application where it is intended to achieve a different function.

Hazards

A hazard can be defined as a situation with the potential for human injury, damage to property, assets or the environment. A hazard has the potential to cause harm. It is not correct to talk of something being 'potentially hazardous'; parachuting does not just become hazardous when the parachute fails and the person hits the ground, it always has the potential for harm. Some examples of hazards are:

■ A cloud of toxic gas
■ An exposed high-voltage cable
■ Loss of radar coverage for air traffic control
■ Corruption of IFF (identification friend or foe) data.

To answer the question 'Is this system safe?', a good starting point is to look at the safety record for a range of everyday activities (see Table 7.5).

Table 7.5 Average probabilities of death for various activities in the UK

Probability of death per year (approximate)	Activity
1 in 100	five hours of solo rock climbing every weekend
1 in 200	smoking 20 cigarettes per day
1 in 5,000	work in the coal mining industry
1 in 50,000	taking the contraceptive pill
1 in 100,000	work in the safest parts of industry
1 in 500,000	passenger in a scheduled air journey
1 in 1 million	electrocution in the home
1 in 10 million	lightning

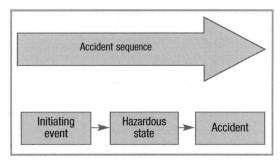

Figure 7.5 Accident sequence

Accidents are undesirable, so time and money are spent trying to make sure that they do not happen or do not have serious consequences. But where should that effort be aimed and how far should it go? This involves the concept of safety risk and the process of safety risk assessment.

Safety risks relate to the occurrence of accidents and the accident sequence (see Figure 7.5). Good safety management will reduce project risk for systems requiring safety certification prior to use. The concept of safety risk starts from the premise that perfect safety (complete freedom from all harm) is not achievable for all but the simplest real-life systems. Risk is the measure which allows different safety issues to be compared according to how serious they are. Although an individual who is killed is probably not concerned whether he dies alone or with 100 other people, it is important that assessments of safety risk should take account of the number of people affected. This leads to the concepts of individual and societal risk:

- *Individual risk* is defined as 'the frequency at which an individual may be expected to sustain a given level of harm from the realisation of specified hazards' (IChemE 1985). It is usually assessed for a typical average person in the group of people at risk.
- *Societal risk* is defined as 'the relationship between frequency and the number of people suffering from a specified level of harm in a given population from the realisation of specified hazards' (IChemE 1985). It therefore takes account of the number of people affected by an accident.

Tolerability of risk (ToR)

A ToR framework, such as the one shown in Figure 7.6, defines three bands of risk – intolerable, tolerable and negligible. In industry, health and safety legislation requires that intolerable risk should be reduced without regard for cost. In these circumstances, there is the ultimate sanction that if a risk cannot be reduced, the activity causing it must cease. The underlying assumption is that the owner of the risk should be responsible for its reduction.

The ToR framework also defines a level of risk which is considered negligible. In this region no measures need be taken to reduce the risk further, but it should be monitored to ensure that the risk remains negligible.

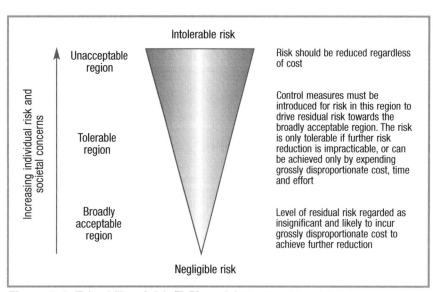

Figure 7.6 Tolerability of risk (ToR) model (The Tolerability of Risk Resource Allocation Strategy, Technical Paper D, The Office of the Deputy Prime Minister, HM Government, UK. http://www.odpm.gov.uk/)

Between the intolerable and the negligible risk zone lies an area where the risk can be described as tolerable. Here, risk must be reduced if it is possible to do so without incurring grossly disproportionate cost. This is generally referred to as the ALARP region, where the risk should be reduced to As Low As Reasonably Practicable. Risks are reduced in this region where it is practicable and cost-effective to do so.

HAZOP studies – safety in the process industries

The HAZOP method (short for HAZard and OPerability study) was first introduced by engineers from ICI Chemicals in the UK, in the mid-1970s. HAZOP studies are recommended by the American Institute of Chemical Engineers to evaluate the risk associated with automated and semi-automated processes. There are a number of recommended techniques for evaluating hazards such as:

- What-if analysis
- Process checklist
- Preliminary hazard analysis
- HAZOP study.

Although the HAZOP method is still new to many companies, it is rapidly becoming the preferred hazard analysis technique. It has been proven that HAZOP, if carried out by experienced personnel, results in the most comprehensive evaluation of a plant's safety and operability.

A HAZOP study identifies hazards and operability problems. This involves investigating how a plant or treatment system might deviate from the intended design. Solutions to these deviations are discussed and noted if appropriate. The method is based on the principle that several experts with different backgrounds can interact and identify more problems when working together than when working separately and combining results, as in a typical design review.

In a HAZOP study, the design drawings developed by project engineers and architects are reviewed by key personnel (for example environmental, safety, industrial hygiene, maintenance and operations personnel), greatly enhancing the effectiveness of the design review. The HAZOP is conducted in a series of meetings where a multidisciplinary team (the HAZOP team) methodically 'brainstorms' the plant design, focusing on specific points in the design (called 'study nodes'), one at a time. The primary

advantage of this brainstorming is that it stimulates creativity and generates ideas.

At each study node, deviations in the process parameters are examined using guide words. The guide words are used to ensure that the design is explored in every conceivable way. The task of the team is to think about each node and what possible deviations can occur, so that their potential causes and consequences can be identified. The guide words are applied to the relevant process parameters, for example flow, temperature, pressure, composition, in order to identify the causes and consequences of deviations in these parameters from their intended values.

Finally, the identification of unintended (or unacceptable) consequences results in recommendations for improvement of the process. These may comprise design modifications, procedural requirements, modifications in written documentation, further investigations and so on.

The best time to conduct a HAZOP study is typically at the 60% design review stage, when the design is fairly firm and the cost is not substantial to make changes from the HAZOP study.

Safety critical applications in projects

Safety critical applications are a category of application where correctness is a prerequisite more than a desirable factor. In the *Arianne 5* incident, 4 June, 1996, the first flight of the *Arianne 5* rocket ended in failure. Approximately 40 seconds after initiation of the flight sequence, *Arianne 5* veered off its flight path, broke up and exploded. Media reports indicated that the amount lost was half a billion dollars. The disaster occurred due to a software error; a reusable component originally implemented for a previous project was not tested when integrated with this project. Fortunately, no lives were lost, although this is not always the case:

- 28 January 1986 – the explosion of the space shuttle *Challenger* killed seven astronauts
- 25 July 2000 – a Concorde jet bound for New York crashed in a ball of fire shortly after taking off from Paris, killing 113 people
- 1 February 2003 – the American space shuttle *Columbia* broke up on re-entry over Texas, killing all seven astronauts on board.

Testing out safety critical systems can impose a great financial risk. Therefore, the previous stages in the development life cycle must be carried out as correctly as possible in order to prevent the discovery of errors at a stage as late as system testing. The risks associated with finding errors at this stage are enormous especially when human lives are at stake.

The development life cycle methodology used to implement these kinds of applications is the same as other applications, the only difference being that a further analysis is carried out to locate hazards and risks in the project. Hazard analysis and risk assessments are carried out to locate and study potential safety critical risks and hazards. Techniques such as reviews and checklists, petri net analysis, formal logic and fault tree analysis are used to perform hazard analyses on these projects.

Both structured and formal methods are used to implement safety critical applications. It is noted, however, that no method should be seen as a panacea. Notwithstanding this, formal logic and fault tree analysis are more popular due to the fact that they force a detailed analysis of the specifications. Most methods also depend on the quality of the personnel involved in applying the techniques since system development is essentially a human activity. Unfortunately, an application might be safe but not complete due to incomplete specifications. For this reason, stress is given to the importance of the requirements stage in the project life cycle.

Quality management

Quality, like communication, is a term often used indiscriminately to describe a broad range of issues that affect organisations. To make sense of this diversity, it is useful to begin with a look at three perspectives of quality: product quality, service quality and process quality.

Product quality

'Quality is never an accident, it is always the result of intelligent effort'; a quote attributed to philosopher John Ruskin, indicating that product quality cannot be taken for granted. Early definitions of product quality in manufacturing organisations tended to focus on a product's specifications; if the product matched the blueprint, the product was good. However, when companies operated to this definition, they were often met with product returns because their products did not meet customer expectations of quality. For example, the new Mini car developed in 2001 by BMW was subject to a recall to the manufacturer because paint used at the fuel tank opening deteriorated more rapidly than designers

expected, creating a minor fire risk. The designers clearly did not understand what strength of coating was needed to withstand everyday use by the customer, leading to product failure.

This type of problem was perceived by quality gurus such as Joseph Juran, who thought up a succinct definition of his own: a good quality product is one which is *fit for use*; it is not up to the producers of the product to decide on their own what this means. Feigenbaum, another guru, would say that product quality is about all the composite product and service characteristics of the contributing functions through which the product in use will meet the expectation of the customers. This includes marketing, engineering, manufacturing and maintenance – a much wider definition of quality than Juran's. Feigenbaum's point is that when defining quality, one has to include a wide range of stakeholders who have contributed elements of quality to the product throughout its life cycle.

David Garvin of the Harvard Business School derived a list of attributes for organisations to take into consideration when managing products (Garvin, 1984). They are:

- **Performance**. A product must do what it claims to do, that is, it must 'do exactly what it says on the tin'.
- **Operation**. This refers to the process of using the product, for example does the DVD recorder enable the user to record the programmes wanted? Are the buttons on the remote control comprehensible?
- **Reliability and durability**. A customer wants a product which will work for a reasonable period of time and be able to tolerate fair wear and tear (see the Mini example above). Organisations can calculate in advance when major components of products are likely to fail. A company's profitability and future prospects depends on design parameters like this – point of failure is typically designed to be slightly after the customer thinks is reasonable; too long after this means the product may be overengineered.
- **Conformance**. A customer wants the one she buys to be the same as the last one she bought and the same as the one her friend bought. US products such as fizzy drinks and fast food restaurants have gained their market share through their ability to manufacture a conforming product around the globe.
- **Serviceability**. Any given product, particularly

complex ones, have to be serviceable. The most popular example of this is the car, for which it is clearly possible to replace tyres, battery, indicator lights and so on without disposing of the entire car. Other items, for example portable compact disc players, are not serviceable; the producer relies on the customer buying another one if they drop and damage the one they have purchased.

- **Appearance and perceived quality**. The product has to look attractive and have a quality image that appeals to its customers. Scotch whisky has long appealed to middle-aged men, but as this sector is only one of many potential imbibers, Scotch's market share over the years has gone down, although attempts are being made to rectify this. Curiously, at the end of the eighteenth century, single malt was perceived to be of low quality because of its variability, so companies introduced blends to improve conformance and customer perceptions. Nowadays the reverse is true.

Service quality

Research by Berry et al. (1994) has contributed significantly to understanding service quality. They proposed an elaborate measurement system called SERVQUAL and tested it on a number of service sectors. Their research identified various areas which make up service quality, and how customers ranked them. The areas are:

- **Reliability** (32%). The reliability of the service was the attribute customers were most interested in. Customers wanted to know that the service would be performed correctly every time they used it.
- **Responsiveness** (22%). This refers to whether the service provider is willing to help the customer within a reasonable timeframe. For example, how long does it take to serve drinks in a restaurant?
- **Assurance** (19%). Ranked third on the list, assurance relates to the inner strengths, knowledge and skills of the employees and the confidence and trust that radiate to the customer. Do the staff understand the products on offer at the bar and, for example, if they have run out of one variety of dry white wine, can they suggest a different brand which the customer might like? Politeness is particularly ritualised in this kind of setting,

but contributes to a professional image for the service, which relates to the next aspect.
- **Empathy** (16%). This is about whether the service provider treats the customer as an individual and appears to care for their particular and unique needs. It is not uncommon in a UK pub to find a bartender who has made it his business to learn the drinking habits for groups of regulars. When he sees a group come in, he is able to prepare the drinks in advance. Bar staff are often a captive audience for the woes of their customers; the best staff know that they should empathise with customers.
- **Tangibles** (11%). Although this area trails considerably in percentage terms, it is the most easy for a manager to do something about. Tangibles relate to how the service facility looks and feels. It includes the equipment, the people and the media used to contact customers.

In summary, the first and last of the above criteria contain the most tangible elements, meaning literally things that can be touched, which are therefore the most easy to manage. The middle three criteria are dependent on the skills, knowledge and personality of all the staff, which is much harder to direct and control. Service quality depends far more heavily on staff skills. The key to managing customer satisfaction is reliability; however, a manager needs to customise a service for each person.

Process quality

Process quality refers to the quality of all the activities that come together to produce and deliver the products and services of an organisation. For example, software development requires a complex web of sequential and parallel steps. As the scale of the project increases, more steps must be included to manage the complexity of the project. The next Insights from Industry: 'Payroll on the loose' illustrates what can go wrong when quality management has taken a back seat. In this project, problems were turned round and valuable lessons learned for the future.

Adhering to a process and achieving high process quality overlaps, to some extent, with the quality of the products. That is, if the process is well designed and is adhered to (high quality), the risk of producing poor quality goods and services is reduced. However, the opposite is not always true – generating high quality products/services is not necessarily an indic-

 **PAYROLL ON THE LOOSE**

The project

The night before the launch of a new payroll system in a major Boston health care organization, project managers were sweating. During a sample run, the off-the-shelf package began cutting checks for large negative amounts and checks that incorrectly matched employee numbers with names, recalls a former director of systems analysis. Called in to review the project before the launch, he wound up sitting in the payroll department for six months to help fix the problem.

Payroll was still delivered on time, and out of 7,000 employees, the fiasco affected the checks of only roughly 50 to 100 people. Still, the payroll office had to pull the bad checks and rerun them manually to create new ones every payday until the application was debugged. The incident damaged the relationship between IS, payroll and finance department staff, and the programming manager resigned in disgrace.

The problem

'It became apparent the entire system was never tested or run in parallel' with the old system, says the director of systems analysis. IS did not check to ensure that an existing human resources database was compatible with the new payroll system software; the problem was that limit controls on hourly rates were not in place. An entry of 8.0 dollars per hour could be read as 800 dollars per hour if the user did not enter the decimal point, which revealed another problem: no one had been adequately made aware of the differences between the old system and the new one. 'There was no turnover between development and production,' the director says. Business managers were signing off on the system without really understanding how the people in their department would be using it, he recalls.

'A lack of clear leadership was a problem from the beginning,' says the director of systems analysis. The main sponsor, the payroll director, suffered a heart attack three weeks before the launch date and was placed on disability; he was gone for months. Throughout the course of the project, the organisation's top IT director was 'uninvolved', the director of systems analysis reveals.

The recovery

The organisation hired a consultant to help and provide support, and eight months after the implementation date hired a new director of IS. An administrator who oversaw all IS-related projects was transferred to another area of the company altogether. With the new management, IS established a more formal reporting methodology and some ground rules. Outside consultants would be used on every major project, and business units had to identify a project manager for every project and provide adequate training for the staff. Overall, project managers began to forge better partnerships with users. 'The effect was really a mandate to change,' says the director of systems analysis. 'It created the demand for a more professional way of managing projects.' The director of systems analysis (who subsequently went on to become CIO of this organisation and others) has a few lessons to share from the experience:

- Test, test and test again: 'It's much harder to fix things afterward.'
- Hire an outside contractor to complete an independent project review.
- Communicate with the business: send a monthly letter to senior management with updates as the project progresses.
- When buying off-the-shelf software, hire a consultant who understands how the application will run in your environment. The former director says that this is the piece of the puzzle software vendors often can't deliver.

Looking back, the director-turned-CIO says that the bungled project was a blessing because it helped raise awareness of the company's growing dependence on IT. 'Without a major catastrophe, there was a perception that IS didn't affect operations.'

Source: Schneider, P. (1998) 'Lessons learned: Payroll on the loose', *CIO Magazine*, 1 Dec

Questions

1. What are the product quality, service quality and process quality issues in this story?
2. What do you think are the key quality-related lessons the organisation has learned?
3. What does this project reveal about the governance of IT projects in an organisation?

ation that an effective process is in place and has been followed. Therefore, process quality and its measurement are not only about establishing the extent to which a process has been carried out, but also the contribution to product quality achieved by the process.

In general, everyone is responsible for implementing and adhering to the agreed or defined process, and making sure that the quality of the products and services produced and delivered achieve the required quality.

Process quality and its relative, continuous process improvement, have become key concerns for many organisations seeking to find new ways of reducing costs and gaining market share. In recent years, attention has moved away from product and service quality and onto process quality. 'A lousy process will consume ten times as many hours as the work itself requires' (Gates, 1999). In particular, a range of quality frameworks focused on improving the quality of processes has become popular. These include techniques and frameworks such as six sigma, design for six sigma, capability maturity models, the balanced scorecard and the EFQM excellence model.

In most cases the underlying principles that these frameworks adopt are grounded in the early quality gurus such as Deming, Shewart and Juran (Ishikawa, 1985). Their value lies in their ability to encapsulate these principles into a single delivery vehicle that organisations can implement on a continuously improving basis.

Capability maturity models (CMMs) originated in the Software Engineering Institute at Carnegie-Mellon University, Pittsburgh as a model to help software organisations improve their development capability (Paulk et al., 1993). The maturity model concept has now been applied to a range of disciplines and remains a growth sector in quality management. There are several CMMs that have been tailored specifically for project management (Foti, 2002; Pennypacker and Grant, 2003). The PMI has developed its own comprehensive maturity model, called the organisational project management maturity model or OPM3.

Quality, grade, reliability

Project stakeholders should also be mindful of the difference between terms such as quality, grade and reliability:

- *Quality*, according to the British Standards Institution is 'the totality of characteristics of an entity that bear on its ability to satisfy stated or implied needs' (BSI, 1995). A critical aspect of quality management in the project context is the necessity to turn implied needs into stated needs through good project scope management.
- *Grade*, on the other hand, is 'a category or rank given to entities having the same functional use but different requirements for quality' (BSI, 1995). Low quality is always a problem, low grade may not be. For example, a software product may be of (PMI, 2000):
  - high quality (no obvious bugs, readable manual) and low grade (a limited number of features)
  - low quality (many bugs, poorly organised user documentation) and high grade (numerous features).
- *Reliability*, however, 'is the ability of a product or service to maintain the standard of its performance for a specified period of time and under stated conditions'. A project may be a one-off venture but its end product may be expected to go on working for many years.

International Organisation for Standardisation (ISO)

The ISO, in recognising the need for the harmonisation of various quality standards used worldwide, issued the ISO 9000 series of standards in 1987. The 9000 series embodies comprehensive quality management concepts and guidance, together with models for external assurance requirements. The basic systems covered in ISO 9001 are shown in Table 7.6.

The series was revised and re-issued in 1994 and again in 2000 – see the Critical Considerations box below for details of the 2000 revision.

The ISO quality standards specify the requirements which determine what elements a quality system has to contain. They do not, however, specify how a specific company shall implement them. They are generic and independent of any specific industry or economic sector, and although they are intended to be used in their present form, some tailoring may be required to suit individual needs.

The basic approach to quality management used in a project should be compatible with ISO, as detailed in the ISO 9000 and 10000 series of standards and guidelines. The approach should also be compatible with:

- proprietary approaches to quality management such as those recommended by Deming (plan–do–study–act cycle), Juran (fitness for purpose) and

	Table 7.6 Key quality system elements in ISO 9001	
Element	Title	Purpose
4.1	Management responsibility	To make certain that executive management takes a leading and visible role in defining, implementing and administering the quality system, with the goal of meeting all customer requirements
4.2	Quality system	To make certain that your quality practices provide product and services that meet your customer needs and will continue to do so consistently in the future
4.3	Contract review	To make certain that you will be able to meet your customers' needs before accepting an order
4.4	Design control	To make certain that the product you produce meets all specified design requirements set by the customer and regulatory agencies
4.5	Document and data control	To make certain that quality system documents and data are controlled so that they are readily available to all users when they need them
4.6	Purchasing	To make certain the product received from your subcontractors meets your requirements
4.7	Control of customer-supplied product	To make certain that the product you receive from your customers will be incorporated into your product and ultimately meet all your customers' requirements
4.8	Product identification and traceability	To make certain that your product is properly identified at all stages of production, and to avoid errors that can cause scrap and rework
4.9	Process control	To make certain that all your processes (production, installation, and servicing) are carried out under controlled conditions to minimise variability in the manufacture of product or service
4.10	Inspection and testing	To make certain that product conforms to all requirements at each production stage; to identify nonconforming product at the earliest possible stage; and to facilitate corrective action
4.11	Control of inspection, measuring and test equipment	To make certain that inspection, measuring and test equipment is capable of consistently providing specified measurement requirements, so that proper decisions can be made for control and acceptance of product
4.12	Inspection and test status	To make certain that only product that passes the required inspections and tests is released
4.13	Control of noncon-forming product	To make certain that you do not use or unintentionally install nonconforming product
4.14	Corrective and preventive action	To make certain that causes of nonconforming product are investigated and an effort is made to eliminate them. You are also to attempt to detect and eliminate potential causes of nonconforming product before they occur
4.15	Handling, storage, packaging, preser-vation and delivery	To make certain that your procedures for handling, storage, packaging, preservation and delivery of product are adequate, and to protect the integrity of product at all stages
4.16	Control of quality records	To make certain that your quality records demonstrate effective operation of your quality system, which will ensure the achievement of required product quality
4.17	Internal quality audits	To make certain that your quality activities meet requirements and demonstrate the effectiveness of your quality system. This strives to ensure the continued capability of all elements of quality practice
4.18	Training	To make certain that employees are trained to do their jobs effectively, so they may avoid mistakes that affect quality
4.19	Servicing	To make certain that after-sale attention is provided for your product, when required, to ensure complete customer satisfaction
4.20	Statistical techniques	To make certain that you have identified places in your process where the use of statistical techniques is necessary to ensure quality or detect potential problems

CRITICAL CONSIDERATIONS

KEY FEATURES OF THE ISO 9000: 2000 SERIES

The main changes in the revised ISO 9000 standards are the increased focus on top management commitment, emphasis on the process approach within the organisation, and continual improvement together with enhancing satisfaction for customers and other interested parties.

The four primary standards are:

■ ISO 9000: *Quality management systems – Fundamentals and vocabulary*
■ ISO 9001: *Quality management systems – Requirements*
■ ISO 9004: *Quality management systems – Guidance for performance improvement*
■ ISO 19011: *Guidelines on quality and/or environmental management systems auditing*

The revised ISO 9001 and 9004 constitute a 'consistent pair' of standards. Their structure and sequence are identical in order to facilitate an easy and useful transition between them. Although they are 'stand-alone' standards, the new structure promotes enhanced synergy between the two and aids organisational efficiency and effectiveness.

The revision of ISO 9001 and 9004 is based on eight quality management principles that reflect best management practice. These eight principles are:

■ Customer focus
■ Leadership
■ Involvement of people
■ Process approach
■ System approach to management
■ Continual improvement
■ Factual approach to decision making
■ Mutually beneficial supplier relationships.

While the 'continual improvement' concept of revised ISO 9001 is intended to promote the effectiveness of the quality management system, the revised ISO 9004 is intended to improve the efficiency of the organisation. Together they will help increase an organisation's competitive advantage in the market, and enable it to better respond to the requirements of its customers.

Other ISO quality standards of special interest to project stakeholders include:

■ ISO 10005:1995, *Quality management – Guidelines for quality plans* – provides guidelines to assist in the preparation, review, acceptance and revision of quality plans.
■ ISO 10006:1997, *Quality management – Guidelines to quality in project management* – guidelines to help ensure the quality of both the project processes and the project products.
■ ISO 10007:1995, *Quality management – Guidelines for configuration management* – guidelines to ensure that a complex product continues to function when components are changed individually.

Source: ISO website, http://www.pmforum.org/

Crosby (conformance to requirements, zero defects)
■ nonproprietary approaches such as total quality management (TQM) and continuous process improvement (CPI).

Deming

Deming encouraged the Japanese to adopt a systematic approach to problem solving, which later became known as the Deming or plan–do–check–act cycle (see Figure 7.7). Deming, however, referred to it as the Shewhart cycle, named after his teacher W. A. Shewhart. He subsequently replaced 'check' by 'study', as that word reflects the actual meaning more

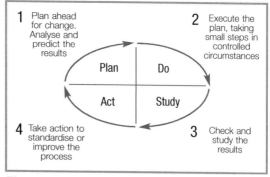

Figure 7.7 The Deming wheel

accurately. The Deming cycle is now often referred to as the Deming wheel or PDSA cycle. Deming also pushed senior managers to become actively involved in their company's quality improvement programmes. His greatest contribution to the Japanese is the message regarding a typical business system. It explains that the consumers are the most important part of a production line. Meeting and exceeding customers' requirements is the task that everyone within an organisation needs to accomplish. Furthermore, the management system has to enable everyone to be responsible for the quality of their own output to internal customers (Ho and Fung, 1998).

Deming's thinking in the late 1980s can best be expressed as management by positive cooperation. He talks about the new climate (organisational culture) which consists of three elements: joy in work, innovation and cooperation. He has referred to this new climate as 'win–win', as opposed to the 'I win–you lose' attitude engendered by competition. In his seminars in America in the 1980s, he spoke of the need for 'the total transformation of the western style of management' and produced his 14 points for management (Deming, 1986) to help people understand and implement the necessary transformation. Deming said that adoption of and action on the 14 points are a signal that management intend to stay in business. They apply to both small and large organisations, and service industries as well as manufacturing – see the Critical Considerations box below.

CRITICAL CONSIDERATIONS

DEMING'S 14 POINTS FOR MANAGEMENT

1. Create constancy of purpose for improvement of product and service.
2. Adopt the new philosophy.
3. Cease dependence on mass inspection. Eliminate the need for mass inspection by building quality into the process and the product.
4. End awarding business on price. Instead, aim at minimum total cost and move towards single suppliers, that is, supply chain management.
5. Improve constantly and forever the system of production and service. Improvement is not a one-time effort. Management is obligated to continually look for ways to reduce waste and improve quality.
6. Institute training. Too often, workers have learned their job from other workers who have never been trained properly. They are forced to follow unintelligible instructions. They cannot do their jobs well because no one tells them how to do so.
7. Institute leadership. The job of a supervisor is not to tell people what to do or to punish them, but to lead. Leading consists of helping people to do a better job and learn by objective methods.
8. Drive out fear. Many employees are afraid to ask questions or take a position, even when they do not understand what their job is or what is right or wrong. They will continue to do things the wrong way, or not do them at all. The economic losses from fear are appalling. To assure better quality and productivity, it is necessary that people feel secure. 'The only stupid question is the one that is not asked.'
9. Break down barriers between departments. Often a company's departments or units are competing with each other or have goals that conflict. They do not work as a team, therefore they cannot solve or foresee problems. Even worse, one department's goal may cause trouble for another.
10. Eliminate slogans, exhortations and numerical targets for the workforce. These never help anybody do a good job. Let workers formulate their own slogans. Then they will be committed to the contents.
11. Eliminate numerical quotas or work standards. Quotas take into account only numbers, not quality or methods. They are usually a guarantee of inefficiency and high cost. A person, in order to hold a job, will try to meet a quota at any cost, including doing damage to his company.
12. Remove barriers to taking pride in workmanship. People are eager to do a good job and distressed when they cannot. Too often, misguided supervisors, faulty equipment and defective materials stand in the way of good performance. These barriers must be removed.
13. Institute a vigorous programme of education. Both management and the workforce will have to be educated in the new knowledge and understanding, including teamwork and statistical techniques.
14. Take action to accomplish the transformation. It

will require a special top management team with a plan of action to carry out the quality mission. Workers cannot do it on their own, nor can managers. A critical mass of people in the

company must understand the 14 points.

Source: Adapted from Deming, D.E. (1986). *Out of the Crisis*, Cambridge University Press, Cambridge

Juran

Juran developed the idea of the quality trilogy: quality planning, quality improvement and quality control. These three aspects of company-wide strategic quality planning are further broken down in Juran's 'quality planning road map', into the following key elements, shown in Table 7.7.

Crosby

Crosby's name is best known in relation to the concepts of 'do it right first time' and 'zero defects'. He considers traditional quality control, acceptable quality limits and waivers of substandard products to represent failure rather than assurance of success. Crosby therefore defines quality as conformance to the requirements which the company itself has established for its products based directly on its customers' needs. He believes that since most companies have organisations and systems that allow deviation from what is really required, manufacturing companies spend around 20% of their revenues doing things wrong and then doing them over again. According to Crosby, this can be 35% of operating expenses for service companies.

He does not believe that workers should take prime responsibility for poor quality; the reality, he says, is that you have to get management straight. In the Crosby scheme of things, management sets the tone on quality and workers follow their example; whilst

employees are involved in operational difficulties and draw them to management's attention, the initiative comes from the top. Zero defects means that the company's objective is 'doing things right first time'. This will not prevent people from making mistakes, but will encourage everyone to improve continuously (Ho and Fung, 1998).

In the Crosby approach, the quality improvement message is spread by creating a core of quality specialists within the company. There is strong emphasis on the top-down approach, since he believes that senior management is entirely responsible for quality.

The ultimate goal is to train all the staff and give them the tools for quality improvement, to apply the basic precept of prevention management in every area. This is aided by viewing all work as a process or series of actions conducted to produce a desired result. A process model can be used to ensure that clear requirements have been defined and understood by both the supplier and the customer. He also views quality improvement as an ongoing process. Crosby's quality improvement process is based upon the four absolutes of quality management:

1. Quality is defined as conformance to requirements, not as 'goodness' or 'elegance'.
2. The system for causing quality is prevention, not appraisal.
3. The performance standard must be zero defects, not 'that's close enough'.

Table 7.7 Juran's quality planning road map	
Quality planning	■ Identify who are the customers ■ Determine the needs of those customers ■ Translate those needs into our language ■ Develop a product that can respond to those needs ■ Optimise the product features so as to meet our needs and customer needs
Quality improvement	■ Develop a process which is able to produce the product ■ Optimise the process
Quality control	■ Prove that the process can produce the product under operating conditions ■ Transfer the process to operations

Source: Ho and Fung (1998).

4. The measurement of quality is the price of nonconformance, not indices.

Quality management processes

Project quality management includes all the processes required to ensure that the project will satisfy the needs for which it was undertaken. Project quality concerns project processes and project deliverables. The project manager and the sponsor should *build in* quality to all project processes and not leave quality to inspection at stage gates and project closure.

The major quality management processes are (PMI, 2000):

■ **quality planning** – identifying which quality standards are relevant to the project and determining how to satisfy them
■ **quality assurance** – evaluating overall project performance on a regular basis to provide confidence that the project will satisfy the relevant quality standards
■ **quality control** – monitoring specific project results to determine if they comply with relevant quality standards and identifying ways to eliminate causes of unsatisfactory performance.

These processes interact with each other to help achieve the project objectives.

Project quality management must address both the management of the process and the end product or service. Failure to meet quality requirements in either dimension can have negative consequences for some or all the project stakeholders. For example:

■ meeting customer requirements by overworking the project team may produce negative consequences in the form of increased employee turnover
■ meeting project schedule objectives by rushing planned quality inspections may produce negative consequences when errors go undetected.

Project Management in Action: 'Taj Mahal Cycle Taxi Improvement Project', at the end of this chapter, is a project with multiple stakeholders that demonstrates this point well.

Quality management complements project management

Determining and delivering the required levels of both quality and grade are the responsibilities of the sponsor, the project manager and the project management team. The project management team should also be aware that modern quality management complements good project management practice. For example, both disciplines recognise the importance of:

■ *customer satisfaction* – understanding, managing and influencing needs so that customer expectations are met or exceeded
■ *prevention over inspection* – the cost of avoiding mistakes is always much less than the cost of correcting them
■ *management responsibility* – success requires the participation of all members of the team, but it remains the responsibility of management to provide the resources needed to succeed
■ *processes within phases* – the repeated plan–do–study–act cycle described by Deming and others is strikingly similar to the feedback loops between project phases discussed in Chapter 2.

The cost of quality

There are three elements to the cost of quality, prevention, appraisal and failure costs.

Prevention costs are the cost of all activities specifically designed to prevent poor quality in products and services. Prevention should always be the predominant quality activity. Examples of prevention activities are:

■ process and product design reviews
■ process capability evaluations
■ quality improvement team meetings
■ quality improvement initiatives
■ preventive maintenance
■ vendor assessments
■ quality education and training
■ statistical quality control tools.

Appraisal costs are those associated with measuring, evaluating, and auditing products or services to assure conformance to quality standards and performance requirements. Examples of appraisal activities are:

■ inspection and testing of purchased materials
■ in-process and final testing and inspection audits of products, processes and services
■ calibration of measuring and test equipment
■ feedback and evaluation.

Failure costs are those resulting from products or services not conforming to requirements or customer/user needs. Failure costs are further broken down into internal failure costs, which are those occurring prior to delivery, shipment or hand over of a product, or the furnishing of a service, to the customer and external failure costs, those occurring after delivery, shipment or hand over of the product, or after the furnishing of a service, to the customer. The following are examples of each kind.

Internal failure costs:
- scrap material costs
- rectification and rework costs
- lower production yields
- delays, downtime, overtime
- reinspection costs.

External failure costs:
- processing customer complaints
- late delivery penalties
- customer returns
- warranty claims
- product recalls
- loss of market share
- legal costs if customer sues.

Total cost of quality

The total cost of quality is given by the equation:

$$\text{Total cost of quality} = \text{Failure costs} + \text{Appraisal costs} + \text{Prevention costs}$$

A balance should be found between the total cost of prevention and appraisal and the total cost of failures. An organisation that does not have quality management processes in place will usually find that failure costs far exceed appraisal and prevention costs. By implementing planned appraisal and prevention audits, the total cost of quality will

reduce. This is a proactive process requiring commitment from all members of the organisation.

Of course the reported cost of quality may not be the same as the actual cost of quality. When asked, most companies cannot tell you how they calculated their cost of quality figure. The actual total cost of quality represents the difference between the actual cost of a product or service, and what the reduced cost would be if there was no possibility of substandard service, failure of products, or defects in their realisation.

Quality control tools

Quality control tools, particularly those associated with statistical quality control (SQC), have proved helpful to identify, quantify and then reduce the costs of quality. These tools have the primary aim of assuring satisfactory quality in all processes. They are designed to be easy-to-use tools for quality control, for use by anyone involved in a project. Some of them are described briefly here.

The tally sheet (or tick chart)

The tally sheet (or tick chart) is a simple method used to collect a wide range of quality related data (see Table 7.8).

The Pareto chart

The Pareto chart is used to distinguish critical problems and shows the magnitude of the different causes. The most frequent cause is usually (but not always) the most important cause. Results are displayed as an ordered bar chart (see Figure 7.8).

Table 7.8 An example of a tally sheet or tick chart					
	Supplier				
Defect	A	B	C	D	Total
Incorrect invoice	IIII	I		II	7
Incorrect inventory	HHI	II	I	I	9
Damaged material	III		II	III	8
Incorrect test doc	I	III	IIII	II	10
Total	13	6	7	8	34

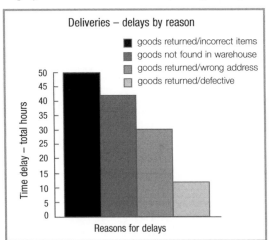

Figure 7.8 An example of a Pareto chart

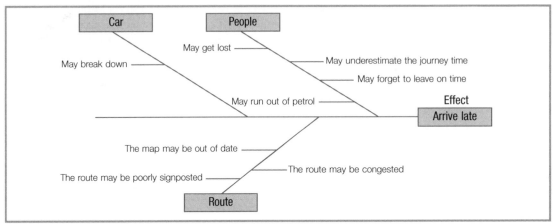

Figure 7.9 An example of a cause and effect diagram (Isaac, 1995)

The cause and effect diagram

The cause and effect diagram is a method of showing possible causes of a problem. Also called a fishbone diagram, the cause and effect diagram is an aid to brainstorming and hypothesis generation. As an illustration, the causes of arriving late from a car journey could be identified with this technique. The aim is to find the underlying causes of a problem by asking questions such as 'Why is this a cause?' several times, until the true underlying cause is discovered (see Figure 7.9).

A scatter diagram

A scatter diagram shows the correlation between two variables, typically a problem and a potential cause. For example, a correlation between the number of design changes (Factor A) and the number of man-days spent on scoping a project (Factor B) could be investigated using a simple scatter diagram (see Figure 7.10).

Control charts

Control charts show the upper and lower allowable limits for a process variable. When the process exceeds those limits or shows a recognisable pattern, action should be taken to adjust the process. Once set up, control charts are effective tools for day-to-day monitoring and management of a process (see Figure 7.11).

The success of these tools has partly been the result of their simplicity and ease of use, while revealing much information about a process. They are designed so that little training is required.

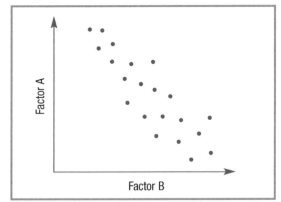

Figure 7.10 An example of a scatter diagram

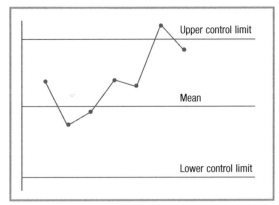

Figure 7.11 An example of a control chart

Special concerns for projects

There is an important difference between a project and other more repetitive operating systems that the project management team need to be aware of. The temporary nature of a project means that investments in product quality improvement, especially defect prevention and appraisal, must often be shared by the performing organisation and the sponsor, since the project may not last long enough to reap the rewards normally expected in an ongoing concern. However, improvements in the quality of the project process, for example by benchmarking current practices against the practices given in the PMI *Guide to the Project Management Body of Knowledge* (PMI, 2000), can be passed on from one project to another. This is particularly important to companies who manage by projects.

Taking cognisance of the external environment

In Chapter 2 projects were described as open systems, interacting with the external environment. Projects themselves can also affect the environment. Large projects with many participants may affect the local economy, with respect to the availability of human resources and specialist services used on the project. Some firms may relocate to take advantage of the business, social and recreational needs of temporary project workers. The nature of the relationships established between a project and its environment will assist or hinder the attainment of the project's objectives.

Environmental impact is a key concern for many stakeholders. Residents near a proposed new airport or runway will be concerned about noise levels; transport projects affect the visual, ecological and economic characteristics of the surrounding land; house prices can fall if noise levels increase or rise if new infrastructure encourages business start-ups, increasing the economic prosperity of an area.

When a road or rail project cuts through an area of outstanding natural beauty or historical or ecological importance, there are often lengthy protests and objections that need to be discussed and considered as part of the planning process – see Insights from Industry: 'Airport and runway projects', which describes some of the difficulties faced by airport authorities and Insights from Industry: 'Australia's fight for a tidal power station', which highlights a project in Western Australia where considerable public pressure was put on the energy minister to consider a new environmentally friendly energy and transmission system, that would also serve 16 aboriginal communities. Note the use of the internet in this project to canvass public support and

> **insights** from INDUSTRY
> **A**
> **PR**
>
> When the British Airports plans to build Terminal 5 inquiry was held. The proje structure ever built on gree cause a major increase in traf air pollution, health risks and d longest public inquiry in the UK, on of the enormous public concern about issue. Thousands of local inhabitants, dozens of community groups and most of the local councils have objected to the plans for Terminal 5.
>
> *Source:* West London Friends of the Earth, http://www.wlfoet5.demon.co.uk/term5.htm
>
> In the USA a growing number of residents cite noise as their biggest concern, deterring many from supporting new runways in their hometowns. In response to these concerns, the Department of Transport (DoT) has suggested using airport revenues for environmental and noise mitigation.
>
> *Source:* Seymour, E. (2001). 'DoT identifies runway roadblocks', *PM Network*, September: 9–10,18)

increase the flow of communication to the minister concerned.

In 1996, the growing concern for the environment resulted in the creation of a new series of international standards, the ISO 14000 series, modelled on the framework of the long-established ISO 9000 series of standards for quality. In a world of competing environmental claims, the appeal of an independent 'seal-of-approval' is a strong driver.

There is nothing terribly new or innovative about the environmental management system (EMS) described in ISO 14001. While its developers and promoters claim that it is based on the best existing practices, many recognise that it has shortcomings that render it potentially less effective than the EMSs that have been in place in the better corporations for some time.

The ISO 14001 EMS model, however, if applied diligently, is an extremely effective model that can assist an organisation to maintain awareness of and control over its environmental performance in an efficient manner.

Some of the key principles that ought to guide the development and implementation of an EMS include:

- …on is better than cure
- …ronmental programmes need not be complex or costly
- environmental management interventions should add value to environmental assets and practices
- access to resources and benefit sharing are fundamental to sound environmental management
- coordination and implementation are vital but separate environmental roles
- influencing policy can be as important as defining practice
- policy formulation and project management should be compatible
- protect the environment to safeguard urban livelihoods.

Some of the grey areas in ISO 14001 involve the identification and analysis of the environmental interactions of an organisation (called environmental 'aspects' in the standard), and the setting of business priorities, objectives and targets with respect to environmental performance. Due to the need for the standard to be applicable to all sorts of organisations, specific procedures for environmental analysis and priority setting are not provided in the standard. The supporting guideline ISO 14004 provides some assistance and mentions terms such as 'risk assessment', but remains quite generic.

It is up to the individual organisations that are trying to use ISO 14001 as their EMS model to define their own internal procedures for identifying and analysing environmental effects, setting performance goals and establishing objectives and targets for achieving them.

ISO 14001 uses the same fundamental systems as ISO 9000 such as documentation control, management system auditing, operational control, control of records, management policies, audits, training, statistical techniques and corrective and preventive action – a deliberate policy of the ISO. Consequently, an organisation with an ISO 9000 registration will find that they are a long way towards an ISO 14001 registration from the outset. Even though there are differences, the management system is generally consistent in both the standards. The approach to management common to ISO 14001 and ISO 9000 serves as a 'model' to be adapted to meet the needs of the organisation and integrate into existing management systems. The standards have been designed to be applied by any organisation in any country regardless of the organisation's size, process, economic situation and regulatory requirements. They are clearly important to project and programme activities as well.

The Project Management in Action: 'Taj Mahal cycle taxi improvement project' below is an example of a project using simple technology in new and creative ways to help solve environmental and economic issues. The project highlights the importance of many key project management processes including stakeholder analysis, risk management and quality management.

AUSTRALIA'S FIGHT FOR A TIDAL POWER STATION

Gannon Media Services have been retained by the community of Derby in the West Kimberley region of Australia to provide public relations services about a proposed tidal power station considered by the Western Australia energy minister for the next stage of the electricity procurement programme.

The innovative proposal by Tidal Energy Australia would see Australia's first tidal power station established at Doctor's Creek near the town of Derby (population 5,000). It would generate 48MW of electricity making it the second largest tidal power station in the world. The proposal also provides for a 500km transmission system serving the towns of Broome, Fitzroy Crossing and a number of remote Aboriginal communities.

Western Australian Energy Minister, Colin Barnett, did not include the tidal power scheme in the short list for further consideration, preferring instead two bidders who propose to burn fossil fuels in three separate stations in Broome, Derby and Fitzroy Crossing. Neither of the two preferred bidders proposes a transmission system leaving over 16 Aboriginal communities without the benefit of a continuous power supply system.

Community support

The overwhelming majority of residents in West Kimberley are in favour of the tidal power option because it is clean and renewable. It also has the capacity to generate significant employment in spin-off industries.

Source: Gannon Media Services, Media and Communications Consultancy, Perth, Western Australia, http://www.gannonmedia.com.au/

Taj Mahal Cycle Taxi Improvement Project

The Taj Mahal Cycle Taxi Improvement Project is a complex development project involving a public–private partnership between India and the USA. The case was written by Walter Hook, Executive Director, Institute for Transportation and Development Policy.

Introduction

The Taj Mahal Cycle Taxi Improvement Project was initiated by the Institute for Transportation and Development Policy (ITDP) based on a request from the Municipality of Agra, the Indian Government, the U.S. Agency for International Development's Energy, Environment, and Enterprise Program, and the U.S. Environmental Protection Agency, which were working together developing strategies to save some of the world's most famous monuments. The Taj Mahal, the Agra Fort, Akbar's Tomb and Sikandra, and Krishna's birth site, the Itmad-Ud Daula are being discolored with orange, black, and brown staining from suspended particulate matter (SPM) and Hydrocarbon (HC) emissions which came mainly from motor vehicles and internal combustion power generators. The adverse effects of these pollutants are quite localised, meaning that the immediate threats to the monuments could be avoided by controlling access to the Taj area by motorised vehicles.

In 1994 a Supreme Court order mandated that motorised vehicles be restricted in the 4 square kilometers immediately surrounding the Taj. Furthermore, the Taj is surrounded on three sides by a neighborhood of narrow winding streets known as the Taj Ganj, which makes access by taxi and bus difficult and congested even without the restrictions. These circumstances have created a lucrative market for all manner of non-motorised vehi-

cles. As most of the travelers to the Taj are tourists, many of them would like to reach the monument using a traditional mode of travel, to give them the flavor of traveling in India. Many tourists already use the horse drawn cart and even camel to make the short trip from the parking lot to the Taj, in trips arranged by various tourist agencies, and many people already travel from the nearby tourist hotels to the Taj by cycle rickshaw.

Tourism is one of the most important sources of income and employment in Agra, and a visit to the Taj Mahal is a major draw for tourists to come to India, bringing critical foreign exchange. Tourist visits to the Taj, however, are quite modest given the fame of the monument. Furthermore, a large number of visitors to the Taj Mahal make a day trip from Delhi, and do not spend the night in Agra or visit the four other world-class tourist sites in the city, three of which are nearby. The environmental and social problems in Agra described below are a large part of why more tourists don't stay longer in Agra, creating more jobs and local revenue. The Associated Chambers of Commerce in Agra, the Agra Tourist Promotion Board, and the Municipality, have therefore taken a serious role in working to improve the environmental and social conditions to make the city a more hospitable place for tourists and residents alike.

The ITDP is not in the business of promoting tourism or preserving international monuments; our mandate is to promote environmentally sustainable and equitable transportation. We became interested in the project because we saw in this very particular set of circumstances an opportunity to build private sector and government support to address critical environmental and social problems in India which we have long been working towards some solution.

Environmental reasons for the project

As an environmental organisation, ITDP

was concerned about the environmental ramifications of the trend in India of rapid increases in motor vehicle use. As incomes rise, individuals switch from using the non-polluting, energy-saving bicycles and non-motorised cycle rickshaw to highly polluting two-stroke engine motorcycles and three-wheeled Bajaj taxis, resulting in a dramatic increase in transport sector air emissions.

As well as damage to the monuments, residents of Indian cities face severe public health risks as a result of being exposed to levels of lead, NOx, CO, SPM, and HC from motor vehicle emissions well above World Health Organization standards. The major threat to public health from motor vehicle emissions in Indian cities is airborne lead, which has been proven to hurt early childhood cognitive development. Incidences of bronchitis, lung cancer, pneumonia, and other upper respiratory illnesses in Agra are also elevated. Finally, motor vehicle emissions are also a major source of CO_2 emissions, which are a major cause of global warming. While currently India is not a major contributor to greenhouse gas emissions, if the country motorises rapidly using available technology, their contribution to global warming will grow sharply.

The cycle rickshaw and wallah (cycle rickshaw driver) contribute minimally to pollution. In Agra the average rickshaw wallah travels around 24,500 km per year. If these trips were changed into trips by highly polluting two stroke IC engines, the annual emission impact would be roughly an additional 11 metric tons of lead in Agra's atmosphere, 4000 tons of particulates, 20,000 metric tons of CO, and 150 tons of NOx. (Based on estimates of 2-stroke motorcycle engines in Chile, from Turner, Weaver, and Reale, 1993). Such increases, particularly of particulates, CO, and lead, would lead to thousands of additional deaths from respiratory and cardiac disease each year.

ITDP was therefore looking for ways of encouraging the use of human powered taxis, cycling, and walking in population centers where the air quality benefits are the most important, and where distances are short enough to make this mode economically and commercially viable. In order to do so, however, many criticisms of cycle rickshaws, both legitimate and unfair, would need to be overcome.

Social reasons for the project

While a city of some of the world's most magnificent monuments, Agra is also a city of severe poverty, underemployment, and low productivity employment. The cycle rickshaw is an important source of employment for many of India's lower income people. In Agra the cycle rickshaws provide employment for roughly 10% of the adult population, and a critical source of low-cost basic mobility for India's lower and middle classes. Even wealthier Indians tend to rely on the cycle rickshaw for bringing their children to school, paying a monthly fee for the service. At the same time, there is a stigma attached to being a wallah, as it is seen as a lower class job.

There are officially 10,000 licensed cycle rickshaws in Agra employing 30,000 wallahs; three wallahs will use a single cycle rickshaw in shifts. While no official count exists of unregistered cycle rickshaws, estimates from Agra residents indicate that there are at least another 10,000 to 20,000 unregistered cycle rickshaws employing another 30,000 to 60,000 wallahs. Thus, the total number of jobs created by the provision of cycle rickshaw service in Agra ranges from 30,000 to 90,000.

Some 30% to 40% of wallahs own and operate their own vehicles, and 60% to 70% rent them from an owner of a cycle rickshaw fleet. Average earnings are $1.30 per day, of which $0.30 goes to the owner of the cycle rickshaw. This puts cycle rickshaw drivers at the World Bank's global poverty line (income of $1.00 per day or less). It also makes the industry a sizable one for the region. Total annual revenue to the region from direct income of the wal-

lahs thus ranges between $14.345 million and $42.7 million.

Agra is also an important regional manufacturer of cycle rickshaws, and is known for producing a high-quality cycle rickshaw. Agra produces between 30,000 and 50,000 cycle rickshaws per year, the majority of which are exported throughout the region within a roughly 80 km radius of the city. The average cycle rickshaw manufacturing firm employs 20 or more people, and there are 5 major cycle rickshaw manufacturers in Agra, producing roughly 10 to 20 vehicles per day. Thus, more than 100 people are employed in the manufacture of cycle rickshaws in Agra, and at least as many in service and maintenance activities. These manufacturers also rely on subcontractors to construct the seats and other specialty components, constituting probably another 100 jobs.

The cycle rickshaw kit which is assembled by a local manufacturer is made in the Punjabi city of Ludhiana, known as the 'bicycle capital of India', which produces bicycles for export all over the developing world, and components for cycle rickshaws all over India. A rough estimate of total employment generated by the manufacture and service side of the cycle rickshaw industry in Agra thus ranges between 500 and 1000 jobs. These are slightly better paying jobs than those of the wallahs.

The cost of the average cycle rickshaw ranges between 4500 and 7000 rupees, or between $100 and $250. Cycle rickshaw manufacturing brings a value added to Agra of roughly $3–$5 million, much of it in export revenues (that is, exported to the surrounding region). The total size of the cycle rickshaw industry in Agra is thus in the range of $20 to $50 million per year, and total employment ranging between 30,500 and 91,000 per year.

Despite the environmental benefits of the cycle rickshaw, and the economic importance of the industry particularly to low income families, public attitudes towards the cycle rickshaw in India are negative, and their use is

being phased out in many Indian cities and elsewhere in Asia. Negative attitudes about the cycle rickshaw are based on views that their use is exploitative to the driver, the vehicles are not safe, the drivers are not trustworthy, they exacerbate roadway congestion, and are in general viewed as backward. While no immediate threat exists to cycle rickshaw operations in Agra, the cycle rickshaw was banned from operating in New Delhi less than a decade ago, although they still operate in Old Delhi, and they face a major battle for their existence in Calcutta this year. Similar trends to restrict the use of cycle rickshaws can be observed in Indonesia, Vietnam, and China.

By contrast, cycle rickshaws have been introduced for the first time in history in over 40 cities in the U.S., as well as in the capitals of many major Western and Central European cities, and recently in Manila as well. Their emergence in Europe and the U.S. is the result of a confluence of factors: growing concern about environmental pollution, the growing popularity of urban planning measures to traffic calm and pedestrianise the street environment in downtown commercial or tourist areas, the growing importance of tourism as an industry, and finally the enormous gains in human powered vehicle technologies which, by dramatic reductions in vehicle weight and specialised gearing, have increased dramatically the ease with which the vehicles are operated and their safety and stability in traffic conditions.

Inducing a process of technological innovation in the Indian cycle rickshaw industry

ITDP realised that unless the legitimate criticisms of the cycle rickshaw could be addressed, the positive environmental and social benefits of the industry would be lost. Much of the stigma against the vehicle was based on its perception of being 'backward.' In fact, the current vehicles in operation are 'backward,' in the sense that the technology being used was developed more than fifty years ago based on indigenous modifications of a British-designed bicycle, and only very limited modifications have occurred since then. We therefore set up a project designed not only to develop a superior vehicle, but to induce a process of ongoing, commercially-induced technological change in the Indian private sector bicycle and cycle-rickshaw industries. Only by demonstrating the technical possibilities of human powered technology, and by introducing technologically superior vehicles to a concrete test market, could we begin to change the image of the cycle rickshaw, reduce the exploitation of the driver, and give the mode a chance to compete with motorised alternatives for certain segments of the transport market.

Lack of innovation is not restricted to the non-motorised vehicle industry, but typifies much vehicle technology in India. The common 'Ambassador' taxi, based on the 'Simca', dates from the 1960s. The three-wheeled motorised Bajaj taxi only recently introduced the first innovation in decades, overcoming considerable resistance.

Technological innovation in the bicycle industry in developing countries, as in other industries, has generally been prompted by an attempt to capture more lucrative export markets, with production developments only gradually being passed on to domestic production where profit margins are not high enough to justify the technological innovation. Most technical innovation in China and India has resulted from technical collaboration with foreigners through joint-ventures. Bicycles produced in Shenzhen (a special economic zone) by Chinese–Taiwanese, Chinese–Hong Kong, and Chinese–American joint ventures, are now producing the most competitive low-end product available. For example, the China Bicycle Company, (CBC), a joint venture with Hong Kong Bicycles and Schwinn Bicycle Company, is now producing one of the most competitively priced bicycles in the world. These firms have focused on producing a higher quality bicycle, cost-

ing around $100, rather than producing the lowest price/lowest quality bicycle. A large share of their market is for exports, but the higher quality vehicles are also entering the domestic market.

In India, the vast majority of bicycles tends to be made using technologies and designs many decades old, with low cost materials and components that are widely available in India. They tend to use low-carbon steel tubing, dipped in molten brass, or 'furnace brazed.' The frame is sand-blasted then chrome plated or painted in an electrostatic painting chamber; a reasonable method but of irregular quality. Most of the vehicles are sold 'completely-knocked-down' (CKD), and assembled locally, to save money on shipping, although some exports are sold 'semi-knocked down' (SKD). Similarly, the cycle rickshaw currently manufactured in Agra is a combination of a 'kit' which is mass-produced in Ludhiana and sent completely knocked down to Agra, where the chassis and carriage are manufactured by hand in small shops.

While there is little technological innovation going on at most of the big bicycle and cycle-rickshaw manufacturers, Hero Cycles is the most advanced Indian manufacturer in terms of technological innovation, has a fairly sophisticated research and development department, and has been slowly modernising its bicycle, both by upgrading its equipment and by setting up new components manufacturers. Hero, in joint venture with Honda Motors of Japan, now has a new bicycle factory with the most modern welding, assembling, and painting machinery in the world, imported from Europe, Japan, and Taiwan, although most of this technical innovation has gone to the development of a moped rather than to a superior bicycle. There has also appeared in recent years on the outskirts of Delhi a cluster of smaller, more innovation-minded bike manufacturers producing specialty mountain bikes and even recumbants. These smaller manufacturers are able

to produce small batch, higher cost specialty orders with high risk designs that the larger manufacturers are unwilling to produce.

Thus, technological innovation is generally a market driven process aimed at producing a more expensive, higher quality vehicle for higher income groups, and the new technology gradually becomes more affordable to lower income groups. The lack of technological innovation in the cycle rickshaw industry was linked to the perception that there is no market for an up-scale, superior vehicle, as it was assumed that higher income taxi drivers and passengers would switch to motorised vehicles. The typical passenger doesn't care how difficult it is for the wallah to pedal, so long as the price is low, and the wallah is generally very poor and wants to buy the cheapest vehicle available that will require the least maintenance.

Previous attempts by NGOs to attempt to induce technological innovation in the cycle rickshaw industry in India and elsewhere have met with only limited success in terms of the commercial dissemination of newly developed technologies. Nonetheless, this institutional experience of both failures and modest success provided valuable insight into how NGOs can facilitate the process of technological innovation, and how they can fail as well.

The best documented attempts to upgrade the rickshaw and the cycle rickshaw come from Bangladesh. Conditions in Bangladesh differ slightly from Indian conditions. The bicycle, cycle-rickshaw, and components industries, as well as industrial producers of alternative metals such as higher grade aluminum, are far better developed in India than in Bangladesh. Nonetheless, the Bangladesh experience offers valuable insights.

The first attempt to improve the Bangladesh cycle rickshaw started as a cooperative venture between the Bangladesh University of Engineering and Technology and the Intermediate Technology Development Group of the

U.K. in the late 1970s. Together, they designed a lighter passenger seat, and introduced gears. In the mid-1980s, Inter-Pares, a Canadian NGO working with engineer Fred Willkie, designed an entirely new cycle rickshaw which was manufactured at two factories in Comilla and Manikganj.

In both cases, improved vehicle designs were developed, but were never incorporated into commercial production. The reasons for the failure to gain commercial acceptance were many. According to our analysis, the two most typical causes of project failure were the failure to work closely with industry and the failure to identify a clear target market for a superior cycle rickshaw that will inevitably cost more in the initial years of production. In most previous projects, all of the work was done by universities and NGO's in isolation from the industry, and then only once the vehicle was designed did they try to convince the industry to adopt it. They tried to introduce the vehicles in a geographically dispersed manner, which meant that the handful that were seen were regarded as oddities and there were no centralised facilities for their maintenance (Gallagher, 1992).

Finally, in the Bangladesh project, the project sponsors decided that the new rickshaws would be sold only to rickshaw puller cooperatives rather than large businesses owned by a single family firm. Their aim was that the benefits should go directly to the pullers, rather than the owners, and also to encourage cooperatives. Furthermore, they manufactured the trial fleet themselves, rather than hiring a current manufacturer of the vehicles, so the current manufacturers viewed the new technology as a threat. In this way, many of the strongest firms in the industry had a vested interest in the failure of the new technology, as it was a threat to their business (Gallagher, 1992).

Several other attempts to introduce commercially viable intermediate transport technologies in India, by IT Transport and the Intermediate Technology Development Group in England, under contract for the International Labor Organization, have been more successful. IT Transport successfully introduced a bicycle trailer in the Indian states of Andhra and Uttar Pradesh (located in Agra Region). After an initial design was developed by IT Transport engineers, four local manufacturing facilities of bicycle trailers began production on a commercial basis, and have produced some 400 trailers as of last reporting. Purchasers of the trailers were said to double their income (Zille, 1989), helping them generate sufficient revenues to repay the cost of the trailer.

World Bank-sponsored projects to develop commercially viable bicycle trailers and small farm vehicles in Ghana also had considerable success. IT Transport in the U.K. developed two bicycle trailers and five small farm vehicle prototypes over a period of several months in cooperation with the Technology Consultancy Center (TCC) in Kumasi. At the same time, a market survey was conducted to identify possible users. Then, several local manufacturing facilities were hired to manufacture 600 bicycle trailers and 500 small farm vehicles (modified wheelbarrows). These vehicles relied on imported wheels, and logistical problems of receiving the wheels and distributing the final product slowed the project down. These first vehicles were then distributed to project beneficiaries at minimal cost for testing the impacts on their basic mobility, and to refine vehicle design.

In the second phase, IT Transport and TCC trained technicians from two local private sector manufacturers, Fatawu Bicycles, and Goodman & Sons, Inc. who were interested in commercial production. Training took approximately two weeks. Fatawu modified the design and developed three prototypes of their own, and another local entrepreneur in Sunyani developed a hand cart. The cost of the vehicles, at $120 (for the bicycle) plus $150 for the trailer was unaffordable to many project beneficiaries. In order to induce the commercial manufacturers to produce these vehicles on a commercial basis, they required the cooperation of the Ministry of Local Government, which in cooperation with the Social Security Bank, set up a revolving loan fund at below-market interest rates, making the vehicle affordable in a hire-to-purchase arrangement over a three year period (Heierli, 1993; Pankaj, 1991). The small farm vehicles were adopted by many small scale entrepreneurs without need for credit and are now in wide commercial production and use throughout Ghana (Amegbletor, 1993).

ITDP's Mobility Haiti project developed innovative designs for human powered ambulatory vehicles which are now used to bring patients from local clinics in Deschapelles to the Hospital Albert Schweitzer based in Haiti's Artibonite Valley. Prototype development took several months, and access to components was a continuing problem. The initial purchaser of these vehicles was the Hospital, and other health facilities in the region also expressed considerable interest, but the Hospital never decided to purchase a trial fleet. As such, the vehicles were successful from the point of view of meeting basic human needs and finding a market niche, but while the product displayed commercial viability, the project partners were not able to take the prototype to commercial production.

The above projects and programs provided critical experience in both the development and viable commercial dissemination of appropriate transport technologies, and outlines some key dangers that the Agra project has tried to carefully avoid.

The market for a superior cycle rickshaw, or a 'cycle taxi'

The particular circumstances in Agra, with the large tourist industry, a famous monument, and thus a private sector and a public sector dedicated to a cleaner environment, created the market and political conditions ideal for the introduction of a superior technology.

ITDP identified three possible markets for a superior cycle rickshaw or cycle rickshaws for use in the Agra area which have the potential of attracting private sector investor interest. First, the tourists represent a significant potential market for a superior vehicle. The 4 square kilometer ban on motorised vehicles around the Taj Mahal means that travel agencies running large tour groups in Agra tend to bring tourists to a bus parking lot still a few kilometers from the entrance to the Taj Mahal. Cycle rickshaws are already providing this service through agreements with the large tourist agencies, as are camel and horse drawn vehicles. Tourists feel somewhat uncomfortable on the current cycle rickshaws as they are not very stable, are often poorly maintained, and the wallahs have to get off the cycle rickshaw and pull the passengers up a modest hill, an experience which many tourists find embarrassing. Discussions with these travel agencies expressed their interest in a superior cycle rickshaw service that would be of lower cost than the horse and camel-drawn vehicles, and several tourist agencies expressed a willingness to explore the possibility of investing in a trial fleet if the prototypes were acceptable.

A tourist can visit four of the five major tourist sites in Agra entirely on cycle rickshaw. Reaching the Taj Mahal from the major tourist hotels is a short trip by cycle rickshaw through the winding streets of the Taj Ganj, a quaint traditional Indian neighborhood of considerable tourist appeal in itself, which is closed to most motorised vehicle traffic. Reaching the three other major sites by cycle rickshaw is less than a half hour ride between destinations. A current cycle rickshaw can be hired for a full day to reach all of these sites for 100 rupees (roughly $3.00). The trip from the train station to the hotels could also be made by cycle rickshaw, though the journey is somewhat longer. Unfortunately, only more adventurous tourists are likely to be willing to make this trip. Casual interviews with tourists indicated their reluctance to travel by cycle rickshaw, despite the pleasure of this mode of travel, because of difficul-

ties in communicating with the driver, fear that the driver is going to charge them an unfair price, discomfort about exploiting the driver, and fear that the driver will take them to a destination they did not intend and place them in a compromising position.

Based on interviews and discussions with the Tourist Promotion Board in Agra, tourists would be willing to pay considerably more than the $3.00 to hire a cycle rickshaw for a day if the cycle rickshaw were more comfortable, more stable, and safer, if the driver was able to pedal up the modest hills surrounding the Taj rather than having to walk, if the service was associated with a travel agency or a hotel, if the rates were made clear at some set rate, and if the destinations were made clear ahead of time. Currently, due to the low esteem in which cycle rickshaws are held, the cycle rickshaw operators are not allowed to ride up to the hotel's front door, unlike motorised vehicles. A superior vehicle, however, might be allowed to pick up passengers from directly from the concierge.

The Tourist Promotion Board estimates that one-third of the 1000 visitors to the Taj per day would be willing to travel to the Taj by cycle rickshaw under these conditions, and would be willing to pay $3.00 just for the trip to the Taj and back to the hotels. If the wallah made three trips per day, they could afford to pay $3.00 a day for the rental of the vehicle (ten times the current rental rate), and the wallah would earn $6.00 per day (six times the average). The estimated number of vehicles to meet this demand would be roughly 100. As the profits on this vehicle owner would be roughly ten times that of a standard vehicle, the cost of the vehicle could be as much as ten times the cost of the existing vehicle and still be profitable. This would allow for a vehicle cost of between $600 and $1000 dollars.

Secondly, the growing use of cycle rickshaws in the cities of the U.S. and Western Europe has also created the possibility of exporting the vehicles.

The most popular cycle rickshaws currently in operation in the U.S. cost $3000 to $4000 per vehicle FOB US Ports. Cycle rickshaws manufactured in India, if they could come close to matching the quality of these vehicles, could readily enjoy an export market. There are already cycle rickshaws being manufactured in Madras for export to Oxford, England, with designs developed with a company in Oxford. Most cycle rickshaw manufacturers have exported a few cycle rickshaws to Europe, but European cycle rickshaw operators prefer more expensive Western vehicles because the Indian vehicles are too heavy, too unstable, and lack gearing.

A third possible market for a superior cycle rickshaw is for the school children of middle and upper income families. Currently most families send their children to school in cycle rickshaws heavily crowded with children. Concerns about their safety might induce some families to switch to a superior vehicle even if more expensive if they felt their children would be safer.

Project design and implementation

ITDP knew that we could not implement the project alone. Many individuals in India had been working for years on possible improvements on the cycle rickshaw, knew the capabilities of the Indian cycle industry, the availability of various specialty components, and the problems encountered in these projects. In order to combine this experience with ITDP's international experience in the field, we negotiated a memorandum of understanding with the Asian Institute for Transport Development (AITD) in New Delhi. AITD was not as interested in developing a higher-end cycle rickshaw for the tourist market, and was more interested in disseminating a superior, lower cost vehicle in the Delhi area. They put together an advisory team of Indian experts familiar with many similar projects in the past, and hired a human powered vehicle designer and a project manager to locate and set up a design facility in Delhi near the new small and innovative bicycle industry on the outskirts of Delhi and cooperate in the design of the new prototypes.

In March of 1998, ITDP's human powered vehicle engineer arrived in New Delhi. In cooperation with AITD staff, a workshop was set up on the outskirts of Delhi and prototype development commenced. Staff had collected a host of information on past cycle rickshaw improvement projects from India and around the world ahead of time. In agreement with our project partners AITD, it was decided to develop three prototypes. The first would be a modest improvement of the existing cycle rickshaw operating in Delhi within very tight cost parameters. The new vehicle should cost no more than 25% more than the cost of the existing vehicle, or no more than $150. The second prototype would be a luxury version of the cycle rickshaw operating in Agra, sticking more or less to the traditional design, but creating an integral frame, a lighter weight vehicle, with superior components. This vehicle would retain the classic hand crafted features of the traditional vehicle but be targeted to a higher end tourist market. The cost of this vehicle would be kept to no more than $400. The third vehicle would be an essentially experimental vehicle which would be the best cycle rickshaw that can be made from the perspective of speed, stability, and style, but using all Indian components, without concern for the cost. The purpose of this third vehicle was to demonstrate the technical possibilities of human powered vehicle technology, which can be made to travel up to the speed of a normal motor vehicle. We would then develop variations on each of these three basic types.

In order to avoid developing a vehicle in isolation of commercial interest, ITDP and AITD decided to set up two advisory boards, one in Agra and one in Delhi. The first prototype and its variations, which we called among ourselves the 'Volkswagen', is targeted to the Delhi low-end market, and AITD has taken responsibility to set up an advisory board of existing cycle rickshaw manufacturers, owners, and experts, who would comment on the prototype, discuss whether and under what conditions they would consider investing the development of a trial fleet, and provide recommendations for further design modifications.

The second prototype, which we called among ourselves the 'Rolls Royce,' is targeted to the Agra tourist market. ITDP set up an advisory board in Agra of potential investors, potential manufacturers of the new designs (the owners of tourist agencies and hotels, all members of the Tourist Promotion Board), local government officials, and the cycle rickshaw wallah's union.

The project is currently developing these prototypes, and their projected completion date is May of 1998. In May, all of the prototypes will be presented to the advisory boards in Agra and Delhi, and a further round of design revisions will be made. Once the further revisions are made, Phase I of the project will be complete.

During Phase II, ITDP and AITD will hold negotiations with potential investors in the trial fleet. The investors in Agra are likely to be from the tourist industry and in Delhi will be cycle rickshaw fleet owners. Through a process of competitive bidding, ITDP and AITD will sign a contract with the investor to purchase and operate the trial fleet for a period of six months, allowing ITDP and AITD to study the financial, economic, and cultural feasibility of expanding operations. ITDP and AITD will also arrange for the manufacture of the trial fleet through a process of competitive bidding, but there is one cycle rickshaw manufacturer in Agra which is technically more proficient than the others, with whom we have a relationship, and it is likely that we will ask this manufacturer to produce the trial fleet. This will require ITDP training of the local manufacturer on how to manufacture these vehicles, which is likely to take several weeks to a month and oversight of the manufacture of the trial fleet. A similar process will occur in Delhi. Once the trial fleet is completed, it will be turned over to the investor for operation.

After six months of operation, ITDP will perform a financial and technical analysis of the business, and make further design changes based on observed cost parameters, customer and operator opinions, and other factors. At the same time, AITD will perform a survey to estimate the total market for such vehicles in Agra, Delhi, and perhaps selected other locations.

Based on the conclusions of this evaluation, and the level of investor interest in the project, ITDP will work on developing a 'kit' for mass production, which could considerably reduce the unit cost of the cycle rickshaw. The hope would be to make an integral frame part of the standard kit and thus possible to mass produce. ITDP and AITD will solicit bids from potential investors and provide sufficient guarantees to the private sector to ensure a willingness to participate in order to reach a minimum order required by the large scale mass manufacturers.

Public policies which would facilitate project implementation

While not necessarily critical to project success, the economic viability of new, human powered vehicle technology adaptation in India will be strongly influenced by the public policy environment in which they are received.

The project would be greatly facilitated by improvements in the traffic safety environment in which these and other human powered vehicles in Agra operate. If the accessibility of the Taj Mahal area and other historical districts were improved with the new vehicle, this would facilitate traffic calming and tighter restrictions on motor vehicle use in these areas. Developing a network of safe cycleways connecting several of the main landmarks, like the New York greenways plan which connects the major parks in New York's five boroughs, would all greatly improve the chances of project success.

Clearly, restrictions on the use of cycle rickshaws in Agra, as have been adopted in New Delhi and more recently in Calcutta, would destroy the chances for project success, and this project is intended in part to demonstrate an environmentally and socially beneficial alternative to these policies.

Excise taxes on commercial vehicles are currently being avoided in the cycle rickshaw industry by informal sector manufacturing, but may be a primary barrier to the adoption of an entirely mass produced cycle rickshaw, which might substantially bring down the cost and improve the quality. An exemption of this commercial vehicle excise tax for non-motorised vehicles would have positive environmental and social consequences, and would greatly enhance the viability of this project.

There are also manufacturing license restrictions on the types of vehicles produced by the large manufacturers which are inhibiting vehicle innovation which would have to be relaxed in order to induce a more continual process of technological innovation.

Local government licensing requirements also affect the market and viability of cycle rickshaws in both positive and negative ways. Currently, cycle rickshaws must meet certain design criteria in order to be eligible for a license. Currently these standards only require mud guards over the rear wheels and a functioning canopy. While even these minor requirements are not really enforced and many vehicles operate without licenses anyway, they do seem to have some normative influence as almost all the vehicles had mud guards and most had functioning canopies. To these requirements could be added better brakes and other safety features such as lighting and warning devices.

An up-market, luxury vehicle might also be eligible for a special license which would allow the vehicle to operate with privileges, such as freedom to operate on hotel grounds, inside tourist areas, in military cantonments, and on other public facilities. Eligibility for the license might require that drivers be uniformed, be required to speak some English, and fares could be fixed for time, distance, or final destination. In the initial stages, this licensing fee could be waived in order to facilitate the adoption of the new technology. The Commissioner of the Municipality has already agreed to grant the current license without fee to the new vehicles.

Conclusions and questions

Several fundamental changes in the global economy have made the reports of the imminent death of the cycle rickshaw premature. First, tourism has grown in its economic importance. Globally, it now accounts for an estimated 7% of world economic output. This change has given municipalities strong incentives to improve the quality of life and the attractiveness of their cities as tourist destinations. Further, it has created market opportunities both for traditional crafts but also for traditional means of transport. Touring a city does not require high speed, it requires slow speeds and safe, unpolluted travel conditions.

Secondly, rapid motorisation has brought with it a host of environmental problems that are causing an increasing public health problems. Restrictions on the use of private motor vehicles in central urban areas to control pollution and congestion are increasingly common around the world and increasingly in Southeast Asia. Exclusive bus lanes have been put in recently in Kuala Lumpur, are being discussed in Manila, and Singapore has long had an area licensing scheme in its downtown. In these conditions, the majority of the congestion is being created by extremely space-intensive private motor vehicles. Average travel speeds in heavily congested Jakarta, Bangkok, and other Asian cities have slowed to levels below those attained by cycle rickshaw due to traffic congestion. Most countries are gradually adopting a fundamentally new approach to traffic planning which focuses on improving the mobility of people rather than of vehicles, facilitating public transit, pedestrian and human-powered vehicle access, and allowing private motor vehicle use only to those willing and able to afford the enormous external pollution and congestion costs generated by this mode of travel.

Several questions about the Taj Cycle Taxi Project remain, and several critical problems. First, it is unclear as yet whether this project will successfully lead to the commercial production of a superior cycle rickshaw. Secondly, it is not yet clear that if such commercial production does commence with an elite vehicle, that the technological advances used will find their way into the manufacture of the cycle rickshaw fleet being used by ordinary people. Third, it is possible that the existence of a superior alternative vehicle will be used by authorities to ban the old vehicles, which would cause a major disruption of the livelihoods of many current cycle rickshaw owners, manufacturers, and operators, significantly increasing their operating costs for a time, if nothing else. Fourth, the interests of all the project partners are not identical. ITDP and AITD would like to see the new technology disseminated and copied by as many manufacturers as possible, while our private sector partners, if the new model is successful, would like to profit from the new product at the expense of their competitors. How this conflict will manifest itself is not yet clear. In a few years we will know a lot more.

Sources: Amegbletor, L. 1993. 'Introducing Intermediate Means of Transport in Ghana – A Solution to Rural Mobility Needs,' International Forum for Rural Transport and Development, First Regional Meeting of Experts in Anglophone Africa, Lilongwe, Malawi

Christoplos, I. *'The Pisces Project: The Tricicleros of Santo Domingo,'* (Washington, D.C.: Inter-American Foundation Occasional Papers, 1984)

Gallagher, R. 1992. *The Rickshaws of Bangladesh* (St. Gallen: Swiss Centre for Development Cooperation in Technology and Management)

Heierli, U. 1993. *Environmental Limits to Motorization: Non-Motorized Transport in Developed and Developing Countries* (St. Gallen, Switzerland: Swiss Centre for Development Cooperation in Technology and Management)

Hook, W. 1994. *Counting on Cars, Counting Out People* (New York: Institute for Transportation and Development Policy)

Hook, W. 1996. 'The Economic Importance of Non-Motorized Transportation,' *Non-Motorized Transportation Research, Issues, and Use* (Washington D.C.: Transportation Research Record No. 1487). p. 14

Non-Motorised Transport in India: Current Status and Policy Issues. 1996. (Delhi: Asian Institute for Transport Development)

Pankaj, T., 1991. 'Designing Low-cost Rural Transport Components to Reach the Poor,' *Infrastructure Notes* (Washington, D.C.: World Bank)

Turner, S., C. Weaver, and M. Reale, 1993. '*Cost and Emissions Benefits of Selected Air Pollution Control Measures for Santiago, Chile: Final Report.*' (Sacramento: Engine, Fuel and Emissions Engineering, Inc.)

World Bank. 1991. *International Competition in the Bicycle Industry: Keeping Pace with Technological Change.* World Bank Industry and Energy Department Working Paper. Industry Series Paper No. 50, Washington, D.C.

Zille, P. 1989. '*The Indian Cycle Trailer: A Case Study in the Development of Appropriate Transport Technologies.*' (Washington, D.C.: Transportation Research Board)

ITDP's website is at www.itdp.org

QUESTIONS TO AID UNDERSTANDING AND DISCUSSION

1. What are the project drivers and critical success factors for this project?

2. Who are the stakeholders – how would you manage their impact on the project?

3. What are the key risks faced by the sponsors and how well have they been managed?

4. What are the product quality, service quality and process quality issues illustrated in this case study?

An update of this project is available in *Current Science*, 83(6): 1–6, 25 Sept, 2002 'Elective and improved cycle rickshaw as a sustainable transport system for India' by Rajvanski, A.K. http://www.worldbike.org/research/MAPRA.pdf

Summary points

- The PMBOK Guide defines project risk as an uncertain event or condition that, if it occurs, has a positive or negative effect on a project outcome.
- All projects carry some level of risk.
- Risks are partially unknown, change with time, can be managed in a project and exist only in the future tense.
- Risk management is about balancing the harmful effects of risk against potential project benefits.
- There are two categories of risk: speculative risk – meaning a chance of a loss or chance of a profit; and pure risk – meaning only a chance of a loss.
- Pure risks are insurable.
- Three key risk processes in a project are risk management planning, risk assessment and risk control.
- Risk management planning defines the objectives and scope of risk management.

- Risk assessment is about identifying, analysing and prioritising risks in a project.
- Risk control is about deciding and implementing a response plan to project risks.
- Risk exposure = probability of risk x impact of risk.
- Risk management is best performed as a team exercise with the help of a facilitator and tools such as a risk checklist, brainstorming and SWOT analysis.
- The use of a risk register and risk information sheets is a convenient way of recording and tracking risk throughout a project, allowing for changes in the severity of risks as the project progresses and the activities in the risk response plan are actioned.
- A contingency plan is a set of planned actions that are activated if the trigger point for a risk is reached or exceeded.
- Safety is 'the freedom from unacceptable risks of personal harm.' (BS 4778).

■ A hazard is 'a situation with the potential for human injury, damage to property, assets or the environment'.

■ Physical safety involves issues such as the working environment; functional safety involves failure, malfunction or poor performance of a system.

■ A tolerability of risk (ToR) framework defines three bands of risk – intolerable, tolerable and negligible.

■ Hazards can be evaluated using tools such as what-if analysis – process checklist, preliminary hazard analysis and HAZOP study.

■ Quality management is about managing the quality of the products, services and processes associated with a project.

■ Quality management processes in a project are quality planning, quality assurance and quality control.

■ There are many quality standards that may be applied and followed in a project, for example the ISO 9000 and 10000 series of international quality standards.

■ The total cost of quality is the sum of prevention costs, appraisal costs and failure costs.

■ Quality control tools such as tick charts, Pareto charts, fishbone diagrams and so on can be applied by anyone in a project to monitor and improve quality.

■ Environmental priorities should be established early in a project, preferably as part of the feasibility study. Guidelines on environmental issues have been issued by the International Organization for Standardisation – the ISO 14000 series.

Visit the website

http://www.palgrave.com/business/gardiner

▶ to test your understanding of the learning objectives for Chapter 7 using multiple choice questions

▶ to access useful websites on risk and quality management

In the next chapter we shall be focusing on the initiation and definition phase of the project life cycle, including the management of expectations and the production of a project charter – an indispensable communication tool in the project manager's toolkit.

References

APM (2000). *Body of Knowledge,* 4th edn, Association for Project Management, High Wycombe.

Bartlett, J. (2002). 'Using risk concept maps in a project or programme', presented at the Fifth European Project Management Conference, PMI Europe 2002, Cannes, France, 19–20 June.

Berry, L., Parasuraman, A. and Zeithaml, V.A. (1994). 'Improving service quality in America: lessons learned', *The Academy of Management Executive*, **8**(2): 32–52.

BS 4778: Part 1: 1987. *Quality Vocabulary*. British Standards Institution, London.

BSI (1995). British Standards Institution, BS EN ISO 8402: 1995 *Quality management and quality assurance – Vocabulary*.

Charette, R. (2002). *'The state of risk management 2002: Hype or reality'*, Industry Report, Cutter Consortium, Arlington, MA.

Deming, D.E. (1986). *Out of the Crisis*, Cambridge University Press, Cambridge.

Foti, R. (2002). 'Maturity (noun), 21st century. Synonym: survival.', *PM Network*, **16**(9): 38–43.

Garvin, D. (1984). 'What does product quality really mean?' *Sloan Management Review*, **26**(1): 25–43.

Gates, B. (1999). *Business@ The Speed of Light*, Time Warner Books, New York.

Ho, S.K.M. and Fung, C.K.K. (1998). *TQM Excellence Model,* Hong Kong Baptist University.

Isaac, I. (1995). 'Training in risk management', *International Journal of Project Management*, **13**(4): 225–9.

Ishikawa, K. (1985). *What is Total Quality Control?*, Prentice Hall, Engelwood Cliffs, NJ.

Jones, D. (1985). *Nomenclature for hazard and risk assessment in the process industries*, IChemE, London.

Lambert, C.A. associate editor, *Harvard Magazine*, Nov–Dec 1997, http://www.harvard-magazine.com/issues/nd97/books3.html.

Paulk, M.C., Curtis, B., Chrissis, M.B. and Weber, C.V. (1993). *'Capability maturity model for software v1.1'* CMU/SEI-93-TR-024, Carnegie-Mellon University, Pittsburgh.

Pennypacker, J.S. and Grant, K.P. (2003). 'Project management maturity: an industry benchmark', *Project Management Journal*, **34**(1): 4–11.

PMI (2000). *'A Guide to the Project Management Body of Knowledge'*, Project Management Institute, Upper Darby, PA.

Visit the website

http://www.palgrave.com/business/gardiner

▶ for additional resources to explore the topics in this chapter further

Project initiation and team building

8

Learning objectives

After reading this chapter, you should be able to:

- describe the process of project scoping and its constituent activities
- participate in the preparation of a project charter
- discuss the need for trade-offs in a project between: scope, cost and time
- demonstrate the importance of and be able to create a work breakdown structure
- advise on the selection of a project team
- explain how to succeed at teamwork in a project using appropriate models

Introduction

Project initiation and definition are about doing the right things in the early stages of a project – it is not about getting everything right. There are few certainties in project management, fewer still at the onset of a project. Less is known about a project and its stakeholders at the start of a project than at any other time, but the project manager's role is to progress the project through its crucial early stages and see that timely decisions get made in the face of uncertainty.

Initiation is the process of formally authorising a new project or recognising that an existing project should continue into its next phase (PMI, 2000: 53). Project initiation is the first phase of the project life cycle. It involves all the pre-planning and project conception activities that help to shape a project and establishes a firm basis for planning, management and control.

In small projects (ones involving just two or three people, and with a simple project plan and goal), the initiation phase may take place informally over a relatively short period of time, say, half a day to three days. In larger, more complex projects with many stakeholders and strategically important deliverables, project initiation may take weeks, months or even years to conduct properly.

An important skill for project managers is to avoid the temptation of getting caught up in the enthusiasm of 'getting on with things' until all aspects relevant to

initiation have been fully considered. Initiation is often the most neglected phase in project management which is why it also underlies many of the problems that can cause a project to fail (Turner, 1999: 74).

Initiation activities include the determination of:

- the project's mission – what are the project's goals and deliverables?
- its constraints – how much money is available, how much time is available, what quality is required?
- its focus – is everyone tuned in to the project, does everyone share the same commitment?
- its critical success factors (CSFs) – what must be achieved to guarantee success, what else would it be nice to achieve, what should not be included as part of the project?
- its objectives – how is it intended to reach the end deliverables, what are the in between stages, the milestones?
- its risks – what can go wrong, how can exposure to risk be reduced, what action can be taken if some things do go wrong?

Project scoping – defining a project's mission and purpose

Scoping is a communication and information-gathering

exercise. It helps to determine how the project fits into the bigger scheme of things and what the individual and combined strengths of the project team are expected to achieve (Briner et al., 1996). Scoping continues the process of defining the project. It is about tuning in all the stakeholders to the project, the goals of the project, and how the project is going to benefit the organisation and its people. It also represents the greatest opportunity for the project manager to unearth and resolve any misunderstandings about the project, for example between senior managers and operations staff or between a sponsor, a contractor and the users of the end product.

A scoping exercise is also often the first real opportunity to create a team environment in which synergy and unity can be fostered and cross-purposes ironed out. In a healthy scoping exercise:

- personalities become known
- relationships are formed and strengthened
- conflicts are aired and resolved
- the rationale behind the project is scrutinised
- proposed solutions are examined for their closeness of fit to the sponsor's needs.

There is often more at stake during initiation than at any other time in a project. A poorly managed scoping exercise is a harbinger of trouble later in the project. This trouble can arise from the mistaken belief that:

- senior managers always give a lot of thought to what they want from a project before they appoint a project manager
- the sponsor's definition of the problem and/or solution should be accepted as correct
- what is obvious to one group of people, for example senior managers, must also be obvious to everyone else involved in the project
- project sponsors usually have a clear idea of what they want and how to achieve it
- if the project's requirements are in writing, they will be understood.

Project Management in Action: 'DataSys knowledge transfer programme', at the end of the chapter, illustrates a wide range of scoping issues and clearly demonstrates that although money and a good idea are necessary, they are not sufficient to deliver a successful project.

Identifying the project's requirements

In many organisations, project initiation and definition are supported by an investment management process that involves evaluating, selecting and financing projects. Chapter 4 describes this process in detail and introduces two important outputs, the feasibility report and the business case, which provide critical information about project risks, benefits and costs. These documents also underpin the scoping process. A project that is not supported by a formal feasibility report and business case must address the same questions during the scoping process as those answered in these reports.

One of the keys to the success of any project is the creation of project requirements that are 'comprehensive and clear, well structured, traceable and testable' (APM, 2000: 32). A project's requirements define the mission or brief of the project and answers questions such as:

- Who is performing the project (the project team)?
- What are they trying to accomplish (the project scope and goals)?
- For whom are they doing this (the project sponsor)?

Scoping is about identifying and writing down the project's requirements. More formally, it can be defined as:

the process of establishing and agreeing with all the stakeholders what the project will involve and where its boundaries are.

Project scoping involves sitting down with the client or sponsor and identifying their individual needs and how the project in question intends to meet them. The aim of project scoping is to arrive at a good understanding of:

- the business need that the project was undertaken to address
- the expectations of the main stakeholders
- the main activities that will need to be carried out
- the main resources required and where they will come from
- the next stage – will there be a follow-on project?

Projects implemented without a thorough scoping exercise and for which clear boundary limits were not established at the start, for example Project Management in Action: 'DataSys knowledge transfer programme', run the risk of delivering end products poorly matched to customer needs. Without strong leadership from the project manager, these projects can drag on indefinitely. Projects that keep on growing in scope during execution are said to suffer from 'scope creep'; ones which undergo a major change are casualties of 'scope leap'.

The project charter

A project charter is a high-level document that records and communicates the results of the scoping process to project stakeholders. It is also a formal document that recognises the existence of a project, giving it official status in an organisation. It documents the project mission and details the overall purpose of the project.

Considerable effort should be put into achieving documented requirements in the project charter that are:

- complete
- correct
- precise
- consistent
- relevant
- feasible
- manageable
- testable
- traceable
- free of design detail.

Although pitched at a fairly high level, a project charter that is too brief will fail to communicate essential information about the project to stakeholders, and one that is crammed full of detailed design, schedule and budget information will be consulted infrequently and may become an undesirable drain on administrative resources in an attempt to keep it updated.

The project charter should be issued by a senior manager at a level appropriate to the needs of the project. It provides the project manager with the authority to apply organisational resources to project activities.

When a project includes work to be carried out by a contractor, a special document called a 'statement of work' (or a statement of understanding, or contractor's terms of reference) is used to communicate the subset of requirements for that part of the project. The statement of work (SoW) forms an agreement between the contractor and the main

provider (sponsor) concerning the extent of the contractor's involvement. In essence it resembles a mini-project charter and therefore should follow a similar development process. The project charter will normally contain a copy of, or make reference to, any contractor statements of work.

Getting the sponsor and main stakeholders to sign the project charter shows that agreement (although not necessarily understanding) has been reached regarding what needs to be achieved and under what conditions. After a successful scoping exercise everyone starts off in agreement. The project charter becomes a communication tool. Each signature shows to the other participants that the person signing supports the information in the document and that input from that person has been received.

Visit the website

http://www.palgrave.com/business/gardiner

▶ to see some examples of project charters

Scoping is iterative – requirements can change

During scoping many people are encouraged to take part in shaping the project. Ideas come and go. This is an important part of the planning phase and helps to secure buy in from the different stakeholders. There are often many changes and iterations to the scope documentation so be prepared to revisit the project charter throughout the course of a project, especially in the early phases.

The originator of a project idea may find it hard to articulate clear and genuine business needs at the outset. It is not enough to put into words what the project must achieve. These are project goals not business requirements. The scoping process must strive to uncover the fundamental business needs behind the project. To do this a project manager should keep asking the questions:

- Why do you want this project?
- What need does it meet for you?

Eventually, after much iteration, the true business need should come to light. Once this has happened the project manager and sponsor can look at alternatives to meeting the same business need in the light of the company's strategic goals. The best solution may turn out to be:

- a completely different project (new and better solution identified)
- a decision to delay the project (changing environment)
- a decision to cancel the project altogether (new business strategy creates different business needs).

For example, a department manager may initiate a project to train staff in the use of a particular project management software package. The manager may identify the business need as 'improving staff efficiency'. After investigating this need further, the manager may discover that staff are being asked to do tasks that exceed the features provided by the software package currently installed. The *real* business need may in turn be identified as 'provide staff with the capability to create monthly project progress reports to senior managers, quickly, accurately, and in an appropriate format'. Finally, the best project solution to meet this need may turn out to be:

1. upgrade all staff PCs
2. install a new operating system
3. install a new project management software package
4. perform staff training.

The project, if carried out as described initially by the department manager, may have only served to frustrate his staff further, failing to deliver any real benefit. Unfortunately, this is all too typical, especially with inexperienced clients and sponsors (take another look at Figure 5.2).

Of course managing a project whose requirements are constantly changing is totally unrealistic. The solution is to put in place a system of requirements control and configuration management (control of project deliverables – see APM, 2000: 35). The best project managers, those that consistently deliver successful projects, control requirements and ensure that there is always a common understanding of requirements between sponsor, customer and participants. Achieving congruence between stakeholders was discussed extensively in Chapter 5. A good idea to help achieve this is to agree and 'freeze' (fix in place allowing, in theory at least, no further changes) project requirements before planning a project in detail, and certainly before the project execution phase begins. Then, later, if requirements do warrant change or additions, replan the project and refreeze the requirements. The scope documentation at the point the scope is frozen is called the 'scope baseline'. The emphasis then changes from defining the scope to implementing it. Any changes to the scope baseline (that is, after the scope has been frozen) ought to be carefully evaluated and strictly controlled. The process for doing this is called 'scope change control' and is discussed in more detail in Chapter 10.

The stakeholders – getting them to say 'Yes'

The sponsor is the strongest project stakeholder. It is the sponsor who controls the purse strings and has the greatest interest in championing the project outcome. But there are often many stakeholders, and dissatisfied stakeholders can cause a project to fail. By defining project requirements, the scoping process should establish and fix the expectations of the project for all the stakeholders. However, getting all the stakeholders to say 'Yes' to the project scope (and keep saying 'Yes') is a dynamic process that requires political and marketing skills. (Chapter 5 showed how the project manager can 'sell' the project to stakeholders).

Critical success factors

Critical success factors (CSFs) are the deliverables that must be achieved in order for the project to succeed. Conversely, if a CSF is not addressed, the project fails. The project manager needs to be careful when scoping out the CSFs not to plunge into a spiral of small details. CSFs should not include such basic items as 'coming to work' or 'surviving the week', but should focus on those tasks within the project scope that must be given extra consideration. A good rule of thumb is not to have more than, say, five CSFs. Too many CSFs will make progress harder to achieve and may suggest a need to split up a project into multiple projects within a programme.

Objectives

Once the CSFs have been determined, the project team can identify what needs to be done to achieve them. This involves planning the steps that need to be taken to move from the starting point to the end point, thus closing the gap between where the sponsor is now and where the sponsor wants to be. Along the way there are certain distinct points of achievement to be made, like checkpoints on a journey. These are called 'project milestones' and become the objectives for everyone involved.

There can be numerous objectives for each project, but it is a good idea to make them SMART:

- *Specific* – clear not vague (so you know what's involved)
- *Measurable* – quantifiable (so you can report meaningfully on progress)
- *Achievable* – attainable in the short term (keeps your enthusiasm going)
- *Result-oriented* – tangible, easily identified (so you know when you've got there)
- *Time-based* – shows when it is required in relation to other objectives (so you can manage your effort accordingly).

Value management

Special techniques have evolved to help organisations maximise the benefit realised from projects. For example, value management (VM) is a technique used by more and more organisations to help define business objectives and identify the best ways to achieve them with a focus on balancing stakeholders' needs and expectations with available resources (APM, 2000: 34; Thiry, 2001; Morris and Harpum, 2003). The technique involves managing the evolution of a project from concept to completion, through the comparison and audit of all decisions against a value system determined by the client or customer (Kelly and Male, 1993).

What's involved – scope, time, resources

Project constraints set an overall tone for the project and provide clear insight for later decision making. There are three universal constraints to any project: scope (including quality), time and resources.

Scope

The project scope (also referred to as 'specification') is defined as:

a description of the sum of the products and services to be provided by the project (PMI, 2000).

It represents a complete listing of all the project deliverables, and defines the functionality (and quality) of the end result. The project requirements form the basis of the project scope; however, the scope defines the project in much more detail. The

project scope provides clarity to everyone concerned with the project, about what work is and what is not included in the project.

For example, an organisation-wide quality audit may involve a team of consultants performing detailed interviews and scoring each department against a recognised quality system, but may not include the actions needed to correct any quality issues revealed by the audit. These may be addressed in a follow-up quality improvement project later. It is important to be clear at the outset what is included and what is outside the project scope boundary.

Time

Project time is the length of time allotted for the project. It is a function of the project's activities and the relationship between those activities. Time is managed in a project with the aid of activity networks and schedules. A project schedule is a representation (usually visual) of the project activities along a time base that enables the time available and the time required to be compared.

Resources

Project activities use resources which in turn cost money. Examples of project resources are:

- people
- material
- equipment
- financing
- knowledge.

Putting a cost against project resources and mapping them onto a schedule produces a time-phased chart or table of project resources, called a 'project budget' or 'cost plan'.

Scope–time–cost triangle

Typically, clients want to maximise their benefit by getting a product to market as quickly as possible with as much functionality as possible and at the minimum cost. In practice, the project team is constrained as to what can be achieved for a given cost, in a given time period.

Choices have to be made in every project. For example:

- In a university project to build a new hall of residence that must also double up as conference accommodation during vacations, a decision may arise about whether it is more important to add additional luxury features to boost conference trade, than it is to finish the project by a given date and be able to receive incoming students that have been promised on-campus accommodation.

■ In an R&D project close to making an important breakthrough, a decision may be required to authorise significant expenditure above the project budget or to slim down the project scope and keep within budget.

Project managers are often judged according to how well they complete a project with respect to scope, time and cost. Projects are labelled as successes or failures depending on how their planned cost, time and scope compare to the final cost, time and scope at the end of the project. For the project manager these three variables are extremely important. See Gardiner and Stewart (2000) for an in-depth discussion about these constraints.

In an ideal world, the project manager would ensure that each constraint remains within the boundaries established at the start of the project. The problem is that, no matter how skilled the project manager is and how well the project has been planned, the unexpected can occur. Therefore, a project manager needs to know (preferably in advance) where adjustments can be made if necessary.

As part of the initiation phase, the wise project manager will help the sponsor to establish the relative priority attached to each of the constraints: scope (including quality), time and cost. One way of doing this is by using the simple process tool shown in Figure 8.1 and asking the sponsor to position the coin inside the triangle to reflect the relative importance of each constraint. For example, placing the coin at the top of the diagram would indicate that time is the unmoveable goal post. Once this is determined, the project manager will know to suggest project trade-offs using only scope and cost whenever an unexpected problem arises. The nature and characteristics of the project will influence the priority given to each constraint.

Some projects may have two constraints that cannot be easily traded, for example in a project to launch a satellite that will observe a major astronomical event, both time and scope may be critical. In this case the coin would need to be positioned between time and scope, leaving cost as the only trading variable.

Unless priorities are established at the outset of a

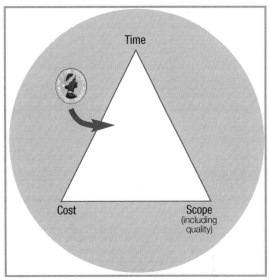

Figure 8.1 Scope–time–cost triangle

project, inappropriate trade-offs might be made. The above tool does not provide answers to the problem, but it does draw attention to it and helps to facilitate a well-thought out position to take. The process is more likely to benefit the occasional or lay client who may be considering these issues for the first time.

Having a clear idea of where priorities lie in relation to project objectives can help project managers make better decisions. Communicating this information effectively to all stakeholders can also improve stakeholder congruence.

TIME
out ✐ Scope, time, cost

Consider the four projects:

(i)   market launch of a new product
(ii) refurbishment of a nuclear reactor
(iii) a publicly funded research project
(iv) fixing the millennium 2000 software bug.

Draw a scope–time–cost triangle for each project and place a coin where you think the project sponsor would place one.

Compare your answers with those suggested in the shaded box overleaf.

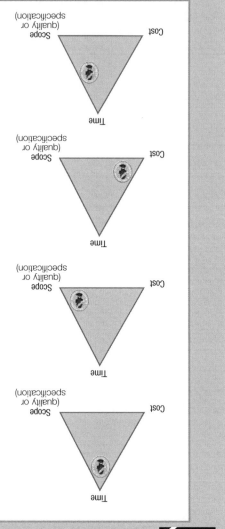

Priority triangle for a new product launch
A project to launch a new product will have time as the number one priority. However, too many trade-offs against quality to achieve a target date can lead to some unpleasant surprises, as Bill Gates can testify following his unintentional 'blank screen' during a live launch of a new version of Microsoft's Windows operating system.

Priority triangle for a nuclear reactor refurbishment
Quality has to be paramount in this project due to its safety critical nature. There is a legal obligation to meet quality specification, and any shortfall would risk serious injury or loss of life. Time and cost must give way to quality issues.

Priority triangle for a publicly funded research project
Typically, cost would be the unmoveable constraint here. Unexpected events, over and above allowances set aside as contingency, would have to be resolved by descoping (that is, reducing the project scope in terms of deliverables or quality) or moving target dates.

Priority triangle for fixing the millennium 2000 bug
This project has a clear time constraint, with no flexibility whatsoever. However, the coin has been placed between time and quality. A poor quality end result may still have grave consequences for any company that relies on information technology for competitive advantage.

Breakdown structures

Deliverables and activities

A project can be defined in two ways:

1. In terms of its deliverables – the products and services that it is going to provide.
2. In terms of its activities, where an activity is any unit of work that results in a deliverable, which can be done by a person or a team of people in a relatively short period of time.

Thus, 'clean carpet in new office' represents a short activity that could be part of a project to do with relocating an office, but 'write management information system software code' might take several months and so is not appropriate as an activity. A task that is too large to be a single activity should be broken down into smaller activities.

Project activities are easier to understand when they are deliverable-oriented, that is, when their description focuses on an action which when completed produces a deliverable. An activity described as 'carpet – new office' might make sense to the person who put it in the project plan but to everyone else it is ambiguous. For example, it could mean:

- choose new office carpet
- fit new office carpet
- remove old carpet from new office
- take measurements for new office carpet.

If the same activity was described as 'clean carpet in new office', most people would have a pretty good idea what this meant. The description this time is deliverable-oriented. The activity will 'deliver' a cleaned carpet in the new office.

To define a *specific* project fully, we need to know all its deliverables and activities. The term 'product scope' is used to define a project's deliverables and the term 'project scope' is used to denote all the work that must be done to make these deliverables appear (PMI, 2000: 51).

Together, the product scope and project scope fully define the project. Every project should have a clear and easily understood scope. The documentation that defines a project's scope is so important that special measures are put in place to make sure that everyone is working to the *same* information, and that they are committed to achieving the *same* product (that is, end deliverables) throughout the entire project. This does not mean that the scope never changes. On the contrary, the scope almost always changes.

The concept of 'chunking'

The idea of breaking up a project into smaller, more manageable 'chunks' was introduced in Chapter 2 in the context of the project life cycle. Each chunk represents a different part of the project. If the resulting parts are still too large to manage as a single 'unit of work', the chunking process can be continued by adding another level. In this way a hierarchy of levels is created. A small project may have only two or three levels. A large project may have more than five or six levels.

Using breakdown structures in project management

The process of chunking breaks up a large system

(that is, a project) into a convenient and logical structure for management and communication purposes. The resulting structure is called a 'breakdown structure'. When using a breakdown structure to communicate project information, you can choose to show some or all the levels. Senior management may want to know the general structure of a project. You might show them a breakdown structure to Level 3, say. Operations managers, on the other hand, may need to see a more detailed picture, say down to Level 5, but only certain portions of the project – the parts that their unit will be delivering.

In project management, breakdown structures can be used to define the:

- *product scope* – the components or elements that make up the end product or service. The breakdown structure used in this case is the product breakdown structure (PBS)
- *project scope* – all the work involved in the project, that is, the project activities. The associated breakdown structure here is the work breakdown structure (WBS)
- *human resources* – the people who will carry out the activities. In this case the organisation breakdown structure (OBS) is used.

A WBS and an OBS should be prepared for all projects. A PBS is used mainly on projects producing complex end products. Product breakdown structures are used extensively in manufacturing.

Because of the importance of the WBS and the OBS, they are considered below in more detail.

The work breakdown structure (WBS)

A WBS is a top-down, deliverable-oriented representation of all areas of work involved in a project. It can be represented diagrammatically or as a structured task list (see Figures 8.2(a) and 8.2(b)).

The work breakdown structure is an important communication tool in the planning phase of a project. It helps all those concerned with the project to visualise the work content and project deliverables. This is vital, especially during the early part of the project life cycle. The WBS helps to generate and create a common understanding of the project and what the project involves for the team members, the sponsor and the customers. It provides a structured view of how the project is broken up into manageable and convenient chunks (APM, 2000: 26). In a WBS it is usual to continue chunking until the end of every branch represents a unit of work

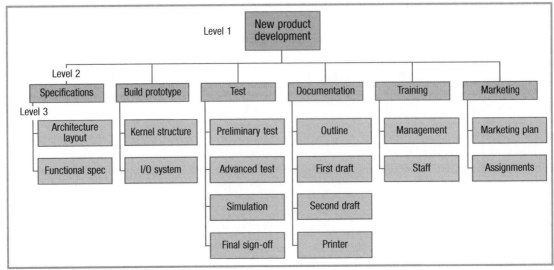

Figure 8.2a Example work breakdown structure – diagrammatic form

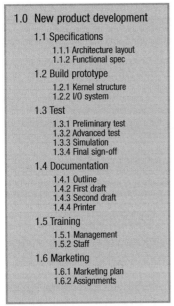

Figure 8.2b Example work breakdown structure – task list form

that can be carried out in a reasonable time by a single unit of manpower resource. The work involved at this level of detail is called a 'work package'. A work package may contain several activities grouped together for management and control purposes and is assigned to a resource unit (that is, work team) for implementation.

An important feature of a WBS is its unique coding system. The WBS is coded using a logical series of numbers to represent the level and position of each of the items in the project. This code can then be used in other documents, for example for responsibility allocation, cost allocation and monitoring and reporting purposes. Each code represents a unique part of the WBS.

It is important that each task and work package is accurately coded to ensure that the ability to control the project is not compromised. The WBS code provides a shorthand method of communicating information about different work packages without ambiguity or long wordy descriptions.

Developing a WBS

By now you will be aware that the process of *defining* a project can involve the sponsor, the project manager, the customers and some or all of the stakeholders. The *management* of this process, however, is usually the responsibility of the project manager. It is his or her job to coordinate everyone's input and make sure that nothing is left out.

So where should one begin when defining a project? A good place to start is with the apex of the WBS, which represents the finished product. Starting at the top (Level 1) encourages a better understanding of the 'big picture' before getting immersed in details. Once the overall project has been described and understood, the team can start breaking it further down, gradually and progressively into more detailed items as required, always maintaining attention on the project's objectives. At

Levels 2 and 3 major milestones can start to be identified. These are intermediate products and deliverables that build towards the project's objectives. The process is continued to create subsidiary milestones. At the lowest level, individual activity plans at the work package level are put in place. Once all the work packages have been defined, the WBS is complete.

Up to this point, the process of creating a WBS has been described using only a top-down approach. It often makes good sense to do it this way. For example, imagine you are going to manage a project for a retail client who wants to open a chain of new showrooms. You might start by helping the client determine how many showrooms to open initially and in which cities to locate them. You will want to establish the purpose of these showrooms and who is likely to use them. You would be unlikely to start by getting the client to agree on the colour of chairs or the type of wine to be served on the opening day of each new facility.

Of course defining a project can also proceed in a bottom-up direction. A brainstorming session with team members to identify lower level activities and work packages might help to generate a higher level structure. More careful thought at each higher level branch may then help to refine the project scope back at the lower levels again. New activities may be added, and some be taken away as the scope of the project becomes clearer.

Thus, the process of defining a project may go through several iterations involving both top-down and bottom-up approaches. Once a draft WBS has been formed, it becomes an excellent tool for communication and discussion during the rest of the planning process.

Common weaknesses in preparing a WBS are a lack of a logical numbering system and organising the structure by discipline or organisation rather than by project objectives and deliverables. There is no one right way to break up a project into its component parts. A WBS should reflect natural groupings or divisions in a project, and not be based on unusual or difficult to understand categories. The most useful WBSs are deliverable-oriented. This means that they take account of the deliverables of the project rather than functional disciplines.

A rolling-wave approach

In a small project, it is desirable to have a complete WBS before work commences on the project. In a large project, the lowest levels of the WBS can be planned on a rolling-wave basis, that is, progressively as and when detailed information becomes available. This means that a project can begin its execution phase before the WBS is complete. Note that it is normally advisable to limit a rolling-wave approach to the lowest levels of the WBS only. The job of detailing the WBS at this level may be delegated to those team members responsible for doing the work.

Using a WBS

A draft WBS can be reviewed with project participants as soon as it has been created. It serves as a checklist for the work required in all areas of the project. A WBS is often included in the project charter. Participants can see clearly what is and what is not expected to complete the project. You may recall that a completed WBS is a good definition of the project scope. The sponsor is able to view the work defined by the WBS and compare it to the project objectives for consistency and completeness. The project manager can use the WBS to curb any unrealistic expectations that the sponsor may be harbouring.

When it comes to doing the work, a WBS can be used to help to allocate responsibilities to the project participants. The WBS can also be used to help to create a schedule and perform a more thorough assessment of project risks than was possible at the initiation phase. In some cases, the identification of a significant risk associated with a work package may mean that it should be further decomposed to isolate the risk and allow preparation of plans to mitigate the risk. Risk mitigation plans should be added to the WBS as activities in their own right. This helps to ensure that they are not forgotten during project execution.

Getting commitment and agreement

As in the case of the project charter, the project manager may ask participants and the sponsor to sign a final copy of the WBS as an indication of their approval of and commitment to it. You may find that doing this results in additional iterations of making improvements and adjustments to the WBS before anyone is prepared to add *their* signature to it. People are often happy to say verbally 'it's OK' but ask them to sign it off and suddenly they want one more look at it! Getting the WBS signed off helps to create a more useful audit trail and ensures a better quality WBS, which in turn will lead to a more successful project. This approach can be applied to all the outputs of project scoping.

Creating a WBS

Given the following incomplete list of activities for making a cup of tea:

Add boiling water to tea leaves in teapot
Add sugar
Boil water
Brew tea in teapot
Bring spoon
Collect tea leaves
Get kettle
Locate and bring teapot
Place cup on table
Put tea leaves in teapot
Stir
Take out sugar
Warm pot

1. Prepare a simple diagrammatic work breakdown structure that has three levels
2. Use the WBS you have created to help identify and add in any missing activities you can think of to prepare your cup of tea

See shaded box for suggested answswer.

The organisation breakdown structure (OBS)

Whereas the WBS maps out all the work packages in the project, the organisation breakdown structure (OBS) shows all the people who are going to do the work. In other words, an OBS shows the human resource (or manpower) requirements of a project. It also shows where they come from, that is, which department, division or company (for example in the case of consultants and contractors) they belong to.

An example of an OBS is shown in Figure 8.4.

The OBS is an important part of the project plan. It establishes for all concerned who the other participants are, both on their immediate team and in the wider project team. An OBS is an excellent source of reference whenever help is needed to resolve a project issue, or when a job needs to be covered because someone is off sick.

The people involved in a project are often selected by a variety of means. The sponsor and the project manager may be responsible for selecting the key project team members. In other cases, the project manager may be assigned manpower by a functional manager, a contracts manager (in the case of a contracting company), or a consulting partner may appoint a junior to oversee smaller value contracts.

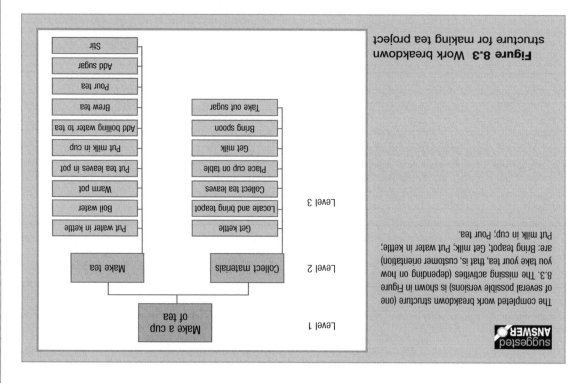

Figure 8.3 Work breakdown structure for making tea project

The completed work breakdown structure (one of several possible versions) is shown in Figure 8.3. The missing activities (depending on how you take your tea, that is, customer orientation) are: Bring teapot; Get milk; Put water in kettle; Put milk in cup; Pour tea.

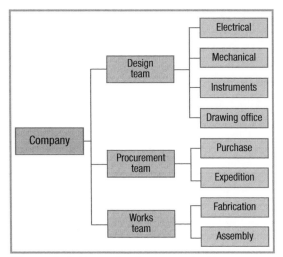

Figure 8.4 Example of an organisation breakdown structure (OBS)

there is no confusion over tasks and the possibility of some tasks being left undone is reduced. Particular attention is needed at organisational interfaces, where the responsibility of one unit ends and another unit begins. There is a greater risk of problems here. When the outputs of two work packages have to combine in some way to produce a larger project deliverable, it is essential that each work unit has a good understanding of how their respective contributions are going to join together. In some projects, much time and materials are wasted as a particular problem is passed from one participant to another, with no one agreeing to take responsibility to resolve the issue.

Integrating the WBS and the OBS

Responsibility at the work package level can be defined in a project by integrating the WBS with the OBS to create a matrix like the one shown in Figure 8.5.

This matrix gives a good visual guide showing who is responsible for which parts of the project. If one area of the project falls behind, it is quickly realised which resource unit is responsible. This open

Allocating responsibilities

A good project plan should make it crystal clear where responsibilities lie in a project. When responsibilities are laid down clearly and unambiguously,

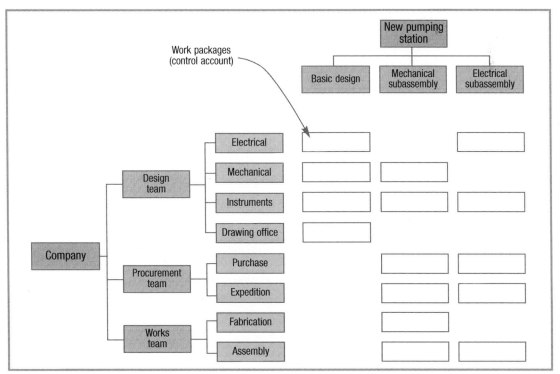

Figure 8.5 Integrating the WBS and OBS to show work package ownership

visibility helps the project manager to control the progress of the project. It also helps to motivate the various resource units to get their part of the project done on time. Genuine problems and concerns can be addressed sooner rather than later.

In larger projects it is common practice to assign each of the segments or boxes in the matrix a cost code. In this case each box is called a 'control account'.

The project team and team building

Selecting the project team

Putting together (and keeping together) a project team includes six areas of accountability for the project manager:

1. *Plan for team building*. Develop the project plan, keeping in mind at every stage the four aspects: what, how, when and who. Remember, the final plan must have the agreement of all project team members.
2. *Negotiate for team members*. The project manager must strive to build the most effective team by obtaining the most promising team personnel. Make every effort to obtain the *correct* personnel (in-house and external) with both technical expertise and favourable personalities. However, obtaining everyone that the project manager wants is unlikely, and rarely necessary. In many cases a line manager is better placed to select appropriate staff. Techniques for selecting contractors are discussed in Chapter 6.
3. *Organise the team*. Allocate activities and tasks using a responsibility assignment matrix (see the next section). Include a mix of tasks to give each team member a challenge. Encourage team members to be responsible for their own planning, deliverables and problem solving. Finally, obtain commitment from each team member for their specific responsibilities.
4. *Hold a kick-off meeting*. This will allow all team members to understand the entire project from the beginning to the end. Everyone will understand the specific responsibilities of each team member and their commitments. The kick-off meeting is the place to begin the team-building process. This will unite the team towards the common project goal shared by all. All this is accomplished by having an effective and well-timed agenda. The project manager should chair the kick-off meeting. How to conduct a kick-off meeting and techniques for managing meetings are discussed in more detail below.
5. *Build communication links*. Establish, and agree with the team, procedures about how the team will communicate; how problems or conflicts are to be reported and resolved.
6. *Conduct team building exercises*. Team building at the kick-off meeting is valuable, but team building is most effective and practical when it is integrated into normal day-to-day project activities. For example, team building can be made an important part of almost every project activity, particularly meetings and group or individual feedback sessions.

The responsibility for team building falls squarely on the shoulders of the project manager. He or she is the only person in the position of being able to ensure that team building occurs and that it is effective. Putting a team together can be an awesome task for many project managers or team leaders, not least because it may feel as if other parts of the organisation are determined to prevent you from succeeding. Assembling an effective team is a challenge that requires the right mix of people and combination of roles to achieve the best result.

Project teams are formed in a variety of ways:

- A top group of managers or a committee decides, producing a list of team members based on a set of selection criteria. The project manager may or may not be in the group and may have to guess why he/she has been allocated the individuals in the team
- A senior manager appoints, the project manager having no choice
- The project manager puts together a team from inside the organisation or hires new full-time recruits or specialist advisers from outside
- After the first few appointments, the project manager and core team members select the rest of the team themselves, to make sure that the fit is optimal
- Where there is no clear or permanent project manager, the team can be self-selecting, or individuals may volunteer.

When selecting a project team, it is important to look for the right personality as well as technical ability. The project manager should use his or her instinct and intuition as well as the analysis of CVs or professional qualifications when making a decision. The most suitable team members will be those that give honest answers rather than those giving the answers they think a manager would want to hear.

Short-listed team members can be invited to spend a day or two together as a team and get involved in some aspects of the work. This can be followed with an evening together and social interaction. By the end of this time, the project manager and existing team members will have a good idea of who would add value to the team and integrate well with them.

Organising the project team and role clarification

Organising a project team means that specific assignments must be allocated to specific people as indicated in the project plan. Work authorisations will be prepared for each of the work packages in the work breakdown structure and assigned to specific people or teams. Project participants are given specific responsibilities and accountabilities. This is the time to prepare and circulate a responsibility chart to the project team.

A more detailed description of an individual's responsibilities in a project can be produced using a special matrix called a 'responsibility chart', also known as a 'responsibility assignment matrix' (RAM). In a responsibility chart, the exact nature of a person's responsibilities for a given task is shown using different symbols. See Figure 8.6 for an example of a completed RAM.

There is no standard format that must be followed. The aim of a responsibility chart is to communicate accurately the responsibilities of the people involved to all the participants. The chart is normally included as a part of the project planning documentation and, when used correctly, can facilitate rapid decision making. This is possible because the person responsible for making a decision can be quickly identified and then contacted. The result is that everyone knows

Key	X – eXecutes the work D – takes Decision solely d – takes decision jointly P – manages Progess T – provides Tuition on the job C – must be Consulted I – must be Informed A – available to Advise	Project manager	Team leaders	Project members	Project support office	Steering committee	Project sponsor
Code	Issue/date:						
	Approved by:						
	Activity/task name						
	Develop milestone plan	PX	X		I	D	D
	Create high-level network	PX			X		
	Develop new activity schedules	DP	X	X	I		
	Update network	P	C	C	X		
	Issue work-to lists			I	X		
	Do work	P	PX	X			
	Return turn-around documents	I	P	X	I		
	Activity review meeting	I	PX	X			
	Identify variances (activities)	DP	PX	X			
	Plan recovery	PI	X	X	I		
	Issue activity progress reports	PX	X				
	Review progress against milestones	PX			X	I	
	Milestone progress meeting	PX			X	X	
	Identify variances (milestones)	PX			X	DX	
	Plan recovery	PX	X		X	D	
	Issue milestone progress report	PX			X	C	I
	Approve progress						D

Figure 8.6 Example responsibility assignment matrix

who is responsible for performing work in the project, who needs to be informed, who can make decisions and so on. Getting to the responsible person quickly when an issue arises is the key to avoiding many project delays. The next step is getting the individuals to work together as a team.

Team members must be made to feel at home and comfortable, reasonably secure, confident that they have good leadership, comfortable that their career objectives are being met, and that they have a significant role in an important project effort. Team members will normally feel considerable anxiety concerning their projected roles in the project. The greatest anxiety usually concerns how their individual goals and objectives will fit with those of the project. The challenge to the project manager is to relieve anxieties by answering the following questions:

1. What are we here to do?
2. How shall we organise ourselves?
3. Who is in charge?
4. Who cares about our success?
5. How do we solve problems?
6. How do we fit in with other groups?
7. What benefits do team members get from the team?
8. Will I be able to achieve my personal goals while working on this project?
9. Will this project help me develop professionally?

Project managers can best relieve these anxieties by clearly spelling out each team member's role in the project effort, and indicating exactly how his or her career and other goals will be advanced while working on the project.

Holding a kick-off meeting or workshop

Often the first action in a new project, and one absolutely critical to the team-building process, is to hold a kick-off meeting or workshop. The principal purpose of a kick-off or start-up meeting is to get the project started on the right foot and initiate the active team-building process. It is here that, for the first time, all the individuals involved in the project are brought together in one place. The project manager should take advantage of this situation to get everyone involved in the project and build a unity of purpose for the accomplishment of the project goals.

Is it always necessary to have a kick-off meeting? Probably not, but something is definitely necessary to get all the factions in a project together, and a

meeting is the simplest, most practical way to do it. However, it need not be a formal meeting with a formal agenda if the major purpose is only to get all the team members to know each other. It can be as simple as an informal group meeting for an hour or so, or as elaborate as a weekend or week-long retreat at a resort or hotel. A social event at a local 'watering hole' often serves the purpose of developing a team spirit, or a social event can be used to supplement a formal meeting. In most cases, an informal get-together will not eliminate the need for a formal kick-off meeting. Project Management in Action: 'City technology college' (in Chapter 1) is a good example of a project where a kick-off meeting helped to develop the project team.

A kick-off meeting, chaired by the project manager, should have all or most of the following objectives:

- Get team members to know one another
- Establish working relationships and lines of communication
- Set team goals and objectives
- Review project status
- Review and formalise project plans
- Identify project risks and problem areas
- Establish individual and group responsibilities and accountabilities
- Obtain individual and group commitments.

Visit the website

http://www.palgrave.com/business/gardiner

▶ to discover ten practical steps to managing meetings more effectively

Opportunities for team building and development

Teamwork is the ability to work together towards a common vision, to direct individual accomplishment towards organisational objectives. It is the fuel that allows ordinary people to attain extraordinary results. The progress of a team is much greater than the individual progress of all its members added together. This effect is called 'synergy' and symbolises the power of teamwork (Owen, 1996).

The role of team building in a project is simply to make sure that every member of the project team is moving in the same direction, and that all the team members recognise, accept and are committed to achieving the same project goals and objectives (Burgess and Turner, 2000). In this way, a team can be viewed as a large arrow consisting of many smaller arrows all interconnected and moving towards the same target. The purpose of the team is to hit the centre of the target. Of course, the probability of achieving this goal increases markedly when all the small arrows are aiming at the same point on the target.

Every project can benefit from a team-building programme. However, some projects have a greater need of it than others. Unless a project consists entirely of people who know each other well from previous project contacts, team building will definitely add value to the project. The safest approach is to initiate a team-building effort as part of every new project.

There is a particular need for team building in a matrix organisation. Here the two-boss situation can result in considerable uncertainty in reporting channels, so that team members are continually pulled from different directions. The result of this can be conflicting policies and work tasks which can only be resolved by a team-building effort to be sure that everyone understands the importance of the project and how it will benefit the organisation. Organisation structures, including the matrix structure, are discussed in Chapter 6.

Conducting an initial project team-building programme is a major step in the right direction. However, it must be recognised that team building is a continuous process throughout the life of a project. One major concern is to keep up the momentum and morale of the team, particularly during very long projects. In addition, there will be periodic infusions of new personnel who must be integrated into the existing project team. At a major project milestone where the project enters a new phase and the emphasis is drastically changed, such as a transfer of the project from research to design or development to manufacturing, the key members of the team may change completely. Occasionally, even the project manager may be replaced because of the change in project emphasis or promotion within the company. In any case, a continued or a renewed team-building effort will be necessary.

Team building is most effective when integrated into normal ongoing project activities. Ongoing team development involves using every possible opportunity during the life cycle of a project to promote and enhance team building. A major opportunity for ongoing project team building occurs every time the

TIME out Team-building scenarios

Consider each of the scenarios below and reflect on what team-building action if any should be taken.

1. You have just finished managing a team of six people on a project to design a new palmtop computer. The design director approves your team's work and reassigns you the same team to come up with an exterior design suitable for teenagers.

2. You are the product manager for a new line of savoury snacks and have been tasked with managing the development of this new product range from initial market research to manufacture and product launch. To date you have built up an effective team during the creation of the product concept and early trials. The next stage of the project requires product testing in different regional locations with the help of a marketing consultancy that has worked on two earlier, successful products.

3. You are a branch manager in a bank and have just been appointed to manage a re-engineering project to increase customer satisfaction and cut operating costs by 30%. If the project is a success, your branch will be used as a benchmark for other targeted branches in the company.

In each case, compare your thinking with the analysis in the shaded box.

ANSWER suggested

1. Your team members all know each other very well and have developed trust and commitment towards each other. Some early teamwork to help orientate the team to the new task would be recommended. It is unlikely that intensive team-building activities would be required.

2. The external consultancy will need to be integrated into the project and adopt the same standards and expectations for the project as your team and the sponsor. The fact that the consultancy has worked on two other products is a good sign and should help to facilitate this. However, it may or may not be the same people working on the project and this will have a bearing on the level of team building required.

3. This project will require the involvement and cooperation of all branch personnel. The stakes are high and the project will probably result in a major change to the work environment and bank working practices. Although branch staff will already know each other, the project team will require a significant team-building effort to establish buy-in and communicate the vision of the project to all concerned. The project is unlikely to succeed without the support and buy-in of the project team and end users, that is, all branch staff. Team-building activities can also be used to create owner-ship and an environment of trust.

project manager holds a scheduled or unscheduled meeting. This includes:

- staff meetings
- planning meetings
- scheduling meetings
- replanning sessions
- technical reviews
- status reviews
- design reviews
- budget reviews
- failure reviews
- top management briefings
- customer briefings and audits.

Actions that the project manager can take to get team members more intimately involved and team conscious are to:

- introduce new team members
- recognise special project performance
- keep the team informed on late developments, both good news and bad
- keep the team informed on client and customer actions and thinking
- report project follow-on potential
- bring in special outside speakers and presenters to emphasise project importance and the views of top management, customer, client and so on
- provide exposure for team members by giving them major roles in every meeting
- get project and team recognition by having representatives from the media and authors of in-house publications attend meetings.

How to recognise an effective team

There are many definitions of a team. However, in this chapter we are less concerned with academically correct definitions than with understanding the characteristics of an effective team, and how these may be harnessed to achieve project goals.

There are four characteristics of a team that successful team members consistently identify (Owen, 1996):

1. A team is more than just a group of individuals working together. Teamwork has a synergistic effect in that the individuals working together achieve more than they could alone.
2. A team shares a common purpose which is clear to each team member.
3. A team requires continuous hard work, but should also be enjoyable, fun and result in a feeling of personal satisfaction for every team member.
4. A team has a 'feel' of 'teamness' about it. Members are open and direct with each other, without anyone feeling personally attacked. Mistakes are openly discussed and seen as opportunities to learn and develop. There is a pride, a sense of belonging to the team, which members find motivating.

The above characteristics can be restated and expanded in the form of a simple inventory which can be used to identify effective teams. Table 8.1 is an example of a team effectiveness inventory.

When you have completed the team effectiveness inventory in the manner indicated, the scores of the nine statement pairs are added up to determine how effective the team is and what action is appropriate to take:

- If the total is between 45 and 63, the team is effective and there is little evidence that the unit needs team building at this time
- If the score is between 27 and 44, there is some evidence but no immediate pressure for team building, unless several items are very low
- If the score is between 18 and 26, a team-building programme should be given serious consideration. If the score is below 18, team building should be a top priority for the project manager.

 Using the team effectiveness inventory

Think of a project team you are currently, or have recently been, a member of. Complete the team effectiveness inventory to assess the effectiveness of this team. Does the score obtained surprise you in any way? Reflect on the strengths and weaknesses of your team and where you believe improvements could be made.

Models for team development

The following section considers five models that can be used in projects to help understand, build and develop effective teams.

Life cycle of a team

New teams coming together for the first time typically operate and pass through different stages in

Table 8.1 Team effectiveness inventory – a simple health check									

Read each statement pair, then tick the box to show your assessment of the team for that characteristic. For example, if the atmosphere is always 'informal and comfortable' and people are always 'involved and interested', tick box 7 for the first statement pair.

Ineffective teams	Tick one box only for each statement pair							Effective teams
The atmosphere reflects either indifference or boredom – for example people whisper to each other	1 ☐	2 ☐	3 ☐	4 ☐	5 ☐	6 ☐	7 ☐	The atmosphere tends to be informal, comfortable. People are involved and interested
Only a few people talk. Little effort is made to keep to the point of the discussion	1 ☐	2 ☐	3 ☐	4 ☐	5 ☐	6 ☐	7 ☐	There is a lot of discussion in which everyone takes part. Everyone keeps to the point
It is difficult to understand what the group task is	1 ☐	2 ☐	3 ☐	4 ☐	5 ☐	6 ☐	7 ☐	Everyone understands the task that has to be done
People do not really listen to each other. Some ideas are not put forward by the group	1 ☐	2 ☐	3 ☐	4 ☐	5 ☐	6 ☐	7 ☐	The group members listen to each other. Every idea is given a hearing
Disagreements are not dealt with effectively. Things are put to the vote without discussing them. Some people are unhappy about the decisions made	1 ☐	2 ☐	3 ☐	4 ☐	5 ☐	6 ☐	7 ☐	There is disagreement. The group is comfortable with this and they work together to resolve it. Nobody feels unhappy about decisions made
People are not open about what they are thinking. They grumble about decisions afterwards	1 ☐	2 ☐	3 ☐	4 ☐	5 ☐	6 ☐	7 ☐	People feel free to criticise and say honestly what they think
One or two people are dominant. What they say goes	1 ☐	2 ☐	3 ☐	4 ☐	5 ☐	6 ☐	7 ☐	Everybody knows how the others feel about the issues being discussed
Nobody takes any interest in what has to be done, and they do not offer help to others	1 ☐	2 ☐	3 ☐	4 ☐	5 ☐	6 ☐	7 ☐	When action needs to be taken, all the participants are clear about what has to be done and they help each other
Only one or two people make the decisions. Leadership is not shared	1 ☐	2 ☐	3 ☐	4 ☐	5 ☐	6 ☐	7 ☐	Different people apply leadership skills from time to time

their life cycle before reaching their full achieving potential (Tuckman and Jensen, 1977). The life cycle stages and their key characteristics are illustrated in Figure 8.7. During the life of a team, the behaviour and performance of team members change as members get to know one another and working practices and values become more clearly defined.

■ A new team begins at the *forming* stage. Productivity is low. Members are learning about each other as well as beginning to understand the project objectives. Through these early interactions, members reveal more of themselves and their personal values and priorities.

■ In the *storming* stage, communication levels will have increased. Brainstorming will have revealed differences of opinions. The group has begun to tap into the resources of its members but there may be several conflicts. The more extrovert members will tend to dominate, often at the expense of valuable contributions from quieter members who may feel isolated from the team. Many teams can fall apart at this stage unless sufficient leadership skills exist to create order from the growing chaos. During the storming stage, the different team roles and responsibilities should be made clear and agreed by team members. Once roles are accepted, procedures for tackling the team objectives can begin to develop – with everyone's involvement.

■ As a team moves from the storming to the *norming* stage, productivity begins to increase. At this point, team development activities can strengthen and help to develop the working and social processes in the team, thus increasing productivity further. The team now learns how to measure performance and act on feedback; their ability to keep focused on the project objectives increases and the commitment of each team member grows. At this point they are entering the performing stage.

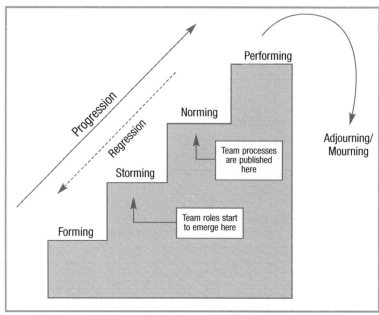

Figure 8.7 Team life cycle model

■ In the *performing* stage, the team has established its interpersonal norms; it becomes an entity capable of diagnosing and solving problems, and making decisions. In this stage, team members may:
  ■ experience insight into personal and interpersonal processes
  ■ be willing to sort through group problems
  ■ develop high conflict resolution skills
  ■ understand members' strengths and weaknesses
  ■ confide in each other, share personal problems and discuss group dynamics
  ■ undertake constructive self-change
  ■ identify closely with the group
  ■ accomplish a great deal of work.

Project teams reaching this stage tend to be effective and will devote time and energy to maintain good group relations.

■ The final stage in the team life cycle is the *mourning* stage. This occurs when the team is about to disband and its members wonder where they will go from here. In this stage, team members may:
  ■ feel elated at the successful attainment of goals
  ■ feel disappointed at unattained goals
  ■ feel a sense of loss when the group is disbanded
  ■ feel relief at the end of the process

  ■ congratulate each other
  ■ celebrate.

Just as individuals go through predictable stages of growth and development depending on age, experience, maturity and other factors, teams go through predictable stages, the duration of which depends on factors such as individual and team maturity, task complexity, leadership, organisational climate and external climate. Because the forming, storming and norming stages of team development result in minimal output, it is tempting to try to rush through or short-circuit these stages and hope that the group can thereby achieve peak productivity. Although seductive, this idea is dysfunctional.

Teams can and do stop developing at various stages. Some teams are never fully functioning. Given that the stages are inevitable, one way to help to reduce the time needed for a new or changing team to be fully productive, while minimising the tension, fear or anxiety common in the forming, storming and norming stages, is to share concerns and expectations about the group. A good way to do this is through a variety of informal and formal team-building activities. Members of the team can contract with one another that there will be no 'surprises' and, therefore, an atmosphere of trust can be achieved earlier, allowing for interpersonal issues to be put aside in favour of task issues. The team can then move easily to the performing stage.

However, without a genuine and positive approach to team building, many teams never reach the performing stage, and in some cases a performing team can regress to the storming stage. Failure to reach and maintain team processes at the performing level can occur for many reasons, including:

- inadequate leadership
- too many members
- unclear or ambiguous objectives
- timescale too tight
- objectives not seen as important
- members having other more pressing priorities
- team membership changes
- too many objectives – lack of focus.

Team-building activities can be used to help tackle and overcome many of these problems. An effective approach to team building can accelerate the progression of a project team through the life cycle stages and enable team members to add value sooner to the project, its sponsor and other stakeholders.

Belbin's team roles

Meredith Belbin is an acknowledged expert in teams. He has carried out one of the most recognised studies of team roles by studying hundreds of managers working to solve exercises in teams. At the time of his study, it was generally accepted that putting all the brightest experts together in the same team would create the most successful team. In fact, these teams, often called 'Apollo teams', did not produce consistently good results. Yet many organisations still believe that the brightest people will automatically outperform any others. This is not always the case (see Belbin, 1981).

In his research, Belbin found that the less brilliant team performed in a mediocre way until they were joined by a creative or task-oriented person. From this, he realised that a successful team needed different 'roles' which related to different processes, and that these could be related to psychometric tests that could be given to individuals. By identifying these roles, a healthy mix could be put together and the team would be more effective. Belbin discovered that for a healthy team, eight different roles had to be filled. He has since added another, the 'specialist', making nine. However, not every team needs every role to the same degree and the nature of the project will influence this. He also found that having all nine roles present does not guarantee high performance. For this reason Belbin's work has been criticised, but

what cannot be disputed is that, whatever the task, a team should reflect the different roles, and each one should be recognised and utilised. Belbin states that too many of one type can lead to conflict and unproductive effort (see Belbin, 1993).

In practice, project teams are often composed for functional purposes with no consideration of team roles. In these circumstances team members have to manage as best they can with the resulting mix of team roles. Most people have one or two strong team roles and one or two weak team roles. This is quite normal. Belbin calls these weak team roles 'allowable weaknesses' that are the consequence of having one or two dominant team roles – called 'natural' team roles.

In a project team it is preferable to have a mix of members whose natural team roles span all nine team roles. It is not recommended for any member to adopt a team role which is one of their weak team roles. This will only interfere with and reduce their effectiveness in performing their natural team roles.

The ideal team size is often cited as having four to six members. In teams of less than eight, some team members will have to adopt more than one team role. This is not a problem because most people have two or three natural roles. The nine team roles, their key strengths and allowable weaknesses are described in Table 8.2.

Visit the website

http://www.palgrave.com/business/gardiner

- to find the Belbin team roles self-perception inventory – can be used to identify strongest and weakest team roles of every team member quickly and simply
- to read an expanded explanation of the Belbin team roles

Using the team roles

A knowledge of the team role profiles of team members can help a project manager in two ways: first, it can be used in the selection of team members alongside other selection criteria; second, it can serve as a diagnostic for an existing team that is underperforming.

It is important never to try and force team members into roles which clearly do not suit their type. This will simply result in disaster. For example, a 'team worker' will perform a constructive role in a relaxed and diplomatic way, but don't ask him or her to make big decisions. If a delicate phone call has to be made which requires a certain amount of diplomacy, then a worried 'completer' may create panic rather than confidence.

Table 8.2 The nine Belbin team roles

Team role	Key strengths	Allowable weaknesses
Plant	Creative, imaginative, unorthodox Solves difficult problems	Ignores incidentals. Too preoccupied to communicate effectively
Resource investigator	Extrovert, enthusiastic, communicative Explores opportunities. Develops contacts	Overoptimistic. Loses interest once initial enthusiasm has passed
Coordinator	Mature, confident, a good chairperson Clarifies goals, promotes decision making, delegates well	Can be seen as manipulative. Offloads personal work
Shaper	Challenging, dynamic, thrives on pressure The drive and courage to overcome obstacles	Prone to provocation. Offends people's feelings
Monitor evaluator	Sober, strategic and discerning. Sees all options. Judges accurately	Lacks drive and ability to inspire others
Teamworker	Cooperative, mild, perceptive and diplomatic Listens, builds, averts friction	Indecisive in crunch situations
Implementer	Disciplined, reliable, conservative and efficient Turns ideas into practical actions	Somewhat inflexible. Slow to respond to new possibilities
Completer	Painstaking, conscientious, anxious. Searches out errors and omissions. Delivers on time	Inclined to worry unduly. Reluctant to delegate
Specialist	Single-minded, self-starting, dedicated Provides knowledge and skills in rare supply	Contributes on only a narrow front. Dwells on technicalities

Usually it is a mistake to try to overcome a team member's shortcomings, and far better to try to make sure that in all cases the team is sufficiently well balanced that the members have complementary qualities.

As was observed earlier, some weaknesses are allowable in the sense that the weakness is the price you pay for the strength. Since an 'allowable weakness' is a common byproduct of a strength, there is a danger that in attempting to remedy the weakness you damage the strength. So team members should be encouraged to learn to control their 'allowable weaknesses' rather than try to correct them. Team members are relieved and reassured when they understand that the team will tolerate and underpin some of their weaknesses.

Finally, a word of warning. Although the application of team roles can be useful, you should avoid 'labelling' people as a 'plant', a 'shaper' and so on. Team role scores are only an indicator of a person's team roles. The method is not foolproof and the project manager should allow team members to be 'themselves' and not expect them to conform to a set of characteristics. If the project manager does try to achieve conformity, team members can become particularly self-conscious and the value of the team role concept can be undermined.

Conflict management

Conflict is generally defined as a clash between hostile or opposing elements or ideas. It can range from a mild disagreement to a win–lose, emotion-packed confrontation. The traditional view sees conflict as being primarily negative and caused by troublemakers, that is, it is something bad and should be avoided. A more contemporary view sees conflict in a positive light and as something that is inevitable and essential in any organisation committed to developing or working with new ideas. It is how the individual views and deals with conflict that determines whether it is constructive or destructive for the organisation.

One of the most important skills a project manager can develop is in the area of conflict management, which requires well-developed skills in managing human interrelationships in a highly conflict-prone environment. Conflicts will exist in all project environments. A failure in these skills and a failure to recognise and carefully manage the details of a conflict situation can easily lead to a total collapse of the project team.

One of the primary, underlying reasons that conflict exists in organisations today is the tremendous amount of change that has occurred in the workplace. Change leads to conflict as people disagree on how organisations should adapt and as they see the results of that adaptation benefiting or damaging their status in the organisation. Some conflict is always present in organisations because they have limited means with which to satisfy the divergent interests of the various employees.

Conflict in the context of project management may be classified into two broad, partly overlapping categories, first, conflict associated with change, and second, conflict associated with the concentration of professionals of diverse disciplines in a more or less autonomous group effort that has a limited life. If a project is to be successful, the project manager must cope with conflict and develop appropriate strategies for its resolution.

Conditions leading to conflict

There are nine antecedent conditions of conflict that exist in all organisations to a greater or lesser degree:

1. *Ambiguous jurisdictions* – when two or more parties have related responsibilities.
2. *Conflict of interests* – when two or more parties want to achieve different or inconsistent goals and desires relative to each other from their association with the organisation.
3. *Communication barriers* – these create misunderstandings and inhibit their resolution by blocking efforts to explain the needs, viewpoints and actions of those involved in the organisation.
4. *Dependence on one party* – in this situation there tends to be a situation of conflict because one person is dependent on the other to provide needed resources.
5. *Differentiation in an organisation* – when different subunits of the organisation are responsible for different tasks. This occurs in all organisations.
6. *Association of the parties* – when people must associate together and make joint decisions, conflict can occur.
7. *Need for consensus* – similar to association of the parties, but when a need for consensus exists, people must willingly agree amongst themselves.
8. *Behaviour regulations* – when the individual's behaviour must be regulated closely, as in a situation involving high levels of safety and security concerns. Individuals resist the tight boundaries placed on their actions.
9. *Unresolved prior conflict* – will build up and create an atmosphere of tension which can lead to more and more intense conflicts. The longer the

conflict is left unresolved, the more severe the conflict will become.

When these conditions are found, it is up to the project manager to avoid the potentially destructive results of conflict by controlling and channelling it into areas that can prove beneficial to the project. Destructive conflict can be highly detrimental to the project and its stakeholders and can significantly affect productivity.

Conflict in a positive light can stimulate the search for new facts, methods or solutions. When parties are involved in conflict about which of two alternatives to accept, their disagreement may stimulate a search for another solution mutually acceptable to both.

Conflict resolution styles

When conflict does occur, there are five distinct styles that can be adopted by the project manager or team members to resolve it, as illustrated in Figure 8.8 (see also Rahim, 1985, 2001). They are:

1. Obliging/smoothing
2. Dominating/forcing
3. Avoiding/withdrawing
4. Integrating/problem solving
5. Compromising.

Each conflict resolution style has a place in the management of conflict during a project, and these are discussed below.

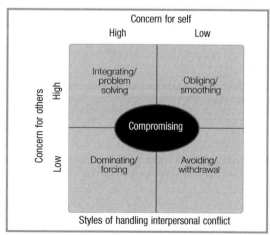

Figure 8.8 Conflict resolution styles

Obliging/smoothing (low concern for self : high concern for others)

If A and B have a conflict and A adopts an obliging approach, A will shift his position to coincide with B's position and the conflict will be resolved. The obliging or smoothing approach is quick and it gives the other party a feeling of ownership and power. It is about de-emphasising differences and emphasising commonalties over conflictual issues. This keeps the atmosphere friendly, but if used over frequently or as the main or only method of dealing with conflict, the conflicts will never be faced. It may be used to resolve conflicts where the other party's position will not adversely affect the team or project objectives. Conflicts involving trivial differences of opinion can be quickly resolved using the obliging or smoothing approach.

Dominating/forcing (high concern for self : low concern for others)

If A and B have a conflict and A adopts a dominating or forcing approach, A will use his authority and/or influence to get B to accept his own position. The dominating approach, like the obliging approach, can also be quick to resolve conflict. It may be used to resolve conflicts of opinion when a decision has to be made quickly and the team have not reached the performing stage. This situation is more likely to occur during the early phases of a project when the team are still establishing norms and accepted procedures. The project manager may use the dominating approach to keep the project moving along. However, exerting one's viewpoint at the potential expense of another party is characterised by a win–lose situation. One party will win while the other loses. This can increase conflicts later as antagonisms build up among the parties involved. It should therefore be used as a last resort. Over-use or inappropriate use of the dominating or forcing approach can lead to resentment, loss of morale and motivation, and impede the development of the team and achievement of the project goal.

Avoiding/withdrawal (low concern for self : low concern for others)

If A and B have a conflict and A adopts an avoiding or withdrawal approach, the conflict is ignored and not acknowledged or made public. B may be completely unaware that a conflict exists at all. The approach essentially involves retreating from actual or potential disagreements and conflict situations. The avoiding/withdrawal approach avoids confrontation but may adversely affect the project if over-used. It is appropriate only in certain situations, for example when a cooling-off period is required to gain perspective on the conflict situation. There is also a danger that a minor conflict perceived and ignored can transform into a more serious conflict, with dysfunctional consequences later in the project.

Integrating/problem solving (high concern for self : high concern for others)

If A and B have a conflict and A uses the integrating approach to resolve it, both parties get together and openly discuss the conflict and its impact on the project objectives. A and B welcome contributions to the discussion from others, and a team meeting is held to find a solution that satisfies everyone concerned. This approach provides a win–win solution. It takes longer to implement but both parties end up with a feeling of ownership and achievement. In this approach the disagreement is addressed directly. The problem is defined, information is collected, alternatives are developed and analysed, and the most appropriate alternative is selected. This method is considered theoretically to be the best way of dealing with conflict. It is a time-consuming process, however, and requires the desire of both parties to resolve the conflict, and a willingness to work together. If a situation requires a quick or immediate solution, the integrating/problem-solving approach is unlikely to work.

Compromising

The compromising approach is a mixture of the other four approaches and reflects what often happens in practice. A conflict may fail to be resolved at the first attempt. The parties move from one position to another before finding an acceptable solution. The compromising approach involves considering various issues, bargaining and searching for solutions which attempt to bring some degree of satisfaction to the conflicting parties. It is an approach where neither party wins, lacks the quickness of the first three approaches and may be long and drawn out as the parties struggle to reach a satisfactory solution. In some cases the conflict may go to a third party to resolve. This may be the project manager, or an arbitrator brought in for the purpose. In severe cases, a conflict may proceed all the way to the law courts for resolution; the construction industry was once noted as the feeding ground for lawyers and solicitors.

In summary, conflict is inevitable in a project and is usually considered to be a disagreement between two or more parties. The conflict, however, can turn out to be good or bad for the organisation and this depends on how the conflict is managed by the project manager. The five methods of dealing with conflict and their general effectiveness give project managers some tools with which to manage conflict in their project environments.

Fundamental needs of an effective team

An effective team is a system composed of an organisational unit (the project team), a common task (the project goal) and a number of individuals aiming to achieve that task (the project members) (see Figure 8.9). All parts of the system must have their needs met for the system to function properly (Adair, 1979). This approach to team building is often called task-centred leadership after its creator, team guru John Adair.

Adair's model focuses on three primary needs:

- individual needs – concerned with developing individuals

- team needs – concerned with maintaining team spirit
- task needs – concerned with achieving the task.

A team may be perfectly 'balanced' even though it consists of individuals who are not, as long as the different concerns of the individual team members are complementary, that is, as long as some team members are primarily concerned with the needs of the task, some with the needs of the individuals in the team and some with the group as a whole.

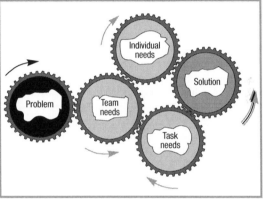

Figure 8.9 John Adair's task-centred leadership model (adapted)

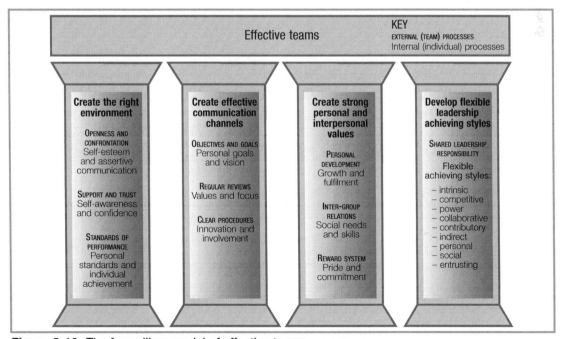

Figure 8.10 The four pillars model of effective teams

The four pillars model of effective teams

The following team-building model, adapted from Owen (1996) and Lipman-Blumen (1996), is based on four essential pillars for creating effective teams (see Figure 8.10):

I Create the right environment
II Create effective communication channels
III Create strong personal and interpersonal values
IV Develop flexible leadership achieving styles

The unique feature of the four pillars model which makes it more suitable for team building than other models is that it incorporates both *external* processes, with a team focus, and *internal* processes, with an individual focus. The model is also consistent with Adair's action-centred leadership approach to team building mentioned above. Each pillar in the four pillars model has a number of processes associated with it. In the first three pillars, these processes occur in three linked pairs, that is, one external process and one internal process working together to improve team effectiveness (Owen, 1996). The fourth pillar on leadership is a special one in which the internal process consists of nine different leadership achieving styles (Lipman-Blumen, 1996).

Pillar I: Create the right environment

The characteristics of the first pillar in the team-building and leadership model are shown in Figure 8.11 and discussed below.

Develop a climate of openness and confrontation in the team: encourage self-esteem and assertive communication

We live in a society where keeping ideas and feel-ings to oneself is still common. In a team there is a need to break down this barrier, for team members to say what they want and feel in a way which doesn't trample over others. Confident and assertive communication comes from having a healthy feeling of 'self', that is, good self-esteem. Low self-esteem leads to aggressive or passive communication, both of which are problematic when it comes to being open and confronting issues. A high performance team opens up by using self-disclosure. This involves sharing both facts and feelings about things that are relevant to the team. It isn't easy for many and does involve an element of personal risk, for example of being threatened by another. However, if this openness is part of the regular feedback procedures it becomes part of the accepted way of doing things.

Aim for total trust and support in the team: promote self-awareness and confidence

Trust implies being allowed to get on with a job on the understanding that individuals will do it the best way they know how. In a team this means everyone trusting the person next to him/her to do the right thing at the right time, so that each person can concentrate on what he or she is doing, without any cross-checking. Total trust and support leads to commitment and open communication. It is generally accepted that trust takes time to establish; people only trust others when they have learnt to trust them-selves first (hence the need for self-awareness) and having the confidence to believe we can do our own job is a precursor to trusting others to do theirs. In a project team, the project manager should set the example by:

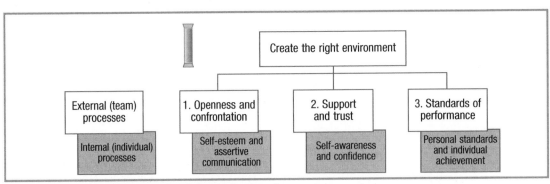

Figure 8.11 Pillar I – create the right environment

- being open and honest in facing problems
- having high personal and team standards
- being true to beliefs and values
- confronting issues as they arise
- using delegation to encourage development and achievement, not just to reduce his or her work-load
- being accessible and receptive
- taking responsibility and using judgement
- giving trust and support to team members, and others outside the core team
- establishing clear goals and objectives with the team.

Define standards of performance for the team: build in personal standards for individual achievement

As well as setting out objectives and goals, team members must be clear about the standard they need to achieve. If there is a feeling that not everyone is working to the same required standard, this can pull a team apart. Once the standard is set, it must be communicated to every team member and all of them should feel they can achieve it. There are links here with personal development and individual achievement and with team rewards and a feeling of pride for success. The project manager should make sure that:

- standards of performance are known to all team members
- each team member accepts responsibility for maintaining these standards
- personal standards are incorporated into project standards.

Pillar II: Create effective communication channels

The characteristics of the second pillar in the team-building and leadership model are shown in Figure 8.12 and discussed below.

A basic prerequisite for a smoothly functioning project team is effective communications within the team and between the team members and all important outside contacts (Müller, 2003). Communication means that meaningful information is passed from one person to another. The process involves more than the transmission of facts; it means that each person understands the intent and real meaning of the information being transferred. A common hazard of project management is the delusion that all communication links are functioning effectively just because people are talking to one another. As indicated by Fulmer (1994): 'One of the most common pitfalls of communication is the assumption that because a message was sent a message must have been received.'

There are many barriers to effective communication, for example:

- *misunderstanding* – may occur when the information sent is ambiguous, unclear, or difficult for the receiver to understand
- *miscommunication* – may occur when the information sent contains errors or is only a partial representation of the facts
- *misrepresentation* – may occur when the information sent is biased, distorted or inaccurate – can be deliberate or innocent – represents a false picture of the facts.

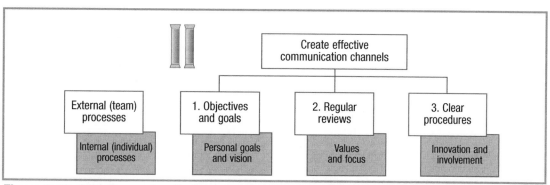

Figure 8.12 Pillar II – create effective communication channels

Critical Considerations: 'Communication – having a strategy helps' emphasises the importance of developing a communications strategy for a project rather than leaving communications to chance.

Establish clear objectives and agree mutual goals for the team: encourage personal goals and vision for each individual

One of the first things a project team does is agree the objectives and goals together. This includes interim milestones and longer term project objectives. Obtaining group commitment is difficult because each team member may subtly perceive the project's goals and objectives in significantly different ways. Even when team members have publicly agreed on project goals and objectives, their individual priorities may differ widely. Some people may hold personal reservations on the practicality or feasibility of portions of the project effort. Differing perceptions of the project tasks may also result in overlapping responsibilities or gaps in the effort.

CRITICAL CONSIDERATIONS

COMMUNICATION – HAVING A STRATEGY HELPS

As well as being aware of organisational issues and influences on a project, the project manager is also the main person responsible for creating a communications structure to meet the needs of the project participants. A good way for any project manager to begin doing this is by developing a communications strategy. A well-thought-out communications strategy can be an invaluable project aid. Such a tool promotes efficient marketing of the project to stakeholders, more accurate reporting on progress, encouragement of teamwork, responsive control and a clear audit trail for project evaluation.

Communication or lack of it is a major cause of project failure. Each element of a communications strategy should consider:

- *the purpose of the communication* – providing for the different needs of the participants and stakeholders (for example progress briefing, progress reporting and review, change control, scoping, marketing, knowledge transfer)
- *the format required* – should suit the intended purpose (for example hard copy – good for audit trails, electronic – rapid but may have limited audience, telephone – quick and informal but hard to check what was said, project meetings, mass meetings and so on)
- *the frequency required* – as and when needed (for example daily, weekly, monthly, ad hoc)
- *the available technology* – technology-based tools can be effective and speed up the process of communication if used wisely (for example cost and schedule tools, intranet, internet, email, groupware, video conference).

In fact, all documentation generated during a project has some value as a communication tool and can help the project manager to maintain a timely flow of information throughout a project. Of course he or she will often delegate parts of this responsibility to other members of the project team, including the sponsor. The following documents can all form part of a communications strategy:

- project charter
- feasibility report
- PBS, WBS, OBS and associated documentation
- responsibility chart
- activity plans
- budget plan
- resource plan
- schedule plan
- monitoring and control data and charts
- change control records
- minutes of meetings
- team reports on progress and issues
- risk management plan
- evaluation report
- lessons learned files.

A communications strategy forms a valuable part of the project planning documentation. Like other elements of the project plan it should be agreed and signed off by all concerned as appropriate. The size and level of formality of a communications strategy will depend on the size and complexity of the project and whether it is internal or external. With external projects, specific communication requirements should be stipulated in the contract conditions.

Real group commitment can only be obtained if the team members not only agree on what the project wants to achieve, but also identify with these goals and objectives because they have helped to develop them. In agreeing the team goals, the team members should also identify their own personal objectives and goals. Personal goals and vision affect the performance of individuals. When people feel help-less or hopeless and lose sight of their personal goals, or feel that what they do does not matter, they won't achieve their goals. It is these beliefs that freeze us and prevent us from achieving – not the fact that the team is short of resources; you can work around that.

Hold regular team reviews to consistently learn: uphold personal values and maintain a personal focus

Two of the most basic processes in high performance teams are the sharing of needed information, ideas and even problems among the group; and the ongoing process of monitoring and giving feedback about tasks and performance. This is done through regular reviews that become part of the procedures and culture of the team. The project manager should use the results of monitoring and feedback to tell people what they have achieved and facilitate the setting of new goals, or assess why current goals were not achieved and agree what action to take to ensure future success. Probably the most important responsibility of project managers involves their handling of project issues in meetings. Technical difficulties, schedule slippage and budget overruns must be discussed as team problems without accusa-tions or blame. Mistakes should be seen as part of the natural learning process, not an excuse to find scape-goats – a view many organisations still struggle with. The underlying process here concerns personal values and the project goal. Values are those things which are important to an individual. It is through self-awareness via an effective feedback system that team members can examine and recognise their own values. Of course, it is important that feedback is positive as well as negative. An often cited complaint in project teams is that people rarely hear motiva-tional feedback. If someone has done well, they should be told so. The purpose of feedback is twofold:

■ *Motivational feedback* tells individuals that good performance has been noticed and gives recogni-

tion for it, so helping their confidence and moti-vating them to repeat the good performance in the future. Motivational feedback is given immed-iately after the performance.

■ *Developmental feedback* tells people what needs to be done better next time and should be given in particular just before the next performance, so that team members are helped and encouraged to do things better next time. This feedback should be given as *support* rather than *criticism*.

Establish clear and meaningful procedures and practices for the team: promote involvement and innovation for each team member

Procedures are actions that take a team forward and help to maximise its synergy. Too often in organ-isations, procedures and practices inhibit innovation and restrict performance. The process to unlock this synergy is to involve all team members and tap into their ideas and innovation as they grow and reach the standards required for the team. Many innovative ideas are smothered by negative thinking before they are given any chance to prove their worth. It is much easier to think of dozens of reasons why something will not work than to figure out how to make it work. People who are prone to this type of thinking, partic-ularly if they overdo the 'devil's advocate' role, will act as communication blockers and seriously impede the process of team building. If there are too many communication blockers in a team, and their way of thinking cannot be changed, perhaps less trouble-some team members should be found. The following types of responses have been termed 'idea killers':

■ It's been done before
■ It will never work
■ The boss won't like it
■ That's interesting, but …
■ It will never fly
■ It's not sexy enough
■ It will cost a fortune
■ Let's be realistic

Pillar III: Create strong personal and interpersonal values

The characteristics of the third pillar in the team-building and leadership model are shown in Figure 8.13 and discussed below.

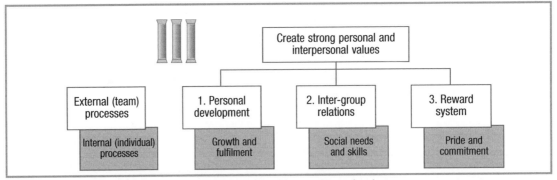

Figure 8.13 Pillar III – create strong personal and interpersonal values

Encourage individual development in the team: enable personal growth and fulfilment

In developing each team member's potential, the whole team will benefit. Feedback is again important, for it is through feedback that individuals can grow – without it, they never know what is possible. It was Goethe who said:

If you treat individuals as they are they will remain as they are, but if you treat them as if they were what they ought to be and could be, they will become what they ought to be and could be.

A project manager who ignores this component will prevent the team from achieving what is possible and giving the team members the experience of feeling fulfilled.

Promote positive inter-group relations with other stakeholders: allow for the social needs of individuals

No team can work totally in isolation. It has to relate to and work with others. If it fails to do this, which is common, the team can fail and collapse. The need to belong or communicate with others differs between team members, and the project manager needs to be aware of this. An engineer on the Red Arrows team comments:

We have quite a busy social scene on the team and there are lots of opportunities to get together and get to know the guys. There's a bit of sport that goes on so we meet in that sort of environment as well. Mainly we work very closely together on a day-to-day basis and you very quickly get to know what the guys are like. There's good healthy interaction that goes on. (Owen, 1996)

Create a reward system for the whole team: encourage pride and commitment among individuals

For a reward system to be effective, the reward should be linked to the performance of the whole team, rather than individual performances. Everyone needs to feel valued and worthwhile. Therefore, a reward should say 'well done' to the team. It ensures commitment and should enable team members to feel proud of their results. An effective reward is rarely financial and is usually part of being something that is considered to be 'the best'. When developing a team reward system care should be taken to:

- identify the key areas for success
- set objectives, goals and performance targets
- monitor progress and measure or evaluate performance
- give feedback and review successes
- identify rewards valued by all team members.

Pillar IV: Develop flexible leadership achieving styles

The characteristics of the fourth and final pillar in the team-building and leadership model are shown in Figure 8.14 and Figure 8.15.

Without leadership skills a project team will surely fail. Project participants expect the project manager to demonstrate good leadership skills both in his or her work and work relationships. Good leadership creates and strengthens trust between a project manager, the project team, the sponsor and all the other project stakeholders. However, it is important to realise that in project management, the project manager does not have a monopoly on leadership skills; all the project participants can and should play

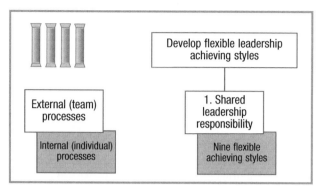

Figure 8.14 Pillar IV – develop flexible leadership achieving styles

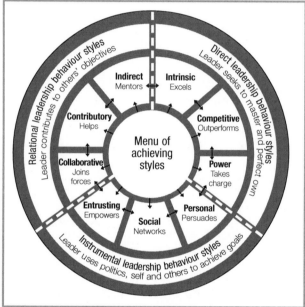

Figure 8.15 Pillar IV in cross-section showing the nine leadership achieving styles

a role in leading a project to a successful conclusion. Although the project manager is ultimately responsible for the completion of the project, there is a real need for shared leadership skills at every level.

The goal of leadership in a project is to achieve project success. This is accomplished at an individual level through the adoption and use of a set of leadership 'achieving' styles from a wide range of styles appropriate to the project environment and conditions. Figure 8.15 presents nine related 'achieving styles' that leaders can consciously and systematically use in several ways. The model allows project managers to assess not only their own leadership

styles and those of others but the leadership behaviours most needed in any particular situation and the leadership styles most valued in a particular organisation – an important factor when dealing with project sponsors and major project suppliers.

The leadership achieving styles describe *how* people go about achieving their goals, not *what* their goals are. They are the means, not the ends, that project participants use to accomplish their objectives. The best leaders of our time use all nine achieving styles more fully and in distinctly different ways to everyone else. The achieving styles fall into three behaviour patterns:

- Direct leadership behaviour (intrinsic, competitive and power styles)
- Relational leadership behaviour (collaborative, contributory and indirect styles)
- Instrumental leadership behaviour (personal, social and entrusting styles)

Direct leadership behaviour

The direct styles focus primarily on the tasks that individuals set for themselves and thrive on individualism and independence. People who prefer the direct styles confront the task or situation directly, rarely requiring the help of others. They are particularly concerned with performance and perfection in carrying out their *own* objectives. People who prefer these styles tightly control the definition of goals and the means used to accomplish them. The best leaders can and do use these styles when appropriate, but unlike other leaders they don't necessarily select them as their first choice. There are three achieving styles associated with direct leadership behaviour:

1. **Intrinsic.** In the intrinsic style, it is the content or intrinsic nature of the task that *excites* the individual. The challenge and importance of the goal is the driving force. Given a project, people who prefer intrinsic action look to themselves, not others, to make it happen. The challenge of personal achievement in completing a task drives these individuals. They don't particularly care whether their performance pleases or disappoints those around them. Instead, leaders applying the intrinsic style are guided by a strict, internal stan-

dard of excellence against which they measure themselves.

2. **Competitive**. The competitive style takes its name from an individual's desire to outdo others. Being the best is what matters to competitive types, and competition is what motivates them to give their best.

3. **Power**. People who favour the power style are turned on by taking charge, coordinating, and organising situations and events, resources and other people. Power types may delegate tasks, but they always retain control over what and how things are done. Individuals using the power style give clear-cut assignments to others, provide detailed implementation plans and set benchmarks and deadlines.

Relational leadership behaviour

The second set of achieving styles, the relational styles, is oriented towards the goals of others. These styles are related to interdependence. People who prefer relational styles easily take part in group tasks or contribute to other people's goals. They willingly relinquish control over both the means and the ends of accomplishment. Their intense identification with others – be they individuals or even institutions – enables them to contribute actively or passively to objectives established by others. In this way, leaders using relational styles derive a strong sense of achievement, pride and pleasure from their enthusiastic participation in the success of others with whom they identify. There are three achieving styles associated with relational leadership behaviour:

1. **Collaborative**. People who use the collaborative style enjoy working with others on teams and joint projects. The synergy of the group gets collaborators going. They share in the glory and hard work that brings success, but they also accept their share of the responsibility for failure. The bonds of friendship and camaraderie strengthen joint efforts and constitute an important part of the reward.

2. **Contributory**. People who prefer contributory styles are concerned with the tasks of others. They are not necessarily prompted to get involved because the other team members lack the talent or determination to do it themselves. Rather, they derive a genuine sense of satisfaction from contributing to others' success.

3. **Indirect**. The indirect style achieves success

without direct participation in other people's activities. Leaders using an indirect style encourage or facilitate others' accomplishments. They act as coaches, offering wisdom, cheering others on, and taking immense pride in the accomplishments of the people and groups with whom they identify.

Instrumental leadership behaviour

The third and final set of achieving styles is called instrumental because people who prefer these strategies treat everything – themselves, their relationships, situations and resources – as *instruments* for achieving their goals. They retain control over goals but allow and even encourage others to shape the means to those ends. There are three achieving styles associated with instrumental leadership behaviour:

1. **Personal**. The personal style involves using the self. Negotiation and persuasion are the territory of personal types who smoothly bring others around to a common point of view. People who prefer the personal behaviour style perceive themselves and others, along with non-personal resources, as tools for brokering agreements. In the role of negotiator, personal types know exactly how to present themselves, how to time the offer, how to get the best deal of the moment.

2. **Social**. The social style focuses less on using the self to muster support and more on using relationships to get things done. People who prefer the social style cultivate and liberally use 'contacts'. They are always aware of how any new individual might fit into their larger scheme – if not now, maybe later. Faced with any task, social individuals immediately flip through their mental name directory to identify people with the needed expertise, talent, experience or other contacts. They build and maintain networks of associates who they call upon as the situation requires. For leaders using the social style, it's *who* you know, not *what* you know, that moves the agenda.

3. **Entrusting**. People who use the entrusting style behave somewhat differently. They simply expect everyone on their horizon to help them achieve what they consider to be their shared goals. They do not look for specific talents or experience, but they do take care to select capable candidates. The expectations that entrusting individuals have

for other people usually bear fruit, largely because their anticipation and trust stimulate motivation, creativity and confidence. Entrusted with the leader's vision, the recipient responds with pride, creativity and a sense of ownership. Unlike direct types, who keep tight control over the goal as well as the path leading to it, people who use entrusting behaviour simply have a goal that they expect others to share and help them reach. They comfortably seek counsel from others and usually leave their team members the choice of method. People who use entrusting behaviour have complete faith that their team members will not disappoint them.

Using the nine achieving styles

Observation reveals that most leaders, having developed a set of achieving behaviours that seems to work, tend to rely on these same styles over and over again. World-class leaders stand out from the crowd because they move easily across all nine achieving styles, using different combinations to respond to various circumstances. When we use the full repertoire of leadership behaviours available to us, we can select styles more appropriate for the unique demands of the situation. Project managers have to confront complex situations, decide what to do and then take action. In a crisis situation, the capacity to react and adapt rapidly is critical.

There are at least six aspects of any particular situation that are central to determining what kinds of achieving styles will work for a project manager or any of the team members:

1. The nature of the task. For example, is it a unique event, like climbing Mt Everest for the first time, or one that has been done before? Although all projects are unique to an extent, some are more unique than others.
2. The importance of the task. Can the project objectives be satisfied if the task is not accomplished? How perfectly must it be done for success?
3. The nature and location of key resources. For example, do you need to negotiate to get resources or do you already possess what you need?
4. The condition of the internal environment in the system or organisation where the task is to be performed. Are things in turmoil, or is life on an even keel?

5. The state of the external environment. Is the world outside changing rapidly? Do you see a crisis on the horizon?
6. The leader's position and reputation within the organisation. Are you an 'old hand' who knows how to get things done through the informal system, or are you a naive newcomer? Are you up high enough in the organisation to wield organisational clout, or do you have to ask permission?

Limitations of team building

The most obvious limitation to team building and leadership is that no amount of team-building or leadership skills will produce a successful project if the project concept is faulty, or if top management is unsupportive. Another limitation involves whether the project is new or whether the project manager has inherited a project in trouble, in which case the new project manager's ability to build an effective team may be limited.

In some organisations the use of team building can only temporarily alleviate the symptoms of a deeper underlying problem. This may be sufficient to help implement small, stand-alone projects, but will not meet the needs of larger project programmes.

For example, in one organisation, the leader was concerned about a lack of teamwork and was about to hire a consultant to do some team building. But when he analysed the problem more deeply, he found that teamwork was inhibited by a number of other deeper issues:

■ People in different business units did not perceive the same priorities: 'When your highest priority is someone else's lowest, it's tough to get their help when you need it'
■ He also found that people were so focused on serving external clients that they broke commitments to each other the moment a client needed their help: 'Of course, if you can't trust your peers to keep their internal commitments, you'll do the work yourself rather than invite them onto your team.'

Team building may enhance interpersonal relations. But no matter how well people like one another, teamwork will not happen when there are systemic obstacles to working together. In this example, team building would have done little good until the organisation changed the way it managed internal priorities and commitments.

In these cases, leaders must first change the way an organisation operates, introducing change at the most fundamental level of the organisation. There are five fundamental systems in every organisation that constitute the bedrock for developing effective teams:

- **Culture**. The behavioural patterns (habits and conventions) generally adopted within the organisation.
- **Structure**. The definition of jobs and the reporting hierarchy (organisation chart), as well as the processes that combine people into teams as work flows across organisational boundaries

- **Internal economy**. The budgeting, priority setting, pricing (chargeback), project approval, and tracking processes that determine how resources flow through an organisation to its clients
- **Methods and tools**. The procedures, methodologies, skills and tools that people in an organisation use
- **Metrics and rewards**. The feedback loops that let people know how they are doing, so they can adjust their behaviour, and the incentives for improving performance.

PROJECT MANAGEMENT *in action*

DataSys knowledge transfer programme

14 October 2003

Tuesday morning, 14 October 2003, found Phil Spencer, co-manager of the knowledge transfer programme (KTP) reviewing his notes from the programme managers meeting three days earlier. At that meeting, he and Dave McKean, his counterpart from the Computer Systems Manufacturing organisation, had presented their plan for reorganising KTP management with a project focus rather than along traditional functional lines. Although the two had shared responsibility for the programme (a process they called 'two-in-a-box') up until this time, Spencer had managed the technology focus of the programme, while McKean had managed the business functions. Under the new plan, both development and operations employees would report directly to the programme manager responsible for their particular project. The programme managers would report directly to Spencer and McKean, who would co-manage the entire programme.

Spencer explained the rationale behind the plan:

The programmes are the primary driver of what we have to achieve in the KTP.

The programme managers have to act among themselves as a team, because there are going to be situations where certain work needs to get done across all the programmes and we only want it done once – not three times in three separate programmes. We figured that the programme manager structure would help eliminate counterproductive behaviours and attitudes by cutting across functional lines. We have to have a total KTP mentality. We also want people to get away from a victim mentality and move towards a 'we can do it' attitude.

On Monday, Spencer and McKean had asked the three most senior managers, James Braithwaite, Bill Jackson and Jan-Pieter Schulz, who were critical to the reorganisation's success, for a two-year commitment as a team to the new model. They had promised to respond by this afternoon.

Genesis of the knowledge programme

The KTP had been envisioned some four years earlier. With DataSys's rapid growth and its subsequent demands on manufacturing, plant managers and staff had very little time to devote to testing and evaluating process improvements that had originated elsewhere. Greg Findlay, senior group manager for the Intelligent Systems Technology Group (ISTG), recalled:

The major projects required a two- or three-year gestation period in the

plants. We realised that if people in the plants are going to be so tremendously busy that they have to concentrate all their efforts on immediate output, then we had better consider other routes for transferring intelligent systems technology and what we had learned into manufacturing.

The KTP was conceived as a learning environment where new technology and skills could be developed, tested, prototyped and then transferred to DataSys's worldwide manufacturing organisation. The KTP would work with leading academics to explore ideas on the cutting edge of manufacturing, and then share the learning within DataSys and with customers and suppliers. Financial support for the programme would be drawn from the central manufacturing funding to which all operating units contributed, so all units would have an interest in the innovations developed. Within the highly volatile and competitive computer industry, DataSys could obtain a real advantage if such a group, dedicated to learning and technology transfer, could spur meaningful innovation in manufacturing processes. Moreover, Findlay noted:

If we really did this right with the participation of the universities and other firms and rotating DataSys people through, if we set up a real-life learning environment with sufficient tools and software simulations and a real production process, we knew of other companies that would be very interested in acquiring a module like the KTP. So we said as the hidden agenda: 'Why don't we think about selling this as a product three years from now?'

Greg Findlay's background

Findlay had played a key role both in designing the PCP line of computers, the cornerstone of the company's early success, and in bringing artificial intelligence (AT) technology into DataSys. ISTG had grown from a single AT project started in 1984, when DataSys was struggling with the problem of checking orders for its complex computer systems before the orders reached manufacturing. Given thousands of possible configurations and hundreds of components to be correctly specified, orders were frequently incorrect. Findlay addressed this costly problem inexpensively by commissioning a university professor to build an 'expert system', an innovative solution initially greeted with scepticism. But Findlay championed and nurtured the project with bits of funding solicited from various functions until its value was apparent to everyone.

By 2001, with funding from corporate manufacturing and the operating units who were its internal customers, Findlay had built DataSys's internal AI capabilities into a technology group that was generally regarded to be the largest and most active centre within any large American corporation. He had drawn upon the expertise of world-renowned academic institutions to put DataSys on the leading edge of implementing AT, which ISTG disseminated in the form of process applications and training throughout the firm. It also developed and marketed AT products for DataSys's customers.

Progress on the knowledge transfer programme

In early 2001, Findlay shared his idea of a learning centre with Dean Jacobs, vice-president of the Computer Systems Manufacturing organisation, with whom he had a close professional relationship. Jacobs, whose background

as a plant manager accorded him tremendous prestige within the company, was similarly frustrated with the pace of learning and innovation in manufacturing. Coincidentally, Jacobs was contending with the underutilisation of a manufacturing plant in Massachusetts. He recalled:

The learning centre originated in part because we knew there had to be a better way to do manufacturing. As we checked the hard data, the costs, the financials, we knew we were not competitive. The KTP was a chance to try something different, learn from it and then transfer the learning. For once in our life at DataSys, we had an empty facility. We weren't pressured to use it for current output. So we said, let's take advantage of the opportunity. Let's see what we can put together to learn something. We'll use a small group with no ties to any other organisations but Greg's and mine. It's kind of a freelance group – an 'intrapreneurial' group.

Findlay and Jacobs agreed to co-sponsor the knowledge transfer programme, conceived of as a 'teaching hospital' where new processes and technology could be developed and implemented on a live experimental production line, and then transferred to DataSys's manufacturing organisation. A committee was formed to explore the concept and assemble an implementation plan.

Findlay selected Phil Spencer to lead the ISTG's participation in the committee. Spencer, who had been with DataSys since 1984, had spent the last 10 years working for Findlay, managing the initial phases of many important projects. Spencer commented:

At the beginning of new functions, Greg usually gives it to me to get it started. He's used me in that role many times. The KTP was another opportunity to start something new, to do something really different.

Jacobs delegated CSM responsibility for the project to Dick McGee, manager of the Options Business Unit (OBU) – the group responsible for logistics and shipping DataSys's computer peripheral products. McGee tapped

Dave McKean, OBU's operations manager, a 15-year DataSys veteran who had recently completed training his successor and had become available for reassignment. McKean explained:

Any time I can find someone to do my job, I'm happy to turn it over to them because there are always other jobs to be done. I never view a job as the one I want to retire to. But each job must have the opportunity for company, personal and business excellence.

For McKean, whose next career move had been unclear, working on the KTP offered a unique opportunity to build something totally new.

Spencer explained what happened next:

The idea that we [Spencer and McKean] would both manage the KTP as a team was our own idea. We were part of the larger task force that Greg and Dean had pulled together to organise the KTP. We couldn't make much progress with a group of that size, so we spun off about five people for a meeting that Dave and I led. We put together a two-page document that we called our Two-Page Straw. We brought that back to the larger group and said 'Here's what we think the KTP should be – does everybody agree? If you don't, what changes do you want to see?' As I recall there were very few changes.

Dave was well linked into Dean's world through Dick McGee. I was linked into Greg's world. Since I came from the AI group, I was going to lead the technology focus, and Dave, as a manager from operations, was going to lead the business focus. Early on we agreed that we had to be able to cover for each other, so no matter who attended a meeting, what people would see was not Phil or Dave but the KTP person. That meant we had to understand exactly what the other person was doing, so that we could answer questions and fill in for each other.

With the two managers in place, Findlay and Jacobs set the team loose with an exciting mandate. As Jacobs related:

It's a unique opportunity. I had been in

manufacturing at DataSys for 20 years, and during that span, I had never had that opportunity to say 'If you had an empty building, no requirements, on your own, and all the money you wanted, whatever talent you needed – what would you do with it?' That was the concept: 'You tell us. By the way, we want different, creative, unique. You can't use today's language – we even want the language different. We don't want you to call people "materials" people, or "finance" people, or personnel. We don't want the metrics to be output per direct labour hour. You've got to make us go "Wow!" when you present this to us. But you've also got to do something that links to better performance. I've got to be able to say "look what they did with 20 people; that used to take 100!" It's got to be a delta like that. It can't be easy.'

Phase one

The first months of the programme were spent putting together the KTP team. Synergy was important, as Dave McKean described:

There's a hereditary strain that goes through this. As you create new teams, you bring together pieces of old teams. But a part of reforming is letting go. If each of the people here acted as a representative of their past as opposed to coming together as a new team, bringing to the new team some strains from the last one, it would prevent the KTP team from bonding together. In the first case it's a United Nations and everyone's the ambassador of their country, and in the latter case, everyone's part of the same country. The hereditary strain is important but being an ambassador of your past is not. It'll block you from becoming part of the new.

McKean and Spencer talked to key managers in DataSys, both to recruit talented people to the project and to try to build support for KTP. They also visited companies across the United States and in Japan that were employing advanced manufacturing techniques and established contacts at Harvard, MIT, the Georgia Institute of Technology and other universities to secure their participation.

Attracting top-notch engineering and operational talent from product design and manufacturing groups proved very difficult, as line managers with profit responsibility were loath to release their best people, particularly to a programme without obvious short-term deliverables. Phil Spencer pointed out:

During our first year, we hadn't developed anything yet. We were looking for help: people who were interested in working with us to develop, to define, what the KTP was. But line managers were looking for a finished product, with definite deliverables. It was the Catch-22: I told them 'I can't give you a finished product unless we get the resources and the problems to work on,' and they said 'We're not going to give you anything until you show us what you can do.' We kept going around in a circle.

Eventually some talented managers signed on, and Spencer and McKean organised the first projects to take advantage of their backgrounds. James Braithwaite, a 15-year DataSys veteran with 25 years of industry experience in shipping and logistics, came on board to develop new ideas for warehousing and distribution. Bill Jackson, with 12 years at DataSys in materials management, was selected to head the Supply-side Business – a project designed to explore possibilities in vendor base and materials management. Finally, Jan-Pieter Schulz, an engineer from Findlay's ISTG, signed on to organise the Concurrent Product and Process Design project, targeted at improving the manufacturability of new products. Phase One of the KTP agenda, expected to cover the first year of operation, involved successfully initiating the three projects and building on them a long-range business plan for the growth and expansion of the KTP. Bill Jackson described the team's focus:

What we were really trying to do was get far enough out in front of the plants, that when they met their goals and were ready for the next step, we had something to pass on to them. The plants look at today, and the future, and how to get there, but we would be looking at the future +1 and the future +2,

out ahead of the plants – a 5–10-year window. Our job was to leapfrog the plants and work on future +1 and +2. When the plants were ready for that technology we would leapfrog them again, so we would always be out in front of them.

The knowledge centre's (KC) preliminary work uncovered long-standing inefficiencies in sourcing policies, and brought the team an early taste of success. As Dean Jacobs related:

The same identical cable but different lengths was sourced from different vendors. That's insane. So if you order a 12-foot cable, and I order 25 feet-identical ends, yours comes from Company X and mine comes from Company Y. Dave looked like a hero, just like that, because he could say 'Look what I found! That's new.' The learning was how to better source these 50,000 little parts that we use a zillion of, in crazy quantities.

The team's early successes put the KTP under the spotlight. Spencer and McKean felt pressured to accelerate the pace of the programme – even with assurances from Findlay and Jacobs that management was comfortable with the KC's progress. The manufacturing plants were implementing new technologies such as sophisticated MRP-II manufacturing control systems. They were continually making huge strides in improving their own operations as they pushed their organisations to achieve the world class 'A' level of manufacturing competence that would make them more cost competitive. With this backdrop, the KTP team felt anxious to show immediate results. McKean and Spencer worked to expand on their initiative and increase the programme's scope. To upper management, it seemed as though the KC group had forgotten their mandate to be different and creative. Jacobs elaborated:

We had to make the knowledge transfer programme into a process, and that's where we got into some real snags. What should the group look like? What kind of people do I need? How do I transfer the learning? What do I have to learn? They got off to a real bad start on that. Right away, they came in with requisitions. They wanted to hire people. They wanted to build an organisation. Dave wanted us to call him the Newcastle plant manager. That really disappointed us. He was getting all caught up in status and traditional thinking. I didn't want him to think about being the 'plant manager'. I didn't want him to think about anything except being one of the two people in the box, running the learning centre.

C-Class

From the early planning stages, Spencer and McKean had intended that the knowledge transfer programme would include an operational manufacturing line to develop and test new processes, and provide an arena for DataSys personnel to come in and learn new skills. In question, however, was what the experimental line would make. Eventually, the decision was made to manufacture cables, for three main reasons:

1. *Political expediency* – No manufacturing group 'owned' cables, they were produced by many groups in many facilities. Therefore, no organisation would find the knowledge transfer programme's manufacturing activities threatening.
2. *Simplicity* – Spencer and McKean wanted the knowledge transfer programme to ship something as soon as possible. Cables – well understood and simple to manufacture – were the least risky choice.
3. *Need* – All product groups in DataSys used C-Class stock (DataSys terminology for Cables and Accessories). Therefore, whatever the KTP team did with C-Class would have relevance to many different product lines and functions. Preliminary studies indicated that problems with C-Class components were a major source of incorrect product shipments.

As Dave McKean explained: 'We were not going to build cables, just to build cables. But at DataSys, without a product, you're not an entity.'

Dean Jacobs discussed his initial reaction to the decision to work with C-Class components:

When they first suggested Class C parts, I said: 'I'm not going to let them touch that, that's nuts! It's not a business that people view as something anyone would want to work on. It's not a challenge. We always just throw Class C parts on the shelf. We don't worry about it. You can order as many as you want – they don't cost anything.' But they laid out all the reasons for working on C parts: 'There's a lot of Class C parts. We spend a lot of money. We don't forecast them. We have a lot of different vendors. It's probably worthwhile looking at them – could have a big impact on performance.' So they kind of convinced us.

Still the decision was a continual source of debate. Bill Jackson, C-Class/Supply Side Business manager, recalled at the time:

I started doing some investigative work into planned and unplanned partial shipments. Cables were not a major hitter. Cables accounted for only 16% of the short shipments and misshipments. I feel that the control of C-Class belongs within the plants that own them. I think that what we have to do within KTP is to not restrict our thinking to just C-Class. We have to go broader than that. Whatever we do, we should apply the skills that we have to an area that will give the biggest payback for the corporation.

It was difficult to get potential sponsors excited about so mundane a product. Spencer noted:

We continually had to justify why we were doing C-Class. Almost everybody was building C-Class, sometimes for their own internal use; or they were subcontracting it out and when business was slow they pulled it back to produce in-house. They used it as a production buffer, as a backfill – so they wouldn't have to lay off people. So when business is good, going in and taking that kind of product hurts no one. It's nonthreatening. But is it sexy and exciting? No.

STRIDe

By October 2002, the core management team was in place (Exhibit 1), the business plan was nearly shipped and the three projects involving (1) shipping and logistics, (2) vendor base research and (3) concurrent product and process design were identified and initiated. Then the KTP received a new challenge. When production was transferred from the Newcastle plant, opening room for the KTP, more than 50 people, most of whom came from an administrative rather than technical background, had been left in Newcastle without jobs. Given DataSys's no layoff

---

Exhibit 1 KTP (October 2002)

We do not have a formal, published organisation chart ... There is no need for one at this time.

The ISTG (Intelligent Systems Technology Group) and CSM (Computer Systems Manufacturing) breakdown as determined by cost centres, is shown below.

CMS
Dean Jacobs
VICE-PRESIDENT

ISTG	*Options Business Unit*	*Strategic Planning*
Greg Findlay	**Dick McGee**	
GROUP MANAGER	GROUP MANAGER	
Phil Spencer	Dave McKean	
Doug Braithwaite	James Braithwaite	Lois Greenberg
Ken Holland	Maryann Franklin	
Jan-Pieter Schulz	Bill Jackson	
Roxanne O'Connell		
Malcolm Reid		

policy, the corporation set up the Strategic & Tactical Resource Identification & Development programme (STRIDe), to place workers made idle. Greg Findlay recalled:

We wanted to be good DataSys citizens, so we volunteered to integrate those 55 people, whoever they were, into the KC programme. If they didn't have the skills, we would help to skill them. A big part of the purpose of this programme is to transfer skills and eventually we will need people with these skills, in the KTP and in other parts of DataSys.

By taking on these workers, the KTP had more than quintupled its size. Said McKean:

We took the group from STRIDe lock, stock, and barrel. We made a tremendous commitment to training – an average of 100 hours of training per person in the skills needed for them to sustain a career at DataSys. A lot of the funds for the training, we begged, borrowed, brokered … One person would go to a training class and come back and teach five. Here was a high degree of commitment, and a high degree of motivation for people to learn and train. We even had training videos during breaks.

The KTP managers differed in their perceptions about the workers. Bill Jackson noted:

Whether we interviewed them or not, we were going to take them. Where do you think the STRIDe people were going to go? They hadn't a job because they didn't want to move from the Newcastle area.

Yet, as James Braithwaite, manager of the logistics project, observed:

I didn't have to waste a lot of time trying to recruit people, because they were already here in Newcastle. A lot of them didn't have the skills, but they were smart folks – retrainable. It was more practical to invest in energy to reskill these folks, than it was to waste time and energy recruiting people. By luck, I was a functional expert in logistics. It was a pure, simple mathematical equation: it would take me less time to teach

these folks what to do than it would take to recruit the 'right' folks.

Phase two

By March 2003, when the knowledge transfer programme business plan was published (see Exhibit 2), Spencer and Mckean presided over an organisation of over 60 people with an initial budget of $2.5 million. The Phase One planning process was complete, and the team was eager to expand the scope of their work. However, with a downturn in the computer industry came an increased emphasis on costs and affordability. The KC had been unable to find engineers with both manufacturing and software experience, and with a freeze on total headcount in the sponsoring organisations, Mckean and Spencer were expected to make do with the personnel on hand. Phil Spencer explained:

To people outside the KC it looked as though we had hired all these administrative people and we hadn't hired any technical people. Then came the hiring freeze and the budget cuts, so we were stuck with what we had, which wasn't the right mix.

Moreover, with the industry slowdown, manufacturing plants were unwilling to allow transfer of C-Class production lines to Newcastle. Said Bill Jackson:

James and I were under the understanding that we were going to have product transferred out of the Augusta plant. In June 2003, we went up to see the materials manager of the plant and he looked at us like we had two heads. They had seen a tail-off in their business, and they didn't feel in a position to transfer product down to us. It became very obvious that we weren't going to have product or a live line in this plant.

Without resources or product the pace of the programme slowed, with the notable exception of James Braithwaite's logistics project. Braithwaite had the necessary personal connections to start up quickly. Working with researchers from the Georgia Institute of Technology, the logistics team set up

DataSys's first paperless warehouse operation, inventorying parts and shipping orders for a variety of plants that were in need of additional warehouse capacity. Braithwaite was able to cut the labour cost of distribution by over 25%. In fact, the demand for the advanced logistics operation's services was great enough that if sufficient warehouse capacity had been available, Braithwaite estimated that his project could have been run at a net profit, despite the overhead costs of his development work. By October, over half the KC's people were working on the warehousing project.

The other pieces of the programme saw sporadic progress. The Concurrent Product and Process Design team created a forum to examine efforts at Design for Manufacturability across the company – identifying and eliminating costly duplications of effort. And the Supply-side Business group initiated the Intelligent Design Engineering Assistant (IDEA). Bill Jackson explained:

There was no catalogue of the cables DataSys produced, so there were a lot of redundant cable designs floating around the company. So we said, 'Let's get one of each cable; take some photographs and list the specs; get it to the design engineers, so when they are designing cables, they can go in and see if there are any that already meet the specs.' Then we said, 'Why not do it electronically?' We figured we needed to get all the cable specs and feed them into a system with a format that would let the designers input all the parameters that they needed. Then the system would do a search to find all the existing cables that could fit those specifications or come close. The system could even go further and suggest changes to specs. Maybe you could take an existing cable and just change the connectors and have what you needed. This application really took off and the engineers got really excited about it. If the system works there, it can work in any number of areas in the company.

In the meantime, DataSys plants continued to improve their operations on their own at a rapid clip, so it was difficult to stay one or two steps ahead. Dean Jacobs described the situation:

> It's tough. Someone is walking, then all of a sudden they're jogging, and now they're sprinting. You started sprinting and you're getting tired and they're not even sweating. It created this feeling in the KTP of 'Oh boy! better come up with something, we'd better do something.' But you can't just say 'Today, I'm going to be creative.' It doesn't work that way.

Reorganisation

By autumn 2003, the entire KC organisation was frustrated. Without the live production line, the operations people chafed for additional work, blaming the technology side for failing to initiate new projects. Technology people, burdened by the scarce technical resources, in turn pointed at operations for lack of cooperation. Recalled Phil Spencer:

> Around the middle of September, Dave and I were having one of our one-on-one sessions. I said, 'You know we haven't built walls, but we sure as heck have got a river flowing between our two organisations (OBU and ISTG). The people that work for me stand on that side and the people who work for you stand on this side. They're very cordial with each other; they say hello and yell at each other and wave at each other, but none of them will cross the river to help each other, to work with each other.'

Dave McKean added:

> We tried to take down fences. The KC programme team very selectively listened and went out and built them up again. Because there was no substance in what they were doing in their jobs, they tried to identify themselves through their relationships with their bosses – with Phil and me.

Near the end of September, the two managers called a management meeting to discuss the situation. Phil Spencer described the response:

> We had a session with the managers about taking more responsibility, and they threw it back on us. They said, 'That's not our job; that's your job.' Dave

and I were trying to do this collaborative management, sharing responsibilities, getting everyone involved in the decision process and they viewed it as if we didn't want to make decisions. We said: 'We're giving you the leadership, we point the direction, show you the way, give you the boundaries, turn you loose.' That's not the way they looked at it.

The simplistic model that Dave and I were trying to follow was that we wanted to provide the leadership and the rest of the team members to provide the management. That doesn't mean that they're only management and can't provide any leadership, but 'management' implies that they make decisions. It was clear from the lack of progress to that point, that they couldn't work closely enough together to make a decision. If they had, I wouldn't have had to make the decision about what organisational form we were going to use. If they had come to a decision, they would have given us their recommendations for the whole KTP rather than a listing of what all the individual projects were, with their individual priorities. Dave and I had expectations for the entire KC and the rest of them were still working in their functional 'stovepipes' – carving out their particular piece of the KTP.

Both McKean and Spencer realised that they needed to address the issue quickly. Said Spencer:

> Dave and I were in a conference room, and I was just furious at the reaction of the managers in the group. I said, 'OK, I've had it up to here; these people want to be managed, I can show them how to be managed; they want decisions, I can show them how to make decisions.' Dave was trying to calm me down but I said, 'We're going put a structure in place, we're going to tell them exactly what their jobs are and they're going to tell us whether or not they will do those jobs and we're going hold them to a set of metrics on those jobs. I won't have it any other way.' Dave and I went around and around for about an hour and a half and we wound up going that way. What Dave said was, 'If we're going to do that then we have to tell them what we're going to do.' So we did.

Restructuring was not without its

detractors. Dean Jacobs believed it was wrong:

> We felt okay that nothing had happened. The difficulty the KC had in following their early success was a learning all to itself. They weren't okay about it. We never gave them a requirement that they had to give us exactly 1.27 ideas every time we meet. They never told us, 'We met with our people, and they have no ideas. Let's have another meeting on why we're not coming up with ideas. Maybe they need help; they need a stimulus; they need an outside consultant; they need to go visit other facilities, other plants, other companies.' We never had that conversation. It was: 'UH! They don't have any ideas. Let's go help them get ideas. We'll give them bosses.' That's traditional thinking – go kickstart them.

On 11 October McKean and Spencer met with Bill Jackson, James Braithwaite and Jan-Pieter Schulz to lay out the proposed reorganisation. In the new KTP hierarchy, these three would have the title 'Programme Manager' and would report directly to Spencer and McKean. Each would have full responsibility and authority for operational and technical aspects of their specific programmes. McKean and Spencer would do joint performance reviews on the programme level and be responsible for strategic administrative functional work (see Exhibit 3).

Spencer and McKean asked the three to commit to the model as a unified team. They would have to speak as one. The length of the commitment would be two to three years, and if they couldn't commit, they would become free agents. Braithwaite, Jackson and Schulz promised to have an answer by noon on 14 October.

14 October, 2003

The meeting began uneventfully, with a litany of business housekeeping items on the agenda. Finally, after an anxious half-hour, the two KTP managers posed their question: 'Do you accept the job as described in the proposal?'

A chronology of the KTP is given in Exhibit 4.

Exhibit 2 Excerpts from the KTP Business Plan, March 2003

I OPPORTUNITY STATEMENT

Success in future manufacturing will require a set of very different characteristics from those needed in the recent past ... because manufacturing firms ... will be operating in a widening set of countries and economic environments including intensive international and domestic competition ...

DataSys's manufacturing enterprises will require state-of-the-art information technologies and manufacturing processes that can respond with flexibility to a stream of product and volume changes. Labour and management must be seen as sources of energy, imagination, and leadership. Manufacturing's human assets must be viewed as proactive and technologically competent, with the potential for perpetual skills development and collaborative learning.

It is no longer possible to develop all or most of the required business process and technologies within a firm or even a single country. To maintain leadership in our industry as we ride these waves of change, we must rapidly integrate and adapt appropriate technologies, whatever their origin. To be successful DataSys must learn new ways to collaborate with a wide variety of international organisations including universities and both competitive and noncompetitive firms. DataSys's knowledge transfer programme will establish a collaborative development environment dedicated to understanding how a variety of functions learn, cooperate, and change in concert.

There are at least five important reasons for establishing such a developmental environment. First, it will provide an industrial laboratory to demonstrate technical feasibility of advanced manufacturing concepts and components. Second, it will help bring in relevant ideas from universities and cooperating firms. Third, it can serve as an integrative function for collaborating and coordinating with other DataSys groups also working on advanced manufacturing projects. Fourth, an embedded norm of continual learning will provide the opportunities for creativity and innovation. Fifth, it will serve as a credible holistic model of integrated manufacturing.

II OVERALL PROGRAMME SCOPE Charter

The knowledge transfer programme (KTP) charter is to design and implement a collaborative industrial laboratory in support of DataSys as a world-class manufacturer. We will focus on learning, teaching, and integrating new business processes into DataSys's manufacturing enterprise. This will be achieved through partner-

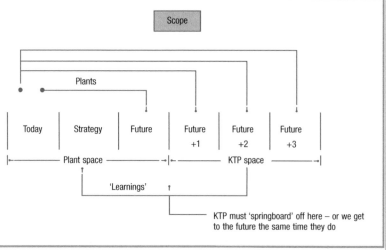

Scope of the KTP

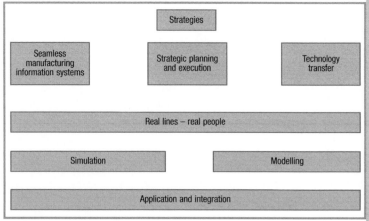

Strategies of the KTP

ships with DataSys plants and organisations, leading universities, and other firms. 'The KTP will establish a Computer Integrated Information Enterprise (CIIE), 'development factory,' and 'learning' environment for DataSys and our customers and suppliers.

The Knowledge Centre

The KTP will focus on learning, teaching, and integrating new business processes into DataSys's manufacturing enterprise.

In order to deliver useful 'prototypes' for operational plants, the KTP will operate beyond the plant's traditional time horizon, developing, testing, and transferring knowledge and technology in support of the corporate business goals. Integration of these business solutions is a vital element of our strategy.

Business Processes

Our objective will be to 'springboard' beyond the technology futures mandated in plants today. Our business processes will be based on operational excellence: the rapid mastery of such things as JIT/TQC, DRP II, and CIM. It is the Manufacturing Centre's belief that these systems skills will be a necessity, not a competitive advantage, in the relatively near future. The elements of operational excellence will be tomorrow's basics.

The KTP will enhance and develop the processes for integration and transferral of new management and control environments such as knowledge-based decision-making support applications, closed-loop and paperless operations, using concepts such as electronic information interchange. We will also set up a CIIE pilot/simulation.

People-knowledge workers

The goal of the Manufacturing Centre is to be far more than a technical laboratory. The primary objective must remain to deliver customer product satisfaction to the end-user through the actions of our people. In parallel with this effort, new advanced skills development projects will be investigated, proposed and developed to address the skills needed for the next generation of business systems and productivity tools. One major goal of the KTP is to provide a flexible learning environment where we learn how people apply knowledge and technologies as a basis for creating newer and better ways to transfer skills and knowledge.

The workers of the future will be knowledge workers. Continual learning and change will be expected and valued. People who will thrive in this work environment will accept the responsibility to continually learn new ways of thinking and doing, constantly teach others, and let go, empower others to learn, change, adapt and then move on to the next cycle. They will also be comfortable working with a widening network of colleagues and collaborators. Terms like 'speed of learning,' 'knowledge turns,' and supporting knowledge-based systems represent some of the key concepts. The quality of the workforce and the workforce management systems will have to be superior. As in many KTP strategies, these new collaborative relationships must still be established.

Change management

A major challenge for the Knowledge Centre is to create an environment where learning happens in such a way that people develop their fullest potential in an effort to create an environment where innovative and integrative thinking are the norm. Within this working system there is a delicate balance of interacting parts:

■ Accomplishment of core work
■ Information and decision systems that support that work
■ People, with their knowledge and skills
■ Measurement and reward systems
■ Organisation with its purpose, leadership, and structure.

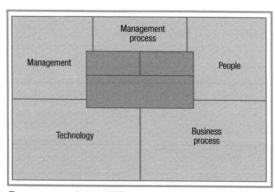

Processes of the KTP

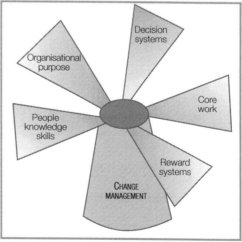

A delicate balance of interacting parts

Just as with a windmill, when any piece of the system changes, the balance may be upset. It is necessary to ensure the integration of all other existing pieces in order for the system to be in balance and operate effectively. It is the integration of the pieces and how they change over time that is key in a change management implementation strategy.

The KTP's people will continually challenge the status quo and always reach out beyond what is currently known. We will provide collaborative leadership in all aspects of our work to develop ideas, test their applicability, implement on a trial basis, learn from our mistakes, celebrate our successes, and continue to develop the next new idea. The KTP provides the opportunity to further develop current change methodologies and to create new ways of thinking about change management.

Integrated solutions
The key is the integration of the business processes technologies and knowledge workers into an environment where continual change is managed as a normal element of the manufacturing task. In the world-class manufacturing enterprise of the future, a variety of functions must learn, cooperate, and change in concert to achieve coordination of activities, cooperation between people and functions, guaranteed integrity of data, optimal use of resources, and a mindset for accepting continual change and improvement.

III THE PROGRAMMES AND PROJECTS
The KTP work, over the next three years, will be focused in three specific programme areas:

■ Seamless Manufacturing Information Systems[a]
■ Intelligent Strategic Planning and Execution Systems[a]
■ Technology Transfer Methodologies[a]

Within these three programmes, there are numerous potential opportunities to develop projects. Examples of opportunities are:

Seamless Manufacturing Information Systems
■ Business planning and execution systems[a]
■ Distribution management systems[a]
■ Vendor base management systems[a]
■ Marketing–engineering–manufacturing interface
■ Collaborative university project opportunities
■ Additional opportunities ...

Intelligent Strategic Planning and Execution Systems
■ Strategic Manufacturing Planning Systems
■ Resource Investment Modelling
■ Collaborative University project opportunities
■ Additional opportunities ...

Technology Transfer
■ KTP Apprenticeship Programme
■ KTP Manufacturing Leaders Programme
■ Collaborative University project opportunities
■ Additional opportunities ...

[a] Initial project planning and sponsorship has been established, and work has begun.

IV INVESTMENT APPRAISAL							
	2003	2004	2005	2006	2007	2008	2009
Program office							
Gross $ ($M)	.6	2.2	3.6	4.1	4.6	5.5	5.5
Capital		.6	.6	1.6	1.5	1.5	1.1
Headcount	5	15	30	35	40	50	50
Offices	5	30	45	65	70	80	80
Manufacturing (K sq. ft.)	0	10	25	30	30	30	30
Baseline operations							
Gross $ ($M)	2.0	7.0	10.0	12.0	13.0	14.0	15.0
Capital	.03	.5	1.0	1.5	1.5	1.5	1.5
Headcount	56	90	120	150	150	150	150
Offices	45	60	70	80	80	80	80
Manufacturing space	0	20	40	50	50	50	50
W/H space (K sq. ft.)	65	65	65	65	65	65	65
Total							
Gross $ ($M)	2.5	9.2	13.6	16.1	17.6	19.5	20.5
Capital	.03	1.1	1.6	3.1	3.0	3.0	3.0
Headcount	61	105	150	185	190	200	200
Offices	50	90	115	145	150	160	160
Manufacturing space	0	30	65	80	80	80	80
W/H space (K sq. ft.)	65	65	65	65	65	65	65

1. Base line operations

		2003		2004				2005				2006				2007			
		3	4	1	2	3	4	1	2	3	4	1	2	3	4	1	2	3	4
Logistics	Completed																		
National acquisition	Completed																		
Physical manufacturing process			X			X													
Simulation lab		X																	
Capital equipment in place				X	X														
Projects defined					X	X													
Visiting prof./research start					X	X					X								X
OEC apprenticeship											X								
Other firms start																			
Showcase																			

2. Seamless manufacturing information systems

	2003		2004				2005				2006				2007			
	3	4	1	2	3	4	1	2	3	4	1	2	3	4	1	2	3	4
Business and technical architecture	X	X	X															
Business planning and executive systems	X	X	X		X					X				X				
Distribution management systems	X	X	X							X								
Vendor base management systems										X								

3. Strategic planning and execution systems

	2003		2004				2005				2006				2007			
	3	4	1	2	3	4	1	2	3	4	1	2	3	4	1	2	3	4
Strategy manufacturing planning systems	X	X										X		X				

4. Technical transfer

Exhibit 3 The knowledge centre (autumn 2003)

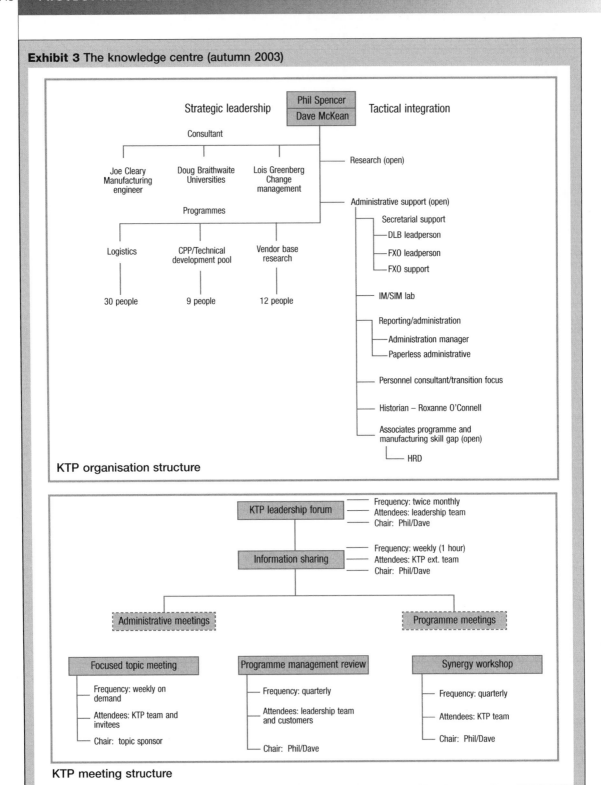

KTP organisation structure

KTP meeting structure

Exhibit 4 Chronology of the KTP

1999	Greg Findlay, senior group manager – Intelligent Systems Technology Group (ISTG), conceives of the idea of a knowledge centre.	
2001	Findlay shares idea with Dean Jacobs, vice-president – Computer Systems Manufacturing.	
April	Newcastle Futures Committee formed to explore the use of the recently idled, Newcastle manufacturing plant as a Knowledge Centre.	
	Phil Spencer joins Newcastle Futures Committee from Greg Findlay's ISTG organisation.	
October	Dave McKean joins the Knowledge Centre team.	
2002 *January*	Two-page Straw developed – presented to team in March.	
March	Straw accepted.	

McKean and Spencer accept co-management responsibilities –'Two-in-a-Box.'

Official kick-off

April McKean and Spencer begin to build support for KT programme and recruit personnel.

Visits to manufacturing sites, other companies, and so on begin.

June Budget Review – presentation to Computer Systems Manufacturing staff.

October Management team in place.

December STRIDe programme transfers 55 workers to the KTP organisation.

2003 *March* KTP business plan published.

End Phase I.

October Knowledge transfer programme is reorganised along project management lines.

QUESTIONS TO AID UNDERSTANDING AND DISCUSSION

1. What was the vision of the project? Was it a good one?

2. What were the project objectives? Were they good ones?

3. How did this project get initiated? Was there a kick-off meeting?

4. Who was in charge of the project? Did this arrangement work?

5. What organisation issues were there in the project?

6. What role did team building and development play?

7. What leadership issues were there?

8. Why was the programme about to be restructured?

9. What decision do you think the three managers would make at the end of the case? Why?

Summary points

■ Project initiation and definition is the first phase in the project life cycle and project managers sow the seeds of success or failure here.

■ Initiation is the process of formally authorising a new project or recognising that an existing project should continue into its next phase (PMI, 2000: 53).

- Initiation activities include the determination of the project's mission, its constraints, its focus, its critical success factors (CSFs), its objectives and its risks.
- Scoping is a communication and information-gathering exercise that determines how the project fits into the business, organisation and information strategies of an organisation and what the project team are expected to achieve.
- The creation of project requirements that are 'comprehensive and clear, well structured, traceable and testable' is the first key to success for any project (APM, 2000: 32).
- Scoping is the process of establishing and agreeing with all the stakeholders what the project will involve and where its boundaries are.
- A project charter is a high-level document that records and communicates the results of the scoping process to project stakeholders and gives official status to a project.
- CSFs are the deliverables that must be achieved in order for the project to succeed; conversely, if a CSF is not addressed, the project fails.
- There are three universal constraints to any project: scope, time and resources.
- The project scope is a description of the sum of the products and services to be provided by the project (PMI, 2000).
- A work breakdown structure (WBS) is a top-down, deliverable-oriented representation of all areas of work involved in a project.
- A WBS can be used to help allocate responsibilities to the project participants, create a schedule and perform a thorough assessment of project risks.
- An organisation breakdown structure (OBS) shows all the people who are going to do work on a project and from which department, division or organisation they belong.
- Integrating the WBS with the OBS creates a matrix of work packages.
- An important event on any project is the kick-off meeting where roles are communicated, objectives are made clear and team protocols are discussed and agreed.
- A successful project launch meeting gives confidence to the key players concerning the value of a project and enthuses them to get involved, put in the extra effort to overcome any difficulties and keep to schedule.
- Team-building activities are required on most projects to help people work together effectively.
- As a temporary organisation, a project has special needs at each phase of its life cycle.

- The project manager should be familiar with several models and theories of team building, for example, the team life cycle, the four pillars of effective teams, Belbin's team role theory and strategies of conflict management.
- Good leadership creates and strengthens trust between a project manager, the project team, the sponsor and all the other project stakeholders.
- Although the project manager is ultimately responsible for the completion of the project, there is a need for shared leadership skills at every level.

In the next chapter we shall be looking at how to estimate project duration and cost, and learning some techniques for scheduling and budgeting.

Visit the website

http://www.palgrave.com/business/gardiner

▶ to test your understanding of the learning objectives for Chapter 8 using multiple choice questions

References

Adair, J. (1979). *Action-centred Leadership*, Gower, Aldershot.

APM (2000). *Body of Knowledge*, 4th edn, Association for Project Management, High Wycombe.

Belbin, M. (1981). *Management Teams: Why They Succeed or Fail*, Butterworth Heinemann, Oxford.

Belbin, M. (1993). *Team Roles at Work*, Butterworth Heinemann, Oxford.

Briner, W., Hastings, C. and Geddes, M. (1996). *Project Leadership*, 2nd edn, Gower, Aldershot.

Burgess, R. and Turner, S. (2000). 'Seven key features for creating and sustaining commitment', *International Journal of Project Management*, **18**(4): 225–33.

Fulmer, R.M. (1994), 'A model for changing the way organisations learn', *Planning Review*, May–June: 20–4.

Gardiner, P.D. and Stewart, K. (2000). 'Revisiting the golden triangle of cost, time and quality: the role of NPV in project control, success and failure', *International Journal of Project Management*, **18**(4): 251–6.

Kelly, J. and Male, S. (1993). *Value Management in Design and Construction*, E & FN Spon, London.

Lipman-Blumen, J. (1996). *The Connective Edge*, Jossey-Bass, San Francisco.

Morris, P. and Harpum, P. (2003). 'Pulling the "levers of value" to deliver genuine business benefit in financial services programs', The Hague, the Netherlands, 22–6 May, PMI Global Congress 2003, Europe.

Müller, R. (2003). 'Determinants for external

communications of IT project managers', *International Journal of Project Management*, **21**(5): 345–54.

Owen, H. (1996). *Creating Top Flight Teams*, Kogan Page, London.

PMI (2000). *A Guide to the Project Management Body of Knowledge*, Project Management Institute, Upper Darby, PA.

Rahim, M.A. (1985). 'A strategy for managing conflict in complex organisations', *Human Relations*, **38**(1): 81–9.

Rahim, M.A. (2001). *Managing Conflict in Organizations*, 3rd edn, Quorum Books, Westport, CT.

Thiry, M. (2001). 'Sensemaking in value management practice', *International Journal of Project Management*, **19**(2): 71–7.

Tuckman, B.W. and Jensen, M.A.C. (1977). 'Stages of small group development revisited', *Group and Organizational Studies*, **2**: 419–27.

Turner, J.R. (1999). *The Handbook of Project-based Management*, 2nd edn, McGraw-Hill, Maidenhead.

Visit the website

http://www.palgrave.com/business/gardiner

▸ for additional resources to explore the topics in this chapter further

9

Estimating, scheduling and budgeting

Learning objectives

After reading this chapter, you should be able to:

- explain the importance of project scheduling and budgeting
- describe the main techniques used in estimating the duration and cost of activities
- construct and analyse project networks
- draw Gantt charts and comment on their value for project control
- use simple techniques to help optimise a schedule
- explain the differences between top-down, bottom-up and iterative budgeting
- construct a cost breakdown structure from a knowledge of the work breakdown structure and organisation breakdown structure
- construct a time-phased project budget from a knowledge of the project schedule, cost estimates and the cost breakdown structure
- draw S-curves to graphically illustrate project cash flows

Introduction

Projects require money, resources and time. How much of each they require is never precisely known until the end of the project; however, by using a range of estimating techniques, it is possible to predict project costs, resources and durations with varying degrees of certainty. These estimates are required for strategy planning, capital budgeting, project budgeting, project scheduling and, later, project control. Although many textbooks consider scheduling and budgeting as separate topics, they are treated together in this chapter to reinforce their strong interdependence. To separate scheduling and budgeting is rather like planning a bicycle ride with reference to distance alone and only later considering the terrain.

The process of estimating may be carried out several times during a project, each succeeding estimate providing greater accuracy and confidence in the predictions obtained than the one before. A number of estimating techniques are reviewed that can be used to help a project to pass through its various stage gates.

The chapter continues with techniques for creating and analysing a project network from an under-

standing of the project's activities and their interrelationships. Gantt charts are an essential part of most project communication tools and these are also developed and discussed, along with the use of baselines. This chapter also deals with allocating human resources and optimising the project schedule in line with the critical success factors identified in the project charter, including a look at how and when to shorten the duration of a project.

The aim of budgeting is to look at situations in advance, think about the impact and implications of things in advance and attempt to take control of situations in advance. The process of budgeting is introduced and top-down, bottom-up and iterative approaches are explored. The close link between budgeting and scheduling is explained, including how the preparation of both these plans uses the work breakdown structure (WBS). The level of detail required in a budget depends on the size and complexity of the project and the needs of the sponsor. With this in mind, the creation of a cost breakdown structure (CBS) from the integration of the organisation breakdown structure (OBS) and the WBS is discussed, including how the resulting matrix can be used as a framework for the accounting system of the project and how this in turn can be linked to the organisation's accounting system. The importance of cash flow is also discussed.

The project schedule

Scheduling is about sequencing project activities and milestones into a sensible and logical order to aid project execution and control. This involves linking activities to form a project network to show how the different activities are related to each other. One of the requirements of scheduling is to establish the timing of a project's activities and resource requirements and so find the expected project duration and milestone dates. Scheduling can also be used to make sure a project is completed by a target date, for example to be ready for the opening day of a new shop.

During the scheduling process, feedback, consensus and eventually signed stakeholder commitment are as important here as they were in the scoping process.

Estimating activity durations

We shall begin our study of scheduling with a look at the estimation of activity durations. Good estimates of activity durations are crucial in project scheduling. They underpin all the outputs of the scheduling process, for example the estimated project duration, the critical path, and the schedule baseline (used later for monitoring and control). The project manager and team members have to agree on a time estimate for every activity in the project.

There are three ways to estimate activity durations:

1. *Use historical data*. Past experience is a good predictor of future events. The more historical data that is available for an activity, the easier it is to predict its duration for the current project.
2. *Time the activity*. It may be possible to do a trial run of an activity and establish an estimate based on the results. For example, in the Calgary Winter Olympics, many of the activities in the presentations and ceremonies were tried out in advance to establish accurate estimates of their duration. This method is useful for relatively simple or one-off activities, but of course it does not allow for the learning that takes place each time an activity is carried out. For example, if a design activity is repeated ten times in the same project, it may take a month to do the first time, three weeks to do the second time, and by the tenth

time the design team may reduce it to four or five days. Learning curve charts can be used to help correct for this.
3. *Use a probabilistic method*. If an activity has never been done before and cannot easily be tested before the project, then a number of estimates can be arrived at using expert judgement or simulation techniques and a probability assigned to each one. A frequently used probabilistic method is the weighted average technique. This method can be used in any situation where significant uncertainty exists. It is explained below.

Weighted average technique

The weighted average technique is based on three estimates of the duration of an activity, often arrived at by expert judgement:

1. Most optimistic (a) – the minimum time this activity would take to complete if everything went exactly as expected without any difficulties or problems whatsoever.
2. Most likely (m) – the most likely duration assuming normal conditions.
3. Most pessimistic (b) – the expected duration if major difficulties are encountered.

The weighted average for the activity duration is calculated using a distribution called a beta distribution approximation. Simply stated, this involves adding together the most optimistic, four times the most likely and the most pessimistic duration and then dividing the total by six:

$$\text{Weighted average} = \frac{a + 4m + b}{6}$$

For example, consider the following time estimates for an activity:

Most optimistic = 24 hours
Most likely = 48 hours
Most pessimistic = 96 hours

$$\therefore \text{Weighted average} = \frac{24 + 4(48) + 96 \text{ hrs}}{6} = 52 \text{ hrs}$$

Issues in estimating duration

Project duration is historically one of the three most important variables in project control alongside budget and scope. Line managers find the simplicity of comparing estimated time, cost and scope with actual time, cost and scope irresistible. The phrase 'on time, on budget and in scope' has long been seen as a defining characteristic of the best project managers. However, it is well known from research in psychology that measures of performance directly affect behaviour and chronic overreliance on the above measures can lead to undesirable effects in project management (Gardiner and Stewart, 2000). New approaches to managing time in the project life cycle have emerged and are now finding their place in the body of knowledge. One of these, considered in Chapter 10, is the application of the theory of constraints (Steyn, 2001) in a project management technique now widely know as *critical chain* project management (Goldratt, 1997), not to be confused with *critical path* project management.

Defining activity dependencies and creating a project network

Sequencing activities in parallel or in series

Having established activity durations, the next requirement is to define the logical relationships between activities and construct a network diagram to reflect these. Let us consider how to approach this. In most projects, there are some activities that are independent of each other and can be done at the same time; these activities should always be sequenced in parallel (see Figure 9.1(a)). Other activities are dependent on each other and must follow one after the other; these should be sequenced in series (see Figure 9.1(b)).

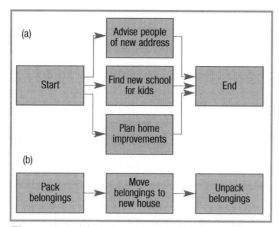

Figure 9.1 (a) Independent activities are sequenced in parallel: (b) Dependent activities are sequenced in series

At this stage no account is taken of the availability of resources – we are *only* concerned with representing the logical relationships between activities. When drawing a project network, we do not place activities in series just because we think (or know) there will not be enough manpower to do them in parallel. On the contrary, the network diagram reflects logical relationships (dependencies) *only* and *not* resource constraints. These are considered later in the scheduling process and affect the timing of activities but not the network logic.

The network diagram

A network diagram not only shows the relationships between activities but can be used to reveal which activities are time-critical, and therefore warrant greater management attention. Over the years, a multitude of labels and acronyms have evolved to describe various kinds of project network and the techniques used to analyse them. When reading books on project management, you will come across terms like CPA (critical path analysis), CPM (critical path method), PERT (programme evaluation and review technique), PDM (precedence diagramming method) and others besides. Morris (1994) gives an excellent historical account of these techniques and their development. However, throughout this chapter we shall use the general term 'network analysis' and the drawing method that uses rectangular activity boxes to represent project activities and arrows to indicate how they are connected.

Visit the website

http://www.palgrave.com/business/gardiner

▶ to see the alternative, activity-on-arrow technique of drawing networks that is often used in construction and engineering projects

Activity boxes

The standard labelling format for an activity box is shown in Figure 9.2.

You will notice that each activity has seven attributes:

- The activity code and name (middle row) – used to identify uniquely the activity in the project. The code should relate to the work breakdown structure. It is important that every activity can be identified quickly and unambiguously in a project, especially during the scheduling process

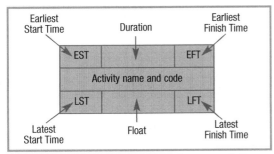

Figure 9.2 Standard labelling for an activity box

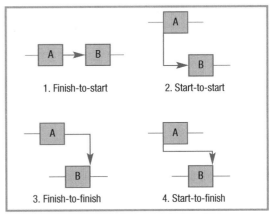

Figure 9.3 The four activity dependency relationships

- The estimated duration of the activity (top row, middle)
- Earliest start and finish times (top row, left and right respectively)
- Latest start and finish times (bottom row, left and right respectively)
- Float or slack (bottom row, middle) – which is basically spare time. We will look again at float and its importance in the section on analysing a network.

Activity relationships

There are four basic relationships that can be expressed between two activities, A and B (see Figure 9.3):

1. **Finish-to-start**. This means activity A must finish before activity B has permission to start. A time lag can be written on the arrow to indicate if there must be a delay after A has finished before starting B. For example, if activity A involves gluing two parts together, there may need to be a delay, to allow the glue to set, before proceeding with the next operation, activity B.
2. **Start-to-start**. This means that once activity A has started, activity B can also start. A time lag can be written on the arrow to indicate if there must be a delay after A has started before starting B. For example, a project may involve painting a rather long fence. Let us say activity A is 'paint fence with undercoat' and activity B is 'paint fence with top coat'. Once we have started painting the undercoat, as soon as it is sufficiently dry, we can begin with the top coat. There is no need to wait until the entire fence has been undercoated before starting with the top coat.
3. **Finish-to-finish**. This means that activity A must finish before activity B can finish. Once again a

time lag can be written on the arrow to indicate if there must be a delay after A has finished before B may also finish. For example, in a software development project, two software engineers may be working on two different modules. If module B makes use of module A in one of its subroutines, procedure B cannot be tested and signed off until the first engineer has completed module A.

4. **Start-to-finish**. This means that as long as activity A has actually started, we can proceed to finish activity B. A time lag can be written on the arrow to indicate if there must be a delay after A has started before B can finish.

Finish-to-start relationships are by far the most common relationships used in project networks.

Creating a network

The most challenging aspect of creating a network is getting the relationships between the activities defined correctly. Often the best way to do this is to ignore the difficulties and start piecing together the network. Ideally, the project activities will have been defined earlier during the creation of a work breakdown structure. To begin, write out the activities on cards or Post-it notes and start arranging them to reflect the logical relationships. The process is one of experimentation and teamwork and should involve the other members of your team.

On the other hand, if you have planned similar projects before, you may have historical records that contain information about the activities you will need to perform and how they should relate to each other. Firms that undertake projects regularly in particular

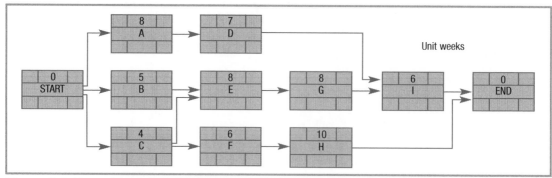

Figure 9.4 Example network diagram

sectors and disciplines develop special knowledge about how to sequence activities on their projects. For most contractors and subcontractors this special knowledge represents their core competencies. This is what the customer wants and is prepared to pay for.

An example network is shown in Figure 9.4. The activities are labelled A to I. Of course in a real project, we would include a summary description of each activity in its activity box or in a key near the network rather than just representing them with a code as we have done here.

A network is a special chart to show the relationships between project activities. In the example project above, every arrow points from the end of one activity box to the start on another activity box. This tells us that all the relationships in our example project are of the finish-to-start type.

Look at activity box E. You will see that it is connected to three other activities. On its left are connections to activities B and C. On its right is a connection to activity G. The direction of an arrow conveys important information about the relationship between the two activities it connects. In the case of activity E, we say that it has two immediate predecessors (activities B and C) and one immediate successor (activity G). What this means is that activity E cannot be started until *both* activities B and C (its predecessors) are complete and activity G cannot be started until activity E is complete. Looking at the network again, we can also say that activity F can be started as soon as activity C is complete and activities A, B, and C can be started any time (and all at the same time) because they are not dependent on the prior completion of any other activities (that is, they have no predecessors).

The logical relationships in a project can also be expressed in the form of a dependency table, as

Table 9.1 Dependency table for network in Figure 9.4

Activity	Immediate predecessor(s)	Duration (weeks)
A	–	8
B	–	5
C	–	4
D	A	7
E	B,C	8
F	C	6
G	E	8
H	F	10
I	D,G	6

shown in Table 9.1. This table defines (without any ambiguity) the equivalent logical relationships represented by the network of Figure 9.4. Notice that the table lists only the *immediate* predecessors of an activity, and that this is sufficient to define fully the network logic. There is no need to declare the successors of an activity as well.

All dependency relationships are finish-to-start with no time delay.

TIME out Using a precedence table to draw a network

Without looking back at Figure 9.4, see if you can use Table 9.1 to draw a network with the same logical relationships. When you have finished, see how you have done. Is your network identical in every respect to Figure 9.4? Does it have to be identical?

See shaded box opposite for a suggested answer to this last question.

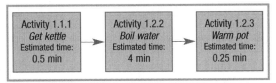

Figure 9.5 Using Post-it notes to establish dependencies and arrange activities into a network

self a cup of tea and use a stopwatch to time the activities as you go. Add this information to the Post-it notes.

3. Now place the activities on a white board or a large sheet of paper and begin arranging the activities into a network to reflect their dependencies, as shown in Figure 9.5. As you do this, remember that activities should only be arranged in series if it is logically impossible (or undesirable) for them to be placed in parallel. The network should proceed from left to right, as in the example network in Figure 9.4.

4. To complete the network diagram, draw in the arrow lines to connect the activities and show the logical relationships between them. (You may wish to restrict yourself to using the finish-to-start relationship.)

5. It is much neater to have a single box to represent the start and end of a network. If your network has several parallel activities at the start and/or end, you can tidy it up by adding a start box and finish box as necessary. These are not real activities and therefore have no duration.

---

suggested ANSWER

Your network may be identical to Figure 9.4 or you may have drawn yours with activities A and D underneath the critical path and activities C, F and H above the critical path. This does not matter, providing the arrows still represent the same logical relationships. Often there are many alternatives to the spatial positioning of the activity boxes in a network (although it is standard practice to draw the network progressing from left to right). This is because it is not the relative position that defines the logical relationships, but the manner in which activity boxes are connected using arrows.

In practice, the first attempt at drawing a network will often end up having arrow lines making all manner of strange looking and difficult-to-draw connections. Do not worry about this. Just get it drawn and the logic put in place. Then you can redraw the network more neatly, taking care to position the activity boxes where they do not require you to perform gymnastics with your arrows!

Using Post-it notes

The process of writing the names of activities on cards or Post-it notes, and arranging them into a logical network, facilitates and encourages input from several team members at the same time and can result in a better first draft of the network (see Figure 9.5). The following questions can be used at any stage to help the process:

- What can be done now?
- What must you have done before that?
- What can be done at the same time?
- What must follow what you do now?

Defining logical relationships and creating a network from scratch

This exercise will give you practice at creating a network from scratch. If you can arrange to do the exercise with a colleague or friend, so much the better.

The WBS for making a cup of tea is given below in Figure 9.6. A WBS defines the scope of a project. The process of creating it helps to ensure that no activities are left out or forgotten, but it does not say anything about the logical relationships between them. When drawing a network, remember that there can be dependencies between any pair of activities, wherever they happen to appear in the WBS.

1. Write each activity on a separate card or Post-it note.
2. Give each activity a reference code and estimate its duration (in seconds or minutes). If you find this difficult, make your-

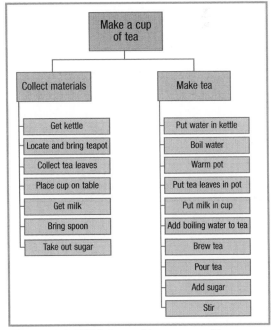

Figure 9.6 WBS for making a cup of tea

Now that you have finished, compare your network with the one given in Figure 9.7. They are unlikely to be identical. Look carefully at any differences and attempt to explain them in terms of the activities and dependencies that you have used. How can you determine which network is the best one?

See shaded box below.

Analysing the network to determine the critical path

The critical path is defined as the path through the network having the longest duration. In fact the critical path defines the expected duration of a project.

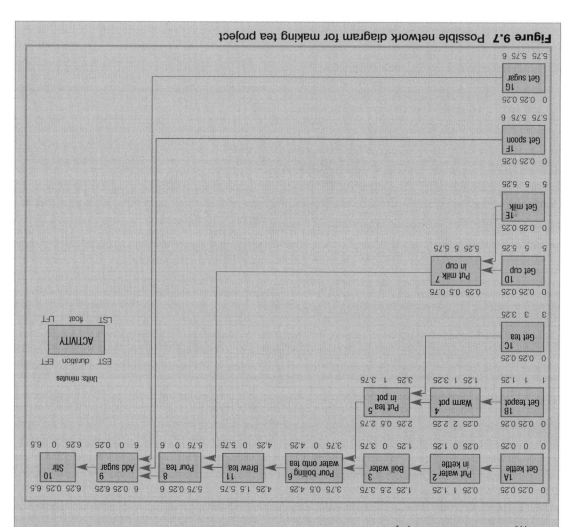

Figure 9.7 Possible network diagram for making tea project

suggested **ANSWER**

Figure 9.7 shows one interpretation of this problem. The best network is the one that will result in a project that meets all the needs and expectations of the customer. This is why it is so important to have the full involvement and commitment of the sponsor and customers in the project definition phase. Otherwise the project schedule may look impressive but it is unlikely to impress an unhappy customer at the end of the project.

The project manager should try to ensure that all the activities on the critical path, called 'critical activities', are completed within their estimated duration. If a critical activity overruns, the project will also overrun (unless special action is taken such as project crashing). In some networks there may be more than one critical path.

Forward pass

The first stage in determining the critical path (and therefore the duration of a project) is to carry out a forward pass through the network. The forward pass begins with the first activity box (the start box in Figure 9.4) and progresses forwards (that is, from left to right) until the last activity box is reached. In the forward pass, the aim is to write down for each activity the earliest start time (EST) and the earliest finish time (EFT):

- The EST for the first activity, whether or not there is a start box, is zero (or the date the project will commence)
- The EFT for an activity is always found by adding its duration to its EST
- The EST for all remaining activities is the same as the EFT of its immediate predecessor
- However, and this is the tricky part, in cases where an activity has more than one immediate predecessor, the EST is taken from the path having the numerically *highest* EFT
- The EFT for the last activity is also the expected duration of the project.

Backward pass

The forward pass gives us the expected project duration but it doesn't identify the critical activities. To find the critical activities and the float of the noncritical activities, we need to complete the analysis by doing a backward pass through the network. This will establish the latest finish time (LFT) and the latest start time (LST) for each activity, from which we can compute the float and find out which activities have zero float – these are the critical activities.

In the backward pass, we proceed from the last activity box in the network (or finish box if there is one) back through the network until the first activity box is reached (that is, from right to left).

- The LFT for the last activity is the same as its EFT (that is, the expected project duration). We

do not allow the project to finish later than its expected duration
- The LST for an activity is always found by subtracting its duration from its LFT
- The LFT for all remaining activities is given by the LST of its immediate successor
- The tricky part of the backward pass is that in cases where an activity has more than one immediate successor, the LFT is taken from the path having the numerically *lowest* LST.

Activity floats

Activities that are not critical are said to have float (or slack). This means that a certain amount of delay can be tolerated without affecting the expected duration of the project. In any given project, there may be many paths through the network, the float associated with activities falling on some paths may be greater than the float of activities that lie on other paths. When an activity has only a very small amount of float relative to the duration of the project, it is said to be 'near critical' and should be monitored closely by the project manager, in a similar way to the critical activities.

Float (spare time for an activity) is calculated by taking the difference between the latest finish time and the earliest finish time *or* between the latest start time and the earliest start time:

$$Float = LFT - EFT$$

or

$$Float = LST - EST$$

Critical activities have zero float.

 **TIME out** Analysing a network

1. Carry out a forward pass and then a backward pass on the example network in Figure 9.4.
2. For each activity, determine the float and write it inside the appropriate activity box.
3. Find and highlight the critical path for the example network.

The fully analysed network can be found overleaf in Figure 9.8.

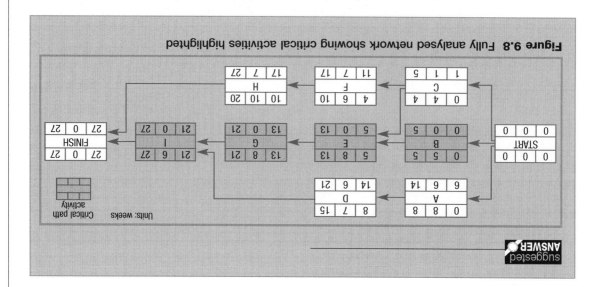

Figure 9.8 Fully analysed network showing critical activities highlighted

Importance of network analysis

Knowing which activities lie on the critical path is important for the project manager and other stakeholders. These are the activities that are most likely to cause a delay to the project schedule. If a critical activity takes longer than expected to complete, this will put severe pressure on all the participants to finish the project by the expected finish date (or target date) that was agreed in the project charter or contract documentation. Project delays are normally the result of slippage in one or more critical activities.

Identifying the critical path helps the project manager to concentrate his or her time on areas of the project that are most likely to cause delays. The critical path is also used to help plan and schedule resources for the project.

Gantt charts

Another way of representing scheduling information is with a Gantt chart. These charts, named after their inventor Henry Gantt in the early twentieth century, are intuitively easier to interpret than networks and are therefore popular progress reporting tools at project review meetings for team members and senior management.

A Gantt chart of the network shown in Figure 9.4 is given in Figure 9.9. Note that:

■ activities are arranged from top to bottom

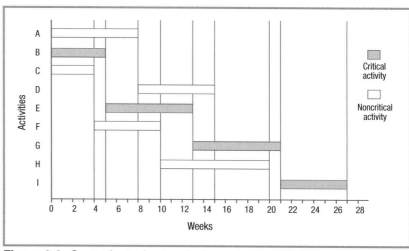

Figure 9.9 Gantt chart of network shown in Figure 9.4

- time is plotted to scale from left to right
- activity bars begin at their earliest start time. When all the activities are in this position, the Gantt chart is referred to as an 'early start Gantt chart'. In a 'late start Gantt chart', the end of all the activity bars are positioned in their latest finish time positions
- critical activities are highlighted.

Gantt charts can be enhanced to show additional information. Float can be shown, for example by adding a dotted bar (float envelope) onto the end of each noncritical activity, with a length equal to the available float. Arrows can also be added to indicate dependency relationships. As more information is included on a Gantt chart, it quickly begins to lose its simplicity and ease of interpretation. Figure 9.10 shows the same Gantt chart after it has been enhanced by adding dotted float envelopes.

Project management software packages can usually toggle between network views and Gantt chart views at the click of a mouse button. The ability to roll up several activities to represent summary levels of the WBS makes the Gantt chart adaptable as a communication tool to a wide range of stakeholders, from project workers to executive board directors and client user groups. High-level charts should be used for reporting to senior management and the client and lower level charts for day-to-day control purposes.

Visit the website

http://www.palgrave.com/business/gardiner

▶ to access additional problems (with solutions) to practise

and develop your network and Gantt chart drawing and analysis skills

Milestones

A milestone is a special event in the life of a project to which you want to draw added attention. Milestones play an important part in planning and managing projects. As they are events rather than activities, they take up no time. Therefore, they are represented in a network diagram as elements with zero duration. The description in a milestone box describes the stage reached rather than a particular job to perform. Sometimes milestones are used to indicate an event in a project for which prior authorisation is required in order to proceed.

Milestones are normally represented on a Gantt chart by a different symbol, often a diamond. Most software packages can produce reports showing only milestones. Such a report – a milestone report – is a useful summary of a detailed plan and can form the basis of higher level project control.

Gantt charts versus network diagrams

Gantt charts play a useful role in a project but are limited in their ability to convey a clear understanding of the logical relationships of the project. Network analysis has some advantages over the Gantt chart, but is limited in other ways. Table 9.2 compares a Gantt chart with a network diagram.

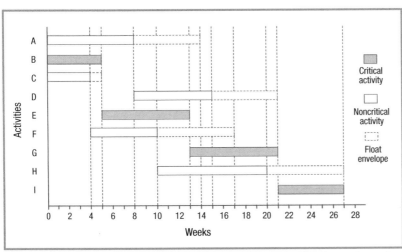

Figure 9.10 Example Gantt chart (enhanced to show float envelopes)

	Table 9.2 Gantt charts and network diagrams compared	
Characteristic	Gantt chart	Network diagram
Timing	Shows project timeline clearly	Does not show project timeline
Activity relationships	Does not show activity relationships clearly	Shows clearly which activities depend on others
Familiarity	Most people find Gantt charts easy to interpret	Most people are not familiar with network diagrams
Presentation	Easy to present and can be scaled down to suit a variety of reports	Plans are hard to read and tend to be quite cumbersome
Resource smoothing and levelling	Suitable	Not suitable
Project crashing	Not suitable	Suitable

Adding people and optimising the schedule

Once the project network is established, staff can be recruited and assigned to activities. The assignment of people who will do the work on a project is best done by referring to the organisation breakdown structure (OBS) and using a Gantt chart. Most Gantt charts are drawn initially with their noncritical activities in the early start position, causing them to appear bunched up. This can lead to an overallocation of staff or conflict hours (where someone is overworked) in the early stages of the project. The bunching up effect can be overcome by resource smoothing and resource levelling. These resource-optimising processes involve:

- taking into account the manpower available for the project and the amount of hours, however limited, that each person is available to work every day
- integrating this information with the flexibility afforded by activity floats and the resource needs of the project activities.

Resource smoothing (a limited form of levelling) involves rescheduling the noncritical activities within their float envelopes; it does not affect the expected project duration. Full resource levelling aims to remove any remaining overallocation of resources or conflict hours by other methods, such as extending the duration of the project or assigning overtime hours.

If the project duration is so long that a target date will be missed, it may be possible to reduce it.

There are several methods available for shortening the duration of a project:

- project crashing – adding resources to selected activities (see below)
- network re-evaluation – looking for ways to increase the parallelisation of the network
- fast tracking – overlapping two or more major project phases (see Chapter 2)
- rescoping – reducing or adjusting the scope of the project
- increased procurement – outsourcing additional parts of the project to a third party
- lean thinking – redesigning work processes to save time and reduce and waste
- renegotiate target dates – does not shorten the duration but buys more time.

In project crashing, additional resources are assigned to one or more critical path activities. However, be aware that increasing the resource units on a work package may actually reduce productivity for a time. This is because the new manpower will take time to climb the learning curve, and the productivity of existing manpower will be reduced while they spend some of their time orientating the new workers. This effect is particularly well known in software engineering projects.

Crashing a project incurs additional costs. The project manager must balance these additional costs against other factors such as earlier project revenue streams, reduced project overhead costs and the impact on the project objectives of finishing late.

The completed schedules, once agreed, should be frozen and signed off. Once this is done they become the project's baseline schedules for project control purposes.

Worked example in resource smoothing

A consulting firm are planning a feasibility study for a new city centre tram scheme. The activities in Table 9.3 have been identified for the final phase of the study.

1. Draw and analyse the network.
2. Give the critical path and the minimum duration for the final phase of the study.
3. Draw the Gantt chart in its early start position.
4. Draw the corresponding resource profile.
5. Calculate appropriate statistics to measure the effectiveness of the allocation of staff.
6. Demonstrate the action that can be taken to reduce the maximum number of staff required for the final phase without affecting its duration. Discuss the implications of this action.

Answer

1. The network diagram is drawn using the method described earlier and then analysed by conducting a forward pass and a backward pass through the network. The fully drawn and analysed network is shown in Figure 9.11.

2. The critical path consists of the activities B, E, G, and I. The minimum duration for the final phase of the development is 27 weeks. You may have noticed that the network in Figure 9.11 is similar to the example network of Figure 9.4. In fact the only difference is that activity G has an additional dependency, activity F. Notice the effect that this has on the float of activity F, although the expected duration and the critical path for the project remain the same.

3. The Gantt chart for the project is shown in Figure

Table 9.3 Activities for the final phase of a feasibility study (resource smoothing example)

Activity	Dependency	Duration (weeks)	Number of Staff Needed
A	–	8	3
B	–	5	3
C	–	4	8
D	A	7	2
E	B,C	8	2
F	C	6	5
G	E,F	8	3
H	F	10	6
I	D,G	6	5

9.12. Dependency arrows and float envelopes for the noncritical activities have been added to the chart. This will help when answering part 5 of the question.

4. The resource profile is drawn by looking at the Gantt chart and the information about staff given in Table 9.3, then plotting a graph of staff required each week against time (see Figure 9.10). For example, in week 9 we see from the Gantt chart that activities D, E, and F are in progress, requiring 2, 2 and 5 people respectively, giving a total of 9 staff required in week 9, as drawn in the resource profile in Figure 9.13.

5. The effectiveness of the allocation of resources is given by the resource utilisation. This is calculated by dividing the area under the resource profile (duration of activity × staff required by each activity, all added together) by the area

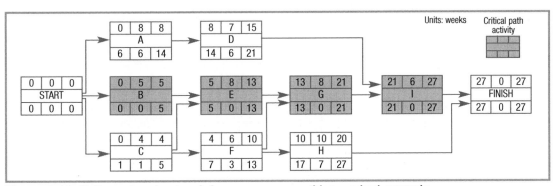

Figure 9.11 Fully analysed network for resource smoothing worked example

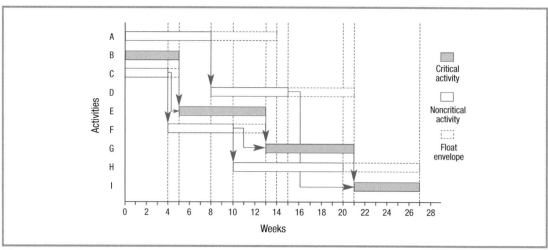

Figure 9.12 Early start Gantt chart (showing dependencies and floats)

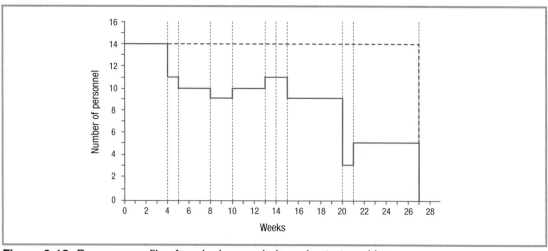

Figure 9.13 Resource profile of worked example in early start position

inside the resource envelope (maximum staff required in any one time period × duration of project, shown dotted in Figure 9.13). Thus

$$\text{Resource utilisation} = \frac{(8\times3)+(5\times3)+(4\times8)+\dots \text{ etc.}}{14\times27}$$
$$= 245 \,/\, 378 = 0.65 \; \textit{or}\; 65\%$$

6. To reduce the number of staff employed, we can smooth the resources by making use of the scheduling flexibility afforded by the noncritical activities and represented by their float envelopes. By moving the noncritical activities along their float envelopes, we can influence the number of staff required in any one week. It is

important to maintain any dependencies when doing this. The process is one of inspection and trial and error. Some project management software packages can give suggested solutions to resource smoothing and resource levelling. In this example we can reduce the maximum number of staff required from 14 to 11 by delaying activities A and D (which both have 6 weeks float) by 4 weeks. The Gantt chart and resource profile have been redrawn in Figure 9.14 to show these changes.

The new resource utilisation is therefore given by

Resource utilisation = 245 / 297 = 0.82 *or* 82%

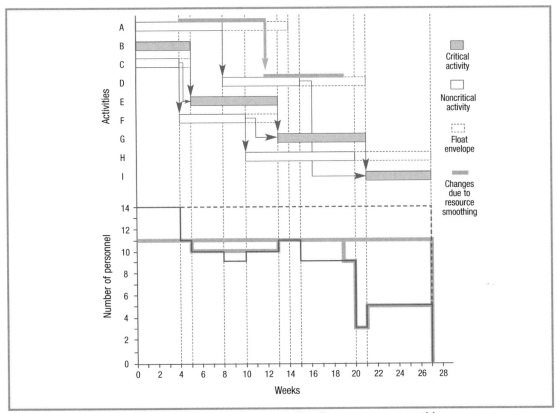

Figure 9.14 Modified Gantt chart and resource profile after resource smoothing

Notice that the manpower required to complete the project is still 245 man-weeks.

The main implication of this action is that noncritical activities delayed during resource levelling lose some or all of their float. This in turn can increase the risk of finishing the project late. After resource smoothing the project manager should revisit the risk management plan.

Worked example in project crashing

Given the information in Table 9.4, establish the cost of crashing this project by:

- one day
- two days
- three days
- four days.

Table 9.4 Data for worked example in project crashing

| Activity | Dependency | Normal | | If crashing used | |
		duration (days)	cost (£)	minimum duration (days)	cost (£) to achieve minimum duration
A	–	2	20	1	40
B	A	4	30	1	60
C	A	2	10	2	10
D	A	2	10	1	40
E	D	3	10	1	30
			Total = 80		Total = 180

If the daily saving in project overheads is £30 per day, comment on what action the project manager may wish to take if cost is the highest priority project constraint.

Answer

The first task is to draw and analyse the network (see Figure 9.15).

To solve the problem the project manager must decide which activities to crash and in what order. The choice of activities to crash is limited to activities on the critical path; these are the activities that determine the total duration of the project. The basis for deciding which critical activities to crash when a choice is available is cost, more specifically cost slope in £/day. The cost slope for each activity can be calculated from the 'normal' and 'crash' information in Table 9.4. In each case the cost slope is the cost interval divided by the time interval. For example, activity B has a cost slope of

(£60–£30) / (4 days–1 day) = £30 / 3 days = £10/day

When crashing a project three variables can change:

- The activity duration can decrease (applies to all activities crashed)
- The float can decrease (may apply to some, all or none of the noncritical activities after crashing a critical activity)
- A noncritical activity may become critical, changing the critical path of the project and the decision process for crashing the project further.

In order to keep track of these variables when solving a crashing problem, it is helpful to construct a table at the start of the process. The table should begin with the following columns completed: activity, cost slope, minimum crash duration, normal duration and normal float. As crashing proceeds an additional two columns should be added for each day crashed to record the new activity durations and floats. At the start of this example, your table should resemble Table 9.5.

The completed table is shown in Table 9.6 and the four-day crashing process is described below. For each day crashed, you should:

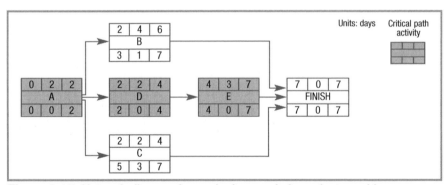

Figure 9.15 Network diagram for worked example in project crashing

Table 9.5 Crash table prepared for start of crashing process (worked example)													
Activity	Cost slope	Min. crash dur.	Norm. dur.	Norm. float	Duration and float when project crashed by:								
					1 day		2 days		3 days		4 days		
					Dur.	Float	Dur.	Float	Dur.	Float	Dur.	Float
A	£20	1	2	0								
B	£10	1	4	1								
C	–	2	2	3								
D	£30	1	2	0								
E	£10	1	3	0								

Durations all in days. Normal project duration is 7 days.

- check the critical path activities
- list the options for crashing and the cost of each option
- decide which actives to crash
- note down the new project duration
- complete the appropriate columns in the table.

The four-day crashing process

Cost   *Cumul. cost*

Crash by 1 day
Critical path   A — D — E

Crash options	A	D	E
Cost	£20	£30	£10

Crash least cost option, 'E'.
Project duration now 6 days.
Complete the next two columns of the table.
Activity B is now also critical.

£10   £10

Crash by 2nd day
Critical path

Crash options	A	B+D	B+E
Cost	£20	£40	£20

Crash 'A', easier to crash 1 than 2 activities.
Project duration now 5 days.
Complete the next two columns of the table.

£20   £30

Crash by 3rd day
Critical path   No change

Crash options	B+D	B+E
Cost	£40	£20

'A' cannot be crashed further, crash 'B+E'.
Project duration now 4 days.
Complete the next two columns of the table.

£20   £50

Crash by 4th day
Critical path   No change

Crash options	B+D
Cost	£40

'A' and 'E' cannot be crashed further, only crash option is 'B+D'.
Project duration now 3 days.
Complete the last two columns of the table.
All activities are now critical.

£40   £90

Table 9.6 Crash table at end of crashing process (worked example)

Activity	Cost slope	Min. crash dur.	Norm. dur.	Norm. float	Duration and float when project crashed by:							
					1 day		2 days		3 days		4 days	
					Dur.	Float	Dur.	Float	Dur.	Float	Dur.	Float
A	£20	1	2	0	2	0	1	0	1	0	1	0
B	£10	1	4	1	4	0	4	0	3	0	2	0
C	–	2	2	3	2	2	2	2	2	1	2	0
D	£30	1	2	0	2	0	2	0	2	0	1	0
E	£10	1	3	0	2	0	2	0	1	0	1	0

Durations all in days. Final project duration is three days.

If the overhead savings are at a rate of £30/day, the project manager is likely to crash the project by a total of three days, giving a total saving of £40. However, he should be aware that crashing by three days makes all the activities critical, except 'B', increasing the management and control burden for the project.

Supplementary question on project crashing

Is there a simple rule that can be used to determine what the effect of crashing a particular activity will be on the float times of the noncritical activities?

Answer

The hardest part of a crashing exercise is working out what happens to the remaining floats after each period of crashing. For example, looking at Table 9.6, how can we predict that:

(a) when crashing the project by one day the float of activity C will change from 3 days to 2 days, but
(b) when crashing the project by a second day, the float of activity C will not change at all but will remain at 2 days?

Project management software is ideal for testing out these kinds of effects when crashing different activities. The software can recalculate the critical path and activity floats very quickly. Doing the same process by hand is much more time-consuming and prone to errors. However, a useful tip is to find the activities with float, activity C in this case, and decide if it is part of a path through the network that also contains the activity being crashed. If they are both on the same path, crashing the one activity will not normally affect the float of the other. However, if they are on separate paths, crashing the critical activity will reduce the float of the noncritical activity by the crash period. Let us examine our example again:

■ In the case of (a) we are going to crash activity E. Look at the network and see if activities C and E can be connected by a single path through the network. No, they can't. So we would expect the float of C to be reduced by one day, which is correct
■ In the case of (b) we are now going to crash activity A. This time we look at the network to see if activities C and A can be connected by a single path through the network. Indeed they can, so we would expect the float of C to be unchanged this time, which again is correct.

Test the technique out a few more times on your own to make sure you understand it. Once learnt, this is a simple and quick technique to use and apply. However, it does require care in a more complex network, especially when a noncritical activity is connected to more than one path through the network.

Visit the website

http://www.palgrave.com/business/gardiner

▶ for additional problems to practise and develop your schedule optimisation skills using resource smoothing and project crashing

Project management software packages

Project management software can be used to help plan and control a project. Most project management software packages, also called cost and schedule tools, allow easy manual input of the names of activities, the dependencies between them and their duration. The software calculates the earliest and latest start and completion dates and enables schedules, charts and reports to be viewed and printed off. Some packages allow resource loading and budgeting calculations, enabling the project manager to see the relationship between time, people and money. A good software package can greatly facilitate communication and consequently teamwork processes in a project. Printouts of the network diagram, bar chart and project reports can be circulated prior to group meetings to resolve any differences at every phase of the project. This documentation can also be used after project implementation as a record of events in case of disputes and contractor claims.

There are many software packages available to choose from. Selecting a suitable package will depend on the current and future needs of the organisation. It may be appropriate to invest in a medium-priced package for small and medium-sized projects, and a more expensive package for programme management and large/complex projects. For example, Microsoft Project is an easily learned package for basic project management needs. However, the increased power and versatility required for reporting and controlling large programmes consisting of many projects may demand the use of a system such as Artemis. Microsoft Project is widely used in industry in small and medium-sized companies.

Project Management in Action: 'Albion Sugar Company' is designed to develop your skills at drawing and analysing project networks, optimising resources, project crashing and writing a report suitable for discussion at a project review meeting.

Visit the website

http://www.palgrave.com/business/gardiner

▶ to find a worksheet for MS Project to develop basic skills in preparation for attempting the questions at the end of Project Management in Action: 'Albion Sugar Company'

Limitations of project management software

Project management software does not incorporate artificial intelligence – the project manager still has to:

- define the work breakdown structure
- analyse activity dependencies
- assign resources to activities
- estimate manpower requirements and activity durations
- monitor progress
- evaluate trade-offs
- make decisions.

Benefits of project management software

Most packages generally include planning, scheduling and controlling functions involving:

- schedule calculations
- critical path identification
- resource loading, smoothing, and levelling
- cost tracking
- planned and actual data comparisons
- report and chart generation
- history tracking
- trouble spot identification
- hypothetical simulations.

Project budgeting

Project budgets are used by managers to fix in advance the resources that a project will use. Budgets represent the planned cost of a project at inception. For example, a manager may allocate a budget of £5,000 to a member of staff to conduct a feasibility study on an idea for a new range of products. The amount of £5,000 becomes the project budget, the budgeted cost. Project budgeting is all about allocating resources to a project. This includes the process that determines *how much money* (or other resources, for example labour) will be allocated to a project. Project budgeting is also

about *how much detail* to include in a budget. At one extreme is a budget that only gives information about the total project cost; at the other extreme a budget can give cost information for every component and activity in the project scope.

In the example above, the budget of £5,000 represents the amount of money available for the *total* project. There is no breakdown of costs to indicate *how* or *where* the money should be spent. Returning to the example, let us assume that in fact there are two managers each looking at a different range of potential new products for development. Let us also assume that each manager has been given a total feasibility budget of £5,000. If the first manager completes his feasibility study for only £4,500, we could say his project came in under budget, saving the company £500. If the second project manager completes her study for £5,500, we would intuitively say her project came in over budget, costing the company an additional £500 of unplanned expenditure.

On the strength of this information, you may decide that the first project manager was the better of the two. But this is not necessarily the case. Look again at these two projects. Notice that no mention has been made of time. That is, the analysis has not considered the project schedule. Does this matter? It most certainly does. Let us assume that each feasibility study gave the go-ahead for its respective product range and that expected profits are £0.5 million per annum in each case. Now suppose the manager of the company had given his two staff 12 months to complete their work and that the work involved for each study was comparable. If it took the first project manager 18 months to complete his feasibility study and the second project manger completed her feasibility study in only 6 months, what can we say about the performance of these two project managers now? We might say that the first project manager failed in terms of schedule but succeeded in terms of budget, while the second project manager failed in terms of budget but succeeded in terms of schedule.

On the other hand, if you were a shareholder in the company, you would be more likely to praise the second project manager and not the first. This is because the second project manager, by bringing in her project 6 months early, enabled her product to enter the market 12 months ahead of the other manager's product, whose study came in 6 months late. What this means for shareholders is an additional £0.5 million profit. You don't particularly care about the £500 overspend to deliver the project; the extra £500,000 of added value (from earlier product sales) is much more important.

The main lesson to learn here is that budgets and schedules should never be considered in isolation when managing a project; they are closely linked. The status of a project cannot be determined without reference to *both* schedule and budget. This concept of project control will be developed in more detail in Chapter 10. Insights from Industry: 'Gambling with high stakes' draws attention to the business risk inherent in very large projects.

---

insights from INDUSTRY | GAMBLING WITH HIGH STAKES

Aircraft manufacturing is a business of enormous risks, for in no other industry is so much capital deployed with so much uncertainty. Launching the Boeing 767 airplane project meant up-front development costs of $1.5–2 billion, lead times of up to four years from go-ahead to first delivery, and the selection and management of thousands of subcontractors. Projects of this scale can put a company's entire net worth on the line.

The building blocks of a budget

Expenditures

Projects consume resources. Resources cost money and are treated as project expenditures. Typical resources in a project would be people, equipment, materials and space, heat and lighting (usually referred to as overheads).

Resources may be provided in-house or they may be provided (wholly or partly) by one or several external organisations such as:

- a firm of consultants (providing advice, knowledge and management skills)
- a contractor (specialising in the delivery of projects in a particular sector, for example building, software or electronic systems)
- subcontractors (smaller, usually highly specialised firms employed by larger contractors and clients to help to resource particular areas of a project requiring expertise in a narrow or technical discipline, for example cladding subcontractors in a building project or data security specialists in a software project)
- suppliers (provide equipment and materials).

The term is also used collectively to mean all the consultants, contractors and subcontractors in a project.

Revenues

Money generated by a project is called 'revenue'. A company owned by shareholders (or any organisation that seeks to make a profit) would normally expect a project to add shareholder value to the company. This means that, when complete, the project must generate revenue. A large project or programme may come on stream in several stages. As each stage is completed, it starts to bring in revenue. If the net present value (NPV) of project revenues exceeds the NPV of project expenditures, a project is said to be profitable and shareholder value added (SVA) is greater than zero.

Cash flow

The money going out and coming in during a project creates what is called a 'cash flow'. In any given month, the project cash flow can be negative or positive. It is determined by the payments going out to consultants, contractors and suppliers, and the revenues generated as a project comes on stream. The cash flow of a project is an important indicator of the health of a project. Too much money going out too quickly and insufficient financing may mean that suppliers do not get paid and work on the project stops. If this happens and additional finance cannot be found, the project may have to be abandoned and the costs written off as sunk costs.

A time-phased plan

The preparation of a budget results in a time-phased plan summarising the planned expenditures and incomes (and therefore the cash flow) throughout the life of the project. One of the key aims of a project manager is to control the cash flow to maintain a healthy bank balance at all times, in other words to make sure that project expenditures do not outstrip project finance plus project revenues.

The budget as a yardstick

A well-designed budget makes the task of project control much easier. It is a key communication document. A detailed budget defines expected costs and expenditures, thus setting the framework of constraints within which a manager is expected to operate. These constraints represent organisational policy and goals.

The well-structured budget is a yardstick that can be used to measure the performance of organisational units and their managers. Managers who participate in the budget development process commit themselves, their subordinates and their unit's resources to the goals specified in the budget. A successful manager is one who can achieve the budget goals with the resources allocated to his or her project. Overshooting a project budget, if unchecked, can lead to a serious drain of organisational resources. This in turn can have serious consequences for the project manager and the organisation.

A good budgetary system allows the project manager to do 'what if' analyses for different project configurations. This becomes important if problems, unforeseen work or delays are incurred which threaten to increase the cost of the project. Typically, when project costs exceed an allowable margin above budget, the project is put on hold until the additional cost has been examined, justified and authorised.

A well-constructed budget enables managers to make rapid decisions about how to steer a project that is overspending back into line with baseline budgets. The budget forms an integral part of the control system that prevents project costs escalating without senior management knowledge, acceptance and approval.

Whilst having a budget is good project management practice, the Insights from Industry: 'The Sydney Opera House – success or failure?' shows that keeping a project to budget can be a major challenge that is often poorly done on large and complex projects.

Approaches to budgeting

Top-down budgeting

In top-down budgeting, senior management sets project budgets (Shtub et al., 1994). These are often fixed before any detailed project planning has taken place. The trigger for this process is usually the strategic long-range plan developed by senior management in response to their perception of the organisation's goals and constraints. The long-range plan, typically budgeted at the programme level, is then passed to the functional unit managers, business managers and project managers who develop mid-range and detailed short-range budgets.

> **insights from INDUSTRY**
>
> ## THE SYDNEY OPERA HOUSE – SUCCESS OR FAILURE?
>
> The Sydney Opera House cost 16 times more than the original budget. Was it a failure? In traditional terms of success, in which a project must meet all its cost, time and functional objectives, the Sydney Opera House failed miserably. However, it has been described as 'the other Taj Mahal' and despite all the criticism it is still in full use today. Originally estimated in 1967 to cost A$6 million, it was completed in 1973 for A$100 million. Of course the scope of the final figure was utterly different from that of those first estimates, and escalation had taken its toll. Perhaps the actual cost and time taken were the real cost and time that it should have taken to build such an ambitious development project. Interestingly, the chairman of the assessors of the project is on record as saying: 'the winning scheme is by far the cheapest to build!' He could still be right and he most certainly can never be proved wrong.
>
> The Sydney Opera House is one of many projects that highlight the importance of 'human factors' and demonstrate the considerable cost implications of not allowing project managers to 'manage'. Many of the problems in the Sydney Opera House project were created by 'committees' who sought to govern. Committee followed committee, administrative bureaucracy grew ever stronger, until Utzon, the original architect, finally left Australia in disgust. However, despite everything, the end result was a building of great grace and beauty. Was the project a success or a failure? You will have to decide for yourself.

The best combination yielding the most efficient schedule for each of the projects involved is not easy to construct, given the constraints imposed by the long-range budget. The question is how to manage the trade-offs in scheduling multiple projects in a suboptimal way. One drawback to this method of setting budgets is rooted in senior management's limited knowledge of the specifics of each project and its activities when the total project budget is set. The necessary information to overcome this problem is simply unavailable when preparing the long-range budget using the top-down approach

Bottom-up budgeting

At the other end of the spectrum is bottom-up

budgeting, in which project budgets are developed at the activity ownership level upwards. Each project manager is asked to prepare a budget proposal that supports efficient and on-schedule project execution. Based on these proposals, functional managers and business managers prepare budgets for their units, considering the resources required in each period. Finally, senior management streamlines and integrates the individual project and functional budgets into a strategic long-range organisational budget. The advantages of this approach are the clear flow of information and the use of detailed data available at the project management level. The disadvantage of the approach is that senior management has limited influence over the budgeting process (Shtub et al., 1994).

Iterative budgeting

Iterative budgeting is a dynamic process involving a two-way flow of information generated by simultaneous or cyclical top-down and bottom-up budgeting. The result is an approach that tries to integrate the two 'pure' approaches described above. Typically, senior management sets a budget framework for each year of the strategic plan. This framework then directs the selection of new projects and serves as a guideline for project managers as they prepare their own budgets. Detailed project budgets are aggregated into functional or business budgets and finally into a top-level or group budget that senior management reviews and, if necessary, modifies. Several iterations of this cycle can take place. The advantages are much better coordination, although the process can be rather time-consuming (Shtub et al., 1994). Insights

from Industry: 'Communication saves projects' highlights the critical role of communications at Boeing.

Risk and management reserve

One unfortunate reality of project management is the ever-looming threat that project costs will be exceeded. To cope with this threat, project managers commonly build some 'fat' into their cost estimates. There are two types of reserves used on projects. The contingency fund is for scope changes that were not considered as part of the original plan, whereas the management reserve is intended to compensate for inaccuracies in estimating and possibly escalation factors. One frequently used procedure is to make as realistic an estimate as possible of project costs and then to multiply this estimate by some 'fudge factor' in order to take into account possible estimating inaccuracies. Building a management reserve of 5 or 10% is typical on projects with low levels of uncertainty; with high-risk projects, the management reserve percentage may be much greater.

 No management reserve!

You work for a global bank. The group finance director has just issued a memo outlining changes to the project budgeting procedures. One item in particular catches your eye. It says: 'From now on project managers will stand by their cost estimates and not depend on the luxury of management reserve to bail them out of troubled waters.' Your project director is soliciting views of the company's project managers on this issue. What response will you make? Will you support or reject the change?

See shaded box opposite for a suggested answer.

---

insights from INDUSTRY COMMUNICATION SAVES PROJECTS

A variety of tools were used in the 767 project to develop realistic schedules and budgets and monitor them over time. One of these tools was a management visibility system, designed to surface problems before they became serious enough to cause delays. Regular communication was encouraged, even if it meant bringing bad news. John Schmick, director of planning explained:

> Early exposure of problems is not a sin at Boeing. We tend not to kill our managers for taking that approach. Here, it's much worse if you bury the problem.

When keeping to budget is seen as one of the measures of success in project management, it is a natural tendency for some project managers to want to inflate cost estimates to protect themselves and act as a cushion against adverse exposure when unforeseen events occur within a defined project scope. However, experience shows that when these inflated budgets are approved, managers frequently still use up all the allocated funds anyway, including contingency reserves, whether or not major problems occur.

There is an alternative view that it is better to try and predict costs accurately and accept that sometimes you will get it wrong, than routinely to add an extra 10–15% on top of your estimate to maintain your reputation in case of problems. A forward-thinking company will encourage this approach and not castigate a project manager every time actual costs exceed budgeted costs. Such companies are usually good at learning the reasons for costs exceeding budget and then making improvements to their project performance.

Project budgeting in action

How much detail

Part of project budgeting is about deciding how much detail to include in a project budget. The level of detail should reflect the planning horizon for which a budget is prepared. A budget prepared for a long-range plan will have less detail than one prepared for tactical short-range plans. The extra detail in the short-range plans allows a more responsive control system to operate. For example, cost overruns can be tracked down to specific activities and work packages. This enables action to be taken at a local level to correct the problem. Cost reporting at a higher level is not suitable for day-to-day project control, but may be sufficient for senior managers who wish to be kept informed on overall progress.

Creating a budget structure

Another important aspect of project budgeting is the ease with which project budgets can be integrated within the existing financial structure in an organisation. A project budget that is compatible with existing systems and uses the same cost codes when aggregating costs should merge more easily with an existing system. The importance of being able to do this increases dramatically in a multiproject environment, when the overall effect of several projects on company cash flow is an important variable for senior managers to control.

Generating a time-phased budget

The simplest approach to budgeting is to estimate the expected costs associated with each activity and milestone. Based on the project schedule, these costs are assigned specific dates and a time-phased budget can be generated. It may be only a partial budget because some of the indirect costs are usually not included at the preliminary stage. Typical indirect costs (overheads) are those for management, facilities, fees, taxes, inflation, quality control and project management support. These costs are not always related to specific activities. However, adding these costs to the budget results in a more complete project budget.

The budgeting process should consider the information needs of the different project stakeholders – who may measure project costs in different ways and at different times. For example, the cost of materials may be measured when committed, ordered, delivered, incurred or recorded for accounting purposes.

Life cycle costing

The budgeting process should also consider the effect of budgeting decisions on the cost of using the end product. For example, limiting the number of design reviews may reduce the cost of the project at the expense of an increase in the sponsor's operating costs. This broader view of project cost management is often called 'life cycle costing'.

Suppliers

Suppliers on a project are a temporary extension of the performing organisation. Good supplier management is essential and includes managing the timing of suppliers' involvement, the integration of their knowledge and expertise into the planning phase,

suggested ANSWER

The proposed change draws attention to a typical trade-off in project management – cost of estimating versus estimating accuracy. Your thinking may go something like this. You know from experience that the costs of some activities are easy to estimate – there are historical figures that have proved their worth, time and time again. No problem here.

Other activities, however, are less easy to predict. You recall a management information system project where the estimated cost was based on the expected number of lines of computer program code. This had given good results on some earlier projects, but in this project, assumptions had been made about the reuse of large 'chunks' of existing code – to save time and money. But the project hit problems when the integration of the new code with the existing code proved troublesome. In the end it required significant overtime and a consultant to resolve. With this experience to go by, you are more likely to fight your corner and lobby for the continued use of management reserve.

To your dismay, the finance director makes the changes anyway. So, from now on, project mangers are instructed to put in realistic, that is, uninflated, cost estimates for projects and monitor their progress carefully.

establishing effective and appropriate communication channels, and providing suppliers with the same quality assurance checks and services that apply to the rest of the project organisation.

This activity needs to be costed and added to the budget like any other. It is easy to disregard supplier management as an unnecessary luxury, but the consequences of so doing can be severe or even catastrophic. It is the project manager's responsibility to advise the sponsor on the value and importance of effective supplier management. Insights from Industry: 'Take good care of your suppliers' shows the care and attention given to suppliers at Boeing.

TAKE GOOD CARE OF YOUR SUPPLIERS

A complete Boeing 767 consists of 3.1 million parts, supplied by 1,300 vendors. Boeing has a policy of working closely with all its subcontractors, from initial planning to final delivery:

> Generally, at Boeing we do not contract with suppliers and then walk away. We feel responsible for them and have to make it work. This was especially true of the 767 programme participants. Because the content of their work was so significant, a failure would have precluded our ability to salvage an industrial operation of this size.

Major budgeting processes

Project budgeting includes the following major processes, the first three being discussed in detail in this chapter:

- *Resource planning* – determining what physical resources (people, equipment, materials) and what quantities of each resource should be used to perform project activities
- *Cost estimating* – developing an approximation of the costs of the resources needed to complete project activities
- *Cost budgeting* – relating cost estimates to schedule and producing time-phased cost and cash flow projections
- *Cost control* – controlling cost in relation to schedule and changes to the project budget (see Chapter 10).

Financial reporting systems

You have recently joined the executive team of Knowledge plc, a relatively new company experiencing rapid growth in the development and management of knowledge systems. Your role is project director. Today you have a meeting with the company's finance director and wish to put forward a budget structure to be used for all new projects. The system you are proposing has been specifically designed to integrate with the existing financial reporting system used by the company.

In the meeting the financial director tells you he can see no need for your project budget structure. In his opinion the company's existing structure will suffice. It already tracks labour costs, equipment costs (ten different categories here), and has many other cost codes for tracking expenditure.

What should you do? Should you:

1. accept defeat gracefully and manage your projects using the existing system only?
2. discuss the difficulties of managing projects using the company's system alone, and explain again how you intend to integrate the project budget structure with the existing financial reporting system so that the two will operate as a single system with no duplication of effort?
3. leave the company – after all you have had offers from two other companies?

See shaded box for a suggested answer.

---

1. You know that this option will only lead to problems and difficulty controlling projects. There will be no easy way to isolate problem areas within a project and your reputation as project manager will almost certainly deteriorate over time.
2. This is by far the best option available. You can explain the reason for needing a detailed project-based budgeting system in order to track, monitor and control performance in all project areas and not just to serve as a financial accounting system. Your proposed system can actually be integrated with the company's existing system, so that the various detailed project levels can be aggregated up level by level until they do align with the existing financial reporting system.
3. This option might work, but you may find the same problems recurring all over again.

Resource planning

Resource planning involves determining what physical resources (people, equipment, materials) and what quantities of each should be used to perform project activities. It must be closely coordinated with cost estimating.

Expert judgement will often be required to assess the inputs to this process. Such expertise may be provided by any group or individual with specialised knowledge or training and is available from many sources including:

- Activity owners (the people who will do the work during project implementation)
- Knowledge workers from other units within the performing organisation
- Consultants
- Professional and technical associations
- Industry groups.

Assigning resources to activities enables resource histograms to be constructed. By plotting resource needs, for example manpower requirements, against time, it is easy to see when specific resources are overallocated and in which periods the available resources are underutilised. This topic was covered earlier in this chapter, under 'Adding people and optimising the schedule'.

Cost estimating

Cost estimating involves developing an approximation (quantitative assessment) of the costs of the resources needed to complete project activities.

Costs must be estimated for all resources that will be charged to the project. This includes, but is not limited to, labour, materials, supplies and special categories

such as an inflation allowance or management reserve. Cost estimates often benefit from being refined during the course of the project to reflect additional detail that becomes available as time goes on. Insights from Industry: 'Learning … the price of success' shows the effect of learning in airplane budgets at Boeing.

When a project is performed under contract, care should be taken to distinguish cost estimating from pricing. Cost estimating involves developing an assessment of how much will it cost the performing organisation to provide the product or service involved. Pricing is a business decision – how much will the performing organisation charge for the product or service – that uses the cost estimate as but one consideration of many.

Cost estimating includes identifying and considering various costing alternatives. For example, in most application areas, additional work during the development phase is widely held to have the potential for reducing the cost of the implementation phase. The cost estimating process must consider whether the expected savings will offset the cost of the additional development work.

Tools and techniques for cost estimating

Analogous estimating (or top-down estimating)

This method uses the actual cost of a previous, similar project as the basis for estimating the cost of the current project. It is frequently used to estimate total project costs when there is a limited amount of detailed information about the project (for example in the early phases). Analogous estimating is a form of expert judgement. It is generally less costly than other techniques, but also generally less accurate. It is most reliable when the previous projects are similar in fact and not just in appearance, and the individuals or groups preparing the estimates have the required expertise.

Parametric estimating

Parametric estimating involves using project characteristics, such as weight, volume, lines of software code and so on, to predict project costs. Models may be simple or complex. Both the cost and accuracy of parametric models vary widely. They are most likely to be reliable when the historical information used to develop the model is accurate, the characteristics are readily quantifiable and it is scaleable (that is, it

PARAMETRIC COST ESTIMATING

Once the basic 767 design was established, costs could be estimated using a parametric estimating technique. This method, adapted by Boeing, had been developed by the New Airplane Programme study group from comparisons of the 707, 727, 737, and 747. It predicted the costs of a new plane from design characteristics, such as weight, speed and length, and historical relationships, such as the number of parts per airplane, that were known well in advance of production.

The critical calculation involved assembly labour hours. Managers began with data from a benchmark (and profitable) programme, the 727, and noted, for every major section of the plane, the number of labour hours per pound required to build the first unit. That number was then multiplied by the expected weight of the same section of the 767; this result, in turn, was multiplied by a factor that reflected Boeing's historical experience in improving the relationship between labour hours and weight as it moved to the next generation airplane. Totalling the results for all plane sections provided an estimate of the labour hours required to build the first 767. A learning curve was then applied to estimate the number of labour hours required to build subsequent planes.

works for a large project as well as small ones). Insurance companies use parametric estimating techniques based on the area of 'living space' to estimate the cost of rebuilding houses. Insights from Industry: 'Parametric cost estimating' reveals how this estimating technique is used at Boeing.

Definitive estimating (or bottom-up estimating)

This technique involves estimating the cost of individual work items, then rolling up the individual estimates to get a project total. The cost and accuracy of bottom-up estimating are generally higher than for other techniques. The project management team must weigh the additional accuracy against the additional cost. Building contractors use bottom-up estimating to prepare detailed bills of quantities before tendering for work.

Cost budgeting

Cost budgeting involves relating individual cost estimates at the work package level to the project schedule to produce projections of expenditure against time. Payment milestones (dates for release of funds from client and payment of subcontractors) can be used to produce projections of cash flow.

The work breakdown structure (WBS) and organisational breakdown structure (OBS) (introduced in Chapter 8) can be combined to form a cost breakdown structure (CBS) (see Figure 9.16). The cost breakdown structure forms the basis of the cost reporting structure for the project. The building blocks for the CBS are called 'control accounts'.

A control account (or cost account) represents a unit of work for which a particular resource unit has sole responsibility to deliver on time, to budget and in accordance with the scope and quality described in the project plan. Each control account appears separately in the budget reporting structure. A control account provides cost control information on work packages for project monitoring and control. A large project will often have hundreds or thousands of control accounts. Control account data are collected and entered into a cost and schedule control system on a computer. The computer software can then perform various calculations and comparisons to determine how the project is progressing with respect to the project plan.

The purpose of a control account is to provide an objective, reliable and systematic method to monitor and control the progress of all the work packages in a project. A whole new discipline called 'earned value analysis' (EVA) has evolved to help project managers in this area. See Chapter 10 for more details of this approach.

A rolling-wave planning horizon is used so that every time the mid-range budget is updated, a budget for the next quarter is added while the budget for the recently completed quarter is deleted.

 A question of detail

You have been assigned programme manager on a group-wide business process re-engineering programme, and are putting together a cost breakdown structure to support the project. Your two assistant planners give you conflicting advice.

The first planner says:

The CBS is created by integrating the WBS with the OBS in such way that *every* item used in the project is represented

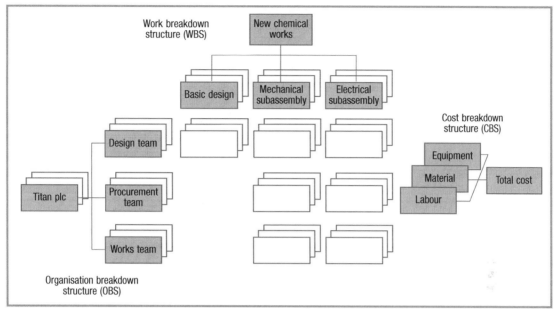

Figure 9.16 Cost breakdown structure (CBS)

in a matrix, no matter how small or trivial it may seem. If we use it, then it must be costed and appear in the CBS.

The second planner says:

The CBS, like the WBS and OBS that are used to create it, is a tool to help communicate, manage and control cost and budget aspects of the project. We should include only as much detail as needed to monitor and control cost. This will save us time and provide us with a more manageable and useful system.

What should you do?

See shaded box for a suggested answer.

S-curves

Cost projections created during the budgeting process are frozen before project implementation starts. They form the baselines for control and performance measurement of the project. Baseline cost projections can be aggregated to higher levels of the WBS for reporting purposes, and used to generate S-curves for visual representation in the project plan and progress reports. An example of an S-curve is shown in Figure 9.17.

An S-curve shows cumulative project cost against time. The S-curve is so named because of its

suggested
ANSWER

After careful thought, you take the advice of the second planner. The CBS does not need to catalogue *every* item separately. This would create a huge and unwieldy document, difficult to read and useless for effective reporting. What you are looking for is a method of identifying which work packages are not progressing as planned – which units are overspending and why – and which areas of the project seem to be causing delays.

You agree that every item needs to be costed and should be accountable, but that the level of breakdown of the CBS should stop at the most appropriate level to control the project, probably the work package level.

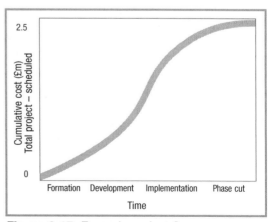

Figure 9.17 Example project S-curve

stretched S-shape. The reason for this shape relates to the project life cycle (see Figure 2.7). Expenditure begins relatively slowly on a project as initial plans are discussed and sketched out. Once a solution is fixed, its development takes place and the rate of expenditure steadily rises. During implementation, the rate of expenditure is at its highest. Eventually, as the project nears completion, activity subsides and the S-curve slope decreases, reaching zero at project closure.

Budgeting decisions made during the early phases of a project typically have their biggest impact during implementation. A poorly structured budget is a hostage to fortune, serving to hinder and obstruct effective control.

Cash flow projections

With the creation of project S-curves, cash flow analysis can be performed and the feasibility of the budget tested. If the resulting cash flow is not acceptable, it is possible to modify the schedule, for example by delaying or bringing forward activities that have float. Projects with large numbers of activities tend to have greater schedule flexibility.

An organisation that tries to avoid the risk of delays may budget its projects according to an early start schedule, which may in turn lead to relatively high expenditures in the project's earlier stages and subsequent cash flow problems. By comparison, a late start schedule results in relatively high expenditures in the later stages.

The choice between an early and a late start schedule affects the risk level associated with the project's on-time completion. Using a late start schedule means that all the activities are started as late as possible without any slack to buffer against

uncertainty, increasing the probability of detrimental delays. The project manager should perform a trade-off analysis of a schedule overrun and a budget overspend.

Creating a cash flow and S-curve

Consider the project defined by the dependencies in Table 9.7, which also shows the estimated costs for each activity. An early start Gantt chart, showing the float envelopes of the noncritical activities, is shown in Figure 9.18.

Cash flows can be generated for this project in both the early start position (as depicted in the Gantt chart of Figure 9.18) and the late start position (assuming the noncritical activities all start as late as possible, using any float available).

Table 9.7 Dependency table showing activity costs			
Activity	Dependencies	Duration (weeks)	Cost (£1,000)
A	–	5	1.5
B	–	3	3.0
C	A, B	8	3.3
D	A	7	4.2
E	–	7	5.7
F	C, D, E	4	6.1
G	F	5	7.2
Total			31.0

Source: Adapted from Shtub et al., 1994.

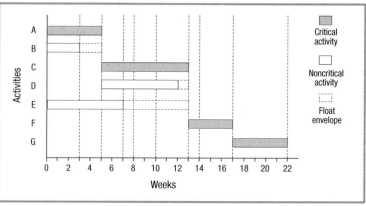

Figure 9.18 Gantt chart showing float envelopes (Adapted from Shtub et al., 1994)

 Project cash flows

Using the Gantt chart to help you, complete the early start cash flow shown below in Table 9.8. The shaded boxes should remain blank. The first two rows have already been completed.

Table 9.8 Part of the early start cash flow for project defined by Table 9.7

| Week | Activity | | | | | | | Weekly cost | Cumulative cost |
	A	B	C	D	E	F	G		
1	300	1,000			814.3			2,114	2,114
2	300	1,000			814.3			2,114	4,229
3									
4									
5									
6									
7									
8									
9									
10									
11									
12									
13									
14									
15									
16									
17									
18									
19									
20									
21									
22									
Total									

Source: Adapted from Shtub et al., 1994.

Now complete the late start cash flow shown in Table 9.9. This time you will need to reposition all the noncritical activities in their latest start position before generating the cash flow. Once again the shaded boxes should remain blank and the first two rows have been completed for you.

Table 9.9 Part of the late start cash flow for project defined by Table 9.7

Week	Activity A	B	C	D	E	F	G	Weekly cost	Cumulative cost
1	300							300	300
2	300							300	600
3									
4									
5									
6									
7									
8									
9									
10									
11									
12									
13									
14									
15									
16									
17									
18									
19									
20									
21									
22									
Total									

Source: Adapted from Shtub et al., 1994.

Compare your completed cash flows with those in Tables 9.10 and 9.11

The completed early start and late start cash flows are presented in Tables 9.10 and 9.11 respectively.

Table 9.10 Completed early start cash flow for project defined by Table 9.7

Week	Activity							Weekly cost	Cumulative cost
	A	B	C	D	E	F	G		
1	300	1,000			814.3			2,114	2,114
2	300	1,000			814.3			2,114	4,229
3	300	1,000			814.3			2,114	6,343
4	300				814.3			1,114	7,457
5	300				814.3			1,114	8,571
6			412.5	600	814.3			1,827	10,398
7			412.5	600	814.3			1,827	12,225
8			412.5	600				1,013	13,238
9			412.5	600				1,013	14,250
10			412.5	600				1,013	15,263
11			412.5	600				1,013	16,275
12			412.5	600				1,013	17,288
13			412.5					412	17,700
14						1,525		1,525	19,225
15						1,525		1,525	20,750
16						1,525		1,525	22,275
17						1,525		1,525	23,800
18							1,440	1,440	25,240
19							1,440	1,440	26,680
20							1,440	1,440	28,120
21							1,440	1,440	29,560
22							1,440	1,440	31,000
Total	1,500	3,000	3,300	4,200	5,700	6,100	7,200	31,000	

Source: Adapted from Shtub et al., 1994.

Table 9.11 Completed late start cash flow for project defined by Table 9.7

Week	A	B	C	D	E	F	G	Weekly cost	Cumulative cost
1	300							300	300
2	300							300	600
3	300	1,000						1,300	1,900
4	300	1,000						1,300	3,200
5	300	1,000						1,300	4,500
6			412.5					412	4,913
7			412.5	600	814.3			1,827	6,739
8			412.5	600	814.3			1,827	8,566
9			412.5	600	814.3			1,827	10,393
10			412.5	600	814.3			1,827	12,220
11			412.5	600	814.3			1,827	14,046
12			412.5	600	814.3			1,827	15,873
13			412.5	600	814.3			1,827	17,700
14						1,525		1,525	19,225
15						1,525		1,525	20,750
16						1,525		1,525	22,275
17						1,525		1,525	23,800
18							1,440	1,440	25,240
19							1,440	1,440	26,680
20							1,440	1,440	28,120
21							1,440	1,440	29,560
22							1,440	1,440	31,000
Total	1,500	3,000	3,300	4,200	5,700	6,100	7,200	31,000	31,000

Source: Adapted from Shtub et al., 1994.

Figure 9.19 shows the weekly cash flow plots for both early start and late start cash flows. The S-curves are shown in Figure 9.20.

In addition to using the project schedule as part of the budgeting process, another option may be available – reduce the duration of the critical path. So far we have assumed that each activity is performed in the most economical way. That is, the combination of resources assigned to each activity is assumed to be selected to minimise the total cost of performing that activity. However, in many cases it is possible to reduce a project's duration by spending more money on the critical path activities (this is called crashing, see earlier in this chapter). The project manager must decide how far to crash a project (if at all).

For each activity, there is a relationship between duration (time) and cost, such as the (simplified) time-cost plot, shown in Figure 9.21. In this case, the plot is simply based on two points: the *normal* point and the *crash* point. The former gives the cost and time involved when the activity is performed in the normal way without extra resources, such as overtime, special materials or improved equipment that could speed things up. By contrast, the crash point gives the time and cost when the activity is fully expedited, that is, no cost is spared to reduce its duration as much as possible.

In some instances, a schedule based on normal durations may produce high indirect costs, for example when a project is going to overrun and a

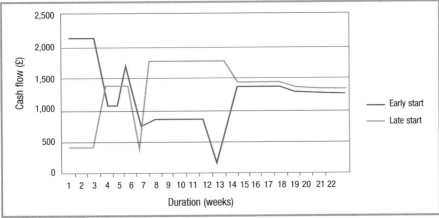

Figure 9.19 Weekly cash flow plots for early and late start schedules
(Adapted from Shtub et al., 1994)

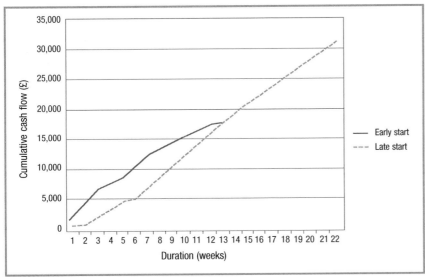

Figure 9.20 S-curves for early and late start schedules (Adapted from Shtub et al., 1994)

penalty is charged for completion after the due date. The resultant penalties must be traded off with the cost of shortening the duration of some of the activities to minimise (or avoid completely) these late charges.

A similar situation occurs when a fixed overhead is charged for a project's duration. Rent for facilities would be such an example. In this case, the project manager might consider shortening some of the critical activities to reduce the project's duration and hence save on indirect costs.

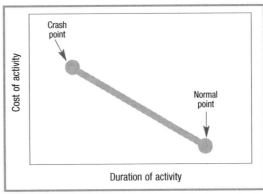

Figure 9.21 Time-cost relationship for project activities (Adapted from Shtub et al., 1994)

TIME out Optimising duration for minimum cost

Budgeting decisions are easier when the time-cost relationship for project activities is known. This exercise requires you to analyse the trade-off between direct and indirect costs for a project.

Suppose that a fixed overhead of £500 per week is charged for a project's duration. Further, assume that the project is due in 18 weeks and that a penalty of £1,000 per week will be imposed starting at the 19th week. The problem you are faced with is to conduct a trade-off analysis between the cost of crashing and the indirect costs of overhead plus penalty. Table 9.12 summarises the three cost components for the normal duration of 22 weeks, and each crash duration down to and including 14 weeks. Figure 9.22 illustrates the same information graphically.

Your task is to choose the best duration for this project.

To do the exercise you will need to complete the total cost column shown in Table 9.12. Add this information to the graph in Figure 9.22. You should now be able to find the project length giving the least total project cost.

See shaded box for a suggested answer.

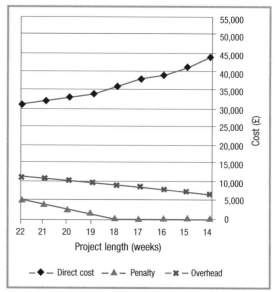

Figure 9.22 Graphical plots of cost data at normal and crash durations (Adapted from Shtub et al., 1994)

Table 9.12 Cost data at normal and crash durations				
Project length (weeks)	Direct cost of activities	Late completion penalty	Overhead cost	Total project cost
22	31,000	4,000	11,000	46,000
21	32,000	3,000	10,000	
20	33,000	2,000	10,500	
19	34,000	1,000	9,500	
18	36,000	0	9,000	
17	38,000	0	8,500	
16	39,000	0	8,000	
15	41,000	0	7,500	
14	44,000	0	7,000	
All costs are in £				

Source: adapted from: Shtub et al., 1994.

suggested ANSWER

The completed table and graph are shown in Table 9.13 and Figure 9.23 respectively.

The minimum cost occurs at a project length of 19 weeks, that is, it is more economical to pay a penalty of £1,000 and an overhead of £500 for the 19th week than to crash activity F for £2,000. Of course, the total project cost may not be the only criterion for budget planning. If, for example, customer satisfaction depends on project completion within 18 weeks, the £500 savings should be evaluated against the customer goodwill that might be otherwise lost. Budgeting decisions should be based on a full evaluation.

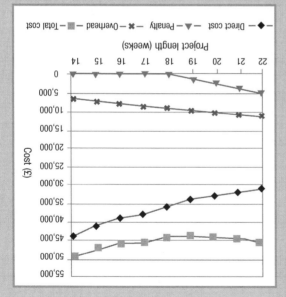

Figure 9.23 Completed graph for exercise showing total cost curve (Adapted from Shtub et al., 1994)

Table 9.13 Completed table for exercise (showing total costs)

Project length (weeks)	Direct cost of activities	Late completion penalty	Overhead cost	Total project cost
14	44,000	0	7,000	51,000
15	41,000	0	7,500	48,500
16	39,000	0	8,000	47,000
17	38,000	0	8,500	46,500
18	36,000	0	9,000	45,000
19	34,000	1,000	9,500	44,500
20	33,000	2,000	10,500	45,000
21	32,000	3,000	10,000	45,500
22	31,000	4,000	11,000	46,000

All costs are in £

Source: Adapted from Shtub et al. (1994).

Albion Sugar Company

Introduction

The Albion Sugar Company, situated in the Caribbean, has been in operation since 1948 and supplies both the domestic and export markets. The company is among the larger manufacturers of sugar in the CARICOM region and also operates a distillery that supplies local companies and foreign markets. In 1976, the government acquired majority shares in the company and made it a subsidiary of the National Sugar Company. A simplified process flow diagram summarising the company's operations is shown in Figure 9.24.

Although the company enjoys the advantage of a virtual monopoly over the domestic market for refined sugar, government control on the selling price and increasing operating costs have combined to erode its profit margins. In the overseas markets, the company enjoys protection by virtue of the quota allocated to the government through the Lomé Convention. In recent years, however, the negotiated prices have not been very attractive and the depressed open market prices have limited the company's options on the marketing side.

In an effort to arrest declining profitability, the company's management has embarked on a critical examination of all aspects of its operations in the hope of identifying areas for realising increased sales revenues or achieving cost savings.

Current operations

The company employs some 900 management and nonmanagement workers. Sugar processing is seasonal as the raw material (sugar cane) is available only during the six-month reaping season, January–June. During the remaining months, the factory equipment undergoes extensive maintenance to ensure its reliability during the grinding season.

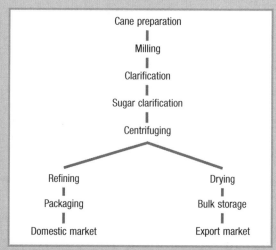

Figure 9.24 Simplified process flow diagram

At present, the distillery also has to be shut down between July and December as it is dependent on low-pressure process steam being supplied from the boilers in the main sugar factory. Because of the prevailing high prices for alcohol, the continuous operation of the distillery throughout the year seemed to offer potential for increasing the company's profitability.

The proposal

Following an engineering economic analysis, the company decided to purchase a 15 tonne/hr, 1 bar, saturated steam boiler to supply the distillery with process steam from July to December when the main factory would be out of operation. Molasses, the raw material needed to manufacture alcohol, would be imported during that period.

After a review of quotations received from boiler equipment manufacturers, the company awarded the contract to a USA-based firm with a well-proven reputation. Its equipment was moderately priced, met the required technical specifications and had the shortest delivery time.

The package boiler was due to arrive in mid-July and the company's management recognised the need to install the unit as quickly as possible to minimise the disruption to alcohol produc-

tion. The following decisions were made:

1. The chief engineer would be responsible for the satisfactory installation and commissioning of the boiler.
2. The installation would be done by company personnel. This was possible since the sugar crop would be finished and work crews could be made available as required from the factory's maintenance personnel.
3. The boiler installation should be phased in with the factory's scheduled 'out-of-crop' maintenance programme. Department managers should be notified in advance when the subordinate maintenance staff would have to be diverted to the installation project.
4. The project should be completed by mid-October, that is, three months after the arrival of the boiler. Sales commitments would be based on this expected date of completion.
5. Unnecessary costs should be avoided. The company was in an unhealthy financial position and could not afford cost slippages in the project budget.

Initial project planning

The project manager assigned responsibility for the boiler installation decided

Job name	Description	Immediate predecessor	Duration (days)*
	Table 9.14 Job list for boiler installation		
A	Excavation of foundations (boiler, feed water tank, oil tank)	start	7
B	Excavation of chimney foundation	start	3
C	Laying out – steam line to process	start	21
D	Laying out of main power cable from substation	start	21
E	Construction of electrical panels and distribution gear	D	21
F	Make electrical connections on boiler	E	15
G	Prepare steel matting for boiler foundation	A	5
H	Prepare steel matting for tank foundation	A	10
I	Prepare steel matting for chimney foundation	B	15
J	Cast all foundations after matting is completed	G, H, I	4
K	Allow concrete to set for 28 days	J	28
L	Construct chimney	K	21
M	Install feed and fuel tanks	K	3
N	Remove and reinstall existing fuel tank	O	3
O	Place boiler on foundation, level and grout	K	3
P	Attach gauges, oil and steam valves, sight glasses, high- and low-level alarms and relief valves	O	7
Q	Place flue gas ducting, forced-draught fan, induced draught fan into position	C	15
R	Connect flue gas duct to chimney	L, Q	3
S	Install feed and chemical closing pumps	M, N	21
T	Connect pipes and dosing lines	P	14
U	Test boiler	F, R, S, T	2

*Based on an 8-hour work day and a 'normal' crew size.

to use Microsoft Project to assist in planning and controlling the project. After reviewing the technical information available on the boiler and discussing the project with the maintenance foremen, he prepared a list of all the jobs required for the project and their immediate predecessors. This included an estimated time for completion of each job (see Table 9.14). From this information, a project network could be created to show the order in which the jobs could be done and identify the critical path, which indicates the shortest time in which the project could be completed and any near-critical activities that should also be closely monitored.

Resource-constrained project planning

The project engineer was well aware that the installation would have to proceed within the following resource constraints (see Table 9.15):

- Only two welders would be allowed at any time
- Only three pipe fitters would be released at any time
- Only three electricians would be available to work on the project
- Only one crane would be available and hence only one crane operator would be needed
- Only three mechanics could be released by the maintenance department
- There would be no limitations on labourers as substitutes would be readily available.

Table 9.15 Normal resource requirement

Job name	Normal duration (days)	Resource requirements					
		Electricians	Pipe fitters	Welders	Crane operators	Mechanics	Labourers
A	7	–	–	–	–	–	4
B	3	–	–	–	–	–	2
C	21	–	2	2	1	–	2
D	21	3	–	–	–	–	2
E	21	3	–	1	–	1	2
F	15	3	–	1	–	–	2
G	5	–	–	–	–	–	3
H	10	–	–	–	–	–	3
I	15	–	–	–	–	–	4
J	4	–	–	–	–	–	4
K	28	–	–	–	–	–	1
L	21	–	–	2	1	–	3
M	3	–	–	1	1	–	2
N	3	–	–	1	1	–	2
O	3	–	–	–	1	–	2
P	7	2	2	–	–	2	1
Q	15	–	–	1	1	2	2
R	3	–	–	2	1	–	2
S	21	–	2	–	–	3	2
T	14	–	2	–	–	2	2
U	2	–	–	–	–	–	–
Maximum resource availability		3	3	2	1	3	No constraint

Project crashing

The 'normal' time estimated to complete certain jobs could be reduced to a minimum or 'crash' time by allocating additional resources at the same hourly rate and incurring extra direct costs. Table 9.16 lists these jobs and summarises their normal and crash times and direct costs. Decisions would have to be made on whether the extra costs of crashing specific jobs would be justified by the additional benefits associated with early project completion. It is also possible that some workers may be prepared to work overtime at evenings (time and a half rate) or weekends (double time rate).

Table 9.16 Normal and crash activity durations and direct costs

Activity	Normal		If crashing used	
	duration (days)	cost (£)	minimum duration (days)	cost (£) to achieve minimum duration
F	15	2,240	12	2,465
G	5	250	4	275
H	10	504	7	579
I	15	1,000	10	1,175
L	21	2.900	15	3,290
P	7	1,240	5	1,410
S	21	3,480	18	3,720
T	14	1,930	10	2,190

Estimated indirect project costs – £100/day

ASSIGNMENT TO AID UNDERSTANDING AND DISCUSSION

You have been appointed project manager for the boiler installation project and have been asked by the operations director to give a PowerPoint presentation of the feasibility of this project at the next management board meeting. The presentation must provide data, charts, analysis and interpretations of the following:

1. Network diagram and early start Gantt chart to identify the critical path (and any near-critical activities), project start and end dates, activity floats.

2. Summary resource histograms for all project resources to show resource conflicts in the early start schedule.

3. Resource smoothing and full resource levelling options.

4. Project crashing options.

Summary points

- Estimating, scheduling and budgeting are key management processes that inform decision makers how best to manage a project throughout the execution phase.
- Scheduling is about sequencing project activities and milestones into a sensible and logical order to aid project execution and control.
- There are three ways to estimate activity durations: use historical data, time the activity, use a probabilistic method.
- When constructing project networks, activities are represented by boxes which are connected with arrows. Activity boxes that are drawn in series imply a precedence relationship, for example A must finish before B can start.
- There are four basic precedence relationships: finish-to-start, start-to-start, finish-to-finish and start-to-finish.
- The most challenging aspect of creating a network is getting the relationships between the activities defined correctly.
- The critical path is defined as the path through the network having the longest duration; activities on the critical path are called critical activities.
- If a critical activity overruns, the project will also overrun unless corrective action is taken such as project crashing.

- Float is a measure of the amount of time an activity can be delayed without affecting the end date of the project.
- When an activity has only a small amount of float relative to the duration of the project, it is said to be 'near critical' and should be monitored closely by the project manager, in a similar way to the critical activities.
- Network analysis is used to determine the expected project duration, the critical activities and critical path, the float of noncritical activities and any near-critical activities.
- A milestone is a significant event in a project which often marks the completion of an important stage in the project. Milestones are not activities and so have zero duration.
- A Gantt chart is a scheduling tool that is easy to interpret which uses activity bars and a timeline to show where activities start and finish. It can also be embellished to show activity relationships, milestones, float and progress information.
- Resource smoothing is a limited form of levelling that involves rescheduling noncritical activities within their float envelopes; it does not affect the expected project duration.
- Full resource levelling removes all overallocation of resources. It may result in an extended project duration and a new critical path due to resource constraints.
- Project management software can be used to help plan and control a project.
- Project budgets are used by managers to fix in advance the resources that a project will use and enable control during project execution.
- The budget forms an integral part of the control system that prevents project costs escalating without senior management knowledge, acceptance and approval.
- Managers who participate in the budget development process commit themselves, their subordinates and their unit's resources to the goals specified in the budget.
- The progress status of a project cannot be determined without reference to *both* schedule and budget.
- Key concepts in budgeting are expenditures, revenues and cash flow.
- Three approaches to establishing a budget are top-down, bottom-up and iterative.
- A contingency fund is money available for scope changes that were not considered as part of the original plan. The contingency fund is not part of the project budget.
- A management reserve is included in the budget to compensate for inaccuracies in estimating and escalation factors. It is typically 5 or 10% of the budget.
- Resource planning involves determining what physical resources (people, equipment, materials) and what quantities of each should be used to perform project activities.
- Cost estimating techniques include analogous estimating, parametric estimating and definitive estimating.
- Cost budgeting involves relating individual cost estimates at the work package level to the project schedule to produce projections of expenditure against time.
- A control account is allocated to each work package or group of related work packages and represents a unit of work for which a particular resource unit has sole responsibility to deliver on time, to budget and in accordance with the project plan.
- A control account provides cost control information for project monitoring and control.
- Cost projections created during the budgeting process are frozen before project implementation starts. They form the baselines for control and performance measurement.
- Baseline cost projections can be aggregated to higher levels of the work breakdown structure for reporting purposes and used to generate S-curves for visual representation in the project plan and progress reports.
- Multiproject environments are considerably more complex and difficult to manage; they require greater software capability and more sophisticated decision-making tools.
- In a multiproject environment, time, resources and benefits are managed interdependently to optimise at the portfolio level rather than at an individual project level.

Visit the website

http://www.palgrave.com/business/gardiner

▶ to test your understanding of the learning objectives for Chapter 9 using multiple choice questions

In the next chapter we will consider project control issues along with special considerations for project closure, project evaluation and the determinants of project success and failure.

References

Gardiner, P.D. and Stewart, K. (2000). 'Revisiting the golden triangle of cost, time and quality: the role of NPV in project control, success and failure', *International Journal of Project Management*, **18**(4): 251–6.

Goldratt, E.M. (1997). *Critical Chain*, North River Press, Great Barrington, MA.

Morris, P.W.G. (1994). *The Management of Projects*, Thomas Telford, London.

Shtub, A., Bard, J.F. and Globerson, S. (1994). *Project Management: Engineering, Technology, and Implementation*, Prentice Hall, Englewood Cliffs, NJ.

Steyn, H. (2001). 'An investigation into the fundamentals of critical chain project scheduling', *International Journal of Project Management*, **19**(6): 363–9.

Visit the website

http://www.palgrave.com/business/gardiner

▶ for additional resources to explore the topics in this chapter further

10

Control, closure and continuous improvement

Learning objectives

After reading this chapter you should be able to:

- explain the difference between monitoring and control
- identify appropriate variables to measure in project control
- design a control system for a given project
- explain the purpose of and describe a process for change management in a project
- apply a variety of project control methods
- discuss the importance and benefits of project closure
- explain the purpose of a final project review
- discuss reasons for project success and failure
- explain the principles of critical chain project management
- identify several approaches to continuous improvement

Introduction

All the plans developed in the early project phases are implemented during project execution, including those made to control the project and ensure that the best (or near-best) outcome is the one eventually delivered. In project management, control is based on a comparison of baseline plans and contracts with actual events, and deciding what to do (that is, replanning) when the two do not match (IPMA, 1999: 49). Project control and replanning activities are applied to the control of cost, schedule, scope, quality, safety and any contracts placed with external contributors. All the information generated during initiation, scheduling, budgeting and procurement planning become inputs for the control phase.

In this chapter, the concept of change and the way in which change is managed in a project is also examined, including the phenomena of scope creep and scope leap. Consideration is given to the use of project plans and progress updates to manage the project towards completion. Both simple and more advanced methods of control are presented and discussed, for example the use of minuted progress meetings and action lists, Gantt charts, milestone monitoring and earned value analysis.

The roles of testing and commissioning in a project are considered, as are project closure activities, leading to the formal end of a project. Post-project review and evaluation are examined with reference to knowledge management and the learning organisation; while a look at the determinants of project success and failure reveals that human factor issues account for more project failures than any other cause.

Continuous improvement is an important aspect of project management for all organisations that engage regularly in project work. A variety of approaches to performance improvement are mentioned, including benchmarking, maturity models, the EFQM excellence model and the balanced scorecard. The role of associations and institutions in continuous improvement is also considered.

Project monitoring and control

When project plans have been approved and signed off, the project team is ready to begin implementing the project. Simply stated, implementation is the execution of the project plan, while project monitoring is about collecting sufficient data to make sure that the project team implements the plan correctly. Project control is the process of ensuring that the project delivers everything it is supposed to – physical products and assets, quality products, documentation and deliverables – such that there is complete assurance on delivery integrity (APM, 2000: 35; ISO 10007, 1995). It is closely related to change management and configuration management (IPMA, 1999: 46).

The elements that make up project monitoring are focused on the:

- selection of control measures
- observation of activities
- collection of control data
- comparison of control data with planning information, such as that contained in schedule, budget and risk management plans.

Performance deviations from the plan are documented and form the basis of corrective project control decisions and actions. The approach is derived from cybernetics – the science of communication and control (APM, 2000: 25)

Project control systems

Project control can be exercised through formal or informal mechanisms. Small projects performed by small teams located in the same place under a single organisational unit may not need a formal control system. This is frequently the case when members of the team are highly motivated and communicate well with each other. Examples of such projects can be found in churches, schools, universities, community action groups and usually involve relatively simple projects.

The decision to introduce a formal control system and the selection of a specific system should be based largely on two aspects of the project – the risk involved and the cost of the control system and its expected benefits.

High-risk situations, where the probability of undesired outcomes is significant due to the complexity of the project, the environmental conditions or other factors, and where the cost associated with such undesired outcomes is high, justify the investment in a formal, well-designed control system.

Project control systems compare actual cost and progress to planned cost and progress as laid down in the baseline cost curves and baseline schedule charts.

Control limits

Control limits are established for important parameters and any deviations outside these limits are flagged. Corrective action is taken when the deviations are considered significant. The ad hoc nature of

many projects often leads to the adoption of control limits that are based on intuition and qualitative risk analysis rather than historical data, as is the case in statistical process control.

The need for an upper control limit is to prevent budget overruns which is a common goal for projects. Actual expenditures below budget are also monitored since they might signal a delay in performing some activities (this lower control limit is important for the detection of delays in noncritical activities that are not monitored by some control systems).

Effectiveness of project control systems

The effectiveness of a project control system can be measured by its average response time, that is, the average time between the occurrence of a deviation outside the control limits and its detection. Another performance measure is traceability, the ability of the control system to identify the source of the problem causing a deviation.

An appropriate data structure is required to achieve traceability. This structure must relate plans and corresponding progress reports to the relevant time periods, work packages and organisational units. Two hierarchical structures are commonly used in an integrated fashion to facilitate traceability – the work breakdown structure (WBS) and the organisational breakdown structure (OBS).

Designing a project monitoring and control system

A monitoring and control system should address the following questions.

- What control measures should be selected?
- What data should be used to estimate the current value of each control measure?
- How should raw data be collected, from which sources and in what frequency?
- How should the data be analysed to detect current and future deviations?
- How should the results of the analysis be reported, in what format, to whom and how often?

Table 10.1 shows a range of control measures that may be monitored as part of a project monitoring and control system. A deviation in any of these measures from the project plan will put strain on one or more areas of the project. For example, if critical tasks are

Table 10.1 Example performance measures for project control

Control measure	Project control area affected
Critical tasks not started on time	Schedule
Critical tasks not finished on time	Schedule
Noncritical tasks becoming critical	Schedule
Milestones missed	Schedule
Due date changes	Schedule
Price changes	Cost
Cost overruns	Cost
Insufficient cash flow	Cost
High overhead rates	Cost
Long supply lead time for material required	Resources, schedule
Low utilisation of resources	Resources, cost
Resource availability problems	Resources, schedule, cost
Changes in labour cost	Resources, cost
Changes in scope of project	Performance, cost, schedule, resources
Lack of technical information	Performance, cost, schedule
Failure in tests	Performance, cost, schedule
Delays in client approvals of configuration changes	Performance, schedule
Errors in records (inventories, configuration, and so on)	Performance, cost, schedule

A fundamental concept in classical project management is the design–freeze–implement model in which carefully laid plans are fixed in place before project execution begins. However, all project managers soon learn that this model is imperfect and so a process is required to allow for changes to a project after execution has begun. Change control is concerned with (PMI, 2000: 47):

■ influencing the factors which create changes to ensure that changes are beneficial
■ determining that a change has occurred
■ managing the actual changes when and as they occur.

Sometimes a project plan needs to be changed as part of the action recommended when a project starts to deviate from its plan. Project change is not normally a cause for alarm. Most projects are one-off endeavours and even the best planning efforts cannot predict every eventuality. A certain amount of change is a normal part of the project management process. However, change should be carefully controlled, especially after planning baselines have been frozen. It is good practice to have written guidelines and procedures for all participants to follow if it becomes necessary to change baseline plans (APM, 2000: 28).

Managing change requires planning, discipline and communication among team members and client representatives. Projects do not fail because of change but because of a lack of clear, consistent direction and leadership when confronted with the challenges of change.

Benefits of effective change management

Effective change management occurs when early identification of the source of change and its effect on a project are realised. Next, a plan to manage change is developed, communicated to all parties and implemented. If these steps have all taken place, the following outcomes are likely:

■ Enhanced client relationships
■ Improved financial performance
■ Reduced project delays
■ Better project teamwork
■ Improved management of project quality.

Change management will enhance client relationships. Because communication is continual and

not started on time this will impact the project schedule. When responding to a deviation, a project manager or team leader would need to assess the size of the deviation, the underlying cause of the problem and decide what action, if any, to take. Even taking no action is a positive response to a situation and may be the best option currently available.

Change management and control

All projects are about change, bringing something new into the world. Project management as a discipline is about the management of projects and therefore, by inference, the management of change.

change is discussed expeditiously, the client is not surprised.

Project budget and schedule performance can be improved and project delays can be minimised with effective change management. Too often a project budget overrun is due to inadequate change management. The cost and time to complete the work may increase because of a number of internal and external factors, including client desires, innovations and changes in the project team. Project Management in Action: 'The $26 million "Oops!"' at the end of this chapter is a striking example of the pitfalls of inadequate change management in a large project.

By practising effective change management techniques, the cost and time required to implement a change are agreed before any new work begins, ensuring buy-in from all parties.

Types and sources of change

Changes encountered during a project generally arise from within the project team, the client, or an external source.

Change arising from the project team

Changes arising from the project team may include the following:

- *Scope creep* – Scope elements increase in small increments until a significant change occurs
- *Increased level of effort* – Unintended additions are made to the amount of work performed in the execution of a task, usually occurring in relation to continual refinement or improvement of concepts or alternatives, for example changes made to improve aesthetics or performance related to constructibility, reliability or operability
- *Quality creep* – A subtle change that occurs when individuals deviate from the quality standard developed for the project. Generally, quality creep occurs as individuals apply their personal preferences to the level of quality of a particular project element
- *New technologies and tools* – The unfocused application of new technologies and tools, which leads to unfulfilled client expectations and project cost increases and schedule delays. This problem is generally associated with scope creep, increased level of effort or quality creep
- *Personnel changes* – Project team members may have to leave the team for a variety of reasons

- *Schedule improvements* – Changes proposed to remove a threat to or improve the chance of achieving milestones on time. These changes often involve the sequencing of tasks, or they may include design or process change to enhance construction or implementation schedules.

Client-initiated change

Client-initiated change may include the following:

- *Personnel changes* – Client representatives may also leave during a project
- *Scope creep* – Client-initiated, incremental increases in scope may also result in a significant change
- *Scope leap* – Clients may request a major change in scope (see, for example, Project Management in Action 'The $26m "Oops!"' at the end of the chapter).

Changes originating from external sources

Changes originating from external sources include the following:

- *Mandated changes* – Changes linked to third-party regulatory requirements, such as code revisions, regulatory changes, permit conditions and discovered conditions
- *Availability changes* – Changes in availability of materials, labour, equipment and other resources
- *Implementation cost changes* – Design, process, or execution sequence changes needed to compensate for implementation costs that were higher than estimated. These cost changes can include cost-saving opportunities.

Whatever its origin, a specific change will often trigger additional changes from the client and project team, resulting in various combinations of the types of change described above. Once this snowball effect begins, it becomes increasingly difficult to analyse or manage change. Therefore, a proactive, disciplined approach to change management is vital to the health of the project.

The change management plan

During the project planning phase, a change management plan should be developed to minimise risk and maximise value from any proposed changes to the project plan. The following five elements are important in a change management plan:

1. Identify the change.
2. Analyse the effects of change.
3. Develop a response strategy.
4. Communicate the strategy and gain acceptance for the change.
5. Revise the project plan and monitor the effects of change.

Each of these is discussed below.

Identify the change

The change management plan must contain a process for identifying change issues, which are actions or circumstances that can cause a change in scope, personnel, cost or schedule. The process should include routine assessments, such as scheduled project reviews, and should prescribe specific techniques that can be applied at any time.

Change issues may be identified by anyone. The project manager should encourage project team members to identify issues that could change the project plan. Even if these issues are ultimately unfounded, it is better to have identified them and discounted them, than to ignore them and have to address them later. The earlier the team can learn about a potential change, the sooner they can track it and plan for it. The change that causes the most damage is the one that is discovered when it is too late to do anything except lament that the project team should have known.

The change management plan should also provide a change issues record: a template for recording change, which will become a part of the project documentation. In practice, the project manager should concisely indicate the type and source of the change issues, as well as any other appropriate information.

Analyse the effects of change

Any change to scope, whether it is additive, deductive or qualitative, will affect the cost, so budgets must be adjusted to reflect the change. Based on the analysis, the project manager should be prepared to explain the effect and value of the change to the client. Gardiner and Stewart (2000) suggest that NPV, an investment management tool (discussed in Chapter 4), should also be used to determine the 'real' impact of change on a project. For example, assume that progress reports show that a project has to absorb a delay to a deliverable on the critical path. Without much thought most project managers will reach the following options:

- move the milestone date
- reduce the scope of the deliverable
- reduce the quality of the deliverable
- apply additional resources

but very few will carry out another investment appraisal to assist in determining what the most appropriate action is.

Develop a response strategy

Once the type and source of change have been identified and their effects on the project have been analysed, the next step is to develop a specific response strategy. Here are some key questions that can be used to build the response:

- What needs to be done?
- Who is going to do it?
- How much will it cost?
- How much time will it take?
- How will quality be ensured?
- How will the project team continue to exceed the client's expectations?
- What will be the effects on other project activities?
- How will the project manager involve and communicate with all stakeholders?

Generally, if the change is client-driven, then funding for the change should be provided by the client in the form of budget modifications, a contract change order or an adjustment to the scope. Externally driven mandatory changes, for example those beyond the control of the project team, should also be paid for by the client. In all cases, the funding for the change should cover all the costs and must be recorded.

Other types of change will depend on the project situation, but all must be acknowledged through adjustment in budget, schedule or scope. If the client will not acknowledge the change and there is no contingency for it, the change may be offset by deleting a lower priority element of scope. However, the project manager must get the client's agreement before deleting any element of scope.

It is important to determine who will assume responsibility for the cost of the change before the work is undertaken. If there is a question regarding responsibility for the change, both parties must be fair and reasonable. In this situation, a healthy client relationship is essential to successful change management. Change issues should be settled promptly but should remain open until the information needed to settle them fairly has been obtained.

Communicate the strategy and gain endorsement for the change

The change management plan should include a process for communicating changes to the client, the firm's management and other key parties. Changes that do not affect the scope may not require the approval of the client, depending on the project contract. As a general rule of thumb, if the change affects the scope, schedule, budget, deliverables or the client's expectations for the final product, the client should be involved.

All changes that are endorsed by the client will require action. Budgets must be adjusted, communication must take place and care must be taken to ensure that elements deleted from the scope do not find their way back into the project. Once the change has been addressed, endorsement by the stakeholders must again take place. For the stakeholders to maintain their commitment to the project, they must be kept fully informed of changes to the project plan.

Revise the project plan and monitor the effects of change

Once the planned response has been communicated and endorsed, it can be implemented. During implementation, two additional tasks should be performed. First, the project manager needs to ensure that the project plan is adjusted to account for the change. Although the effect of the change upon project plan elements may already have been assessed and endorsed, the actual revisions must now be documented in the project plan. Second, the project manager should install a means to monitor the effects of change. Depending on the magnitude of the change, the monitoring may be either incorporated into the next standard project review or conducted more frequently.

The remainder of this chapter will consider two techniques for project monitoring and control.

Milestone monitoring

Milestone monitoring is a simple method that project managers can use to control a project. The method is less effective and less detailed than other methods, but it has the advantage of needing only a modest amount of management effort to set up and maintain. It also requires less sophisticated cost and accounting techniques and can be used even when the project plans or schedules are not particularly detailed.

The success of milestone monitoring depends on the identification of clear, well-defined milestones, concrete milestones, before implementation begins. When choosing milestones, there is only one relevant rule. Milestones must be specific, measurable events, defined with unambiguous boundaries. A milestone is either achieved or not achieved. Milestone monitoring does not attempt to give a percentage complete value to a milestone: the milestone is regarded as being either 100% complete or 0% complete. This is what makes the method so powerful. Project contributors are unable to hide behind phrases such as 'we're almost there', 'another week and we'll do it' or 'we are about 99% complete'.

Ideally, milestones should coincide with the completion of work packages from the work breakdown structure. For each milestone, two essential pieces of data are required in the project plan:

1. the date on which the milestone is scheduled to be achieved
2. the budgeted cost of all the work needed specifically to achieve the milestone.

 Use of milestone monitoring

Table 10.2 shows some milestone and cost information for a project.

Notice that progress and cost information have been gathered up to week 32. The resulting graphs of planned budget and actual cost are shown in Figure 10.1. Comment on project performance to date, expected project completion date and expected final cost.

See shaded box overleaf for a suggested answer.

Table 10.2 Planned and actual milestone information for example project

Code	Milestone description	Planned			Actual		
		Week no.	Budget £000	Cum. budget £000	Week no.	Cost £000	Cum. cost £000
1.10	Project go-ahead given	0	0	0	0	0	0
1.15	Design approved	5	8	8	6	9	9
1.20	Construction drawings issued	11	16	24	13	18	27
1.25	Engineering drawings issued	15	12	36	17	18	45
1.30	Main foundation work done	22	10	46	22	10	55
1.35	Building shell complete	26	24	70	29	30	85
1.40	All doors and windows fitted	27	14	84	30	15	100
1.45	Roof completed	33	34	118	32	30	130
1.50	Fire and safety inspection done	35	24	142			
1.55	Electricals complete	40	12	154			
1.60	All services installed	42	20	174			
1.65	Landscaping complete	47	4	178			
1.70	Internal finishes complete	49	20	198			

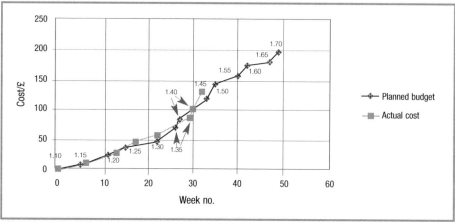

Figure 10.1 Milestones and monitoring

ANSWER suggested

The graph shows that the project schedule slipped by several weeks after milestone 1.30 and that costs exceeded budget by about £15,000. However, it appears that appropriate control action has helped bring the schedule back on target although cost remains about £15k over budget. There are 17 weeks remaining. There is no reason to expect a significant schedule delay. Cost seems to have stabilised so we may expect the project to come in about £15k over budget. If this is unacceptable, some minor descoping may be necessary (for example by reviewing the remaining work packages for cost-saving ideas, but without changing the original intent of project).

Project control using earned value analysis (EVA)

EVA is a widely used cost and schedule control system (APM, 2000: 29; PMI, 2000: 90: IPMA, 1999: 19; Fleming and Koppelman, 1996). It is also known as 'cost/schedule control system' (C/SCS) and 'baseline performance measurement' (BPM). The basic principle of EVA is to compare the value of actual work completed (known as the earned value) against planned progress and actual expenditure. The technique requires the project manager to schedule and budget project work using a time-phased plan and monitor progress against this plan.

Origin of EVA

EVA has its roots in the US Department of Defense and was developed to help contractors on large government projects control cost and schedule. The system is currently described in detail by a set of 32 criteria for measuring the adequacy of management control systems through, among other things, the application of earned value analysis concepts (Fleming, 1993). These criteria were adopted by the US Department of Defense for large value projects as a means of keeping cost overruns under some sort of control. It was created as Department of Defense Instruction 7000.2 (DODI 7000.2) in 1967 under the title of 'Performance Measurement for Selected Acquisitions'.

The primary measurement variables in EVA

The main variables used in EVA relate to planned cost, planned schedule, actual cost and actual progress.

 Missing information

A work package in a project plan has a planned cost of £10,000 over a 10-week period, that is, £1000 per week for 10 weeks. If the task owner has been working on this package for 6 weeks and has spent £6000, should we conclude that his package is proceeding to plan?

See shaded box for a suggested answer.

Three variables are needed to determine project performance in terms of cost and schedule:

1. *Value of actual work done*, that is, earned value. This is the value of completed work expressed in terms of the budget assigned to that work. More formally, it is called the 'budgeted cost of work performed' (BCWP).
2. *Value of planned work*, that is, planned value or, more formally, the 'budgeted cost of work scheduled' (BCWS).
3. *Actual expenditure*, that is, the 'actual cost of work performed' (ACWP).

In EVA, percentage complete means the value of actual work done (earned value), expressed as a percentage of the total planned value of the same work package or project. BCWP, BCWS and ACWP are used by project managers to calculate variances and performance indices useful for project control.

Schedule variance (SV)

SV is the difference between the value of planned work and the value of actual work:

$$SV = BCWP - BCWS$$

The difference between the cost of work performed (BCWP) and the budgeted cost of work scheduled (BCWS) indicates (in monetary units) the deviation or variance between the work content performed and the work content scheduled for the control period. If the absolute value of the difference is very small, then, in terms of work content, the project is on schedule. A positive difference indicates that the project is ahead of schedule and a negative difference implies that the project is late.

This measure, together with a simple critical path chart, for example Gantt chart, provides the means for tracking critical activities and detecting overall trends in schedule performance. Although a delay in noncritical activities may not cause immediate

 ANSWER suggested

Before we can answer this question, we need some additional information on the percentage complete of the work package. Consider the following possibilities:

■ If the work package is 60% complete, we conclude that it is on target and budget

■ If it is 40% complete, we conclude that the package is behind schedule and over budget

■ If it is 80% complete, we conclude that the package is ahead of schedule and under budget.

project delays, if these activities are not performed on schedule, the resources required to perform them will be needed in a later period. This shift in resource requirements may cause a problem if the load on resources exceeds the available capacity.

Schedule delays detected by EVA should be monitored closely. When the delay extends beyond the control level, analysis of resource requirements should be initiated to test whether, due to resource limits, the entire project may be delayed.

Cost variance (CV)

CV is the difference between actual expenditure and the earned value:

CV = BCWP – ACWP

A positive CV indicates a lower actual cost than budgeted for the control period, while a negative CV indicates a cost overrun.

Schedule and cost performance indices

Schedule variance and cost variance are absolute measures indicating deviations between planned performance and actual progress, in monetary units. A relative measure is also useful. A £1,000 cost overrun of an activity originally budgeted for £500 is clearly more troublesome than the same overrun on an activity originally budgeted for £50,000. Schedule performance index (SPI) and cost performance index (CPI) are proportional measures of schedule and cost performance, respectively. They are also known as schedule index (SI) and cost index (CI).

The schedule performance index of a work package or project is defined as the ratio of BCWP to BCWS:

SPI = BCWP / BCWS

An SPI value equal to 1 indicates that the associated activity is on schedule. Values larger than 1 suggest that the activity is ahead of schedule, and values smaller than 1 indicate a schedule overrun.

The cost performance index is defined as the ratio of BCWP to ACWP:

CPI = BCWP / ACWP

When the CPI equals 1, a work package is on budget. CPI values larger than 1 indicate a better than planned cost performance, and values smaller than 1 indicate a cost overrun.

The SPI and the CPI can be calculated for a single

activity, a work package, a group of work packages or the whole project. This is done by aggregating the values of BCWS, BCWP and ACWP for the appropriate activities and calculating the values of SPI and CPI based on these totals.

Earned value analysis can be performed period by period and on a cumulative basis.

A few more metrics

Budget at completion (BAC)

Budget at completion is the total original budgeted cost:

BAC = BCWS at completion

Estimate at completion (EAC)

An EAC is a forecast of total project costs, usually based on current project performance. Three methods of forecasting EAC are:

1. EAC is equal to actual costs to date plus the remaining project budget modified by a performance factor, often the cost performance index. This approach is most often used when current variances are seen as typical of future variances. It is the most common method of calculating EAC:

    EAC = BAC / CPI

2. EAC is equal to actual costs to date plus remaining budget. This approach is most often used when current variances are seen as atypical and the project management team's expectation is that similar variances will not occur in the future:

    EAC = ACWP + (BAC – BCWP)

3. EAC is equal to actual costs to date plus a new estimate for all remaining work. This approach is most often used when past performance shows that the original estimating assumptions were fundamentally flawed or they are no longer relevant due to a change in conditions.

Any of the above approaches may be the correct approach for a given project.

Variance at completion (VAC)

The variance at completion is a forecast of the final cost variance:

VAC = BAC – EAC

Schedule at completion

The schedule at completion is an estimate of the total duration of the project based on current schedule performance:

$$\text{Schedule at completion} = \frac{\text{Original estimated duration}}{\text{SPI}}$$

 **Care with cost curves**

Study the cumulative cost curves shown in Figure 10.2. The graph shows the baseline cost curve for the entire project and the actual cost curve to date. Which of the following statements are true?

1. Actual project costs at the date line are greater than planned project costs.
2. If the current rate of expenditure continues unchecked, the final project costs will exceed the planned project budget.

See shaded box below for a suggested answer.

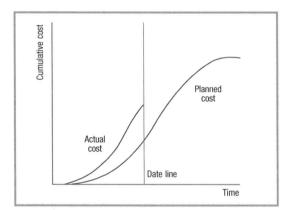

Figure 10.2 Cumulative cost curves

---

suggested ANSWER

Lemonade project status after 10 days:

1. BCWS = 10 days × 20 cups per day × £0.50/cup budget
   = £100
2. BCWP = 150 cups × £0.50/cup budget
   = £75 (earned value)
3. SV = BCWP − BCWS = £75 − £100 = −£25
   SPI = BCWP / BCWS = 0.75
   CV = BCWP − ACWP = £75 − £90 = −£15
   CPI = BCWP / ACWP = 0.833
   The project is therefore behind schedule and budget.
4. Lemonade project forecast:
   EAC = BAC / CPI = £500 / 0.833 = £600
   VAC = BAC − EAC = £500 − £600 = £100 (unfavourable)
   Schedule at completion = 50 days / SPI = 50 days / 0.75
   = 66.67 days

 **Applying EVA to a project**

You have been given a project to make 1,000 cups of lemonade over 50 days. You decide to produce the lemonade at a steady rate of 20 cups per day. The budgeted cost per cup is £0.50. The total project budget is £500.

At the end of day 10, you carry out a cost/schedule control check:

- 150 cups have been made
- Total actual cost is £90 (ACWP)

Answer the following questions:

1. What is the planned value, that is, the budgeted cost of the work scheduled (BCWS)?
2. What is the earned value, that is, the budgeted cost of the work performed (BCWP)?
3. Calculate appropriate statistics to determine if the project is ahead or behind schedule and budget.
4. Calculate the forecast at completion for cost, variance and schedule.

See shaded box above for a suggested answer.

---

 suggested ANSWER

Statement 1 is true. There is no ambiguity here. Statement 2 appears to be true, but there is not enough information to decide. In order to know if statement 2 is true or false, we need information about the physical progress of the project. Is the project on schedule, behind schedule or ahead of schedule?

Figure 10.2 tells us that we have spent more money than we expected to spend at this point in time. If the progress of the project is on schedule (or behind schedule), statement 2 is true. However, if the project is ahead of schedule, this might explain the higher than expected costs. In other words, the project is ahead of schedule and will finish early. The final cost need not exceed the baseline budget, it may even come in under budget.

This example demonstrates that, to be effective, a project control system must monitor both project cost and progress against time.

Difficulties with EVA

One of the main difficulties in EVA is the calculation of earned value (BCWP) because of the need to estimate the percentage complete.

One of the most important (and neglected) project management skills is progress measurement. Not the progress measurement which counts the number of days which have elapsed or the number of cheques which have gone out, but the measurement which counts what work has been done. People can have difficulty in measuring completed work because some activities seem too complex or do not have clearly defined deliverables.

A good example is the software project which seems to achieve 90 or 95% completion very quickly but then starts to go backwards until people start to wonder if it will ever be finished at all. This is because of the difficulty of measuring the percentage complete, where the deliverable is intangible like software, knowledge or cultural change. The remaining duration cannot be estimated reliably without knowing the value of what has already been done.

Estimating physical progress using the 0/100 rule

The basic and fundamental rule for measuring progress is the 0/100 rule. Either something is done or not. There is no way for something to be half done, unless the half corresponds to something measurable. Usually there is something measurable if you go into enough detail. For example, to have constructed half a key, half a lamppost, half a chair or half a penny would be meaningless unless you understand the fabrication process and could identify a 50% milestone. An objective 50% milestone for cleaning or repairing a pair of shoes might be one shoe done, but for designing the shoe in the first place would be something else, such as 'shoe mould complete'.

Estimating physical progress using a variation of the 0/100 rule

For work which lasts several months, it is unsatisfactory to wait until the end of an activity before checking to see if the work has been done. Therefore, intermediate milestones are established. As these are reached, a given percentage of physical progress is considered to have been achieved. This is a popular way to measure progress. Between each 0/100 milestone, some progress is taking place which has not yet been measured. This can cause a slight contortion because the real progress is being underestimated. This is why many people replace 0/100 with 20/80 or 50/100 or some other rule to balance the effect of work not being finished, or else they make an informed but subjective estimate about the stage work is at for any given moment. These are the sort of estimates which a client likes to validate.

One advantage of using the 0/100 rule or one of its variations is that it eliminates the necessity for the *continuous* determination of the percentage complete.

Estimating physical progress using units or standards

Two other methods are worth considering in certain circumstances. The 'units' method records the number of finished units, for example one building out of ten, one document out of a hundred. But care should be taken to ensure that the units are equivalent. The 'standards' method is based upon the principle of a standard effort for a given quantity of work. If the job always takes 100 hours and 80 have already been spent, the physical progress will be 80%, until the standard improves.

 Measuring physical progress when cleaning a car

Consider the task of cleaning a car. How would you effectively measure and report task progress to someone else?

See shaded box for a suggested answer.

One method would be to regard the task as 0% or 100% complete. The task is either finished or it isn't. Another method would be to use the 50/100 rule. As soon as you make a start on the task, it is recorded as 50% complete, and it stays this way in the system until it is completely finished, that is, 100% complete. Alternatively, you may ask yourself the following questions before you begin:

- Is the inside to be cleaned as well as the outside?
- How messy/dirty is the inside?
- What standard of work is required for the inside?
- Are the wheels to be cleaned?
- Are they especially filthy?
- Is the car to be polished?

Once specific activities have been defined, it becomes possible to assign an acceptable percentage of cleaning work, that is, a weighting factor, for each of them, for example the inside of car might equal 33%.

Visit the website

http://www.palgrave.com/business/gardiner

▶ to access a comprehensive bibliography on earned value analysis

Project closure

Despite common misconceptions, project closure should begin during the planning phase of a project when the work plan is developed, not in the final stages in a project. Closure activities should be ongoing throughout the life of a project. In this way, project closure can be completed in an efficient and timely manner as a part of budgeted activities and not as a poorly executed afterthought that is a burden on the project budget. Project closure essentially combines two processes (IPMA, 1999: 40): 'first the commissioning of the project deliverables and their acceptance by the sponsor, and second to document all experiences in the project.' The manner in which the end products and services of a project are handed over to the sponsor should be defined in the project charter and any contractual documents (APM, 2000: 46). The handover process may include testing, commissioning and start-up.

Project closure as a defined project phase is frequently overlooked, yet it is an essential activity in successful project delivery. The project manager who recognises project closure as a strategic part of the project delivery process will have greater success managing the outcome of the project and meeting the expectations of the stakeholders.

Benefits of efficient project closure

Project closure provides a unique opportunity for the project manager to capture and distribute the experience, skills and knowledge that have been developed during a project. This knowledge and intellectual capital should be captured and passed on to other projects in the organisation. So, even though a project is complete, it can still contribute to the strategic objectives of the firm.

A well-planned project closure provides benefit to all the project stakeholders. For example, project closure has value for the client if it results in a thorough project record with easy to retrieve information.

A good closure plan paves the way for the project team members' feelings of personal accomplishment. Items such as deliverables, project references, project résumés, project evaluations provided by the client, project write-ups, press releases and publications all help to provide a tangible sense of completion of the project and a sense of personal satisfaction and recognition. In order for this to occur effectively, closeout activities that emphasise personal accomplishment must be defined at the beginning of the project, during project work plan development. Planning for closure should result in written instructions known as the closure plan, which is a component of the project work plan.

The closure plan

In preparing the project closure plan, the project manager has several goals. First and most important, the project must have well-defined tasks in the WBS and an adequate budget for closure activities. The project manager should not plan on using the contingency budget to support closure activities. Much of the closure process should occur during the project as tasks are completed and will most probably be part of other ongoing activities including:

- project reviews
- coordination with the client
- periodic removal or purging of temporary items from the files
- records management
- demobilisation.

The project manager must budget for project archiving, project closure meetings and any follow-up activities that will support the development of promotional material for the client.

The project manager should communicate to the team members their roles and responsibilities in project closure. All members of the team should be aware of what is expected of them during the project and at its end. Although there is no prescribed format for a closure plan, the guidance for its development can come from several sources, including:

- discussions with the client
- requirements of the firm
- requirements of the contracts.

Although the specifics of the closure plan will vary depending on the requirements of the client, the firm and the contract, most closure plans will contain procedures for the following activities:

- Phased closure based on tasks in the work breakdown structure
- Demobilising staff and resources
- Recommending staff development opportunities

- Closing the technical elements of the project
- Conducting a project closure meeting with the client and reconciling the client's vision with the final product and service
- Closing the financial elements of the project
- Evaluating, rewarding, and recognising project team members
- Archiving project material
- Supplying information to the firm's business development database.

Extending a project schedule is expensive, and early identification of these activities in a closure plan will help to ensure that they are accomplished in a timely manner.

Closing the project

Project closure marks the fulfilment of all client needs and expectations and the end of project administration. All tasks must be closed, all financial details completed and the project records must be archived. The project manager must provide the client with all deliverables, including a complete project record, and must offer a final opportunity for the client to provide feedback.

Final project evaluation

The processes of review and evaluation are applied at different stages throughout a project, for example at the feasibility stage and all major milestones. The end of a project marks the last major milestone and provides an important opportunity to capture lessons learned during the project, both with respect to personal development of staff, evolution of the project management methodology and also to reward and recognise everyone appropriately for their efforts. It is also an opportunity to revisit the project's critical success factors: Did the participants deliver? Were all the project objectives met? Such a review is often called a post-implementation review (PIR). Lessons learned are opportunities for organisational learning that can benefit future programmes and projects (APM, 2000: 46; PMI, 2000: 125).

There are often business development opportunities to explore with clients in terms of follow-on work or new services associated with the completed facility or asset. In partnership arrangements, such as build–operate–transfer (BOT) or public finance initiative (PFI), the relationship between sponsor and project provider may continue for many years after the 'completion' of the project (partnerships are discussed more fully in Chapter 6).

The following considerations are important when conducting a project review:

- Process – post-project evaluation should be an embedded process in the organisation
- Budget – allocate a budget at the outset of a project to conduct a satisfactory post-implementation review (PIR)
- People – the review should be led by independent people with no vested interest and the appropriate experience and skills
- Documentation – include all project files, reports, minutes of meetings and so on
- Economic climate – take into account the economic climate and the project's impact on society
- Include all major players – projects are complex, so use a reasonable representation of all the key players
- Use a standardised methodology – this enables comparison between projects and future benchmarking studies
- Use appropriate technology for the scale of the review
- Interviews – where possible try to triangulate findings for enhanced validity
- Feedback – feed back results before drawing final conclusions
- Outcomes of the review:
  - Identify mistakes/successes
  - Determine impact, avoidance, strategy/best practices
  - Initiate changes in policies and processes
- Guidelines for conducting a project review:
  - Establishing trust
  - Philosophy: it is not a witch-hunt
  - Keep to project issues
  - Be sensitive to human emotions and reactions
  - Give adequate notification of an impending audit
  - Accuracy of data used is of paramount importance
  - Ensure senior management lends their support to the review
  - Complete the review as soon as possible.

The IPMA *Competence Baseline* also lists a set of project review activities for continuous improvement (IPMA, 1999: 40).

At British Petroleum, project reviews are performed to (Cleland, 1994: 297):

- Determine costs accurately
- Anticipate and minimise risk
- Evaluate contractors more thoroughly
- Improve project management.

Many companies now perform project reviews as a matter of course. The concept is also built into modern performance and improvement systems such as TQM, six sigma, CMM, lean manufacturing, EFQM, balanced scorecard, programme management and knowledge management. The growing number of organisations that have established project or programme offices is another driver of regular project reviews.

Determinants of project success and failure

Debate continues about what is meant by project success; a topic that is widely acknowledged as a complex issue (Pinto and Slevin, 1988a; Lechler, 1998; Turner, 1999: 71). Indeed, there are no silver bullets in project management and therefore any consideration of the determinants of project success and failure must be tempered with caution. Pinto and Slevin (1988b) point out that the importance of success factors change as a project moves through its life cycle. Research has shown that when stakeholders agree before they start how they are going to evaluate the success of a project, the probability of achieving success increases (Wateridge, 1995).

This book emphasises the wide variety and types of project that exist, and the equally diverse range of environments into which they are conceived. Consequently, any list of success or failure factors should be used as a guiding principle only and modified according to the nature and context of each project (IPMA, 1999: 38). If this were not so, research into project success and failure would have concluded long ago and all projects would be successful. Some of the key lessons learned in project management over the last 30 years are cogently discussed in Winch (1996).

Project success

The list of critical success factors reported by Pinto and Slevin (1988b) from a questionnaire-based survey to over 600 members of the Project Manage-

ment Institute (PMI) has much to commend it and remains a useful reference. Their study produced a list of ten critical success factors:

1. *Project mission* – initial clarity of goals and general directions.
2. *Top management support* – willingness of top management to provide the necessary resources and authority for project success.
3. *Project schedule and plans* – a detailed specification of the individual action steps required for project implementation.
4. *Client consultation* – communication, consultation, and active listening to all impacted parties.
5. *Personnel* – recruitment, selection and training of the necessary personnel for the project team.
6. *Technical tasks* – availability of the required technology and expertise to accomplish the specific technical action steps.
7. *Client acceptance* – the act of 'selling' the final project to its ultimate intended users.
8. *Monitoring and feedback* – timely provision of comprehensive control information at each phase in the implementation process.
9. *Communication* – the provision of an appropriate network and necessary data to all key factors in the project implementation.
10. *Troubleshooting* – the ability to handle unexpected crises and deviations from the plan.

There are an additional four factors largely 'beyond the control of the project team' but still regarded as critical to project success:

11. *Characteristics of the project team leader* – competence of the project leader (administratively, interpersonally and technically) and the amount of authority available to perform his/her duties.
12. *Power and politics* – the degree of political activity within the organisation and perception of the project as furthering the self-interests of an organisation's members.
13. *Environmental events* – the likelihood of external organisational factors impacting on the operations of the project team, either positively or negatively.
14. *Urgency* – the perception of the importance of the project or the need to implement the project as soon as possible.

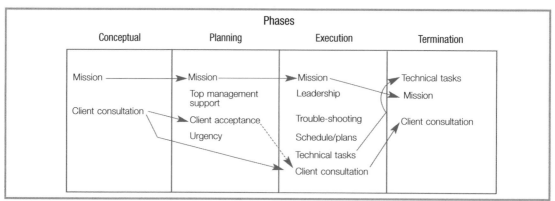

Figure 10.3 **Project success factors at different stages in the project lifecycle** (Pinto and Slevin, 1988b)

Figure 10.3 shows the relationship between these success factors and the life cycle of the project.

More recent literature focuses on the human factor issues in project management (Lechler, 1998). For example, Gray (2001) establishes a clear association between project outcomes and the social and management climate in which those projects are implemented. This acknowledges that the often-cited time–cost–scope triangle is too simple to represent the interacting objectives of most projects and that the personal objectives and feelings of the people involved must also be taken into account. He concludes that a supportive organisational environment is a key factor in successful project outcomes.

In another study, Cooke-Davies (2002) identifies 12 factors that he calls the 'real' factors to project success. His research draws attention to the difference between project success and project management success, the former being linked to success criteria defined by the project objectives, the latter being linked to the 'inputs to the management system that lead directly or indirectly to the success of the project'. His findings are shown in Table 10.3.

Table 10.3 The 'real' critical success factors of project success	
Factors critical to project management success	1. Adequacy of company-wide education on the concepts of risk management 2. Maturity of an organisation's processes for assigning ownership of risks 3. Adequacy with which a visible risk register is maintained 4. Adequacy of an up-to-date risk management plan 5. Adequacy of documentation of organisational responsibilities on the project 6. Keep project (or project stage duration) as far below 3 years as possible (1 year is better) 7. Allow changes to scope only through a mature scope change control process 8. Maintain integrity of the performance measurement baseline
Factors critical to success on an individual project	9. The existence of an effective benefits delivery and management process that involves the mutual cooperation of project management and line management functions
Factors that lead to consistently successful projects	10. Portfolio and programme management practices that allow the enterprise to resource fully a suite of projects that are thoughtfully and dynamically matched to the corporate strategy and business objectives 11. A suite of project, programme and portfolio metrics that provides direct 'line of sight' feedback on current project performance, and anticipated future success, so that project, portfolio and corporate decisions can be aligned 12. An effective means of 'learning from experience' on projects, that combines explicit knowledge with tacit knowledge in a way that encourages people to learn and to embed that learning into continuous improvement of project management processes and practices

Source: Cooke-Davies, 2002.

Project failure

In addition to the research carried out to identify project success factors, another body of literature has emerged looking at the flip side of the coin – determinants of project failure. The following tongue-in-cheek list compiled by Pinto and Kharbanda (1996) highlights 12 methods to ensure project failure:

1. Ignore the project environment (including stakeholders) – unhappy internal and external stakeholders can ruin an otherwise successful project.
2. Push a new technology to market too quickly – tried and tested technology lowers the risk level in a project.
3. Don't bother building in fallback options – 'I didn't expect that to happen' is no recourse in the middle of project execution.
4. When problems occur, shoot the one most visible – finding and firing a scapegoat (often the project manager) when a project is going off course, rarely solves the problem.
5. Let new ideas starve to death from inertia – organisations that are purely numbers driven and always take the lowest risk route will stultify innovation.
6. Don't bother conducting feasibility studies – the benefits of conducting a feasibility study have been covered in Chapter 4.
7. Never admit a project is a failure – terminating a project that is heading for failure is a difficult but correct decision on some projects (Staw and Ross, 1987; Nulden, 1996).
8. Overmanage project managers and their teams – high levels of bureaucracy can strangle a project; decision making at lower levels increases responsiveness and flexibility.
9. Never, never conduct post-failure reviews – most managers prefer to bury their failed projects; the best organisations capture the learning potential from every project.

Table 10.4 Summary of classic mistakes

People-related mistakes	Process-related mistakes	Product-related mistakes	Technology-related mistakes
1. Undermined motivation 2. Weak personnel 3. Uncontrolled problem employees 4. Heroics 5. Adding people to a late project 6. Noisy, crowded offices 7. Friction between developers and customers 8. Unrealistic expectations 9. Lack of effective project sponsorship 10. Lack of stakeholder buy-in 11. Lack of user input 12. Politics placed over substance 13. Wishful thinking	14. Overly optimistic schedules 15. Insufficient risk management 16. Contractor failure 17. Insufficient planning 18. Abandonment of planning under pressure 19. Wasted time during the fuzzy front end 20. Short-changed upstream activities 21. Inadequate design 22. Short-changed quality assurance 23. Insufficient management controls 24. Premature or too frequent convergence 25. Omitting necessary tasks from estimates 26. Planning to catch up later 27. Code-like-hell programming	28. Requirements gold-plating 29. Feature creep 30. Developer gold-plating 31. Push me, pull me negotiation 32. Research-oriented development	33. Silver-bullet syndrome 34. Overestimated savings from new tools or methods 35. Switching tools in the middle of a project 36. Lack of automated source-code control

Source: McConnell, 1996, reproduced with permission.

10. Never bother to understand project trade-offs – hard decisions are the prerequisite of project management, uninformed decisions are its bane.

11. Allow political expediency and infighting to dictate crucial project decisions – political decision making emphasises parochial needs often at the expense of organisational effectiveness.

12. Make sure the project is run by a weak leader – in the absence of a strong project leader to keep the project team operating on track, most projects begin to experience the vacuum of indecision, orders given and rescinded, and a general sense of aimlessness.

The software development industry has been the focus of project success and failure traits in recent years (Brooks, 1995). Table 10.4 summarises the classic mistakes identified by McConnell (1996) in rapid development software development projects.

Critical chain project management (CCPM) – a critical perspective

Introduction to the theory of constraints (TOC)

The theory of constraints (TOC) is a management philosophy first developed by Dr Eliyahu Goldratt for running and improving a manufacturing organisation (Goldratt and Cox, 1984). TOC maintains that every system is subject to at least one constraint, which prevents the system from achieving infinitely high levels of performance. Thus, an organisation's performance is dependent on its weakest link. Their bestselling book, *The Goal*, identified core principles and techniques applicable to constraints within manufacturing organisations as well as a five-step process of ongoing improvement, shown in Key Concepts: 'Goldratt and Cox's five-step process for ongoing improvement'.

 Goldratt and Cox's five-step process for ongoing improvement

Goldratt and Cox (1984) identified the following five-step process as a solution to deal with the constraints in an organisation:

1. Identify the system's constraint (or weak link).
2. Decide how to exploit the system's constraint.
3. Subordinate everything else to the system constraint.
4. Elevate the constraint.

5. If in the previous step a constraint has been broken, go back to step one, but do not allow inertia to cause a system constraint.

A system's constraint is anything that limits the system from achieving higher performance towards its goal. In the case of a moneymaking organisation, the system constraint limits the profit level. In a manufacturing environment, the constraint may be a machine which will determine the overall capacity of the plant. Exploiting the system constraint involves getting the most out of this machine to improve throughput. The constraint can be exploited by ensuring that the quality of the parts entering the machine prevents the machine from wasting time on defective parts.

Goldratt and Cox (1984) suggest that all other planning decisions need to be subordinated to the schedule required to keep the constraining machine running. Running other machines at a higher production rate than the constraint will increase inventory and costs and will not increase the throughput of the plant. The fourth step in the process is to elevate the constraint to improve the objective of the organisation. This can be achieved by running an additional shift on the constraining machine to increase its output. The application of step four may have changed the system's constraint. To ensure that continuous improvement occurs the new constraint must be identified.

Applying TOC to project management: the critical chain

In *Critical Chain*, Goldratt (1997) applies TOC and the five-step process to project management, where the constraint of a project is defined as the critical chain:

the sequence of dependent events that prevents the project from completing in a shorter interval. Resource dependencies determine the critical chain as much as do activity dependencies. Goldratt (1997: 215)

Goldratt (1997) suggests that duration is the major constraint of projects. He suggests that project costs often escalate as a result of extended duration and that the contingency costs of project delays are high. Steyn (2002) argues that extended project duration not only leads to escalation of overhead costs but also leads to scope changes, since there is more time for stakeholders' needs to change. The minimisation of project duration is a key project goal and it can enable an organisation to create a competitive advantage over other firms.

The critical chain takes resource limitations into account and is composed of sections that are dependent on precedence relationships and other sections that are dependent on resource availability. Resource dependencies might exist between activities because they require the same resource. An improvement anywhere on the critical chain means the project can complete earlier. Goldratt's application of TOC to project management departs from the Project Management *Body of Knowledge Guide* (PMBOK Guide) by specifying the critical chain, rather than the critical path, as the project constraint, where critical path is defined as 'the series of activities which determines the earliest completion of the project' PMI (2000).

Steyn (2000) claims that the critical path is traditionally determined by precedence relationships only and resource limitations are taken care of after the critical path has been defined, but this practice varies considerably from one organisation to the next. Of course, if an organisation does not have resource constraints, or has infinite resources, the critical chain will be the same as the critical path, whether or not resource levelling has been applied.

It should be noted, however, that critical path software packages, such as Microsoft Project, contain options to level the resources and use late start as opposed to early start schedules. This suggests that the main difference between the critical chain and the critical path method relates to the estimations of task durations and the use of buffers rather than fundamental differences between their definitions.

According to Goldratt (1997), the main reason for project overrun is because of the misuse of the safety time created within the estimated times for each project activity. He argues that task estimates given in projects are much bigger than the actual time needed to complete a task and that on average a project will contain about 200% safety time. Thus, if a project is scheduled to last for 300 days, 200 days safety time has been estimated. He further identifies a number of different mechanisms by which safety is inserted into the time estimates of almost every step of a project.

Goldratt (1997) argues that time estimates are based on pessimistic experience and people are likely to give estimates that give them a good chance of finishing their step on time. In addition, people will add in extra safety because they think that management will ask them to reduce their durations in order to reduce the overall lead time of the project. He argues that since employees know that safety time is built into estimates, they do not need to start tasks on time. Goldratt refers to this as the 'student syndrome', which he describes as leaving everything until the last minute. Schuyler (2000), Leach (1999), Patrick (1999) and Newbold (1998) all suggest that people have a tendency to wait until activities become really urgent before they work on them. If an unanticipated problem appears, the resource does not have time to complete the task on time due to the late start. Delays are frequent because of the uncertainties or unknowns that exist in projects (referred to as Murphy's Law).

We can't know what problems will crop up until we start the work. Due to the fact that tasks are started later than planned there isn't enough time left to recover from the problems in time to meet the due date. Patrick (1999: 59)

Goldratt (1997) also argues that safety time is wasted through multitasking. Multitasking is the performance of multiple project activities at the same time. He argues that in the majority of organisations a resource has several tasks for various projects to complete and attempts to work on them simultaneously, thereby increasing the lead time for a specific task. He claims that Parkinson's law exists in projects, that is, 'work expands so as to fill the time available for its completion'. Therefore, projects do not tend to benefit from early activity completions.

In summary, despite the fact there is an excess of safety time inserted into projects, it is wasted due to the student syndrome, Parkinson's law and multitasking. Goldratt's solution to managing safety time within projects is to remove safety time from tasks and allocate a project completion buffer instead.

The TOC approach to managing safety time

Traditionally we protect the schedule by padding individual tasks or spreading the slack throughout the schedule. Using the critical chain approach we don't protect individual tasks; we protect the project completion. We do this by means of lumps of protection, scheduled blocks of time called buffers. Newbold (1999: 5)

CCPM requires that the schedule be built with only the time to do the work, without the safety. This is the time the work is expected to take if allowed to focus a full sustainable level of effort on it and if there are no significant problems. Goldratt (1997) recommends that task times should be reduced to the best estimate, which he describes as the level where the resource has a 50% chance of completing on time. To protect the completion date of the project, Goldratt (1997) argues that safety time should be inserted into a project buffer at the end of the critical chain. The project buffer is called the 'critical chain completion buffer'. In terms of its size, Goldratt suggests that one half of the sum of the critical chain activities should be used. If the length of the critical chain on a project is 60 days, the project buffer would be 30 days. The total duration of the project would be 90 days. Aggressive task estimates, reflecting only the amount of work required, will have the effect of reducing the length of the project.

Figure 10.4 shows that the TOC method reduces the project duration when compared with the traditional critical path method. The safety times have been removed from tasks A, B and C and have been placed into a project buffer at the end of task C. This minimises the impact of student syndrome since resources have less time to complete their specific tasks and they should not wait as long to start. Much project management guidance recommends that project managers use an early start schedule. However, Leach (1999) claims that early start means permitting all the noncritical chain activities to start earlier than is necessary to meet the schedule date. This results in multitasking and a loss of focus on the critical activities. Critical chain uses late start for all project activities and requires the elimination of task due dates from project plans:

If we are building a schedule on the basis of aggressive, 50% confidence durations, we can't expect people to meet them all the time, and therefore there is no way we can think in terms of due dates. Patrick (1999: 60)

Critical chain project plans only provide dates for the start of activity chains and the end of the project buffer (points 1 and 2 in Figure 10.4). For the rest of the project, the plan provides approximate start times and estimated activity durations. The elimination of task due dates allows the project to take advantage of early task finishes and avoids delays caused by Parkinson's law.

Feeding buffers

Goldratt (1997) suggests that protection is required every time a noncritical chain task feeds into the critical chain. This protection time is called a 'feeding buffer' and is inserted at the end of noncritical paths. Goldratt recommends that the size of the feeding buffer should be one half of the sum of the feeding path activities. In Figure 10.5 the critical chain consists of activities A, B and C. The activity path of tasks D and E merge into the critical chain and must be completed prior to activity C commencing. A feeding buffer has been inserted at the end of this task to protect the critical chain from a potential delay in the feeding path. Once the feeding buffer in Figure 10.5 is fully penetrated, any further delay on activity D or E will translate into additional penetration into the project buffer. The chain consisting of activities D, E and C might cause a higher penetration into the project buffer than the critical chain. Whilst the critical chain never changes, it may not be

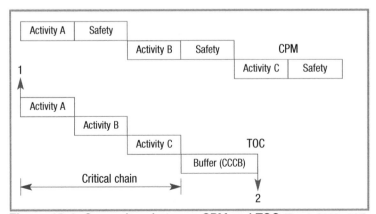

Figure 10.4 Comparison between CPM and TOC (Rand, 2000: 175)

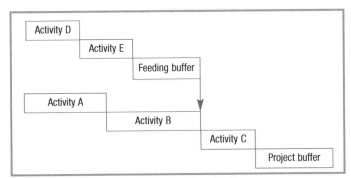

Figure 10.5 The location of feeding buffers

the chain that is causing the highest penetration into the buffer.

The critical chain methodology described can be applied to a single or multiple project environment.

To improve the lead time of the project (elevating the constraint) the critical chain tasks must be reduced. This could be achieved by employing more resources on the critical chain tasks or by subcontracting a critical task to a vendor that can complete the task quicker. In doing so the constraint may have been broken and a new constraint must be identified.

Multiple projects

Planning projects in isolation means that resource contention between projects is likely. Therefore, multiple projects need to be planned together. The multiple project critical chain process is also based on a five-step TOC process (Leach, 1999; Steyn, 2002):

1. Identify the multiproject constraint: the company constraining resource (CCR).
2. Schedule the work to be performed by the constraining resource.
3. Subordinate the schedule of other resources to the CCR.
4. Elevate the constraint: increase capacity of the CCR.
5. If the resource under consideration is no longer the constraint, go back to step 1.

The CCR limits the number of projects that an organisation can execute. Leach (1999) suggests that the CCR is most often a certain type of person, but may be a physical or even a policy constraint. The schedule of the CCR determines the sequencing of projects and ensures that projects are staggered to resolve resource contention. In order to schedule the CCR, decisions have to be made in terms of the organisation's priorities. The overall progress of a project is determined by the work schedule of the CCR. To protect the CCR from delays a buffer is inserted before each task is performed by the CCR. Leach (1999) claims that the CCR buffers ensure that they never starve the capacity constraint for work. Such buffers are illustrated in Figure 10.6.

The CCR buffers prevent the CCR from having to wait when a preceding activity has been delayed. Step 4 of the multiple project method focuses on elevating the CCR. This can be achieved by acquiring additional resources to increase the capacity of the CCR. By elevating the constraint, the resource under consideration may no longer be the constraint, therefore a new constraint must be identified. The multiple project method still requires that each individual project is planned using the critical chain methodology. Thus, each project plan will have project and feeding buffers. The multiple project method does not attempt to schedule all resources across all projects. Only the constraining resources are scheduled in this way.

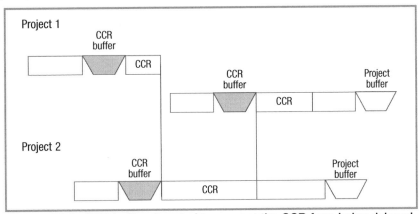

Figure 10.6 CCR buffers inserted to prevent the CCR from being delayed

Controlling the process – buffer management

The critical chain scheduling approach requires the elimination of task due dates from the project plan, except for activity chain start dates and the end of project buffers. The buffers are used to monitor the status of projects and determine whether drastic actions are required to bring the schedule back on track. The project buffer is the most important buffer since it protects the customer commitment date from disruptions along the critical chain. Newbold (1998) claims that project managers need to analyse how much of the project buffer has been used up, compared with how much work remains on the path feeding it. Ideally, the percentage of work complete through the critical chain should match the percentage of penetration into the project buffer. It is evident that the monitoring of buffers to review project status is similar to using float and earned value analysis on a resource levelled critical path network.

Goldratt (1997) recommends that the project manager should monitor the feeding buffers and make adjustments before a noncritical chain causes problems on the critical chain. In order to monitor the buffers, resources must provide regular updates of their current estimate of the time to complete their current task:

Compared to traditional project management, this is a bit of a shift away from focusing on what we have done via reporting percent of work complete to focusing on what counts to assess and address project status: how much time is left to accomplish unfinished tasks. Patrick (1999:60)

However, as in EVA, progress can be difficult to measure precisely on project tasks. Both methods suffer from the fact that the remaining 5–10% of task durations can take longer than expected and delay the completion of the project.

Benefits and criticisms of critical chain project management

Proponents of CCPM (for example Goldratt, 1997; Newbold, 1998; Leach, 1999; Patrick, 1999; Schuyler, 2000) all claim that its application to project management reduces project duration and provides a substantial step in continuous improvement to the PMBOK. They argue that the process helps the project manager to stay focused on a few critical tasks instead of dividing his attention among all the project's tasks and resources. However, it could be argued that the critical path method also enables the project manager to stay focused on the key project activities. These views are contrasted by other authors, for example Raz et al. (2003), who argue that CCPM successes seem to be 'mainly in organisations that started out with weak or nonexistant project management methodologies'.

However, it is questionable whether the critical chain is simple compared to the critical path and EVA method, since the hardest part of both methods is estimating durations and determining the estimate to complete activities.

Leach (2000) suggests that CCPM provides major benefits compared to the critical path theory. He identifies a number of organisations that have reduced project durations by implementing CCPM. These include Lucent Technologies, Harris, Honeywell Defense Avionic Systems, Siemens and the Israeli Aircraft Industry. These examples do not prove CCPM theory; they only provide confidence that it is not fatally flawed. It would be useful to hear from organisations that have implemented CCPM and have not seen any improvements. Raz et al. (2003) caution that since CCPM has been out for such a short period of time 'it is impossible to assess any sustainable long-term benefits'.

The critical chain process has received criticism from a number of authors. Elton and Roe (1998) admit that Goldratt's *Critical Chain* works well when dealing with individual projects but argue that the book falls short in explaining how companies can best manage a portfolio of projects. Elton and Roe (1998: 156) argue that 'the book's only advice is to make sure to allocate resources carefully across projects to minimise the constraints on the shared resources'. They suggest that managing project portfolios is far more complicated because most organisations have too many projects relative to their available capacity.

CCPM is criticised for underestimating the influence that senior managers have on the performance of projects. Elton and Roe (1998) claim that many of the delays in individual projects arise from problems at the senior management level rather than from mistakes made by the project manager. They suggest that the progress of any individual project is limited by factors outside an individual manager's control:

Too often, projects fall short of resources or lose direction because of a lack of agreement among senior business and functional managers. Thus, executives may slow a project down by failing to take necessary actions or by limiting the available resources. Elton and Roe (1998: 156–7)

Conflicts over the allocation of resources are common in a matrix structure. Project managers advocate for their own project and attempt to get the best resources assigned to their project. Newbold and Lynch (1999) suggest that in matrix organisations resource managers tend to give the highest priority to jobs for the most vocal people. Whilst CCPM recognises the conflict that exists within a matrix structure, it does not highlight what changes should be made to resolve the conflict.

CCPM is also criticised for underestimating the skills and abilities that a project manager requires when running a project. Schuyler (2000) argues that project performance is often less a matter of understanding the constraints of the project and more a function of the personal skills and capabilities of the potential project leaders available. Elton and Roe (1998: 159) also identify the importance of the leadership function:

Critical chain starts with a set of talented and driven project managers and assumes the resource constraints are inside the work of the project, not in its leadership. In truth leadership may be the larger constraint.

Both proponents and critics of Goldratt's critical chain method recognise that major behavioural changes must take place within organisations for the process to be implemented.

Behaviour changes required to implement CCPM

Putting critical chain scheduling in place requires major change in how projects, resources and priorities are managed. Patrick (1999) suggests that project managers must not criticise performers that overrun estimated activity durations. This is because there is a 50% probability that tasks will overrun. CCPM requires resources to provide tasks durations without any safety time and regular updates of their current estimate of the time to complete the task.

In order for critical chain to be implemented those involved must understand the theory of constraints philosophy and should receive training and education accordingly. Leach (2000) highlights this point and recognises that successful implementations occur in organisations that can continually adapt to change:

Critical chain project management implementation is greatly aided by an organisation's understanding of TOC and a successful change history of adapting new practices. Leach (2000: 256)

Adapting to change has become a prerequisite for all organisations, not just those implementing critical chain project management. A number of authors (Newbold, 1998; Newbold and Lynch, 1999; Leach, 2000) have developed detailed plans for implementing critical chain in a multiproject organisation. They all stress that senior management leadership is the critical success factor for multiproject implementation. The senior managers must take direct responsibility over the implementation and must ensure that they involve the entire organisation in the plan.

Continuous improvement

All organisations are perfectly aligned to get the results they get. That's one of the major problems in organisations. (Covey, http://www.franklincovey.com.)

The principles and tools of continuous improvement evolved from the original contributions of quality gurus such as Edwards Deming and Joseph Juran. The philosophies of these masters were introduced in Chapter 7.

Put simply, performance improvement is an ongoing effort in an organisation to find new and better ways of doing things. The goal of performance improvement is to solve performance problems or realise performance opportunities at the organisational, process and employee levels in order to achieve desired organisational results. It can involve some or all of the work areas of an organisation to:

- improve productivity
- gain and maintain competitive advantage
- optimise resources
- increase profit and shareholder value
- deliver high quality, sustainable, products and services
- meet customer expectations and demands.

Performance improvement achieves results through a systematic process that:

- considers the organisational context
- describes desired performance
- identifies gaps between desired and actual performance
- identifies root causes
- selects, designs and implements interventions (that is, activities to be carried out) to fix the root causes

■ measures changes in performance.

It is a continuously evolving process that uses the results of monitoring and feedback to determine whether progress has been made and plan and implement additional appropriate changes.

The performance improvement process is most likely to achieve its goal and desired result when:

■ Managers and staff from the organisation actively participate in all stages of the process improvement effort and change process
■ Performance improvement managers identify and build on existing performance standards and successes as well as address performance problems.

Performance measurement

The goal of making measurements is to permit managers to see their company more clearly, from many perspectives, and hence to make wiser long-term decisions. The Baldridge criteria (Brown, 1997) reiterate this concept of fact-based management:

Modern businesses depend upon measurement and analysis of performance. Measurements must derive from the company's strategy and provide critical data and information about key processes, outputs and results. Data and information needed for performance measurement and improvement are of many types, including: customer, product and service performance, operations, market, competitive comparisons, supplier, employee-related, and cost and financial. Analysis entails using data to determine trends, projections, and cause and effect that might not be evident without analysis. Data and analysis support a variety of company purposes, such as planning, reviewing company performance, improving operations, and comparing company performance with competitors' or with 'best practices' benchmarks.

Establishing the right performance measures is the key to successful performance improvement. A firm must be able to tell whether progress is being made on its critical goals and whether stakeholder expectations are being met.

A good way of doing this is to develop performance measures that are cross-functional and which are linked to strategies, objectives and performance criteria. These measures form the framework for a firm's performance measurement system. Several

well-known frameworks for measuring performance already exist. They are mentioned briefly below:

■ **Balanced scorecard:** A strategic, measurement-based management system, originated by Robert Kaplan and David Norton (1996, 2001), which provides a method of aligning business activities to the strategy, and monitoring performance of strategic goals over time.
■ **Baldridge Award:** A prestigious award, developed by Malcolm Baldridge in 1984 to offer an incentive to companies that score highest on a detailed set of management quality assessment criteria. The criteria include leadership, use of information and analysis, strategic planning, human resources, business process management, financial results and customer focus and satisfaction. The award is currently administered by the National Institute for Standards and Technology.
■ **Benchmarking:** The process of learning by making comparisons. For centuries and even today, comparisons are made in an informal sense. Benchmarking has come to mean a formal process of comparison between organisations as a way of generating ideas for improvement, preferably improvements of a major or 'breakthrough' nature (Boxwell, 1994).
■ **BPI (business process improvement):** A methodology for focused change in a business process achieved by analysing the AS-IS process using flow charts and other tools, then developing a streamlined TO-BE process in which automation may be added to result in a process that is better, faster and cheaper. BPI aims at cost reductions of 10–40%, with moderate risk.
■ **BPR (business process reengineering):** A methodology for radical, rapid change in business processes achieved by redesigning the process from scratch and then adding automation. Aimed at cost reductions of 70% or more when starting with antiquated processes, but with a significant risk of lower results (Hammer and Champy, 1993; Hammer, 1996).
■ **CMM (capability maturity model):** Measures process capability across a wide range of processes in a given discipline. The measurement scale goes from Level 0, with no formal process, to Level 5, with a continuous, rigorous and self-improving process. Developed by the Software Engineering Institute of Carnegie Mellon University, and now being extended to a broader range

of applications in management and manufacturing (Humphrey, 1989).

■ **EFQM:** The European Foundation for Quality Management's model of excellence (formerly called business excellence model), which provides benchmarking and self-assessment tools in a framework similar to that of the Malcolm Baldridge criteria.

■ **ERP (enterprise resource planning).** The collection and use of information in an organisation to improve and optimise performance. Executives and managers use the information produced by the enterprise information system to reinforce initiatives, reward behaviour and change strategies. Employees use it to adjust operations and respond to strategic needs. By linking timely accurate measures to specific goals and objectives, process management becomes more of a science and less of an art (Bocij et al., 2003).

■ **IIP (investors in people):** A national UK standard that seeks to encourage organisations to train and develop all their people. It is based on the practical experience of organisations that have improved their performance by investing in their people. The standard requires that an investor in people: is fully committed to developing its people in order to achieve its aims and objectives; is clear about its aims and objectives and what its people need to do to achieve them; develops its people effectively in order to improve its performance; and understands the impact of its investment in people on its performance.

■ **ISO 9000:** ISO, the International Standards Organization, has established a series of performance and quality measurement procedures for industrial organisations; if they implement these procedures they may receive certification by ISO.

■ **Six sigma:** Literally, refers to the reduction of errors to six standard deviations from the mean value of a process output or task opportunities, that is, about 1 error in 300,000 opportunities. In modern practice, this terminology has been applied to a quality improvement methodology for industry.

■ **SPC (statistical process control):** A mathematical procedure for measuring and tracking the variability in a manufacturing process; developed by Shewhart in the 1930s and applied by Deming in TQM.

■ **TQM (total quality management):** A methodology for continuous monitoring and incremental improvement of a supply line process by identifying causes of variation and reducing them. Originated by Deming in the 1950s, and widely applied in the US Federal government, where it was sometimes called total quality leadership (TQL) (Evans and Lindsay, 1989).

■ **Knowledge management (KM):** A business philosophy, incorporating an emerging set of principles, processes, organisational structures and technology applications that help people share and leverage their knowledge to meet business objectives. KM is fundamentally about sharing knowledge and putting that knowledge to use (Fernie et al., 2003).

Each system has its own strengths and weaknesses; consultants and business experts agree that there is no perfect measurement or improvement system. The way in which a measurement system is used as part of a continuous performance improvement programme is often more important than the specific system used.

PROJECT MANAGEMENT *in action*

The $26 million 'Oops!'

By CHIP ALEXANDER, BOB WILLIAMS and MATTHEW EISLEY, Staff Writers of *The News & Observer* on the Web

The steel and concrete skeleton of an arena has been taking shape on Raleigh's skyline for more than a year, waiting to be brought to life. As construction dragged on, and the tab kept rising, one question has overshadowed the project: Why is it costing so much?

The committee in charge of building the Sports and Entertainment Arena has always had an answer: bad weather, funding problems, a tight labour market, the need to reconfigure the design to accommodate the Carolina Hurricanes hockey team.

Then last week, when members of the Centennial Authority went before the Raleigh City Council to ask for more money because they had misjudged the cost by almost $26 million, they had a new explanation: They had blundered.

Reef Ivey, a Raleigh lawyer and a member of the authority, offered a condensed summary for the council. Try to alter a circular arena intended for college basketball so that it can also handle big-league hockey, he said, and everything changes. The architects and engineers learned that adding luxury suites and an extra level of seating would be too much for the foundation.

'They said, "Oops,"' Ivey said.

An extensive review of Centennial Authority documents by The News & Observer has found, in fact, that the authority, its contractors and its consultants vastly miscalculated the impact the design changes would have on the arena's structure and its cost.

Beyond the cost increases, the documents also show the building process to be politicised and contentious. And they show the Centennial Authority – composed of 13 unpaid political appointees charged with overseeing the job – has had difficulty settling disputes among contractors, the Hurricanes, the architects and others.

Ray Rouse, who heads the authority's construction and design committee, echoed Ivey's characterisation of the huge miscalculation on the redesign costs and on the money needed to speed up construction to finish the building by September 1, 1999.

'It was an "oops" all right,' Rouse said. 'It was a $26 million "oops."' The documents, supported by interviews with authority members, architects and others involved in the project, show that the initial estimates of what the changes would cost were little more than rough guesses. Nonetheless, the authority relied on those estimates during critical negotiations last fall with the Hurricanes over an arena lease. The $25.7 million gap in funding did not come to light until months after the lease was signed and the Hurricanes' financial commitment was set at $20 million.

Authority members say they did not fully grasp the magnitude of the error or its cost until March – more than eight months after construction began.

Those eight months were filled with extensive bickering and complaining among contractors, the Hurricanes and the Centennial Authority. Construction stalled while contractors waited for the redesign. One company submitted a bill for $72,000 to cover the cost of 'idle equipment.' Another contractor likened the project to the Titanic.

'To radically change the design once the building was under way is your worst nightmare,' Rouse said. 'All of a sudden the building changed, from the foundation to the top.'

The projected cost of the Entertainment and Sports Arena (the working name of the facility until an individual or corporation pays for the right to give it a name) is now $158 million – up from $120 million when construction started 15 months ago.

While N.C. State and the Hurricanes have chipped in, about two-thirds of that money is coming from taxpayers. This week, the authority hopes to get the remainder of the money it needs to cover its cost overruns from Raleigh and Wake County.

Members of the authority maintain that despite the delays, it will open in September 1999, in time for N.C. State University's basketball season and the Hurricanes' first season in Raleigh.

Almost from the beginning of construction, critics have contended that the authority is not providing good leadership on the project. A 'partnering' approach among contractors, consultants, architects and the authority that was intended to provide quick resolution of construction disputes is faulted by almost everyone involved. Authority members and others have criticised the general contractor, Hensel Phelps Construction, which has been called 'lackadaisical' and 'nonprofessional.'

Rouse contends that much of the criticism is unfair. Delays and cost overruns are nearly inevitable on a project this large, this complex, this political, he said. And the decision by the Hurricanes to make the arena their home, while welcome, came at an awkward time – after a building design had been adopted and just as construction was about to start.

'All that matters in the end is what happens in the end, and we will have a great building,' Rouse said. 'Right now, it's like trying to judge a painting before all the paint is on the canvas. When all is done, how we got there, all the struggles, people won't remember all that.'

Not everyone agrees, and among the most vocal of critics is Mayor Tom Fetzer.

'Taking a project of this size and scope and putting it in the hands of a bunch of part-time political appointees was a prescription for unmitigated disaster,' Fetzer said. 'I don't think they're bad people. I think they've conducted the public's business badly.'

'The irony is that all of those guys are successful business people. ... The reason they're all successful business people is that none of them run their business like they've run this project.'

One party has been on the sidelines, watching with interest: N.C. State. The arena was conceived as a new basketball home for the NCSU Wolfpack, and the university had committed $22 million as its share of what was once a $66 million project.

Now, at little additional cost to the university – $6 million – the team looks forward to competing next year in a far more luxurious setting. While not directly involved in the negotiations, the university has had its interest represented by the Centennial Authority, on which nine of 13 have close ties to NCSU.

Two days in May

Hensel Phelps Construction of Colorado was named the general contractor and given the job of building the arena, then pegged at $120 million, on May 8, 1997. Two days earlier, Hartford Whalers owner Pete Karmanos announced that he was moving the National Hockey League club to North Carolina – and into the new arena if a lease agreement could be reached.

Construction began as scheduled on July 1, 1997, even though negotiations about design changes were just getting started between the hockey team – rechristened the Carolina Hurricanes – and the Centennial Authority. At the job site, not even preliminary drawings of the proposed changes would be received until September.

It didn't take long for complaints to

surface. An early one was expressed by Rouse, the head of the authority's construction committee, in a September 26, 1997, letter to Peter Hellekjaer, a Detroit-based construction financial consultant hired by the Hurricanes. Rouse said the team's requests had changed several times. He asked for an 'official and final list of improvements.'

The Hurricanes' list included a group of luxury suites, a new ring of seating for the press atop the arena and improvements to the locker rooms. At the same time, the Centennial Authority added some items of its own: an expanded concourse and ticket area at the south end and some more office space. The authority also decided to upgrade the flooring from concrete to terrazzo at a cost of $750,000.

In the lease negotiations, the Hurricanes made clear their willingness to pay for the hockey improvements. To keep the process moving, it was accepted by all parties that they would not wait for final calculations and drawings; the Hurricanes would accept an estimate determined by the authority and the principal members of its construction team: the architectural firm of Odell Associates; the consulting firm McDevitt Street Bovis, and the major contractors.

Based on the preliminary drawings, the contractors issued an estimate in October: $15.8 million for all the changes.

Why so low? Michael Woollen, then an architect with Odell, said everything was based on preliminary concept drawings and a list of 'gross assumptions.'

'The Hurricanes wanted this, they wanted that – suites, press ring,' said Woollen, now with a Miami architecture firm. 'But everything the press ring added – dead weight, added height, gravity loads, wind loads – translates to the foundation. After all, the whole structure is one animal.'

'It was like adding a second floor to a house and pricing the second floor,' Rouse said. 'Then, later, you realise the foundation needs to be enlarged to hold the second floor.'

The initial price sounded fine to the Hurricanes. On November 7, they signed a lease with the authority, agreeing to pay $13.8 million to cover their share of the added construction costs. Separately, the team would also pay $6.2 million for some nonconstruction items, including a scoreboard.

'That was to be our one bite of the apple,' Hurricanes president Dean Jordan said. 'We gave $20 million and that was to be it.'

Meanwhile, construction had bogged down awaiting a decision on the design changes. Minutes from a Nov. 5 meeting of the authority's construction committee quote Rouse as saying, 'The contractors are very frustrated. ... Something has to be done.'

According to those minutes, Rouse observed that 'for all practical purposes the project [has] stopped,' and he estimated that work on the site was being done at about 25 percent efficiency.

'It was like trying to hit a moving target,' Rouse recalled last week. 'Prices were changing weekly. The designers were trying to catch up with the changes while we were trying to catch up with an estimation of the costs. It was like chasing your tail.'

One subcontractor, Seaboard Foundations, sent a letter to Hensel Phelps noting a 27-day delay. It also sent a bill for $189,000, for which $72,000 was itemised as 'idle equipment.'

By the end of November, Hensel Phelps' project manager, Harmon Anderson, said the project was 56 work days behind schedule. Central to the delay was that 80 percent of the foundation work had been put on hold, he said.

The extent of the confusion is hinted at in a January letter from the structural engineers to the architects. David Campbell, CEO of Geiger Engineers, noted that the expansion of the south end was first cancelled, then revived. Geiger wasn't sure whether a staircase should be in or out until December, then after a re-evaluation, discovered the foundation load had increased.

Campbell said the arena had become 'a very difficult and complex

project to execute. Frankly, we would just as soon not do it.'

A partnering session in mid-January was large and contentious, with about 40 people attending. Minutes of the meeting note that a 'conflict' between the contractors and architects was discussed, without elaboration.

Structural steel, already expected to be on the site, would not arrive until August, the minutes say. Hensel Phelps said the arena might not be finished until March 2000, which the authority deemed unacceptable.

The January meeting did produce one clear decision: A moratorium was declared on additional design changes. Before long, it would be disregarded.

Leadership vacuum

In the early weeks of 1998, the redesign plans had advanced enough that much of the construction work could resume, but the weather turned foul. Heavy rain in January and February – about double the average level in both months – halted work day after day.

In February, Hurricanes' owner Karmanos was demanding answers. In a letter to the authority, he expressed 'serious concerns' about the arena and said the team would not be responsible for paying for any construction delays.

'Our contribution is fixed,' Karmanos wrote. 'We are more concerned that there appears to be more emphasis on defending positions and assigning blame for cost and schedule problems rather than working towards a more positive effort.'

'There is no apparent sense of urgency. ... There seems to be no one in charge of this effort. Someone needs to provide leadership.'

Rouse quickly answered, urging Karmanos not to be upset by 'alarmist reports' in the media. In another letter, authority chairman Steve Stroud assured Karmanos that the authority had enough money to cover cost overruns, even though the final pricing hadn't been determined.

For the first eight months of construction, the authority was operating without a full-time chief of staff; its first executive director, Sims Hinds, was hired away by the Hurricanes in May 1997. As a result, the Hurricanes dealt directly with Odell Associates, the architect, on the design changes.

It wasn't until March, when Curt Williams, a former legislative lobbyist for Governor Jim Hunt, was hired as executive director, that the authority put an end to the Hurricanes' direct dealings with Odell.

'It was a bad time for us,' authority vice chairman Perry Safran said. 'Communication was a problem. ... We cut off Odell as middleman when Curt came in, but we did not get a handle on it fast enough.'

One low point came in April, when steel subcontractor Eddie Williams sent Hensel Phelps' Anderson a letter complaining about the lack of a 'real schedule' and the delays.

'Someone needs to "step up to bat" and get this project back on track or it will go down like the *Titanic*,' wrote Williams, president of Buckner Steel Erection. 'I plan to be on a life raft when that happens.'

Hensel Phelps replied that anyone not committed to the project 'had better get off at the next port, or be thrown overboard.'

By the time the final pricing from the contractors was completed, it was mid-March, Rouse said. The tab on the arena would be substantially higher than the October estimates – $25.7 million higher, a figure that included costs of accelerating the project for the September 1, 1999, opening.

To authority members, it was a shocking figure – one they chose not to make public until June.

'All in all, it was a rough stretch,' Rouse said. 'In midstream, we learned we had a different building.'

Blamestorming
If blame and complaints could be converted to money, the Centennial Authority would have more than enough to finish the arena.

Hundreds of documents in the authority's files deal with a wide range of real or perceived shortcomings on the part of project participants.

A frequent target is the performance of Hensel Phelps as general contractor.

The personal notes of authority executive director Williams refer to a March 25, 1998, conference call in which Rouse, the authority member who heads the construction committee, called Hensel Phelps 'lackadaisical.' Two months later, Williams' notes have authority member Reef Ivey saying, 'We are probably going to hire a construction lawyer to address HPCC [Hensel Phelps].' Williams' notes indicate Bob Ferguson of McDevitt Street Bovis, the authority's on-site construction consultant, as saying he believed that 'we are dealing with nonprofessionals' while adding that he did not know if it was possible to 'terminate' Hensel Phelps.

Ferguson could not be reached for comment last week. Williams and authority vice chairman Safran said no vote was ever taken by the authority on whether to terminate Hensel Phelps.

In a letter last month, Williams complained again to Rouse about Hensel Phelps and the pace of work, which he said was falling further and further behind.

'There seem to be continuing problems with HPCC,' Williams wrote on Aug. 5. 'We are enjoying perfect weather for accelerating work, but NONE has occurred.'

In a renewed push to meet the September 1, 1999, target date, all contractors adopted a new construction schedule in June. But Williams noted in the letter: 'HPCC is already 2 weeks behind after only 6 weeks since June 19 schedule agreement.'

As of last week, the project was 15 work days behind the new schedule, Rouse said.

Hensel Phelps blames the rainy weather last winter for robbing it of building days. It says finding qualified workers has also been difficult in the tight Triangle labour market.

'It has been a complex job,' said Bob Daniels, executive vice president in charge of the project for Hensel Phelps. 'The labor situation has been very difficult.'

Contributing to the discontent with Hensel Phelps, according to authority documents, was the structure of the chain of command. In compliance with state regulations, the arena actually has three 'prime contractors': Hensel Phelps is the general contractor, J. J. Kirlin is the mechanical contractor and Aneco the electrical contractor.

The three were hired independently, and construction people say it leaves the architect, Odell Associates, as the 'quarterback' of a team with no real coach.

'There's no boss other than the owner [authority] and the owner in this case has to be removed,' Curt Williams acknowledged. 'The architect interprets the contracts and has some administrative role there. He's the final decision-maker on the interpretation of the specs [design specifications]. I don't think the contractors have particularly liked that nor are they used to that.'

Harmon Anderson, the project manager for Hensel Phelps, apparently has ruffled his counterparts.

'Some reckon that HPCC is having a difficult time dealing with the multiprime system,' Williams wrote to Rouse on Aug. 5. 'Harmon seems to be able to upset the other primes regularly.'

Williams declined in a recent interview to discuss Anderson's performance, although he said, 'From time to time, there have been personality clashes.'

Authority vice chairman Safran says some of the criticism of Hensel Phelps is misplaced. The authority should have been more active in resolving disputes and personality clashes at the construction site.

'It's the authority's fault,' Safran said. 'We were supposed to set the tone and set the people in the right direction. To blame anybody but us would be a mistake.'

Furthermore, authority officials emphasise, the work that has been performed has been satisfactory.

'It's not a matter of the quality of work,' Williams said. 'There have been no faulty beams or columns.'

On that point, everyone agrees. There has been no 'showstopper,' as construction people call a major structural defect.

'It's hard to judge a contractor or anybody in midstream,' Rouse said.

'It's easy to find fault, but it was not the typical project with all the stops and starts.'

The Hurricanes, meanwhile, seem less worried about the project than they were a few months ago.

'A building this size, this complex, is always a battle,' owner Karmanos said.

'I'm not looking to blame anybody. I just want to get it done.'

The Hurricanes also expect the keys to the building on September 1, 1999.

'We haven't been told otherwise by anyone,' team president Jordan said.

'It's not a gimme we're going to hit that September date,' Rouse said. 'It is going to be a struggle.'

QUESTIONS TO AID UNDERSTANDING AND DISCUSSION

1. What are the signs that this project appears to be out of control?

2. Identify the reasons for this. Look for evidence relating to human factors, technical specifications, integration management, conflict management, team building, leadership, contractual, time management, client or owner, stakeholders, project champion, change management.

3. What measures (if any) could have been taken to avoid these problems?

4. List any lessons you can learn from this case for your own projects.

Summary points

- Project implementation is the execution of the project plan while project monitoring is about collecting sufficient data to make sure the project team implements the plan correctly.

- Project control is the process of ensuring that the project delivers everything it is supposed to – physical products and assets, quality products, documentation and deliverables such that there is complete assurance on delivery integrity.

- Project control systems compare actual cost and progress to planned cost and progress as laid down in the baseline cost curves and baseline schedule charts.

- The effectiveness of a project control system is measured by its average response time and its ability to identify the source of any problems.

- Project management is about delivering value to the project stakeholders and this sometimes means changing well-laid plans in response to changing conditions; however, change should be carefully controlled, especially after planning baselines have been frozen.

- Projects do not fail because of change but because of a lack of clear, consistent direction and leadership when confronted with the challenges of change.

- Changes encountered during a project generally arise

from three sources: within the project team (for example scope creep), from the client (for example scope leap) or from an external source (for example new regulatory requirements).

- During the project planning phase, a change management plan should be developed to minimise risk and maximise value from any proposed changes to the project plan.

- Milestone monitoring is a simple method that project managers can use to control a project. Its success depends on the identification of clear, well-defined milestones before implementation begins.

- Earned value analysis (EVA) is a widely used cost and schedule control system which compares the value of actual work completed (known as the earned value) against planned progress and actual expenditure.

- The main variables used in EVA relate to planned cost and schedule (BCWS), actual cost (ACWP) and real progress (earned value) (BCWP).

- One of the main difficulties in EVA is the calculation of earned value because of the need to estimate the percentage complete.

- Project closure should begin during the planning phase of a project when the work plan is developed, not in the final stages of a project.

- The processes of review and evaluation are applied at different stages throughout a project, for example at feasibility stage and all major milestones, and provide an opportunity to revisit the project's critical success factors.

- At the end of a project is it important to capture and distribute the experience, skills and knowledge that have been developed during a project, both with respect to personal development of staff, evolution of the project management methodology and also to reward and recognise everyone for their efforts.

- When stakeholders agree before they start how they are going to evaluate the success of a project, the probability of achieving success increases (Wateridge, 1995).

- Critical chain project management (CCPM) is derived from the theory of constraints (TOC) and is focused on the critical chain as the main schedule constraint in a project (Goldratt, 1997).

- The critical chain is defined as the sequence of dependent events that prevents the project from completing in a shorter interval. Resource dependencies determine the critical chain as much as do activity dependencies (Goldratt, 1997: 215).

- The principle of CCPM is to remove safety time from activities and allocate a project completion buffer instead.

- Performance improvement is an ongoing effort in an organisation to find new and better ways of doing things.

- The goal of performance improvement is to solve performance problems or realise performance opportunities at the organisational, process and employee levels in order to achieve desired organisational results.

Visit the website

http://www.palgrave.com/business/gardiner

▶ to test your understanding of the learning objectives for Chapter 10 using multiple choice questions

References

APM (2000). *Body of Knowledge*, 4th edn, Association for Project Management (APM), High Wycombe.

Bocij, P., Chaffey, D., Greasley, A. and Hickie, S. (2003). *Business Information Systems – Technology, Development and Management for the e-business*, Financial Times/Prentice Hall, Harlow.

Boxwell, Jr., R.J. (1994). *Benchmarking for Competitive Advantage*, McGraw-Hill, New York.

Brooks, Jr, F.P. (1995). *The Mythical Man-Month: Essays on Software Engineering Anniversary Edition*, Addison-Wesley, Reading.

Brown, M.G. (1997). 'Measuring up against the 1997 Baldridge criteria', *Journal for Quality and Participation*, **20**(4): 22–8.

Cleland, D.I. (1994). *Project Management – Strategic Design and Implementation*, 2nd edn, McGraw-Hill, New York.

Cooke-Davies, T. (2002). 'The "real" success factors on projects', *International Journal of Project Management*, **20**(3): 185–90.

Elton, J. and Roe, J. (1998). 'Bringing discipline to project management', *Harvard Business Review*, March–April: 153–9.

Evans, J.R. and Lindsay, W.M. (1989). *The Management and Control of Quality*, West Publishing, St. Paul, MN.

Fernie, S., Green, S.D., Weller, S.J. and Newcombe, R. (2003). 'Knowledge sharing: context, confusion and controversy', *International Journal of Project Management*, **21**(3): 177–87.

Fleming, Q.W. (1993). *Cost/Schedule Control Systems Criteria*, rev. edn, Probus, Chicago.

Fleming, Q.W. and Koppelman, J.M. (1996). *Earned Value Project Management*, Project Management Institute, Pennsylvania.

Gardiner, P.D. and Stewart, K. (2000). 'Revisiting the golden triangle of cost, time and quality: the role of NPV in project control, success and failure', *International Journal of Project Management*, **18**(4): 251–6.

Goldratt, E.M. and Cox, J. (1984). *The Goal : Excellence in Manufacturing*, North River Press, Great Barrington, MA.

Goldratt, E.M. (1997). *Critical Chain*, North River Press, Great Barrington, MA.

Gray, R.J. (2001). 'Organisational climate and project success', *International Journal of Project Management*, **19**(2): 103–9.

Hammer, M. (1996). *Beyond Reengineering – How the Process-centred Organization is Changing Our Work and Our Lives*, HarperCollins Business, London.

Hammer, M. and Champy, J. (1993). *Reengineering the Corporation – A Manifesto for Business Revolution*, Harper Business, New York.

Humphrey, W. (1989). *Managing the Software Process*, Addison-Wesley, Reading, MA.

IPMA (1999). *IPMA Competence Baseline* (ICB) Version 2.0, International Project Management Association (IPMA), Monmouth.

ISO 10007 (1995). 'Guidelines for configuration management'.

Kaplan, R.S. and Norton, D.P. (1996). *The Balanced Scorecard – Translating Strategy into Action*, Harvard Business School Press, Boston, MA.

Kaplan, R.S. and Norton, D.P. (2001). *The Strategy-focused Organization – How Balanced Scorecard Companies Thrive in the New Business Environment*, Harvard Business School Press, Boston, MA.

Leach, L.P. (1999). 'Critical chain project management improves project performance', *Project Management Journal*, **30**(2): 39–51.

Leach, L.P. (2000). *Critical Chain Project Management*, Artech House, London.

Lechler, T. (1998). 'When it comes to project management it's the people that matter', Proceedings of the 3rd International Research Network on Organizing by Projects (IRNOP III), University of Calgary, Alberta, Canada, 6–8 July, 317–23.

McConnell, S. (1996). *Rapid Development*, Microsoft Press.

Newbold, R.C. (1998). *Project Management in the Fast Last: Applying the Theory of Constraints*, St Lucie Press, Boca Raton, FL.

Newbold, R.C. (1999). 'Introduction to critical chain project management', accessed online [8 July 2004] at http://www.prochain.com/articles.asp.

Newbold, R.C. and Lynch, W. (1999). 'Critical chain: critical success factors', accessed online [8 July 2004] at http://www.prochain.com/articles.asp.

Nulden, U. (1996). 'Failing projects: harder to abandon than to continue', Projectics, Bayonne, France, Communications Proceedings.

Patrick, F.S. (1999). 'Getting out from between Parkinson's rock and Murphy's hard place', *PM Network*, April, 57–60.

Pinto, J.K. and Kharbanda, O.P. (1996). 'How to fail in project management (without really trying)', *Business Horizons*, **39**(4): 45–53.

Pinto, J.K. and Slevin, D.P. (1988a). 'Project success: definitions and measurement techniques', *Project Management Journal*, **19**(31): 67–72.

Pinto, J.K. and Slevin, D.P. (1988b). 'Critical success factors across the project', *Project Management Journal*, **19**(3): 67–75.

PMI (2000). *Guide to the Project Management Body of Knowledge*, Project Management Institute, Pennsylvania.

Rand, G.K. (2000). 'Critical chain: the theory of constraints applied to project management', *International Journal of Project Management*, **18**(3): 173–7.

Raz, T., Barnes, R. and Dvir, D. (2003). 'A critical look at critical chain project management', *Project Management Journal*, **34**(4): 24–32.

Retief, F. (2002). 'Overview of critical chain project management', Critical Chain Symposium.

Schuyler, J. (2000). 'Exploiting the best of critical chain and Monte Carlo simulation', *PM Network*, January: 56–60.

Staw, B.M. and Ross, J. (1987). 'Knowing when to pull the plug', *Harvard Business Review*, **65**(2): 68–74.

Steyn, H. (2000). 'An investigation into the fundamentals of critical chain project scheduling', *International Journal of Project Management*, **19**(5): 363–9.

Steyn, H. (2002). 'Project management applications of the theory of constraints beyond critical chain scheduling', *International Journal of Project Management*, **20**(1): 75–80.

Turner, J.R. (1999). *The Handbook of Project-based Management*, 2nd edn, McGraw-Hill, London.

Wateridge, J.H. (1995). 'IT projects: a basis for success', *International Journal of Project Management*, **13**(3): 169–72.

Winch, G. (1996). 'Thirty years of project management: what have we learned?', Proceedings of the British Academy of Management, Aston, UK.

Visit the website

http://www.palgrave.com/business/gardiner

▶ for additional resources to explore the topics in this chapter further

Index

Page numbers in *italic* indicate figures and tables